Public Libraries and the Internet

PUBLIC LIBRARIES AND THE INTERNET

Roles, Perspectives, and Implications

John Carlo Bertot, Paul T. Jaeger,
and Charles R. McClure, Editors

LIBRARIES UNLIMITED

AN IMPRINT OF ABC-CLIO, LLC
Santa Barbara, California • Denver, Colorado • Oxford, England

Library of Congress Cataloging-in-Publication Data

Public libraries and the Internet : roles, perspectives, and implications / John Carlo Bertot, Paul T. Jaeger, and Charles R. McClure, editors.
    p. cm.
Includes bibliographical references and index.
ISBN 978–1–59158–776–7 (pbk. : acid-free paper) — ISBN 978–1–59158–777–4 (ebook)
1. Libraries and the Internet—United States 2. Internet access for library users—United States. 3. Public libraries—Information technology—United States.
I. Bertot, John Carlo. II. Jaeger, Paul T., 1974– III. McClure, Charles R.
Z674.75.I58P84   2011
025.042—dc22   2010032376

ISBN: 978–1–59158–776–7
EISBN: 978–1–59158–777–4

15 14 13 12 11   1 2 3 4 5

This book is also available on the World Wide Web as an eBook.
Visit www.abc-clio.com for details.

Libraries Unlimited
An Imprint of ABC-CLIO, LLC

ABC-CLIO, LLC
130 Cremona Drive, P.O. Box 1911
Santa Barbara, California 93116-1911

This book is printed on acid-free paper ∞

Manufactured in the United States of America

Contents

Acknowledgments

First and foremost, we would like to thank all of the contributors to this volume. In taking the time and effort to share their research, experiences, and insights on some of the innumerable facets of the interrelationships between public libraries and the Internet, they have made this book a representation of the diverse perspectives on these important issues.

This book was inspired by the *Public Libraries and the Internet* series of surveys/studies and all of the data they have provided over the years. The various versions of the *Public Libraries and the Internet* study have now been ongoing for more than 15 years. Over time, a large number of granting agencies have supported the work, and many friends and colleagues have been involved in these studies.

Support for the studies comes from the Bill and Melinda Gates Foundation, the American Library Association, the Institute for Museum and Library Services, and the National Commission on Libraries and Information Science, among others. Without the support of these organizations, this book would not exist. Nor would we have the longitudinal data that charts public library involvement with and use of the Internet.

The surveys involved many researchers in data collection and analysis. During the past 15 years, these individuals have included: Kristen M. Barton, Larra M. Clark, Denise M. Davis, Elizabeth J. Decoster, Justin M. Grimes, Elise Jensen, Lesley A. Langa, Jonathan Lazar, Sunshine Lewis, Jessica McGilvray, Joe Ryan, Kathryn Sigler, Shannon N. Simmons, John T. Snead, Susan Thomas, Kim M. Thompson, Carla B. Wright, and Douglas L. Zweizig.

Most importantly, public libraries deserve tremendous appreciation for providing Internet access and assistance to everyone who needs it. Public libraries have been great supporters of the survey over the years, and their patience in answering the annual survey questions reflects their overall dedication to ensuring Internet access for all, in spite of the extra expenditures and responsibilities that the Internet has added to their workloads.

We hope that this book will serve as a valuable resource for librarians, library students, and scholars, as the relationships between the public library and the Internet continue to change, expand, and redefine the roles of the public library in society.

Part

I

Overview

Chapter 1

Evolving Relationships between Information Technology and Public Libraries

Paul T. Jaeger, John Carlo Bertot, and Kenneth R. Fleischmann

INTRODUCTION

The integration of technology into public library services has been a continual process across the eighteenth, nineteenth, twentieth, and twenty-first centuries, in which libraries have responded to new technologies, altering the ways that information could be recorded, accessed, and used. The Internet is a prominent recent example, but it is part of a larger continuity in public library history in the United States. In order to frame the explorations of the Internet and related technologies in public libraries today, this chapter briefly considers the historical relationships between public libraries and information technologies, how these relationships have shaped the maturation of public libraries, and the new roles in communities that have been created for libraries through increased provision of information technology.

Public libraries "are intricately intertwined with the greater social patterns of society as a whole and of the communities in which they are situated" (Burke & Martin, 2004, p. 422). As public libraries began to organize around professional associations and develop professional standards in the late 1800s, technology played an important role in shaping libraries and the profession of librarianship. Melvil Dewey in particular was keenly focused on the creation and novel employment of technology to improve library operations (Garrison, 1993; Wiegand, 1996). As new means of the electronic dissemination of information became widely used, libraries reacted by eventually incorporating many of these developments into the services and types of materials provided by libraries (Preer, 2006). By the 1960s, Jesse Shera (1964) foresaw that information technology could greatly reduce manual tasks performed by librarians. Now, computers, Internet access, and online services are vital components of public libraries, not only in reducing manual tasks for staff but in providing access to an increasing and evolving range of information and services far beyond what print materials alone could.

The important historical role of technology in libraries requires additional attention, especially as computer and Internet provision by libraries are now significantly reshaping the roles, expectations, and values of public libraries. Though some recent work helps us understand when libraries adopted information technologies and the ways in which the profession reacted to these technologies (McCrossen, 2006; Pawley, 2005; Preer, 2006), the intertwined historical development of modern information technologies and modern librarianship merits more detailed exploration. Information technology has not merely served as a tool to perpetuate existing services or a force that libraries have had to react to, but acts as a direct partner in the maturation of public libraries into a uniquely important entity that is widely trusted in the public sphere (Jaeger & Fleischmann, 2007). Ultimately, the progression of modern information technology has been a major influence on what libraries have tried to provide to their patrons and what patrons have in turn expected from their libraries.

PUBLIC LIBRARIES AND TECHNOLOGICAL CHANGE

When they first became common in the 1800s, "public libraries took shape within an extraordinarily vibrant market for culture" (McCrossen, 2006, p. 171). In the early 1900s, many public libraries had begun to acquire popular fiction of the day, newspapers, and magazines to add to their collections, and started to delve into multimedia by offering musical concerts, motion picture viewings, and art exhibitions. In the early days of radio, libraries began to use radio to advertise library services and activities (McCrossen, 2006). As they became widely popular, many libraries sponsored or hosted radio programs and used movies for educational purposes in the 1930s (Preer, 2006). In 1940s, LPs, radio transcripts, educational films, art reproductions, and other audiovisual materials became standard parts of the collection (Preer, 2006).

Over time, many librarians went through much conflict and anxiety about the provision of fiction, periodicals, newspapers and multimedia, with these materials being seen as lowering the standards of libraries, reducing their value, catering to the basest instincts of the public, and attracting the unemployed and the homeless (Garrison, 1993; McCrossen, 2006). However, "from the early part of the century, the library was portrayed as an institution that served all in the community" (Beckerman, 1996, p. 3). To best serve as many members of the community as possible, the preponderance of libraries found it worth the perceived risks to broaden the range and types of materials in libraries. Further, libraries were inspired by the increasing availability of information from other sources to expand their offerings.

During the 1930s and 1940s, the free distribution of information through new technologies (radio, movies, and television), lower costs, and easier access to mass market trades (books, periodicals), brought information to many people who had previously relied heavily on public libraries for information (Raber, 1997). Ultimately, the embrace of new forms and types of information became the norm in libraries. "As new technologies were introduced they embraced them, expanding the library's realm to include information in the latest formats and using them to promote library usage" (Preer, 2006, p. 494).

Since the 1950s, technological change has accelerated at a previously unimaginable pace. The invention of many home-use entertainment technologies led libraries to begin to include new types of media—audiocassettes, videocassettes, compact discs, DVDs, and CD-ROMs, among others—in the mission to offer a diversity of materials with many perspectives for users (Pittman, 2001). There now exists an expectation that the public library will provide equal access to a wide range of information and views in numerous formats, often in multiple languages, that represent a diverse array of perspectives on social and political issues (Jaeger & Burnett, 2005). For people with limited or no other access to published and electronic materials, the expected social function of public libraries became ensuring access to newspapers and periodicals, books of non-fiction and fiction, art, music, movies, and much more. Because of their accessibility and their ideology of equal access for all, libraries became socially sacred places in the minds of the public (Jaeger & Burnett, 2005; McCrossen, 2006).

Libraries first began to adopt the Internet and provide free public Internet access in mid-1990s, and this adoption has been swift. Public library Internet connectivity jumped from 20.9% in 1994 to 99.1% in 2009 (American Library Association, 2009). Today, librarians report that in nearly 75% of communities, the public library is the only source of free public access to the Internet (Bertot, McClure, & Jaeger, 2008). Yet, public libraries typically receive less than one half of one percent of a local community's budget (Beckerman, 1996).

As the Internet swiftly gained social prominence and significance in the late twentieth and early twenty-first century, public libraries began to add Internet access and a range of new services via numerous media through which patrons could gain access to a wide expanse of information and ideas. Many assertions have been made that the provision of Internet access and these services in libraries can serve as a natural extension of the established social roles of libraries. By providing a new avenue through which to access information and by providing access to many materials that the library could not otherwise provide for reasons of cost, space, or scarcity, the Internet can be considered a robust source of diverse, and often otherwise unavailable, information for patrons.

The public library's historical position as the marketplace of ideas might seem to be enhanced by the growth of Internet usage. In many ways, the Internet is akin to a marketplace of ideas where a dialogue on myriad topics is generated in cyberspace between users, based on their information needs and personal interests. As a result, Internet access and services are now becoming an essential part of public libraries and the services they provide to patrons. For most patrons, walking into a library and finding no public Internet access would be as unexpected, and as unacceptable, as walking into a library and finding no printed materials. As such, the social roles, expectations, and values of public libraries now include being a provider of Internet access—computers, connectivity, and Internet-based services and materials—to patrons (McClure & Jaeger, 2008; Bertot, 2009).

It has been suggested that certain aspects of the Internet and related technologies, however, run contrary to or undermine the established social roles of public libraries as a marketplace of ideas. New technologies are often expensive, and in many libraries, the costs of these new technologies are cutting into spending on more traditional and permanent materials, while much of the information provided by the Internet—particularly commercial information—falls outside of the parameters of information provided by other media in the library (Brown & Duguid, 2002; Buschman, 2003). Critics—both in the popular media and in LIS—have criticized libraries' perceived confusion of purpose and rush toward the Internet, which is seen as entertainment, and away from books, which is viewed as a more pure service to communities (Baker, 1996, 2001; Buschman, 2003; Tisdale, 1997).

These fears include concerns that computers in libraries will encourage the dissipation of authority, of history, and of continuity through a "technocracy" that replaces the traditional purpose of libraries (Buschman, 2003, p. 158). Part of this resistance is likely due to the increasing appearance of computers in libraries that may make them appear similar to many other social institutions. "At this historical moment, the changes that libraries are undergoing make them appear to be complicit with other contemporary forces that are eroding access to history and unraveling the connections of past and future generations" (Manoff, 2001, p. 374). A further factor may be that libraries have historically been considered refuges in times of social change (Rayward & Jenkins, 2007), but these social changes—in the tangible form of computers in the library buildings—reach into the essence of the library itself.

PUBLIC LIBRARIES AND THE MYRIAD IMPACTS OF THE INTERNET

One area of agreement between proponents and critics of the Internet in public libraries is that it has significantly shaped the roles of public libraries and the expectations of public library patrons in the past fifteen years. Over this period of time, the annual *Public Libraries and the Internet* studies—led by John Carlo Bertot and Charles R. McClure—have documented the rapid changes in Internet access and services in public libraries and the accompanying successes and challenges that the Internet has raised for libraries. Beginning in 2006, the *Public Libraries and the Internet* survey became part of the larger *Public Library Funding & Technology Access Study* (PLFTAS) study conducted by the American Library Association.

Many of the problems faced by libraries in dealing with new technologies and information sources through the years are similar to those faced now in relation to the Internet by forcing a reconsideration of the roles that the library wants to play in society. As examples among countless others, the digital age has forced libraries to redefine the meaning of intellectual freedom in libraries and the meaning of the library as public forum (Dresang, 2006; Gathegi, 2005). Laws related to the technology and Internet access provided by libraries—such as the USA PATRIOT Act, the Children's Internet Protection Act, the Homeland Security Act, and the Library Services Technology Act, among others—have added new constraints in information provision and access in libraries, from mandating filtering of Internet access to creating new guidelines for what electronic information can be requested from libraries in investigations. All of these laws impact how the library can serve in its role as marketplace of ideas. Along with these challenges to maintaining existing social roles, however, the Internet has also opened up opportunities for libraries to expand their social roles in recent years.

For example, by the late 1990s, the role of public libraries as a marketplace of ideas was augmented by the public library's burgeoning role as the primary public access point for Internet services to limit gaps in access (McClure, Jaeger, & Bertot, 2007). From its initial appearance, the Internet has resulted in gaps in access due to income level, educational attainment, social networks, geography, and other factors, creating a large number of residents unable to access Internet services except through the public library (Burnett, Jaeger, & Thompson, 2008; Jaeger & Thompson, 2003, 2004). To ensure the social role as a marketplace of ideas, public libraries serve as a guarantor of public access to Internet service for all. The degree to which this was a conscious decision on the part of the public library community is unclear—but many national leaders and policymakers have found that this social role of public libraries does, in fact, meet important societal needs of access and inclusiveness.

The Internet and related technology have also allowed libraries to take on previously unthinkable social roles, with e-government and emergency response being perhaps two of the most prominent new social roles. E-government is the provision of government information and services via electronic means, most prominently through Web sites and email. As a result of the early embrace of providing free public Internet access, public libraries have come to be seen as centers of Internet access in society, with patrons, communities, and governments all relying on the availability of Internet access (Bertot, Jaeger, Langa, & McClure, 2006a, 2006b; Jaeger, Langa, McClure, & Bertot, 2006). As a result, many local, state, and federal governments direct residents to the public library to access local e-government when residents lack other means of access or need help using the Web sites (Bertot, Jaeger, Langa, & McClure, 2006a, 2006b). To meet this social role, nearly 80% of public libraries offer training for patrons in the use of the Internet and e-government (Jaeger & Bertot, 2009).

More dramatically, the provision of Internet access has drafted libraries into new emergency service roles. For example, during the unprecedented 2004 and 2005 hurricane seasons, many Gulf Coast communities relied on public libraries to provide access to vital government information and services after being hit by major hurricanes, like Katrina, Rita, Wilma, Dennis, and Ivan. Libraries ensured access to e-government information and communication; guided people through the process of filling out e-government and insurance forms, created means for searching for missing family, friends, and pets; and provided access to news and satellite images of their homes and communities. The levels of assistance that libraries were providing to damaged communities and to displaced persons were extraordinary. In Mississippi, one library completed over 45,000 FEMA applications for patrons in the first month after Katrina made landfall (Jaeger, Langa, McClure, & Bertot, 2006). This heroic level of service was achieved even though the situation that the libraries found themselves in was unplanned and unprecedented.

More commonplace crises have also led to new ways that patrons rely on the public library. In the current economic downturn, use of public libraries and library computers for job seeking activities, social services, email access, entertainment, and other purposes has skyrocketed (Carlton, 2009; CNN, 2009; Van Sant, 2009). Further, as many people consider home Internet access to be a luxury that can be cut to save money in harsh economic times (Horrigan, 2008), this usage of libraries for information access and exchange is likely to continue to increase.

These examples clearly demonstrate how new technologies can simultaneously reinforce and force the re-examination of traditional roles and create complimentary new roles for public libraries. As an extension of their traditional roles of providing equal access to a range of information, libraries have committed to ensuring access not only to the Internet in general, but to socially beneficial online content like e-government and emergency information. As such, Internet access has evolved to become part of the social roles of public libraries in society and the expectations of libraries by patrons, communities, and governments, while simultaneously becoming a critical component of the core value of librarianship to provide access to information (Jaeger & Fleischmann, 2007). Further, libraries are thus playing a significant role in providing universal access to various services provided through information technology, reconfiguring both how the technology is delivered and, necessarily, how the development process is conceptualized. These new ways of serving the public, however, create extra responsibilities and burdens for libraries, creating challenges in terms of funding, staffing, space, and other issues of cost and support.

THEMES OF THIS BOOK

The chapters in this book explore the successes and challenges of the relationship of the public library and the Internet. To present these myriad topics and perspectives, the contributors to this volume include researchers and practitioners who have devoted large portions of their careers to engaging with these issues.

Following this chapter, the book provides a chapter authored by John Carlo Bertot that offers a detailed exploration of the longitudinal data, trends, and findings that have been collected through the *Public Libraries and the Internet* and the *Public Library Funding and Technology Access* studies during the past fifteen years. As the only source of longitudinal information about the Internet in public libraries since the early 1990s, this data is used to trace the development of the Internet access, services, costs, and expectations in libraries. Together, the first two chapters present the overall context and development of the Internet in public libraries.

The book then presents a set of chapters examining different situations in which the Internet access and services in libraries play an important part in supporting the needs and interests of members of the community. The first chapter in this section, written by Paul T. Jaeger and John Carlo Bertot, explores the newly developed, but important, role of libraries in ensuring that all citizens have access to and assistance using e-government information and services, which is the provision of government information and services through the online environment. Over the past several years, the Internet access and training provided by public libraries has combined with the public trust of libraries to make libraries the primary public outlet for e-government. This intersection between public libraries and e-government has many significant implications and impacts for library activities and management, and expectations for libraries, the activities of librarians, and library education.

A chapter by Lorri Mon then focuses on the use of social networking and other Web 2.0 technologies by public libraries to create a virtual presence and services. Exploring the potential roles for communications modes such as instant messaging, SMS text messaging, and virtual worlds, as well as new participatory publishing technologies such as wikis, blogging, and social networking in libraries, the chapter examines the extent to which public libraries can serve local users who never physically set foot within the physical library, and the challenges of conceptualizing and providing virtual branch collections and services.

As noted above, one key area in which the Internet and e-government access and services provided by libraries have played a major role is in disaster preparedness and recovery. Charles R. McClure, Joe Ryan, Lauren H. Mandel, John Brobst, Charles C. Hinnant, and John T. Snead discuss the range of hurricane and disaster preparation and response roles that public libraries are able to accomplish with the capacities provided by the Internet. This chapter catalogues major roles, important available resources, and best practices in disaster preparation and response roles for libraries.

A chapter written by Kenneth R. Fleischmann explores the impact that the public library has had on the Internet in terms of the development and adoption of Internet services and technologies. Building on the core service orientation and values of librarianship, this chapter articulates the oft-neglected mutual shaping of technology and society that has occurred as a result of the rise of the public library as the primary public access point for Internet access and services.

The final chapter in this section, authored by Lauren H. Mandel, Charles R. McClure, and Bradley Wade Bishop, discusses the service roles and capacity demands that have developed around the availability of broadband in libraries. While many libraries now have broadband-level access, the access speed often remains too low to provide quality access for all of the service demands in the library, especially as libraries add more computers and provide wi-fi service, while users consume ever increasing amounts of high-bandwidth content, from social media to videos. This chapter explores the ways in which libraries are balancing these demands.

The next group of chapters in the book explores specific populations that have the potential to be better served as a result of the rise of the Internet as a core part of library services. Kim M. Thompson's chapter on the potential of the Internet to meet the needs of the information poor begins the section. This chapter focuses on the ability of libraries to addresses gaps in access and technological literacy through not only the provision of information, but also through education and training that link patrons to socioeconomic and employment opportunities. The chapter culminates with recommendations for ways in which public libraries can use these approaches to create better information service for and foster social participation among all user groups.

Erin V. Helmrich and Erin Downey Howerton provide an informative overview regarding Internet-enabled youth services in public libraries. Their chapter discusses the impact of the Internet on young adults, and how this impact in turn shapes the services that public libraries provide. The chapter also identifies policies, legislation, and other issues that shape the context in which public libraries offer a range of Internet services and resources to young adults.

At the opposite end of the age spectrum, Bo Xie, Amy Cooper White, Chadwick B. Stark, David Piper, and Elizabeth Norton discuss the ways in which public libraries can foster Internet access to vital health and wellness information for older adults through the provision of age-appropriate training to help them learn to navigate, evaluate, and use the wide range of reliable health information available there. In response to major societal and technological trends, libraries are creating special programs to train older adults to access and use health information online. This chapter includes both case studies and recommendations for developing programs to meet the health information needs of older adult patrons.

The last chapter in this section deals with the issues of providing equal access to patrons with disabilities both to the technology in the library and to the virtual services offered by the technology. While public libraries have long been committed to providing services to persons with disabilities, the complexity of access to Internet services makes the consideration of the accessibility and usability of electronic resources an important issue for all patrons. In this chapter, Jonathan Lazar, Paul T. Jaeger, and John Carlo Bertot provide strategies for providing inclusive services for patrons with disabilities and recommendations for developing partnerships to enhance library efforts to provide equal access.

The fourth section of the book focuses on the institutions and financial support structures that underlie the ability of libraries to provide Internet access and services to patrons. Denise M. Davis offers a detailed examination of public library funding. Her chapter offers an historical perspective on public library funding in general, and provides detailed budgetary information regarding public library technology funding. This chapter sheds light on the myriad funding approaches to U.S. public libraries, and the impact on these funding streams in difficult economic times.

Next, Robert Bocher discusses the important roles of state library agencies in supporting the provision of access to the Internet in public libraries. These support structures include broadband access, provision of databases and other electronic resources, digitization, integration of system and resource sharing, grant-making, advocacy, and education, among others. This chapter examines these roles in detail and offers key examples of states that are doing exemplary work in providing these supports.

Based on a series of case studies of public libraries, Larra M. Clark provides an in-depth view of the issues and challenges public libraries face when providing Internet-enabled services to the communities that libraries serve. The chapter identifies key areas of challenge—buildings, funding, staff expertise, and user needs—that public libraries encounter as they maintain, expand, and upgrade their public access technology environment.

The final section of the book contains two chapters that tie together the broad themes explored in the book that point to the future of public libraries and the Internet. Paul T. Jaeger and John Carlo Bertot examine the policy environment that shapes the provision and management of Internet services by public libraries. Information policy affects access, management, content, and training in the provision of Internet access and training in public libraries, but libraries are frequently not involved in the policymaking process. This chapter explores the centrality of information policy to library activities and the ways in which public libraries can become more active in influencing these policies.

The book concludes with a chapter by Charles R. McClure, John Carlo Bertot, and Paul T. Jaeger examining the impacts on libraries and their communities that result from increased demands for a range of public access computing services and resources in a time of diminished capacity to provide such services and resources. A number of economic, social, government, and technological factors contribute to this situation, forcing libraries to formulate possible strategies that public librarians might consider to mitigate this situation and better provide public access computing services in the future.

CONCLUSION

The development of the public library through the nineteenth and twentieth centuries solidified the library's social position so that, at the beginning of the twenty-first century, the public library stands as a primary source of information that is equally available to all citizens and residents. This provision of information has created certain social roles of and expectations for public libraries in the United States. Nearly 90% of Americans believe public libraries to be as valuable as or more valuable than other tax-supported public services, and accord libraries a high level of trust (*Economist*, 1998). A study conducted in 2006 found that "public libraries seem almost immune to the distrust that is associated with so many other institutions" (Public Agenda, 2006, p. 11). As such, the recent additional services that libraries are providing through the Internet-related technologies are serving to increase the trust accorded to libraries and the roles they play in society (Jaeger & Fleischmann, 2007).

However, for all of the significant accomplishments and new roles of public libraries in the lives of their patrons and communities that have developed as a result of Internet access, the situation that libraries now find themselves in is far from ideal. As the economic troubles of recent years have eaten into state and local budgets, funding for public libraries has diminished, quite substantially in some states. Yet, at the same time, the economic circumstances have driven up library use as people seek places to file job applications and forms for assistance, as well as people seeking a place providing free entertainment, resulting in few libraries being able to meet demands for access and training. In addition, some of these new Internet-enabled social roles through which libraries are able to support communities—such as e-government access point and emergency support center—place considerable new burdens on library staff and technology. Service expectations add further complications, as patrons expect more computer access, wi-fi access, and the ability to use high-bandwidth applications, all of which tax library access to the limits.

Throughout the chapters in this book emerges a clear theme demonstrating the enormous popularity among patrons of Internet access and the wonderful new contributions and services that libraries have been able to provide to their patrons, communities, and governments. However, there is also an undercurrent of unease, if not sorrow, and a sense of time running out. There is a real danger of libraries' ability to provide access, training, and assistance being overwhelmed by economic, technological, social, and governmental factors. To continue to provide the quality of access and assistance that libraries want to provide, new models of collaboration and partnership among libraries, new approaches to seeking funding, increased emphasis on demonstrating value to communities, and greater levels of direct engagement in policymaking and political processes will likely become necessary.

The essays in this book serve not only to catalogue library developments, achievements, and programs over the past 15 years. They also paint a picture of the current state of Internet and computing services and, perhaps most importantly, identify strategies and models that will help libraries continue to meet patron, community, and government expectations. Libraries are justifiably proud of everything that they achieved in the age of the Internet, but they must continue to evolve and innovate to ensure that they provide patrons, communities, and governments with the access, training, and assistance that have become central to the roles of public libraries in society.

A NOTE ON THE DATA AND SURVEY REPORTS

The Public Libraries and the Internet surveys, now part of the larger Public Library Funding and Technology Access study, continue to be conducted and reveal new and evolving practices regarding public access technology use and involvement in public libraries. The data reported in various chapters in this book were current as of January 2010. As new surveys are conducted, readers will find updated data, reports, and other items of interest at the Center for Library & Information Innovation's *Public Libraries and the Internet* portal at http://www.plinternetsurvey.org.

REFERENCES

American Library Association. (2009). *Libraries Connect Communities: Public Library Funding & Technology Access Study 2008–2009*. Chicago, IL: American Library Association. Available at http://www.ala.org/plinternetfunding.

Baker, N. (1996). The author vs. the library. *New Yorker, 72*(31), 51–62.

Baker, N. (2001). *Double fold: Libraries and the assault on paper*. New York: Random House.

Beckerman, E. (1996). *Politics and the American public library: Creating political support for library goals*. Lanham, MD: Scarecrow.

Bertot, J. C. (2009). Public access technologies in public libraries: Effects and implications. *Information Technology and Libraries, 28*(2), 81–92.

Bertot, J. C., Jaeger, P. T., Langa, L. A., & McClure, C. R. (2006a). Public access computing and Internet access in public libraries: The role of public libraries in e-government and emergency situations. *First Monday, 11*(9). Available at http://www.firstmonday.org/issues/issue11_9/bertot/index.html.

Bertot, J. C., Jaeger, P. T., Langa, L. A., & McClure, C. R. (2006b). Drafted: I want you to deliver e-government. *Library Journal, 131*(13), 34–39.

Bertot, J. C., McClure, C. R., & Jaeger, P. T. (2008). The impacts of free public Internet access on public library patrons and communities. *Library Quarterly, 78,* 285–301.

Brown, J. S., & Duguid, P. (2002). *The social life of information.* Boston: Harvard Business School Press.

Burke, S. K., & Martin, E. (2004). Libraries in communities: Expected and unexpected portrayals in state case law. *Libraries and Culture, 39,* 405–428.

Burnett, G., Jaeger, P. T., & Thompson, K. M. (2008). The social aspects of information access: The viewpoint of normative theory of information behavior. *Library & Information Science Research, 30,* 56–66.

Buschman, J. E. (2003). *Dismantling the public sphere: Situating and sustaining librarianship in the age of the new public philosophy.* Westport, CT: Libraries Unlimited.

Carlton, J. (2009, January 19). Folks are flocking to the library, a cozy place to look for a job: Books, computers and wi-fi are free, but staffs are stressed by crowds, cutbacks. *Washington Post,* A1.

CNN. (2009). Hard economic times: A boon for public libraries. *CNN.com.* Available at http://www.cnn.com/2009/US/02/28/recession.libraries/index.html.

Dresang, E. T. (2006). Intellectual freedom and libraries: Complexity and change in the twenty-first century digital environment. *Library Quarterly, 76,* 169–192.

Economist. (1998, September 12). Off to the library: Buildings, books, and bytes. *Economist, 348,* 30.

Garrison, D. (1993). *Apostles of culture: The public librarian and American society, 1876–1920.* Madison: University of Wisconsin Press.

Gathegi, J. N. (2005). The public library and the (de)evolution of a legal doctrine. *Library Quarterly, 75,* 1–19.

Horrigan, J. B. (2008). *Home broadband adoption 2008: Adoption stalls for low-income Americans even as many broadband users opt for premium services that give them more speed.* Washington, D.C.: Pew Internet and American Life Project.

Jaeger, P. T., & Bertot, J. C. (2009). E-government education in public libraries: New service roles and expanding social responsibilities. *Journal of Education for Library and Information Science, 50,* 40–50.

Jaeger, P. T., & Burnett, G. (2005). Information access and exchange among small worlds in a democratic society: The role of policy in redefining information behavior in the post-9/11 United States. *Library Quarterly, 75*(4), 464–495.

Jaeger, P. T., & Fleischmann, K. R. (2007). Public libraries, values, trust, and e-government. *Information Technology and Libraries, 26*(4), 35–43.

Jaeger, P. T., Langa, L. A., McClure, C. R., & Bertot, J. C. (2006). The 2004 and 2005 Gulf Coast hurricanes: Evolving roles and lessons learned for public libraries in disaster preparedness and community services. *Public Library Quarterly, 25*(3/4), 199–214.

Jaeger, P. T., & Thompson, K. M. (2003). E-government around the world: Lessons, challenges, and new directions. *Government Information Quarterly, 20*(4), 389–394.

Jaeger, P. T., & Thompson, K. M. (2004). Social information behavior and the democratic process: Information poverty, normative behavior, and electronic government in the United States. *Library and Information Science Research, 26*(1), 94–107.

Manoff, M. (2001). The symbolic meaning of libraries in a digital age. *Portal: Libraries and the Academy, 1,* 371–381.

McClure, C. R., & Jaeger, P. T. (2008). *Public libraries and Internet service roles: Measuring and maximizing Internet services.* Chicago: ALA Editions.

McClure, C. R., Jaeger, P. T., & Bertot, J. C. (2007). The looming infrastructure plateau?: Space, funding, connection speed, and the ability of public libraries to meet the demand for free Internet access. *First Monday, 12*(12). Available at http://www.uic.edu/htbin/cgiwrap/bin/ojs/index.php/fm/article/view/2017/1907.

McCrossen, A. (2006). "One more cathedral" or "mere lounging places for bummers?" The cultural politics of leisure and the public library in Gilded Age America. *Libraries and the Cultural Record, 41*, 169–188.

Pawley, C. (2005). History in the library and information science curriculum: Outline of a debate. *Libraries and the Cultural Record, 40*(3), 223–238.

Pittman, R. (2001). Sex, democracy, and videotape. In N. Kranich (Ed.), *Libraries and democracy: The cornerstones of liberty* (pp. 113–118). Chicago: American Library Association.

Preer, J. L. (2006). "Louder please": Using historical research to foster professional identity in LIS students. *Libraries and the Cultural Record, 41*, 487–496.

Public Agenda. (2006). *Long overdue: A fresh look at public and leadership attitudes about libraries in the 21st Century.* New York: Author.

Raber, D. (1997). *Librarianship and legitimacy: The ideology of the public library inquiry.* Westport, CT: Greenwood.

Rayward, W. B., & Jenkins, C. (2007). Libraries in times of war, revolution, and social change. *Library Trends, 55*(3), 361–369.

Shera, J. H. (1964). Automation and the reference librarian. *Reference Quarterly, 3*(July), 3–7.

Tisdale, S. (1997). Silence, please: The public library as entertainment center. *Harper's Magazine*, March, 65–73.

Van Sant, W. (2009, June 8). Librarians now add social work to their resumes. *St. Petersburg Times.* Available: http://www.tampabay.com/.

Wiegand, W. A. (1996). *Irrepressible reformer: A biography of Melvil Dewey.* Chicago: American Library Association.

Chapter 2

Public Libraries and the Internet: A Retrospective, Challenges, and Issues Moving Forward

John Carlo Bertot

INTRODUCTION

Public libraries were early adopters of Internet-based technologies, and the *Public Libraries and the Internet* and *Public Library Funding and Technology Access* national surveys have charted the involvement with and use of the Internet by U.S. public libraries since 1994. Since 1994, 11 national studies—funded over the years by the American Library Association, the Bill & Melinda Gates Foundation, the National Commission on Libraries and Information Science, and the U.S. Institute of Museum and Library Services—provide longitudinal data that track trends in the public access computing and Internet access provided by public libraries to the communities that they serve. This chapter provides findings based on surveys conducted through January 2010. As more surveys are conducted, readers will find current reports, findings, and other items at the University of Maryland Center for Library & Information Innovation's Public Libraries and the Internet Web portal http://www.plinternetsurvey.org.

This chapter is not a general review of public library Internet involvement and use, but rather:

- Provides an overview and review of selected *Public Libraries and the Internet* national survey data;
- Identifies key trends and changes in Internet-enabled services and resources provided by public libraries to their communities over the course of the 15 years of conducting the national surveys;

- Identifies key issues that emerge from the data regarding public library Internet use and involvement; and

- Identifies selected future issues regarding public library Internet-enabled services, particularly as the public access that libraries provide their communities takes on increasing importance in supporting a range of services such as e-government, jobs/employment, health information, and education.

The chapter therefore seeks to provide an evolutionary perspective on public library Internet connectivity. A full reference list of all the *Public Libraries and the Internet* and *Public Library Funding and Technology Access* studies and their findings is available at the end of the chapter.

BACKGROUND

The *Public Libraries and the Internet* national surveys began in 1994 with the purpose of tracking the growth of public library Internet connectivity and uses as a basis for (1) proposing and promoting public library Internet policies at the federal level; (2) maintaining selected longitudinal data as to the connectivity, services, and deployment of the Internet in public libraries; and (3) providing national estimates regarding public library Internet connectivity. Through 2004, the surveys were conducted roughly every two years. Beginning in 2006, the surveys switched to an annual data collection cycle, and became part of a larger *Public Library Funding and Technology Access* study (http://www .ala.org/plinternetfunding) funded by the American Library Association (ALA) and the Bill & Melinda Gates Foundation.

Though the survey remains true to its core goals, the survey evolved over time and has experienced four clear shifts in data collection, methodology, and approach:

- Prior to 1998, the surveys collected data at the system level (i.e., total number of workstations across all library branches, if applicable);[1]

- Between 1998 and 2004, the surveys collected data at the building/outlet level (i.e., number of workstations in a particular branch, speed of connectivity at the branch), as well as system level data (i.e., E-rate applications);

- Beginning in 2004, the surveys expanded to collect data at the state and national levels, and include both building/outlet level and system level data; and

- Beginning in 2002, the survey offered participants a fully online version of the survey as well as a printed version of the survey to complete. Each year, more surveys were completed online, and in 2009, the survey became an online-only survey.

Throughout these shifts, the survey has maintained core longitudinal questions (e.g., numbers of public access workstations, bandwidth), but consistently explored a range of emerging topics (e.g., jobs assistance, e-government).

Due to its longevity, longitudinal data, and unique data, data from the surveys appeared over the years in Congressional testimony, filings with the Federal Communications Commission (particularly the development of the National Broadband Plan), filings with the National Telecommunications and Information Administration (particularly regarding the recent Broadband Technology Opportunity Program grant program), in the Children's Internet Protection Act U.S. Supreme Court decision, in U.S. Senate hearings on the E-government Act, and many other critical policy venues. State librarians have also used the data in state legislative testimony, and in a range of state policy documents and initiatives. In short, the data from the surveys are used by a number of stakeholders in a wide range of ways.

METHODOLOGY IN BRIEF

The survey's methodology has evolved over time to meet changing survey data goals. As of this writing, the survey provides both national and state estimates with the following objectives:

- To provide branch-level national data regarding public library Internet connectivity and use;
- To provide state branch-level data (including the District of Columbia) regarding public library Internet connectivity and use;
- To provide system- (administrative) level data (including the District of Columbia) regarding E-rate use and library operating and technology funding and expenditures; and
- To include assessment questions for selected public libraries that were the recipients of certain Foundation grants.

The latter objective is beyond the scope of this chapter, as selected libraries receive particular survey questions related to Foundation grants.

The survey has additional objectives of obtaining data to conduct analysis using metropolitan status[2] (e.g., urban, suburban, and rural) and poverty[3] (less than 20% [low], 20%–40% [medium], and greater than 40% [high]) variables. Over the years, the poverty variable has not demonstrated any statistical significance in terms of the survey's findings, and thus the poverty variable was removed beginning with the 2009–2010 survey.

The survey uses a stratified "proportionate to size sample" to ensure a proportionate national sample. The sampling approach taken ensured high quality and generalizeable data within the states analyzed, nationally, and across and within the various strata. The study team uses the now Institute of Museum and Library Services public library dataset (formerly maintained by the U.S. National Center for Education Statistics) to draw its sample. Foundation grant recipient data are overlaid on the national library dataset. The survey asks respondents to answer questions about specific library branches and about the library system to which each respondent branch belonged. Respondents typically answer the survey between September and November of each survey year. In each year of the survey, except for the 2006–2007 survey, the survey response rate is between 70.0 and 79.0%, and provides between 5,500 and 6,100 survey responses. The data are weighted for both national and state level analysis, and have a margin of error of ±3%. The high survey response rate and representativeness of responses demonstrate the high quality of the survey data and the ability to generalize to the public library population.

SELECTED LONGITUDINAL AND KEY FINDINGS

This section provides an overview of selected longitudinal data. The section provides longitudinal data for as many survey years as possible. It is important to note, however, that key survey questions, such as broadband connectivity speeds, have changed substantially over the years to reflect the evolving nature of Internet connectivity. For example, the first surveys asked about dial-up connections and their speeds, versus today's questions that explore fiber optic and other types of Internet connectivity and corresponding higher speeds. Thus some longitudinal comparisons would not make sense. Finally, the section provides selected findings regarding newer services, particularly as they have an impact on future public library Internet-enabled services.

Infrastructure

The survey asks a number of questions about a public library's public access infrastructure, e.g., public access to the Internet, numbers of workstations, wireless (wi-fi) access, and connectivity speed. As Figure 2.1 shows, nearly

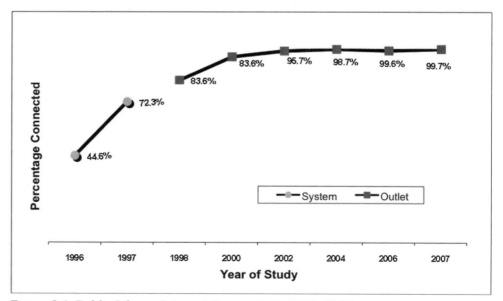

Figure 2.1 Public Library Internet Connectivity 1996–2007.

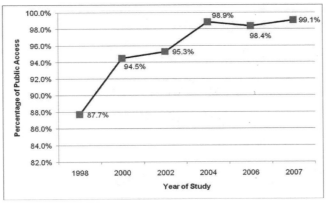

Figure 2.2 Public Access to Public Library Internet Connectivity 1998–2007.

100% of public libraries are connected to the Internet. Libraries achieved this growth in connectivity quite quickly, from 20.9% of public library systems connected to the Internet in 1994 to nearly 100% by 2002. Indeed, so prevalent is Internet connectivity in public libraries, that the survey discontinued asking this question in 2008. And, as Figure 2.2 shows, nearly all connected public libraries provide public access to the Internet. Interestingly, nearly all libraries that reported an Internet connection indicated the provision of public access to the Internet—even in 1998, with 87.7% of connected libraries providing public access to the Internet.

Along with Internet connectivity, public libraries also rapidly increased the average number of workstations that they provided for public use. Between 1996 and 2009, the average number of workstations grew from 1.9 to 11.0 (see Figure 2.3). Of note is that the average number of workstations, except for 2008 with a reported average of 12.0, hovered between 10.0 and 11.0 since 2002. Libraries reported that cost, staff, and space issues were impediments to adding more workstations.

Public library adoption of broadband continued to increase over time (see Figure 2.4). Libraries continue to enhance their connection speeds annually.

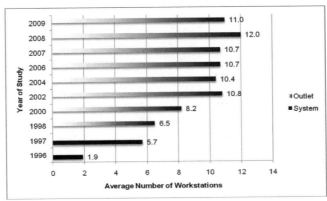

Figure 2.3 Average Number of Public Access Workstations: 1996–2009.

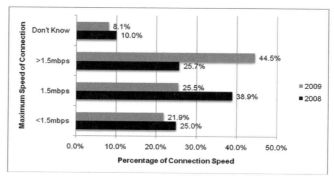

Figure 2.4 Public Library Speed of Internet Connection 2008–2009.

Indeed, from 2008 to 2009, public libraries reported an increase in connectivity speed, with 44.5% of libraries reporting connection speeds of greater than 1.5 MBPS in 2009 as opposed to 25.7% in 2008. Libraries reported a corresponding decline in speeds of 1.5 MPBS or less in 2009 as compared to 2008.

Libraries report a substantial increase in the availability of wireless (wi-fi) services for public use (see Figure 2.5). In 2009, 76.4% of public libraries provide public wireless access, as compared to 54.2% in 2007. And, if libraries that indicate they are planning to provide wireless access within the year do so, the figure will approach just over 80.0%. The adoption of wi-fi in public libraries has been quite rapid, and is likely to become almost as ubiquitous as Internet connectivity in libraries.

Connectivity, however, is a prerequisite to providing a range of Internet-enabled services and resources to the communities that libraries serve.

Services

Public libraries use their Internet connectivity and public access computers to provide databases, e-books, digital reference, training, and a number of Internet-enabled services to their users—both from inside and

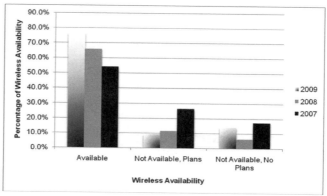

Figure 2.5 Wireless (Wi-Fi) Internet Connectivity Availability: 2007–2009.

outside of the library's walls. More specifically, as reported in 2009, public libraries:

- Offer licensed databases (89.6%), homework resources (79.6%), audio content such as audio books (72.9%), and digital reference (62.4%) (see Table 2.1).
- Offer a substantial amount of information technology training (see Table 2.2) on a wide range of topics, including general Internet use (92.8%), general computer use (91.3%), online searching (76.9%), and general software use (70.5%).
- Provide innovative support services to meet community needs in such areas as e-government by helping users understand and use government Web resources (80.5%), helping patrons apply for government benefits (54.1%), and through immigration services (32.1%) (see Table 2.3).

There are other services provided by public libraries, but these demonstrate the depth and breadth of public library Internet-enabled services.

If one looks at the survey data over the years, there is a sense that public libraries quickly incorporated public access technologies into their libraries, made public access a critical service provided to their communities, offered training and instructional programs to facilitate the ability of users to interact with Internet technologies, and responded to community needs such as e-government. Libraries do not provide these services without challenge, however.

CHALLENGES IN PUBLIC ACCESS SERVICES AND TECHNOLOGIES

Increasingly, the Public Library Internet surveys show conflicting results. This section focuses on these somewhat contradictory results, by way of findings reported in the latest (2008–2009) survey. On the one hand, public libraries continue to offer enhanced public access computing and Internet access surveys to their communities. As presented above, public libraries:

- Offer wireless (wi-fi) access to the Internet;
- Have faster public access broadband speeds;
- Offer technology and Internet training; and
- Offer a range of other services such as databases, digital reference, e-books, and e-government.

And, as libraries report, over 70% are the only free public access computing and Internet centers in their communities (see Figure 2.6). Thus, public libraries provide critical public access computing and Internet services that support their communities in a wide range of areas.

On the other hand, however, public libraries indicate that:

- *Their broadband speeds are inadequate.* At the same time, 59.6% (up from 57.5% in 2007–2008) of respondents reported that their connectivity speed is insufficient some or all of the time (see Figure 2.7).

TABLE 2.1 Public Library Services Available to Users by Metropolitan Status and Poverty

Services	Metropolitan Status			Poverty Level			Overall
	Urban	Suburban	Rural	Low	Medium	High	
Licensed databases	96.6% (n = 2,648)	95.2% (n = 4,839)	83.4% (n = 6,461)	89.3% (n = 11,702)	91.0% (n = 2,091)	93.4% (n = 155)	89.6% (n = 13,948)
Homework resources	90.5% (n = 2,480)	83.4% (n = 4,242)	73.3% (n = 5,683)	79.1% (n = 10,374)	82.1% (n = 1,888)	86.7% (n = 144)	79.6% (n = 12,40)
Audio content (e.g., podcasts, audio books, other)	84.1% (n = 2,305)	77.6% (n = 3,948)	65.8% (n = 5,098)	73.0% (n = 9,566)	72.1% (n = 1,657)	77.1% (n = 128)	72.9% (n = 11,351)
Digital reference/virtual reference	75.1% (n = 2,059)	70.8% (n = 3,601)	52.5% (n = 4,066)	62.5% (n = 8,194)	61.4% (n = 1,412)	71.9% (n = 120)	62.4% (n = 9,726)
E-books	79.4% (n = 2,176)	64.1% (n = 3,261)	41.2% (n = 3,191)	55.5% (n = 7,273)	54.3% (n = 1,249)	64.1% (n = 107)	55.4% (n = 8,629)
Video content	63.4% (n = 1,738)	52.8% (n = 2,687)	46.2% (n = 3,578)	51.6% (n = 6,768)	48.9% (n = 1,124)	66.9% (n = 111)	51.4% (n = 8,003)
Online instructional courses/tutorials	52.1% (n = 1,427)	44.2% (n = 2,246)	39.6% (n = 3,072)	42.9% (n = 5,625)	45.4% (n = 1,044)	45.8% (n = 76)	43.3% (n = 6,745)

Will not total 100%, as respondents could select more than one option.
Weighted missing values, n = 385.
Source: Bertot, et al. (2009).

22

TABLE 2.2 Formal Technology Training Classes Offered by Public Library Outlets by Metropolitan Status and Poverty

Technology Training Classes	Metropolitan Status			Poverty Level			Overall
	Urban	Suburban	Rural	Low	Medium	High	
General Internet use (e.g., set up e-mail, Web browsing)	94.7% (n = 1,356)	93.2% (n = 1,960)	91.0% (n = 1,690)	92.5% (n = 4,062)	94.9% (n = 852)	90.2% (n = 92)	92.8% (n = 5,006)
General computer skills (e.g., how to use mouse, keyboard, printing)	93.9% (n = 1,343)	88.7% (n = 1,865)	92.3% (n = 1,714)	90.5% (n = 3,976)	94.5% (n = 849)	97% (n = 98)	91.3% (n = 4,923)
General online/Web searching (e.g., using Google, Yahoo, others)	72.0% (n = 1.030)	81.5% (n = 1,715)	75.4% (n = 1,401)	78.2% (n = 3,433)	71.3% (n = 640)	72.5% (n = 74)	76.9% (n = 4,147)
General software use (e.g., word processing, spreadsheets, presentation)	66.9% (n = 957)	72.5% (n = 1,524)	71.0% (n = 1,319)	70.3% (n = 3,089)	71.8% (n = 645)	66.3% (n = 67)	70.5% (n = 3,801)
Using library's Online Public Access Catalog (OPAC)	44.2% (n = 632)	52.3% (n = 1,100)	47.3% (n = 878)	50.4% (n = 2,212)	39.5% (n = 355)	42.6% (n = 43)	48.4% (n = 2,610)
Using online databases (e.g., commercial databases to search and find content)	51.0% (n = 730)	51.1% (n = 1,075)	41.1% (n = 762)	48.7% (n = 2,139)	42.8% (n = 384)	42.6% (n = 43)	47.6% (n = 2,566)
Accessing online job-seeking and career-related information	36.9% (n = 528)	23.2% (n = 488)	23.4% (n = 434)	25.0% (n = 1,099)	34.6% (n = 311)	40.2% (n = 41)	26.9% (n = 1,451)

(Continued)

23

TABLE 2.2 (Continued)

Technology Training Classes	Metropolitan Status			Poverty Level			Overall
	Urban	Suburban	Rural	Low	Medium	High	
Safe online practices (e.g., not divulging personal information)	24.8% (n = 355)	23.7% (n = 498)	26.1% (n = 485)	24.2% (n = 1,064)	27.8% (n = 250)	22.8% (n = 23)	24.8% (n = 1,337)
Accessing online government information (e.g., Medicare, taxes, how to complete forms)	35.4% (n = 507)	19.0% (n = 399)	22.9% (n = 426)	22.2% (n = 974)	36.1% (n = 324)	33.3% (n = 34)	24.7% (n = 1,332)
Digital photography, software and online applications (e.g., Photoshop, Flickr)	15.9% (n = 228)	24.9% (n = 524)	20.6% (n = 383)	21.6% (n = 948)	18.5% (n = 166)	19.8% (n = 20)	21.0% (n = 1,134)
Accessing online medical information (e.g., health literacy)	20.5% (n = 294)	15.0% (n = 315)	19% (n = 352)	17.4% (n = 766)	20.6% (n = 185)	9.9% (n = 10)	17.8% (n = 961)
Web 2.0 (e.g., blogging, RSS)	16.4% (n = 234)	10.4% (n = 218)	8.3% (n = 154)	10.1% (n = 444)	15.5% (n = 139)	22.8% (n = 23)	11.2% (n = 606)
Accessing online investment information	11.8% (n = 169)	11.2% (n = 236)	6.6% (n = 123)	9.7% (n = 424)	11.1% (n = 100)	3.0% (n = 3)	9.8% (n = 527)

Will not total 100%, as categories are not mutually exclusive.
Weighted missing values, n = 63.
Source: Bertot et al. (2009).

24

TABLE 2.3   E-government Roles and Services Provided by Public Library Outlets by Metropolitan Status and Poverty.

E-Government Roles and Services	Metropolitan Status			Poverty Level			Overall
	Urban	Suburban	Rural	Low	Medium	High	
Staff provide assistance to patrons applying for or accessing e-government services	59.3% (n = 1,580)	53.7% (n = 2,651)	52.6% (n = 3,903)	54.0% (n = 6,819)	55.3% (n = 1,236)	48.8% (n = 78)	54.1% (n = 8,133)
Staff provide as-needed assistance to patrons for understanding and using e-government resources	83.5% (n = 2,225)	81.8% (n = 4,039)	78.6% (n = 5,831)	80.5% (n = 10,161)	80.6% (n = 1,800)	83.8% (n = 134)	80.5% (n = 12,095)
Staff provide immigrants with assistance in locating immigration-related services and information	52.7% (n = 1,405)	33.9% (n = 1,675)	23.5% (n = 1,742)	31.0% (n = 3,911)	38.4% (n = 859)	32.3% (n = 52)	32.1% (n = 4,822)
The library offers training classes regarding the use of e-government resources	21.8% (n = 582)	6.8% (n = 337)	4.6% (n = 343)	7.4% (n = 935)	13.1% (n = 293)	21.2% (n = 34)	8.4% (n = 1,262)
The library is partnering with others to provide e-government services	17.8% (n = 474)	14.0% (n = 689)	11.5% (n = 852)	13.3% (n = 1,680)	14.3% (n = 319)	10.6% (n = 17)	13.4% (n = 2,016)

(Continued)

25

TABLE 2.3 (Continued)

E-Government Roles and Services	Metropolitan Status			Poverty Level			Overall
	Urban	Suburban	Rural	Low	Medium	High	
The library has at least one staff member with significant knowledge and skills in provision of e-government services	33.1% (n = 882)	18.3% (n = 903)	18.4% (n = 1,366)	20.1% (n = 2,539)	25.4% (n = 569)	26.7% (n = 43)	21.0% (n = 3,151)
Other	2.5% (n = 66)	3.0% (n = 149)	2.9% (n = 213)	2.9% (n = 365)	2.7% (n = 60)	1.9% (n = 3)	2.8% (n = 428)
The library does not provide e-government services to its patrons on a regular basis	10.0% (n = 266)	12.4% (n = 613)	17.7% (n = 1,316)	14.9% (n = 1,880)	13.2% (n = 295)	12.4% (n = 20)	14.6% (n = 2,195)

Will not total 100% as categories are not mutually exclusive.
Weighted missing values, n = 935.
Source: Bertot, et al. (2009).

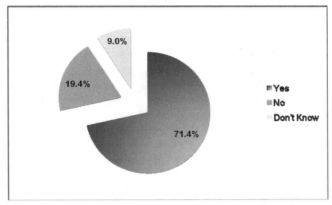

Figure 2.6 Public Libraries as Only Provider of Free Access in Community.

- *Their numbers of public access computers are inadequate.* 81.2% of libraries reported that they have insufficient availability of workstations some or all of the time (see Figure 2.8).
- *They implement limitations on the use of their public access workstations.* 94.1% of libraries have time limits imposed on the use of their public access workstations. Of those libraries that have time limits, nearly 70% (67.6%) have time limits of 60 minutes or less, with nearly 25% (22.4%) having time limits of up to 30 minutes (see Table 2.4).
- *Costs, space, and buildings are real barriers to the public access environment public libraries can offer.* 77.4% of libraries reported that cost factors, 75.9% reported space limitations, and 34.0% reported that the building infrastructure (e.g., cabling, wiring, electrical outlets) influence their decisions to add public access workstations/laptops (see Table 2.5).
- *They rely on non-professional IT staff for technology support.* 62.8% of libraries report that they rely on non-IT public service staff or library

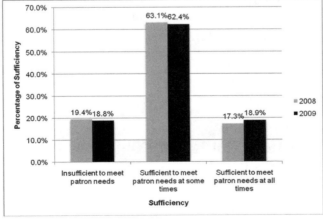

Figure 2.7 Sufficiency of Public Access Workstations: 2008–2009.

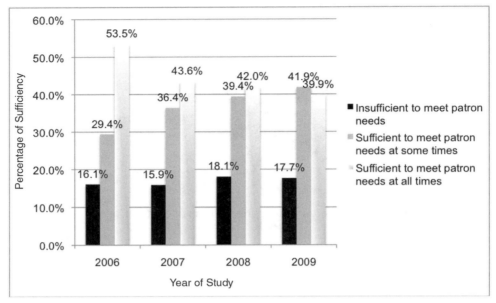

Figure 2.8 Sufficiency of Internet Connection: 2006–2009.

directors for support for their technology. This percentage climbs to 74.6% for rural libraries and drops to 36.8% for urban libraries. 42.3% of libraries support their IT with system-level IT staff, but only 28.7% of rural libraries have access to such support as compared to 72.2% of urban libraries (see Table 2.6).

The real significance of these findings is that some libraries continue to face the same challenges *in spite of upgrades to their technology infrastructure*. And, more significantly, libraries continue to offer a significant amount of services to the communities that they serve—licensed databases, technology training, e-government, and more—while often being the only free public access point within their communities.

Thus, public libraries increasingly report that they are unable to meet patron demands for services due to inadequate technology infrastructure, costs associated with operating and maintaining that infrastructure, and bandwidth quality/availability issues—but not for lack of trying to enhance their services. What is unclear is how libraries will maintain their levels of public access computer and Internet access services, much less extend and augment them in the current economic downturn. It is in this mixed and paradoxical context that public libraries provide their public access services.

FUTURE ISSUES AND CONSIDERATIONS

The surveys have demonstrated the embracing of the Internet and public access technologies by public libraries—not just from an infrastructure perspective, but also from a service and resource perspective. Public libraries, on average, increased the number of public access workstations by several

TABLE 2.4 Public Library Outlet Time Limits for Patron Use of Workstations by Metropolitan Status and Poverty

Method	Metropolitan Status				Poverty Level			
	Urban	Suburban	Rural	Low	Medium	High	Overall	
This library does not have time limits for public Internet workstations	2.2% (n = 62)	5.2% (n = 273)	7.4% (n = 586)	6.0% (n = 803)	4.8% (n = 112)	3.5% (n = 6)	5.8% (n = 921)	
This library does have time limits for public Internet workstations	97.8% (n = 2,731)	94.6% (n = 4,927)	92.4% (n = 7,290)	93.8% (n = 12,544)	95.2% (n = 2,236)	96.5% (n = 167)	94.1% (n = 14,947)	
Do not know if this library has time limits	*	*	*	*	*	*	*	

Weighted missing values, n = 69.
Key: * : Insufficient data to report.
Source: Bertot, et al. (2009).

TABLE 2.5   Factors Influencing the Addition of Public Access Workstations/Laptops by Metropolitan Status and Poverty

Factors Influencing Workstation/Laptop Upgrade Decisions	Metropolitan Status				Poverty Level			Overall
	Urban	Suburban	Rural	Low	Medium	High		
Space limitations	79.0% (n = 2,176)	77.0% (n = 3,930)	74.2% (n = 5,806)	75.5% (n = 9,973)	78.7% (n = 1,820)	72.3% (n = 120)		75.9% (n = 11,912)
Cost factors	79.9% (n = 2,202)	72.4% (n = 3,695)	79.9% (n = 6,252)	77.2% (n = 10,193)	78.7% (n = 1,822)	80.7% (n = 134)		77.4% (n = 12,149)
Maintenance, upgrade, and general upkeep	10.7% (n = 294)	17.8% (n = 911)	24.0% (n = 1,877)	19.8% (n = 2,621)	18.9% (n = 438)	13.8% (n = 23)		19.6% (n = 3,082)
Availability of public service staff	11.5% (n = 316)	9.4% (n = 479)	7.8% (n = 609)	8.4% (n = 1,111)	12.0% (n = 277)	10.2% (n = 17)		8.9% (n = 1,404)
Availability of technical staff	13.9% (n = 382)	10.3% (n = 524)	12.7% (n = 995)	11.9% (n = 1,573)	13.0% (n = 301)	16.3% (n = 27)		12.1% (n = 1,901)
Availability of bandwidth to support additional workstations	16.8% (n = 462)	18.2% (n = 929)	12.9% (n = 1,007)	14.9% (n = 1,967)	16.8% (n = 389)	25.1% (n = 42)		15.3% (n = 2,398)
Availability of electrical outlets, cabling, or other infrastructure	50.1% (n = 1,380)	36.2% (n = 1,846)	27.0% (n = 2,114)	33.1% (n = 4,366)	37.7% (n = 873)	60.8% (n = 101)		34.0% (n = 5,340)
Other	1.6% (n = 43)	2.9% (n = 149)	3.2% (n = 252)	3.0% (n = 399)	1.9% (n = 45)	*		2.8% (n = 444)

Will not total 100%, as categories are not mutually exclusive.
Weighted missing values, n = 270.
Key: * : Insufficient data to report.
Source: Bertot et al. (2009).

TABLE 2.6 Sources of IT and Computer Support Provided to Public Library Outlets by Metropolitan Status and Poverty

Source of IT Support	Metropolitan Status			Poverty Level			Overall
	Urban	Suburban	Rural	Low	Medium	High	
Non-IT specialist public service staff	30.7% (n = 849)	33.1% (n = 1,701)	27.4% (n = 2,154)	29.4% (n = 3,894)	41.8% (n = 71)	31.9% (n = 739)	29.9% (n = 4,704)
Non-IT specialist library director	6.1% (n = 168)	25.7% (n = 1,318)	47.2% (n = 3,701)	35.5% (n = 4,710)	20.0% (n = 463)	8.2% (n = 14)	32.9% (n = 5,187)
Non-IT specialist other	6.4% (n = 176)	10.3% (n = 529)	12.5% (n = 982)	10.7% (n = 1,414)	11.5% (n = 267)	3.5% (n = 6)	10.7% (n = 1,687)
Building-based IT specialist	11.4% (n = 316)	13.7% (n = 705)	7.6% (n = 593)	10.2% (n = 1,349)	10.4% (n = 242)	13.6% (n = 23)	10.2% (n = 1,614)
System-level IT staff	72.2% (n = 1,994)	47.1% (n = 2,420)	28.7% (n = 2,251)	40.4% (n = 5,356)	50.5% (n = 1,169)	81.7% (n = 138)	42.3% (n = 6,663)
Library consortia or other library organization	5.8% (n = 161)	16.3% (n = 835)	12.8% (n = 1,005)	13.9% (n = 1,841)	6.0% (n = 140)	12.4% (n = 21)	12.7% (n = 2,002)
County/city IT staff	20.8% (n = 574)	16.4% (n = 843)	10.0% (n = 784)	13.5% (n = 1,794)	16.1% (n = 374)	19.4% (n = 33)	14.0% (n = 2,201)
State telecom-munications network staff	6.7% (n = 185)	1.6% (n = 84)	2.7% (n = 213)	2.5% (n = 338)	5.4% (n = 125)	11.2% (n = 19)	3.1% (n = 482)
State library IT staff	7.2% (n = 198)	2.1% (n = 106)	6.5% (n = 513)	4.3% (n = 567)	10.0% (n = 231)	11.2% (n = 19)	5.2% (n = 817)
Outside vendor/contractor	17.7% (n = 489)	22.1% (n = 1,138)	33.8% (n = 2,651)	27.4% (n = 3,636)	26.2% (n = 608)	20.6% (n = 35)	27.2% (n = 4,279)
Volunteer[s]	1.6% (n = 43)	5.2% (n = 266)	13.2% (n = 1,034)	9.3% (n = 1,240)	4.4% (n = 101)	1.8% (n = 3)	8.5% (n = 1,344)
Other source	*	1.6% (n = 84)	2.9% (n = 226)	2.2% (n = 297)	1.5% (n = 35)	*	2.1% (n = 332)

Weighted missing values, n = 209.
Key: * insufficient data to report.
Totals will not equal 100% as respondents marked all that applied.
Source: Bertot et al. (2009).

hundred percent in a period of eight years; they substantially increased their Internet speeds; expanded service to include wi-fi public access; and now offer a large range of Internet-enabled services and resources such as databases, digital reference, and e-books/audio books; and provide technology and Internet resource training services. But the data also show that libraries are stretched, and increasingly challenged to maintain and/or enhance their levels of services.

Other chapters in this book discuss a range of issues regarding public library Internet connectivity. Rather than be repetitive, this concluding section offers insights into key issue areas that public libraries, policymakers, and others need to consider as public libraries continue to fulfill their role as community-based providers of cost-free public access to the Internet and computing:

- *How much is enough? It's never enough.* A question that the surveys have never adequately addressed is "How much access (workstations, broadband) is enough?" In fact, as the bar gets higher in terms of service provision, so too does the assessment of how much is needed. Libraries—even the smallest in the most rural areas—are rapidly approaching the need for fiber optic connections. Nearly half of all libraries report a T1 (1.5 MBPS) connection—something that only a few short years ago was considered robust bandwidth. And yet, a vast majority of libraries report that this increase in bandwidth is inadequate.

- *Better understanding of the relationship between infrastructure and services.* The initial Public Library Internet surveys showed that libraries viewed Internet connectivity as an experimental service—one that had substantial potential, but it was unclear at the time (after all, the Mosaic browser was introduced in 1993, the same year that the first survey went into the field) just how revolutionary the Internet would be to public library service. As Internet-enabled services are a mainstay of the public library, there is a substantial need to better understand which services require what amount of bandwidth. Increasingly, for example, streaming video content is in high definition format, which consumes substantially more bandwidth than Web browsing.

- *The need for comprehensive capacity planning.* Public access services and resources require libraries to look across their Internet-enabled services and resources comprehensively. Public access workstations, broadband, and wi-fi are part of a collective public access technology environment that directly impacts the ability of libraries to offer patrons high quality Internet services and resources—and moreover, high quality user experiences. A library that has seven public access workstations and offers wi-fi, but has a DSL connection, ultimately provides a dial-up experience to its users. Capacity planning needs to include not just that last mile, but also internal library infrastructure, including routers, switches, and up to date workstations, at the least, to provide quality public access services.

- *Continual upgrades to technology and staff.* As the surveys demonstrate, public access computing and Internet infrastructure and services are not a one-time investment. There is a continual need to upgrade computing technology, Internet connectivity, and buildings. Also, the surveys show that, given the demands placed on libraries for training, e-government, education, employment, and other critical service areas, there is a need to continually train library staff on a range of technologies as well as services (such as how to help patrons apply for government benefits, seek employment, take certification exams, and more).

- *Setting service quality benchmarks.* Given increasing demands, and libraries that report the inability to keep up with demand, libraries may need to consider setting levels of service quality benchmarks. Libraries will need to decide whether they will offer as many services at the highest level of quality as possible, or set levels of service quality, realizing that a library may not be able to meet all requests and demands. In some cases, service quality levels may be dictated by the, for example, broadband that is available to a library due to cost and geography.

- *The library divide.* One factor across all the surveys conducted in the last 10 years remains: rural libraries in general have fewer resources, less connectivity, fewer workstations, less access to technology support, and other factors. This does not mean that urban libraries are infinitely better off—in fact, urban libraries often report similar issues in terms of keeping up with demand. But the survey data are clear: rural libraries face substantial challenges in supporting their public access technology environment, and there is no indication of abatement in this circumstance.

The above are a selection of issues that will need consideration and resolution if public libraries are to continue their role as critical providers of community public Internet and computing access.

Future *Public Libraries and the Internet* surveys will need to continue exploring the evolving service context of public access Internet and computing services within public libraries. Public libraries have clearly moved beyond issues of "getting connected" and into critical services provision via the Internet. Indeed, one cannot imagine a public library that is not connected to the Internet, not providing public access computers, or not offering users a number of online resources such as licensed databases, assistance with using technology and/or the Internet, or, increasingly, wi-fi access. One can no longer separate the public library from public Internet access. The issue is not one of measuring connectivity, but rather, better understanding the nature and roles of public libraries as providers of community-based public access.

NOTES

1. By system we mean the central authority for the library—that is, the entity that makes budget decisions, applies for E-rate, and makes other management decisions. The survey does not use the term "system" to mean regional cooperatives or other forms of federated libraries.

2. Metropolitan status was determined using the official designations employed by the Census Bureau, the Office of Management and Budget, and other government agencies. These designations are used in the study because they are

the official definition employed by the Institute of Museum and Library Services (IMLS), which allows for the mapping of public library outlets in the study.

3. In previous studies, the authors have used the less than 20%, 20–40%, and greater than 40% poverty breakdowns. The poverty of the population a library outlet serves is calculated using a combination of geocoded library facilities and census data. More information on this technique is available through the authors as well as by reviewing the 1998 and 2000 public library Internet studies (Bertot & McClure, 1998, 2000).

REFERENCES

American Library Association. (2007). *Libraries Connect Communities: Public Library Funding and Technology Access Study: 2006–2007*. Chicago, IL: American Library Association.

American Library Association. (2008). *Libraries Connect Communities: Public Library Funding and Technology Access Study: 2007–2008*. Chicago, IL: American Library Association.

American Library Association. (2009). *Libraries Connect Communities 3: Public Library Funding and Technology Access Study: 2008–2009*. Chicago, IL: American Library Association.

Bertot, J. C., & McClure, C. R. (1998a). *Moving toward More Effective Public Internet Access: The 1998 National Survey of Public Library Outlet Internet Connectivity*. Washington, D.C.: National Commission on Libraries and Information Science. Available at http://www.plinternetsurvey.org.

Bertot, J. C., & McClure, C. R. (1998b). *The 1998 National Survey of U.S. Public Library Outlet Internet Connectivity: Final Report*. Washington, D.C.: National Commission on Libraries and Information Science. Available at http://www.plinternetsurvey.org.

Bertot, J. C., & McClure, C. R. (2000). *Public Libraries and the Internet 2000: Summary Findings and Data Tables*. Washington, D.C.: National Commission on Libraries and Information Science. Available at http://www.plinternetsurvey.org.

Bertot, J. C., & McClure, C. R. (2002). *Public Libraries and the Internet 2002: Internet Connectivity and Networked Services*. Available at http://www.plinternetsurvey.org.

Bertot, J. C., McClure, C. R., Barton, K., Thomas, S., & McGilvray, J. (2007). *Public Libraries and the Internet 2007: Survey Results and Findings*. Tallahassee, FL: Information Use Management and Policy Institute. Available at http://www.plinternetsurvey.org.

Bertot, J. C., McClure, C. R., & Fletcher, P. D. (1997). *The 1997 National Survey of U.S. Public Libraries and the Internet: Final Report*. Washington, D.C.: American Library Association, Office for Information Technology Policy. Available at http://www.plinternetsurvey.org.

Bertot, J. C., McClure, C. R., & Jaeger, P. T. (2004). *Public Libraries and the Internet 2004: Survey Results and Findings*. Tallahassee, FL: Information Use Management and Policy Institute. Available at http://www.plinternetsurvey.org.

Bertot, J. C., McClure, C. R., & Jaeger, P. T. (2006). *Public Libraries and the Internet 2006: Survey Results and Findings*. Tallahassee, FL: Information Use Management and Policy Institute. Available at http://www.plinternetsurvey.org.

Bertot, J. C., McClure, C. R., Wright, C. B., Jensen, E., & Thomas, S. (2008). *Public Libraries and the Internet 2008: Survey Results and Findings*. Tallahassee, FL: Information Use Management and Policy Institute. Available at http://www.plinternetsurvey.org.

Bertot, J. C., McClure, C. R., Wright, C. B., Jensen, E., & Thomas, S. (2009). *Public Libraries and the Internet 2009: Survey Results and Findings.* College Park, MD: Center for Library & Information Innovation. Available at http:// www.plinternetsurvey.org.

Bertot, J. C., McClure, C. R., & Zweizig, D. L. (1996). *The 1996 National Survey of Public Libraries and the Internet: Progress and Issues.* Washington, D.C.: National Commission on Libraries and Information Science. Available at http://www.plinternetsurvey.org.

McClure, C. R., Bertot, J. C., & Zweizig, D. L. (1994). *Public Libraries and the Internet: Study Results, Policy Issues, and Recommendations.* Washington, D.C.: National Commission on Libraries and Information Science. Available at http://www.plinternetsurvey.org.

Part

II

Contexts and Connections

Chapter 3

Public Libraries and E-government

Paul T. Jaeger and John Carlo Bertot

INTRODUCTION

E-government is the provision of government information and services through the online environment, including such diverse interactions as applying for Medicare prescription drug plans, paying taxes, and e-mailing a public official. E-government content is generated at the local, state, and federal government levels in the United States. E-government interactions can occur over multiple devices, such as computers, personal digital assistants (PDA), smart phones, and other mobile devices. A new but extremely important social role for public libraries is ensuring that all citizens have access to and assistance using e-government information and services (Bertot, Jaeger, Langa, & McClure, 2006a, 2006b). This chapter explores the intersection between public libraries and e-government, identifying many significant implications and impacts for library activities and management, including expectations for libraries, the activities of librarians, and library education.

THE CONTEXT OF E-GOVERNMENT ADOPTION

E-government is a dynamic socio-technical system encompassing issues of governance, societal trends, technological change, information management, interaction, and human factors (Dawes, 2009). Governments at all levels are showing a strong preference for delivering services via the Internet, primarily as a means of boosting cost-efficiency and reducing time spent on direct interactions with citizens (Ebbers, Pieterson, & Noordman, 2008). However, citizens still show a preference for in person or phone-based interactions with government representatives when they have questions or are seeking services, though individuals with higher levels of education are typically more open to using online interactions with government (Ebbers, Pieterson, & Noordman, 2008; Steib & Navarro, 2006). E-government services are limited often by difficulties in searching for and locating the desired information, as well as by lack of availability of computers and Internet access for many segments of the general population (Bertot & Jaeger, 2008; Singh & Sahu, 2008). In the United States, the scope of e-government is enormous—federal e-government now encompasses more than 30,000 Web sites and well over 100 million pages (Evans, 2007). And, governments and agencies are increasing their digital presence and services through the use of social media technologies such as Twitter and YouTube.

Such problems are exacerbated by a general lack of familiarity of the structure of government, including which agencies to contact, and by attitudes toward technology and government among many citizens (Jaeger & Thompson, 2003, 2004). Also, as many e-government sites give more emphasis to presenting political agendas rather than promoting democratic participation, users are becoming less trusting of the sites themselves (Jaeger, 2005, 2007). Further complications arise from the fact that many government agencies are ambivalent about direct citizen participation in the political process (Roberts, 2004).

Nevertheless, many citizens look to e-government as a valuable source of information, considering e-government sites to be "objective authoritative sources" (Anderson, 2002, p. 1). Currently, the primary reason that people use e-government is to gather information (Reddick, 2005). In the United States, 58% of Internet users believe e-government to be the best source for government information and 65% of Americans expect that information they are seeking will be on a government site, with 26 million Americans seeking political information online every day (Horrigan, 2006; Horrigan & Rainie, 2002). But increasingly, people expect to be able to interact with government through a range of digital media and devices—not just seek information.

Public satisfaction with the e-government services available, however, is limited. As commercial sites are developing faster and provide more innovative services than e-government sites, public satisfaction with government Web sites is declining (Barr, 2007). Public confidence in government Web sites has also declined as much of the public policy related to e-government since 9/11 has been the reduction of access to information through e-government (Feinberg, 2004; Halchin, 2004; Kirtley, 2006; Relyea & Halchin, 2003). The types of information that have been affected include many forms of socially useful information, from scientific information to public safety information to information about government activities (Jaeger, 2007). For these and other reasons, the majority of citizens, even those with a high speed Internet connection at home, seeking government information and services, prefer to speak to a person directly in their contacts with the government (Horrigan, 2004).

Issues of acceptance and use of e-government can vary between different levels of government. For example, larger local and state governments are generally better equipped to pursue e-government initiatives, often because larger governments have greater financial, technical, or personnel capacities available for e-government projects (Moon, 2002). In many local communities, support for e-government implementation is countered by various forms of resistance to the idea of e-government initiatives (Ebbers & van Dijk, 2007). The success of government initiatives are dependant on managerial leadership and political support within the government (Ho & Ni, 2004). At the government agency level, the acceptance of the importance of e-government by government employees is also vital to the success of e-government programs and initiatives (Ho & Ni, 2004; Jaeger & Matteson, 2009; Mahler & Regan, 2002).

E-GOVERNMENT USAGE IN THE PUBLIC LIBRARY

Nearly half of the residents of the United States do not have access to broadband services on which e-government services rely (Horrigan, 2008). Internet penetration in public libraries has now reached nearly 100%, and perhaps more significantly, the only free public Internet access is that which is provided by public libraries in almost 75% of communities in United States (Bertot, McClure, & Jaeger, 2008). As a result, Internet access in public libraries serves as the guarantor of access to e-government for those with no other access, those with insufficient access, and those who need assistance using e-government (Bertot, Jaeger, Langa, & McClure, 2006a, 2006b). Among patrons using e-government in libraries, 52.4% do not own a computer, 42.4% lack access both at home and at work, 40% are there because access is free, and 38.1% rely on the assistance of librarians (Gibson, Bertot, & McClure, 2009).

The vital roles that public libraries played in the aftermath of the major hurricanes of 2004 and 2005 by providing access to FEMA forms and other e-government materials essential for emergency response and recovery may have permanently cemented the public and government perception of public libraries as hubs for e-government access (Jaeger, Langa, Bertot, & McClure, 2006). E-government access and training will continue to grow in importance for public libraries, as more government information and services migrate to online formats due both to availability of access and trust of the library.

The public library "is a trusted community-based entity to which individuals turn for help in their online activities—even if they have computers and Internet access at home or elsewhere" (Bertot, Jaeger, Langa, & McClure, 2006a, n. p.). As a result, citizens not only seek access to e-government at the public library because access is available, but also because they know that they can get help using it and they trust the help that they will receive there (Jaeger & Fleischmann, 2007). Many individuals who are otherwise confident Internet users will seek help at the public library when preparing their taxes online, applying for government assistance and/or services, or emailing a government official. "When people struggle with, become frustrated by, or reject e-government services, they turn to public libraries" (Jaeger & Fleischmann, 2007, p. 42). When using e-government in libraries, 28% of patrons report needing help with e-government, 24% struggle with time limits, 16% have difficulty using Web sites, and 13% have difficulty with forms (Gibson, Bertot, & McClure, 2009).

People often use e-government as part of major life events—requesting social support, filing taxes, registering children for school, signing up for Medicare, protecting water rights, getting help from FEMA, paying fines, emailing officials, finding out where to turn for assistance, and countless other activities of sizeable importance in the life of the patron. About one-third of library patrons using e-government are seeking state e-government, 31% are seeking federal e-government, and 28.1% are seeking local e-government (Gibson, Bertot, & McClure, 2009). In terms of specific services, more than 40% are looking for forms, nearly 40% are working on issues related to taxes, 24.3% are searching for government jobs, and another 24.3% are looking for education information (Gibson, Bertot, & McClure, 2009). As such, e-government access and training activities encompass Internet services and government information provision, as well as include a unique element of personal importance from the perspective of the patrons.

However, few patrons enter the library and describe their information needs in terms of e-government, and most users of the Internet access in libraries are not there to surf government sites aimlessly. This attitude is even reflected in how patrons search for government information. A 2008 study found that 77.4% of U.S. citizens seeking e-government information check Google or a similar search engine, while only 16.5% check the main portal of U.S. e-government (www.usa.gov) (Burroughs, 2009).

The complex relationship between public libraries and e-government raises increasingly significant issues for libraries. For example, the provision of e-government access:

- Contributes to the plateau in the quality of Internet access that libraries are able to provide (McClure, Jaeger, & Bertot, 2007);
- Redefines the notion of quality public access technology services in the public library context (Bertot & McClure, 2007);
- Encourages governments to rely on libraries as the public provider of e-government access and assistance (Bertot, Jaeger, Langa, & McClure, 2006a, 2006b);
- Places libraries in the position of ensuring access to government information during emergency situations (Jaeger, Langa, McClure, & Bertot, 2006);
- Creates new social expectations for libraries from patrons and communities (Jaeger & Fleischmann, 2007; McClure & Jaeger, 2008);
- Reveals new educational challenges for the education of future librarians by Library and Information Science (LIS) programs (Jaeger, 2008);
- Creates new educational obligations for libraries (Jaeger & Bertot, 2009);
- Alters relationships between libraries and other agencies of local government (Jaeger, 2009).

These issues are representative of the range of opportunities and challenges that e-government presents to libraries, librarianship, and library education.

E-GOVERNMENT AND TRUST IN THE PUBLIC LIBRARY

Several different factors have contributed to public libraries becoming the trusted source of e-government access in society. Public libraries were one of the first societal institutions to commit to the provision of Internet access, with many having provided access since the early 1990s. Now, such access is nearly universal and universally free among public libraries in the United States

(Bertot, McClure, Jaeger, & Ryan, 2006). This availability of free access combines with the historical trust that libraries have long cultivated as providers of information. "The public library is one place that is culturally ingrained as a trusted source of free and open information access and exchange" (Jaeger & Burnett, 2005, p. 487). As a result, people have been far more willing to rely on public libraries for Internet access than public schools, government offices, or the Community Technology Centers (CTCs) that were created in 1990s to provide public access to the Internet.

The 2007 *Public Libraries and the Internet* survey found that nearly 75% of the public libraries responding reported that in their communities the public library is the only source for free public access to the Internet (Bertot, McClure, & Jaeger, 2008). Only 17.4% of communities have another public access point to consistently rely on beyond the library to ensure access to federal, state, and local e-government information and services. This means that public libraries truly are the guarantors of public access to the e-government in the United States.

The access to Internet technology provided by libraries is extremely important to the large percentage of the U.S. population that has no other access or has insufficient access. While 73% of Americans are Internet users, 27% of Americans live in a household that has no Internet connection and 58% of Americans with home access do not have broadband (Fox, 2005; Madden, 2006). The former group clearly needs a public outlet for access to the Internet and e-government. The latter group frequently turns to public libraries for access as Internet-based information and services, including e-government applications, are increasingly sophisticated and require higher levels of bandwidth (Bertot, McClure, & Jaeger, 2008). As lack of access and lack of sufficient access will likely be continuing problems for large numbers of people for economic and other reasons, the role of public libraries as guarantor of access will remain socially significant.

Another major part of the provision of Internet access in public libraries has been providing assistance. It is evident that "even if Americans had all the hardware they needed to access every bit of government information they required, many would still need the help of skilled librarians whose job it is to be familiar with multiple systems of access to government systems" (Heanue, 2001, p. 124). A 2001 study of users of public libraries and the Internet identified the key preferences that users had for seeking information in the public libraries: the ease of use, the accuracy of the information, and the availability of the library staff to provide assistance (D'Elia, Jorgensen, Woelfel, & Rodger, 2002; Rodger, D'Elia, & Jorgensen, 2001). As such, the fact that public libraries provide assistance increases the trust in the information provided by the library. The value of such trusted help continues to increase in importance as the scope and number of e-government activities has grown, because greater numbers of people need to accomplish ever-more complicated e-government tasks that they may not feel confident they can accomplish on their own.

Trust of public libraries is another important part of public libraries' role as e-government access point. The historical trust in the United States of public libraries as a place that provides information equally to all is a key factor in their being trusted as providers of e-government access and training (Jaeger & Fleischmann, 2007). Exactly one half of the respondents to a 2007 Pew

Research Center study agreed with the statement "You can't be too careful in dealing with people" (p. 2). However, a 2006 study conducted by Public Agenda found that "public libraries seem almost immune to the distrust that is associated with so many other institutions" (p. 11). Public libraries have managed to maintain the trust of their users and communities even when most other social institutions have not due to the provision of user-centered services, the availability of knowledgeable assistance, a focus of all activities on meeting the needs of the library user, and active engagement with users, including connecting users to new information sources (Carr, 2003).

The trust of libraries also has been sustained through their core values of intellectual freedom that have manifested in the defense of free speech and expression, opposition to censorship, and the provision of access to materials that represent a wide range of perspectives (Jaeger & Burnett, 2005). Such trust-building stances have influenced the perceptions of e-government in the library. Librarians are able to make the experience of using e-government less difficult and overwhelming for many users simply by directing them immediately to the sites that the users are seeking and providing further assistance if needed. Trust of public libraries as e-government access providers can overcome a patron's hesitancy in using e-government. A lack of trust in e-government parallels an overall lack of trust in government among many citizens (Horst, Kuttschreuter, & Gutteling, 2007). For many e-government users, trust of public libraries and librarians trumps any distrust of e-government (Jaeger & Fleischmann, 2007).

In addition to members of the public, government agencies also trust and rely on public libraries to ensure public access to e-government, frequently directing Web site users to public libraries for assistance using their Web sites and materials provided on them (Bertot, Jaeger, Langa, & McClure, 2006a, 2006b). While public libraries did not set out to intentionally become the primary public access point for e-government when they began commonly providing Internet access, the reliance on the Internet for so many government, education, employment, and other functions necessitated the availability of societal guarantors of Internet access. As part of this role, public libraries now serve to ensure e-government access and assistance for those who have not other means of access and for those who have access but need help in completing their e-government tasks.

Ultimately, by providing assistance along with access to the Internet, libraries matured into the trusted societal access points for e-government. In contrast, CTCs—which had no established trust in their communities and which often lacked any assistance for users—primarily disappeared due to lack of usage around the turn of the millennium. No commercial institutions can play the same access role as libraries, either, as commercial institutions tend to concentrate on providing free wi-fi. Since libraries provide free access to both the Internet and to computers, they ensure access to people who do not own a laptop to take advantage of free wi-fi. As the socially trusted providers of e-government access and assistance, libraries have become a critical part of governmental processes and societal infrastructure in the United States. If libraries were not providing this e-government access and assistance, many members of the public would be at risk of being partially or completely disenfranchised from e-government.

E-GOVERNMENT AND EMERGENCIES

The most dramatic role of public libraries in supporting e-government may be in emergency situations. During the unprecedented 2004 and 2005 hurricane seasons, many Gulf Coast communities from Texas to Florida relied on public libraries to provide access to vital government information and services after being hit by major hurricanes, like Katrina, Rita, Wilma, Dennis, and Ivan. The public libraries and their Internet access played several major disaster response and recovery roles related to those major hurricanes:

- Completion of online FEMA forms and insurance claims.
- Location of and communication with dispersed and displaced family members, friends, and pets.
- Provision of news, images, and satellite maps of the areas that had been evacuated and affected, including homes and places of employment.
- Assistance for emergency service providers through information, local knowledge, and Internet access (Bertot, Jaeger, Langa, & McClure, 2006a, 2006b).

The provision of e-government information and assistance in filling out e-government forms was a central function of these libraries in helping their communities. The levels of assistance that libraries were providing to damaged communities and to displaced persons were extraordinary. In Mississippi, one library completed over 45,000 FEMA applications for patrons in the first month after Katrina made landfall (Jaeger, Langa, McClure, & Bertot, 2006). This heroic level of service was achieved even though the situation that the libraries found themselves in was unplanned and unprecedented.

Federal government agencies were of little help in the immediate aftermath of any of these situations (Arnone, 2007; Brinkley, 2006; Cooper & Block, 2006). Instead, public libraries, in conjunction with other local community organizations and local government agencies, used whatever information technology recourses were still functional to seek help, apply for and distribute aid, search for missing community members, and much else. The confluence of public libraries and local e-government in these situations allowed public libraries to keep local e-government online, distribute local emergency information, coordinate local response, direct aid to areas of the community most needing assistance, allow rescue personnel to communicate, support emergency responders with directions, maps, and information about where people most needed help, and numerous other life-saving functions (Jaeger, Langa, McClure, & Bertot, 2006). Because of this local knowledge, and connections with their communities, public libraries were able to leverage responses that were far more tailored to local needs that state or federal agencies.

The Internet access in public libraries also helped to hold communities together by helping to find missing community members. Many libraries created online lists of community members (people and animals) who were being sought to help in establishing contacts between people in the community and those who were displaced or missing. These efforts allowed patrons to locate missing family, friends, and pets, as well as to have, in the words of the librarians, "contact with family members outside of the disaster area," "communication with family and friends," and the ability to "stay in touch with family & friends due to lack of telephone service" (Jaeger, Langa, McClure, & Bertot, 2006).

The successes of public libraries in helping to meet community needs, including local e-government access, demonstrated the depth of the importance of public libraries in local government, particularly in extreme circumstances. As e-government becomes used more frequently as a tool of emergency response and recovery, the public library—through its role of guarantor of access—will likely be considered an essential part of making sure residents have e-government access in an emergency (Jaeger, Fleischmann, Preece, Shneiderman, Wu, & Qu, 2007; Jaeger, Shneiderman, Fleischmann, Preece, Qu, & Wu, 2007).

PUBLIC LIBRARIES AND COMMUNITY-LEVEL E-GOVERNMENT

In the delivery of e-government as it impacts local communities, public libraries perform several different functions. The most basic function is simply through providing access. Many governments direct residents to the public library to access local e-government when residents lack other means of access or need help using the Web sites (Bertot, Jaeger, Langa, & McClure, 2006a, 2006b). However, along with the major federal-level e-government activities that people engage in, there are also many smaller-scale community (local and state level) e-government activities that are used on a daily basis.

Community-level e-government services frequently used in public libraries now include (Bertot, McClure, Wright, Jensen, & Thomas, 2009; Bertot, Jaeger, Langa, & McClure, 2006a; Jaeger, 2009):

- Finding court proceedings;
- Submitting local zoning board information;
- Requesting planning permits;
- Searching property and assessor databases;
- Registering students in school;
- Tasking driver's education programs;
- Applying for permits;
- Scheduling appointments;
- Developing and maintaining local government Web sites;
- Training to use e-government;
- Paying fees and taxes; and
- Completing numerous other local government functions online.

By making e-government access available to those who have no other way to reach it effectively, public libraries ensure that all citizens can access their community-level e-government.

The expertise of public libraries in e-government and ability to support community-level e-government can even extend beyond the library itself. Local governments have relied on public librarians to assist in community planning processes by sorting through and identifying the relevant local e-government materials and information sources (Quinn & Ramasubramanian, 2007). As such, public librarians can assist local government officials in using community-level e-government resources.

E-GOVERNMENT EDUCATION IN PUBLIC LIBRARIES

Since the implementation of the Internet in public libraries in the early 1990s, training patrons to use the Internet has been an important function of libraries. Internet penetration in public libraries has now reached nearly 100%, and perhaps more significantly, the only free public Internet access is that which is provided by public libraries in almost 75% of communities in United States (Bertot, McClure, & Jaeger, 2008). As a result, education about the Internet is a very sizeable activity for librarians. These educational activities are important to individual patrons and to entire communities.

E-government education is an activity that will continue to grow in importance for public libraries, as more government information and services migrate to online formats. A key aspect of e-government service delivery and availability is the ability of citizens to successfully use e-government services. It is not the case that all citizens are familiar with computing and Internet-based technologies (Bertot, 2003). Education about using e-government can be as basic as the ability to use a mouse, a word processing program, a browser, a dropdown menu, or a hyperlink (Cilan, Bolat, & Coskun, 2009; van Deuesen & van Dijk, in press). Further, e-government education encompasses attitudinal issues such as desire to use and confidence in e-government (Hamner & Al-Qahtani, 2009). Most e-government educational issues deal with issues of understanding, locating, and successfully using the information or services needed.

There is a wide spectrum of major impacts of information technology training provided to patrons by public libraries. In the 2008 national survey of public libraries, providing information literacy skills was the most commonly reported major impact of the technology training (47.5%), while forms of technology skills training were the second (39.5%) and fourth (38.3%) most frequently reported major impacts of information technology training by libraries (Bertot, McClure, & Jaeger, 2008). Helping students with school and homework assignments was reported by 38.4% of libraries, but facilitating local economic development (1.8%) and helping local business owners (1.9%) were rarely cited as impacts.

Yet, while only 21.8% of libraries saw helping users with e-government access and use as a major impact of the information technology training, the vast majority of libraries provide assistance and education about e-government. This discrepancy is due to the fact that many librarians and library directors do not actually think of e-government services as a specific library activity, instead viewing e-government as an aspect of Internet access or an aspect of traditional government documents services (Jaeger & Bertot, 2009). These beliefs may be a factor contributing to the fact that 21.8% of libraries include e-government in the important benefits of information technology training. But it is also a factor in how libraries continue to measure their activities and performance. By and large, e-government transactions are simply tallied as part of an overall reference service, even though the level of effort required to provide e-government services is substantial in terms of time and expertise, and basic measures such as surveys and logs fail to capture these efforts effectively (Jaeger & Bertot, 2009).

In 2008, 74.0% of public libraries were providing access to and assistance with government Web sites, programs, and services (Bertot, McClure, & Jaeger, 2008). Additionally, over half of public library systems (51.9%) provide assistance to patrons applying for or accessing e-government services, such as taxes or Medicare applications. More advanced forms of e-government assistance, like partnering with government agencies (11.8%) and providing e-government training courses (9.6%), have not yet been as widely embraced by public libraries.

In different public libraries and library systems around the country, e-government educational activities in libraries can include:

- Formal and informal e-government training, ranging from scheduled courses to one point-of-delivery assistance when requested;
- E-government Web resources that can include instructions, references, and important links;
- E-government support services, such as those available through digital reference;
- Librarians hired specifically to coordinate and oversee e-government services and education provided by the library;
- E-government partnerships through which libraries and agencies work together to reach intended service recipients, thus serving as instructional outlets for programs and services;
- E-government development for local government agencies, training local government employees about how to develop their own e-government sites (Jaeger & Bertot, 2009).

The activities listed above are indicative of the range of e-government educational activities of libraries, but are not exhaustive.

E-government education also serves important community engagement functions for libraries. The availability of e-government access and assistance in libraries is bringing people into libraries who would not otherwise use them, as well as building trust in e-government among library patrons (Jaeger & Fleischmann, 2007). As noted above, in many communities, the public library is the only source for free public access to the Internet (Bertot, McClure, & Jaeger, 2007). This means that public libraries serve as the guarantors of public access to and education about e-government in the United States. In three-quarters of the communities in the country, the residents have only the public library to ensure access to and education about federal, state, and local e-government information and services.

These educational activities involve both teaching patrons to access information and services and to learn to communicate electronically with the government (Jaeger & Bertot, 2009). Educating patrons about using e-government is far beyond previous technology training or Internet training activities—the educational responsibilities extend to teaching patrons to access government information, use government services, and engage in communication with government officials. As such, an emphasis on e-government education in libraries is an important and growing aspect of information technology training in libraries. E-government access and education are vital services to patrons and communities, but libraries need to find ways to make stronger links between e-government provision and community awareness, support, and participation.

EXTERNAL SUPPORT FOR E-GOVERNMENT PROVISION

While public libraries have made significant contributions in access to and use of e-government by residents, communities, and governments themselves, public libraries still face challenges in the delivery of e-government. The most significant challenges are related to the limited external support provided to libraries in relation to e-government, to the infrastructure plateau that many libraries are reaching, and to the limited input that libraries have in policy decisions about e-government.

External pressures also contribute to the difficulties of providing adequate e-government education for patrons. Many major e-government responsibilities of libraries are driven entirely by government decisions far outside the control of libraries. Federal and state governments direct citizens to public libraries for help with taxes, Medicare, and many other e-government services, without libraries being informed or consulted (Bertot, Jaeger, Langa, & McClure, 2006a, 2006b; McClure, Jaeger, & Bertot, 2007). As a result, libraries often must react to the e-government services they are being asked to provide. Other e-government roles, such as playing a major role in response to natural disasters, occurred unexpectedly out of necessity (Jaeger, Langa, McClure, & Bertot, 2006). As a result, libraries have not been in the position to develop e-government education programs that anticipate the types of assistance patrons will be requesting.

In becoming guarantors of e-government access, public libraries have taken on significant extra expenses in terms of hardware, software, connections, physical space, maintenance, upkeep, networking, staff time, electronic resources, and staff training, among other expenses. In a 2007 survey of public libraries, 83.3% of libraries indicated that the use of e-government in the library had increased overall library usage (McClure, McGilvray, Barton, & Bertot, 2006). However, with no significant forms of external support for e-government access and training, public libraries in different communities have widely varying access to e-government as a result of differences in numbers of computers, connection speed, and many other factors (Jaeger, Bertot, McClure, & Rodriguez, 2007). These differences, in effect, create "digital divides" between libraries that can provide high quality e-government access and training and those that cannot.

At the same time, only 21.9% of libraries can always meet demand for public Internet access; the vast majority of libraries have insufficient workstations to meet patron demand part (58.8%) or all of the day (18.7%) (McClure, Jaeger, & Bertot, 2007). These numbers indicate that public libraries are reaching an infrastructure plateau—a point where their infrastructure can no longer meet demands for Internet access (McClure, Jaeger, & Bertot, 2007). As infrastructure issues slow down connectivity speed (and thereby work speed) in libraries, governments are sending more and more people to libraries to use and get help with accessing e-government. This creates a vicious circle that puts ever increasing strain on the public libraries in providing e-government access and assistance that needs to be addressed. The lack of sufficient funding to provide high quality Internet access is a key contributor to the Infrastructure Plateau (McClure, Jaeger, & Bertot, 2007). But so too is the lack of a clear understanding, definition, and evaluation framework for what constitutes quality public access technology services and resources (Bertot & McClure, 2007). Financial and definitional constraints extend to the ability of libraries to afford to (1) determine their capacity to provide training services; and (2) allocate staff time to education activities, including e-government education.

Public libraries, if they had a larger voice in the public policy process, might be able to better argue for greater funding and support in upgrading their infrastructure to meet the demands being placed on them in providing e-government access. Unfortunately, the third major challenge—the limited input that libraries have in policy decisions about e-government—serves to perpetuate the first major challenge. Public libraries need to work to better articulate their roles, and need for support, to governments, particularly local government that provides the majority of their funding. This can be done by libraries working together—perhaps coordinated by state library organizations—to craft a consistent message to all levels of government that accurately details what they are doing in relation to e-government and the types of support they need to provide these services.

At the same time, governments need to be more cognizant of the needs of public libraries in order to sustain their role as e-government access point. "The maintenance of traditional services, the addition and expansion of public access computing and networked services, and now the addition of a range of e-government services tacitly required by federal, state, and local governments, in combination, risk stretching public library resources beyond their ability to keep up" (Jaeger, Bertot, McClure, & Rodriguez, 2007, p. 13). Increased financial support for and involvement in the policy process for public libraries will help to ensure that libraries can continue to serve as the community access point for e-government.

E-GOVERNMENT IN LIS EDUCATION

There is also an extremely important role for Library and Information Science (LIS) programs in ensuring that public libraries are able to continue to meet user and community expectations for e-government access and assistance, while also perpetuating the success of public libraries in linking citizens and local e-government. As more government information, communication, and services occur primarily or exclusively through online channels, the reliance of users and communities on public libraries for e-government access and assistance will continue to grow.

To meet these user and community expectations, graduates of LIS programs must be adequately prepared to provide access to and assistance with e-government information and services, as well as understanding the professional, management, social, economic, usage, community, patron, and governmental issues associated with e-government access in public libraries (Jaeger, 2008).

However, LIS education has so far paid scant attention to preparing future public librarians to fulfill the e-government access and service expectations of individual patrons, communities, and government agencies. As this is of quickly growing significance within the profession of public librarianship, more LIS programs should begin to emphasize e-government in the pedagogy.

Preparing future librarians to be proficient with e-government as both users and educators should be a priority in LIS programs. Many LIS programs offer law and information policy-related courses and programs, while courses related to government information and services tend to be government documents or government information courses (Gathegi & Burke, 2008). For public librarians to be ready to meet patron e-government needs, however, LIS programs must work toward:

- Creating master's level coursework that can be used to more effectively prepare LIS students to provide e-government training, services, and tools in public libraries;
- Conducting research that advances understandings about and creates actionable solutions for public libraries in the provision of e-government access and services;
- Increasing the number of e-government savvy LIS faculty and library professionals;
- Developing means to share ideas and best practices between libraries;
- Increasing the number of faculty members of LIS programs with a specialization in the intersections of public libraries and e-government (Jaeger, 2008).

A larger number of LIS programs bringing e-government into library education through the development of new classes and programs, or the incorporation of e-government into existing courses, would be a valuable starting point.

At the College of Information Studies at the University of Maryland, a concentration in e-government is available to students enrolled in the Master of Library Science program (http://ischool.umd.edu). The University of Maryland also has a companion research and education facility, the Center for Information Policy and Electronic Government (http://www.cipeg.umd.edu/), to further research in this area. These types of education and research options for future librarians who wish to specialize in e-government will be of growing importance as users, communities, and government agencies rely on public libraries for greater amounts of access to and assistance with e-government.

The University of Maryland is also expanding its e-government librarian coursework to include the digital government information context, and received an Institute of Museum and Library Services Laura Bush 21st Century Librarian scholarship grant to bring this program of study online in the fall of 2010. In particular, the program entails four key components (Bertot, Jaeger, & Shuler, 2009):

- *Coursework.* The coursework serves as the intellectual and conceptual basis for the evolving government information and e-government service environment;

- *Practice*. Though internships with the Government Information Online (http://www.govtinfo.org/) program, students will develop applied government information and e-government skills;

- *Professional*. By bringing students together annually to attend the Fall Federal Depository Library meeting, students will become integrated into the larger government information and e-government community and engage key issues in government information;

- *Scholarship*. Though inclusion in the review process of Government Information Quarterly (http://www.elsevier.com/locate/govinf), students will publish government resource reviews, contribute to furthering scholarship in government information, and learn the publication process. The project principles will also work with students to publish manuscripts in key areas of government information and e-government.

This comprehensive approach will push the boundaries of e-government services in libraries. This is important, as graduates of LIS programs need to be prepared to fulfill the vital role of meeting patrons' e-government information needs. If LIS programs are not properly preparing graduates to be e-government savvy librarians, they will have difficulty meeting the needs of many patrons. In conjunction with an increased educational focus on e-government, LIS programs also need to engage in more research on the affects of and expectations for e-government information, communication, and services in public libraries.

CONCLUSION: PUBLIC LIBRARIES AND THE FUTURE OF E-GOVERNMENT

Increases in information access have historically been tied to increases in the inclusiveness of the democratic process (Bennett, 2001; Burke & Martin, 2004; Smith, 1995). E-government is a new manifestation of the public library's contributions to the health of the democratic process. In many ways, e-government education is a natural continuation of the long-standing library roles of educating patrons about technology and of promoting civic participation and citizen engagement among patrons and communities (Kranich, 2001, 2005). Information technology has not merely served as a tool to perpetuate existing services or a force that libraries have had to react to, but a direct partner in the maturation of public libraries into a uniquely important entity that is widely trusted. E-government education is becoming a key component of the role of the public library in society (Fleischmann, 2007; Jaeger & Fleischmann, 2007); as a result, ensuring equal access to and education about e-government not only helps patrons meet their own needs, it also has the potential to help promote civic literacy, political awareness, and involvement in government among patrons.

By ensuring access to e-government, public libraries are having a profound, if subtle influence on the development of e-government. Simply put, their commitment to ensuring access is allowing governments to develop e-government without having to be concerned about leaving behind large numbers of residents who have no access to the Internet. Though public libraries are not the only possible points of free e-government access in many communities, they have demonstrated the strongest commitment to providing access and help for all.

Overall, the provision of e-government access assistance by public libraries has been a tremendous benefit to individuals, communities, and governments in the United States. Ensuring that the technology, staff, and resources exist to meet these expectations of patrons, communities, and governments, however, is one of the primary issues that public libraries face in continuing to meet patron and community needs. However, a key challenge of advocating for libraries in providing e-government support is that many librarians conceive of the provision of e-government education and services as part of other activities rather than a unique activity (Jaeger & Bertot, 2009). As a result, libraries often cannot fully articulate their e-government activities. E-government is a unique activity, and conceiving of it as a government documents activity or an Internet activity alone is an insufficient portrayal of the role of e-government in library services. Thus there is a need to develop measures of e-government activities within public libraries that disaggregate e-government efforts from larger library services such as reference and technology training.

Several further challenges come from within the library community. First, library professionals need to articulate within the library community the e-government expectations of patrons and the role of e-government within other library services. Doing so will help libraries better understand the impacts of e-government on their activities and describe these activities to those beyond the library community. Thus far, e-government has been only infrequently discussed in the professional literature (e.g., Bertot, Jaeger, Langa, & McClure, 2006b; Oder, 2007). Second, library professionals—particularly those involved in the more advanced types of e-government activities—need to develop best practices in e-government education that can be shared between libraries. Articulating and sharing such practices will help to identify the ways to most effectively provide e-government education to patrons (Gibson, Bertot, & McClure, 2009). Third, LIS programs must do a much better job of preparing future professionals to meet e-government needs of patrons (Jaeger, 2008).

Ultimately, until the governments that send citizens to libraries to use e-government recognize the need to better support libraries for their contributions to e-government access and training, public libraries will continue to deal with issues of funding, technology, connection, maintenance, and personnel in continuing to provide e-government access and training.

REFERENCES

Anderson. (2002). *A usability analysis of selected federal government web sites.* Washington, D.C.: Author.

Arnone, M. (2007). Storm watch 2006: Ready or not. *Federal Computer Week* (2006, June 5). Available at http://www.fcw.com.

Barr, S. (2007, March 21). Public less satisfied with government web sites. *Washington Post.* Available at http://www.washingtonpost.com/wp-dyn/content/article/2007/03/20/AR2007032001338.html.

Bennett, S. (2001). The golden age of libraries. *Journal of Academic Librarianship, 27,* 256–259.

Bertot, J. C. (2003). The multiple dimensions of the digital divide: more than the technology "haves" and "have nots." *Government Information Quarterly, 20*(2): 185–191.

Bertot, J. C., & Jaeger, P. T. (2008). The e-government paradox: Better customer service doesn't necessarily cost less. *Government Information Quarterly, 25,* 149–154.

Bertot, J. C., Jaeger, P. T., Langa, L. A., & McClure, C. R. (2006a). Public access computing and Internet access in public libraries: The role of public libraries in e-government and emergency situations. *First Monday, 11*(9). Available at http://www.firstmonday.org/issues/issue11_9/bertot/index.html.

Bertot, J. C., Jaeger, P. T., Langa, L. A., & McClure, C. R. (2006b). Drafted: I want you to deliver e-government. *Library Journal, 131*(13), 34–39.

Bertot, J. C., Jaeger, P. T., & Shuler, J. A. (2009). Next generation E-government librarians and digital government librarians. Available at http://clii.umd.edu/libegov.

Bertot, J. C., & McClure, C. R. (2007). Assessing sufficiency and quality of bandwidth for public libraries. *Information Technology and Libraries, 26*(1): 14–22.

Bertot, J. C., McClure, C. R., & Jaeger, P. T. (2008). The impacts of free public Internet access on public library patrons and communities. *Library Quarterly, 78,* 285–301.

Bertot, J. C., McClure, C. R., Jaeger, P. T., & Ryan, J. (2006). *Public Libraries and the Internet 2006: Survey Results and Findings* for the Bill & Melinda Gates Foundation and the American Library Association. Tallahassee, FL: Information Institute. Available at http://www.plinternetsurvey.org.

Bertot, J. C., McClure, C. R., Wright, C.B, Jensen, E., & Thomas, S. (2009). *Public Libraries and the Internet 2009: Survey Results and Findings.* College Park, MD: Center for Library & Information Innovation. Available at http://www.plinternetsurvey.org.

Brinkley, D. (2006). *The great deluge: Hurricane Katrina, New Orleans, and the Mississippi Gulf Coast.* New York: Harper Perennial.

Burke, S. K., & Martin, E. (2004). Libraries in communities: Expected and unexpected portrayals in state case law. *Libraries and Culture, 39,* 405–428.

Burroughs, J. M. (2009). What users want: Assessing government information preferences to drive information services. *Government Information Quarterly, 26,* 203–218.

Carr, D. W. (2003). An ethos of trust in information service. In Rockenbach, B. & Mendina, T. (Eds.), *Ethics and Electronic Information: A Festschrift for Stephen Almagno,* pp. 45–52. Jefferson, NC: McFarland & Company.

Cilan, C. A., Bolat, B. A., & Coskun, E. (2009). Analyzing digital divide within and between member and candidate countries of European Union. *Government Information Quarterly, 26,* 98–107.

Cooper, C., & Block, R. (2006). *Disaster: Hurricane Katrina and the failure of homeland security.* New York: Times Books.

Dawes, S. S. (2009). Governance in the digital age: A research and action framework for an uncertain future. *Government Information Quarterly, 26,* 257–264.

D'Elia, G., Jorgensen, C., Woelfel, J., & Rodger, E. J. (2002). The impact of the Internet on public library uses: An analysis of the current consumer market for library and Internet services. *Journal of the American Society for Information Science and Technology, 53,* 802–820.

Ebbers, W. E., Pieterson, W. J., & Noordman, H. N. (2008). Electronic government: Rethinking channel management strategies. *Government Information Quarterly, 25,* 181–201.

Ebbers, W. E., & van Dijk, J. A. G. M. (2007). Resistance and support to electronic government, building a model of innovation. *Government Information Quarterly, 24,* 554–575.

Evans, K. (2007). *E-government and information technology for the federal government.* Talk presented at the Center for Information Policy and Electronic Government, University of Maryland.

Feinberg, L. E. (2004). FOIA, Federal information policy, and information availability in a post-9/11 world. *Government Information Quarterly, 21,* 439–460.

Fleischmann, K. R. (2007). Digital libraries with embedded values: Combining insights from LIS and Science and Technology Studies. *Library Quarterly, 77,* 409–427.

Fox, S. (2005). *Digital divisions.* Washington D.C.: Pew Internet & American Life Project.

Gathegi, J. N., & Burke, D. E. (2008). Convergence of information and law: A comparative study between i-Schools and other ALISE schools. *Journal of Education for Library and Information Science, 49,* 1–22.

Gauld, R., Gray, A., & McComb, S. (2009). How responsive is e-government?: Evidence from Australia and New Zealand. *Government Information Quarterly, 26,* 69–74.

Gibson, A. N., Bertot, J. C., & McClure, C. R. (2009). Emerging roles of public libraries as e-government providers. Paper presented at the *42nd Hawaii International Conference on Systems Sciences.*

Halchin, L. E. (2004). Electronic government: Government capability and terrorist resource. *Government Information Quarterly, 21,* 406–419.

Hamner, M., & Al-Qahtani, R. (2009). Enhancing the case for electronic government in developing nations: A people-centric study focused in Saudi Arabia. *Government Information Quarterly, 26,* 118–127.

Heanue, A. (2001). In support of democracy: The library role in public access to government information. In Kranich, N. (Ed.), *Libraries & Democracy: The Cornerstones of Liberty* (pp. 121–128). Chicago: American Library Association.

Ho, A. T-K., & Ni, A. Y. (2004). Explaining the adoption of e-government features: A case study of Iowa County Treasurers' offices. *American Review of Public Administration, 34,* 164–180.

Horrigan, J. B. (2004). *How Americans get in touch with government.* Washington D.C.: Pew Internet & American Life Project.

Horrigan, J. B. (2006). *Politics online.* Washington D.C.: Pew Internet & American Life Project.

Horrigan, J. B. (2008). *Home broadband 2008.* Washington, D.C.: Pew Internet & American Life Project.

Horrigan, J. B., & Rainie, L. (2002). *Counting on the Internet.* Washington D.C.: Pew Internet & American Life Project.

Horst, M., Kuttscreuter, M., & Gutteling, J. M. (2007). Perceived usefulness, personal experiences, risk perception, and trust as determinants of adoption of e-government services in the Netherlands. *Computers in Human Behavior, 23,* 1838–1852.

Jaeger, P. T. (2005). Deliberative democracy and the conceptual foundations of electronic government. *Government Information Quarterly, 22*(4), 702–719.

Jaeger, P. T. (2007). Information policy, information access, and democratic participation: The national and international implications of the Bush administration's information politics. *Government Information Quarterly, 24*(4), 840–859.

Jaeger, P. T. (2008). Building e-government into the Library & Information Science curriculum: The future of government information and services. *Journal of Education for Library and Information Science, 49*, 167–179.

Jaeger, P. T. (2009). Public libraries and local e-government. In C. G. Reddick (Ed.), *Handbook on research on strategies for local e-government adoption and implementation: Comparative studies* (pp. 647–660). Hershey, PA: IGI Global.

Jaeger, P. T., & Bertot, J. C. (2009). E-government education in public libraries: New service roles and expanding social responsibilities. *Journal of Education for Library and Information Science, 50*, 40–50.

Jaeger, P. T., Bertot, J. C., McClure, C. R., & Rodriguez, M. (2007). Public libraries and Internet access across the United States: A comparison by state from 2004 to 2006. *Information Technology and Libraries, 26*(2), 4–14.

Jaeger, P. T., & Burnett, G. (2005). Information access and exchange among small worlds in a democratic society: The role of policy in redefining information behavior in the post-9/11 United States. *Library Quarterly, 75*(4), 464–495.

Jaeger, P. T., & Fleischmann, K. R. (2007). Public libraries, values, trust, and e-government. *Information Technology and Libraries, 26*(4), 35–43.

Jaeger, P. T., Fleischmann, K. R., Preece, J., Shneiderman, B., Wu, F. P., & Qu, Y. (2007). Community response grids: Facilitating community response to bio-security and bioterror emergencies through information and communication technologies. *Biosecurity and Bioterrorism, 5*(4), 1–11.

Jaeger, P. T., Langa, L. A., McClure, C. R., & Bertot, J. C. (2006). The 2004 and 2005 Gulf Coast hurricanes: Evolving roles and lessons learned for public libraries in disaster preparedness and community services. *Public Library Quarterly, 25*(3/4), 199–214.

Jaeger, P. T., & Matteson, M. (2009). E-government and technology acceptance: The implementation of Section 508 guidelines for e-government web sites. *Electronic Journal of E-Government, 7*(1), 87–98. Available at http://www.ejeg.com/volume-7/vol7-iss1/v7-i1-art8.htm.

Jaeger, P. T., Shneiderman, B., Fleischmann, K. R., Preece, J., Qu, Y., & Wu, F. P. (2007). Community response grids: E-government, social networks, and effective emergency response. *Telecommunications Policy, 31*, 592–604.

Jaeger, P. T., & Thompson, K. M. (2003). E-government around the world: Lessons, challenges, and new directions. *Government Information Quarterly, 20*(4), 389–394.

Jaeger, P. T., & Thompson, K. M. (2004). Social information behavior and the democratic process: Information poverty, normative behavior, and electronic government in the United States. *Library & Information Science Research, 26*(1), 94–107.

Kirtley, J. E. (2006). Transparency and accountability in a time of terror: The Bush administration's assault on freedom of information. *Communication Law and Policy, 11*, 479–509.

Kranich, N. (2005). Civic partnerships: The role of libraries in promoting civic engagement. *Resource Sharing and Information Networks, 18*(1/2), 89–103.

Kranich, N. C. (2001). Libraries, the Internet, and democracy. In N. C. Kranich (Ed.), *Libraries & democracy: The cornerstones of liberty*. Chicago: American Library Association, 2001.

Madden, M. (2006). *Internet penetration and impact*. Washington D.C.: Pew Internet & American Life Project.

Mahler, J., & Regan, P. M. (2002). Learning to govern online: Federal agency Internet use. *American Review of Public Administration, 32*, 326–349.

McClure, C. R., & Jaeger, P. T. (2008a). *Public libraries and Internet service roles: Measuring and maximizing Internet services*. Chicago: ALA Editions.

McClure, C. R., & Jaeger, P. T. (2008b). Government information policy research: Importance, approaches, and realities. *Library & Information Science Research, 30,* 257–264.

McClure, C. R., Jaeger, P. T., & Bertot, J. C. (2007). The looming infrastructure plateau?: Space, funding, connection speed, and the ability of public libraries to meet the demand for free Internet access. *First Monday, 12*(12). Available at http://www.uic.edu/htbin/cgiwrap/bin/ojs/index.php/fm/article/view/2017/1907.

McClure, C. R., McGilvray, J., Barton, K. M., & Bertot, J. C. (2006). *E-government and public libraries: Current status, meeting report, findings, and next steps.* Tallahassee, FL: Information Use Management and Policy Institute. Available at http://www.ii.fsu.edu/announcements/e-gov2006/egov_report.pdf.

Moon, M. J. (2002). The evolution of e-government among municipalities: Rhetoric or reality? *Public Administration Review, 62,* 424–433.

Oder, N. (2007). E-government and libraries: After consciousness-raising, could new law and funding be coming? *Library Journal, 132*(5), 17.

Pew Research Center. (2007). *Americans and social trust: Who, where and why.* Washington, D.C.: Author. Available at http://pewresearch.org.

Public Agenda. (2006). *Long overdue: A fresh look at public and leadership attitudes about libraries in the 21st century.* New York: Author. Available at http://publicagenda.org.

Quinn, A. C. & Ramasubramanian, L. (2007). Information technologies and civic engagement: Perspectives from librarianship and planning. *Government Information Quarterly, 24,* 595–610.

Reddick, C. G. (2005). Citizen interaction with e-government: From the streets to servers? *Government Information Quarterly, 22,* 338–357.

Relyea, H. C., & Halchin, L. E. (2003). Homeland security and information management. In D. Bogart (Ed.), *The Bowker annual: Library and trade almanac 2003* (pp. 231–250). Medford, NJ: Information Today.

Roberts, N. (2004). Public deliberation in an age of direct citizen participation. *American Review of Public Administration, 34,* 315–353.

Rodger, E. J., D'Elia, G., & Jorgensen, C. (2001). The public library and the Internet: Is peaceful coexistence possible? *American Libraries, 31*(5), 58–61.

Singh, A. K., & Sahu, R. (2008). Integrating Internet, telephones, and call centers for delivering better quality e-governance to all citizens. *Government Information Quarterly, 25,* 477–490.

Smith, E. (1995). Equal information access and the evolution of American democracy. *Journal of Educational Media and Library Sciences, 33,* 158–171.

Streib, G., & Navarro, I. (2006). Citizen demand for interactive e-government: The case of Georgia consumer services. *American Review of Public Administration, 36,* 288–300.

van Deursen, A. J. A. M., & van Dijk, J. A. G. M. (2009). Improving digital skills for the use of online public information and services. *Government Information Quarterly, 26*(2): 333–340.

Chapter 4

Public Library 2.0: New Technologies, Roles, and Challenges for Public Libraries

Lorri Mon

INTRODUCTION

As each new information technology arises, U.S. public libraries seek to evaluate and integrate useful innovations into library services. In 1876, Alexander Graham Bell invented the telephone and by 1880, Samuel Swett Green of the Worcester Free Library was advocating its use for library services (Richardson, 1999). In the 1930s, public libraries were answering questions by telephone and even in some cases via teletype, which was first used in 1927 by the Philadelphia Free Library (Garnett, 1936; Becker, 1969; Ryan, 1996). These ongoing patterns of technological change and experimentation with new technologies in the public libraries have continued through the present day, as shown in Table 4.1.

The most recent technological challenges for U.S. public libraries involve meeting an increasing public demand for remote access to library resources and services, including 24/7 access to downloadable articles, books, movies, virtual reference question-answering, and other online interactive services. This chapter offers insights emerging from a 2008 study supported by a grant from the Florida State University Information Use Management and Policy Institute in which surveys and interviews examined the implementation of innovative technologies in 242 U.S. public libraries across 49 states (Mon & Randeree, 2009). Researchers contacted 813 U.S. public libraries via e-mail

TABLE 4.1   U.S. Public Library Technology Firsts

1942	First U.S. public library to have a computerized circulation system, on IBM punch cards, Montclair Public Library. (Montclair Public Library, 2004)
1994	First public library Web site, St. Joseph County Public Library (Library Journal Staff, 2005)
1995	First entirely Internet-based public library, including asynchronous e-mail and live, synchronous MOO-based question answering, the Internet Public Library. (Ryan, 1996; Shaw, 1996)
2000	First U.S. public library to offer a live chat reference question-answering, Santa Monica Public Library, California. (Seattle Public Library, 2004)
2003	First public library to offer downloadable e-books, Cleveland Public Library, Ohio. (Business Editors, 2003)
2005	First U.S. public library to offer RSS feeds, Orange County Library System, Florida. (Orange County Library System, 2009)
2006	First U.S. public library to offer downloadable movies, Denver Public Library, Colorado. (Gathright, 2006)
2007	First U.S. public library to integrate LibraryThing tagging and tag clouds into its online catalog, Danbury Public Library, Connecticut. (Blumenstein, 2007)
2009	First public library iPhone application, District of Columbia Public Library (District of Columbia Public Library, 2009)

during 2008, receiving a 29.8% response rate. Research questions sought to identify:

- Web 2.0 technologies (if any) being used in U.S. public libraries, and
- Challenges, barriers, and strategies in implementing these technologies in the libraries.

This chapter draws upon responses from the study participants at U.S. public libraries in 2008 in order to highlight issues with new technologies, existing challenges, emerging roles, and trends to watch in the future.

BACKGROUND

An increasing number of Americans turn to the Internet when seeking information and services. In 2008, more than three-quarters of Americans between ages 12 and 54 were Internet users, and teenagers ranked highest in Internet use with 93% of those aged 12 to 17 being online users (Jones & Fox, 2009, p. 2). These users are not merely passive readers of online information. Internet users engage in many highly interactive online activities including shopping and selling; game-playing; blogging; social networking; exploring virtual worlds; creating and sharing music, videos, photos, and artwork; and communicating via e-mail, chat, and instant messaging.

Due to two converging trends, Internet users have become accustomed to not only being able to find information online but also to using online services. One strong influence has been the e-government/e-commerce movement, which since 1995 has shifted a great deal of consumer information and services to the Web. Users can now go online for everything from paying taxes and applying for government services, to online banking and bill-paying. Windham (2005) described a "Net Generation" lifestyle for today's college students of banking and paying bills online, and registering for classes and ordering books online; she presciently added that "If it were a possibility, we would probably order pizza online" (p. 5.13). Today Pizza Hut, Dominos and other pizza chains offer exactly that: online pizza-ordering service. From e-Bay Internet auctions and online distance education classes to Web-based newspapers, movies, and music downloads, an increasing range of online goods and services fulfills the needs and desires of consumers—some of whom have grown to adulthood without ever knowing a world in which computers and the Internet did not exist.

The second strong trend has been the emergence of highly interactive "next generation" Web 2.0 Internet sites and services, such as the social networking sites MySpace and Facebook, social tagging sites del.icio.us and LibraryThing, content sharing sites YouTube and Flickr, and interactive publishing sites Wikipedia, Livejournal and Blogger (O'Reilly, 2005; Maness, 2006). This new participatory style of Internet presence sparked off discussion of how Web 2.0 might impact libraries, often referred to as "Library 2.0" (Miller, 2005; Stephens, 2006; Crawford, 2006). These innovative and interactive Web 2.0 sites began to appear around 1999 and later, as seen in Figure 4.1.

Today's library users have grown accustomed to the interactivity of Web 2.0 sites and services; posting their own videos and photos to YouTube and Flickr; blogging their daily thoughts on Blogger, LiveJournal, and social networking pages on MySpace or Facebook; sharing their knowledge on Wikipedia, and book reviews on LibraryThing and Amazon; and tagging and organizing their favorite Web links on del.ici.ous and Connotea. They expect to find similar convenience in online interactive services from their local library's Web site. However, where they may have hoped to be able to use the library's Web site in the same interactive ways in which they use Web 2.0, e-government, and e-commerce sites, instead library patrons sometimes find themselves being told that they must take time off from work, school, or personal business to come into the public library and complete what they may see as simple e-business tasks, such as asking a question, paying library fines or getting a library card. A library staff member in Massachusetts described a typical patron response: "Why can't I use your services the way I'd use any other online site?" Library users want to interact with the library Web site in the same way that they do

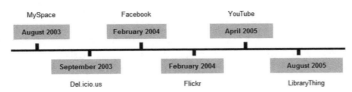

Figure 4.1 Web 2.0 Timeline.

online shopping or bill-paying with their banks—as a full service, fully-featured virtual representation of the physical library.

THE VIRTUAL BRANCH LIBRARY

We began referring to our Web site as our Online Branch Library.

—a public library staff member in Iowa

User expectations today are that the online library should be as fully functional as the physical library. This new paradigm of the public library Web site as not merely a shadow or vestigial representation of the "real" public library, but as a fully-fledged branch library in its own right, was repeated in comments from librarians across the country to the 2008 Innovative Technologies study (Mon & Randeree, 2009). In states such as New Jersey, New Hampshire, Massachusetts and Iowa, public library staff members spoke of the idea of transforming the library's Web site into a fully-featured "online branch library" or "virtual branch."

Such a virtual branch library would serve as a destination in its own right, regardless of whether the online library user ever visits the physical, brick-and-mortar library. The virtual branch would offer the same services made available to in-person patrons, such as requesting a library card, placing holds on books, and paying fines. Indeed in some cases, these types of services are already available online. At the Public Library of Charlotte and Mecklenburg County, teenagers using Teen Second Life are able to pay their public library fines from within the virtual world by touching a device that lets them type in their library card number, look up the balance owed on their overdue books, and pay it off using virtual world Linden dollars, the currency of Second Life (Czarnecki, 2008). Today's users can not only use credit cards in online payment interactions, but also online banking and Web-based PayPal accounts.

Working adults, the core taxpayers supporting local public libraries through tax millages, may find it difficult to visit the physical library during open hours, particularly in times of budget cuts when hours and staffing in public libraries are reduced. However, providing virtual branch collections and services for the online library user may offer an effective alternate approach in targeting services to those users whose work schedules conflict with the open hours of the physical library. The public library can also digitize special collections of interest to users of the library's virtual branch. In Ohio, a public library staff member described how the library was scanning and placing online "old rare books . . . city directories and other material," which attracted members of the public to visit its virtual branch. It is not uncommon for public libraries to have special collections of interest to the local community, such as historic local photographs, old and rare books, letters, memorabilia, and librarian-created "fact files" of answers to commonly-asked questions (also sometimes known as "knowledgebases"). When made digitally available, these unique local resources can provide online collections that attract local community members to visit and use the virtual branch.

VIRTUAL BRANCH COLLECTION BUILDING

Library teens maintain the MySpace.

—from a public library in Arizona

The physical branch of the public library is situated and embedded within the local neighborhood; and this raises the question of how the virtual branch of the library might be similarly embedded and situated within the "online neighborhood" as part of local people's online lives. There is an oft-quoted phrase "If you build it, they will come" from the movie *A Field of Dreams*, but what is not at all clear is whether this philosophy actually works when applied to the building of public library Web sites. In fact, it may be that users are less likely to come "If you build it" than if they themselves are personally involved in the building process, making the virtual branch truly their own.

Dervin and Schaefer (1998) pointed to the problem that information systems tend to be most used and most useful to people just like those who designed them. A good example of this dynamic at work is the International Children's Digital Library (http://en.childrenslibrary.org/), an online digital library of children's books which was created by a design team including young children. The search interface allows users to search on facets that children identified as important such as whether books were "short," "medium," or "long," whether stories were "make believe" or "true," what kinds of characters inhabited the books (such as "kids," "imaginary creatures," or "real animals") and the color of the book cover—none of which are choices that librarians traditionally would deem important in searching for books.

Public libraries experimenting with patron-inclusive, participatory approaches to building the virtual branch mentioned a variety of different methods for gaining user participation. Some public libraries have considered as part of their design process that library patrons may be even more likely to come to your virtual branch if they themselves have participated in building it into the kind of resource they would be likely to use.

This actual participation can take many forms. A commonly described method was to involve Teen Advisory Boards (TABs) in the creation of teen areas within the library Web site, such as blogs or social networking pages. Libraries in the states of Washington, New Mexico, Arizona and Colorado reported local teens being involved in creating and maintaining their library's MySpace pages. At the Public Library of Charlotte and Mecklenburg County, it was the library's teenaged patrons who conceptualized and carried out the idea of creating a library fine-paying device that they could use in looking up and paying their own overdue book fees from within the virtual world of Teen Second Life (Czarnecki, 2008).

Public libraries can involve users in creating and contributing a variety of content for the library's virtual branch such as audio, video or written user book reviews and poetry that could be posted on library Web pages, blogs, podcasts or linked through the library's YouTube site. Contests with prizes given to the library users who submitted winning entries have been successfully used in soliciting creative content from library patrons. Libraries in Colorado, Maryland, California, Florida, North Carolina, New York, Georgia, and Louisiana also created podcasts of storytimes, local oral histories, or of local authors reading their work; and "vodcasts" or video podcasts were created by libraries in Colorado and Florida. Even interactive online book catalogs have been explored through the integration of LibraryThing within a library's online catalog, allowing library users to contribute toward improved metadata via tagging. More interactive library Web pages can also allow library users themselves to help spread the word through clicking links that facilitate emailing of library Web site links to friends and family, or that post library-authored content onto sites such as Technorati, Furl, and StumbleUpon. In New Jersey, a public library staff member commented about the use of e-mail forwarding links that "our patrons are becoming viral marketers."

VIRTUAL BRANCH EVENTS

Brick and mortar public libraries serve as the loci for community as people come in to attend events such as author lectures, book groups, and children's story hours. Physical library spaces also serve as places for holding community meetings, and attending or teaching workshops for practical lifelong learning. Often physically situated in central locations within the community, the library's physical buildings are hard to overlook and can attract new patrons by serendipity as local people walking by decide to walk in.

However the virtual branch of the public library has no such inherent centrality in people's online lives. A public library staff member in West Virginia commented: "We have found it hard to reach the core group of internet users in our area due to the fact that this demographic is not as likely to use the library." In the course of a typical day's Internet searching and browsing, it is unlikely that local community members will serendipitously stumble into the public library Web site unless some effort has been made to situate links to the library strategically within virtual spaces that online users are likely to visit.

This philosophy of somehow situating the virtual library in the users' path was famously referred to by Anne Lipow (1999) as "in your face reference" when applied to digital reference question-answering services. Librarians sought to position links to chat question-answering services right where people were located when they needed the help—such as within the library's online catalog, within databases and on the browser itself.

In positioning the virtual branch so that local users might serendipitously find it, some of public libraries from the 2008 Innovative Technologies study leveraged the popularity of Web 2.0 sites to establish links and increase visibility. A public library in North Carolina reported success in using MeetUp to attract 20- and 30-something aged users to library book group events. "We have very high attendance and most of our members found us through meetup." Meetup (http://www.meetup.com) is an interactive site for finding or starting local area group meetings. The local newspaper's Web site may afford another opportunity for online positioning of the virtual branch.

Another strategy used by the public libraries to attract teen and young adult users was the creation of MySpace and Facebook pages. Library staff had already observed the popularity of social networking sites among their library patrons, just by seeing increased patron use of these sites on the library's computers.

An Arkansas library staff member commented, for example: "When we have 20 or so people all on MySpace & Runescape we run real slow." Runescape, a virtual world role-playing gaming environment, is popular among pre-teens and teen-agers. Libraries increasingly have sought to go out to where their teenaged and young adult users are and to establish a local public library online presence for the teens and young adults to serendipitously find among the social networking sites. In Colorado, Denver Public Library gained a 41% increase in traffic to the library's regular teen Web page following the 2006 launch of their library MySpace page (Gauder, 2007). Other efforts by public libraries to "go to where the online users are" have included establishing a library presence within virtual worlds such as Second Life, Teen Second Life, and Whyville (Pope et al., 2007).

While relatively few U.S. public libraries as yet have established outposts within virtual worlds, early adopters such as Alliance Library System in Illinois, Cleveland Public Library in Ohio, and Clearwater Public Library in Florida exemplify a key trend for the future—that increasing numbers of Internet users are not only involved with social networking sites but also with gaming and virtual worlds. Gartner Group (2007) has predicted that by 2011, 80% of all Internet users will be involved with virtual worlds. Among the variety of different types of services that public libraries have attempted to provide in virtual worlds such as Second Life, one of the most successful appears to be the staging of public events such as reading group discussions, training workshops, and author presentations. Establishing the virtual branch equivalent by implementing online technologies such as Webinars and virtual worlds may offer a way to engage online library patrons in virtual branch book talks and virtual classes, without requiring that they come into the physical library.

Gaming is another event-based way of bringing users into the library and represents a rapidly growing trend for the future. In 2008, the American Library Association proclaimed November 15 as national "Gaming @ Your Library Day." A library staff member in Virginia commented: "Teens love our gaming programs, and we see 2–4 times as many teens at gaming programs as we see at other programs targeted at them." In Ann Arbor, Michigan, the public library developed and distributed a game tournament software called GT System that allows gamers at participating public libraries across the country to play against each other, thus competing not only to find out who is best at the local library but who is best among libraries nationwide (Swope, 2008). Potentially this type of event participation could be extended to online patrons as well, attracting home players to be part of the virtual branch library's gaming team.

VIRTUAL BRANCH QUESTIONING AND ANSWERING

People love it and the ability to be able to ask their question when they want to ask it.

—from a Maryland public library, on chat and e-mail reference services

In the virtual branch, the library online reference service is located "where and when" the user is at their time of information need. By joining collaborative reference services, today's public libraries have been able to expand hours of question-answering service coverage for chat and e-mail reference to 24 hours, 7 days a week and 365 days per year, although the libraries have had to accept the tradeoff that the service is not always staffed by local librarians.

Online question-answering in the public libraries began with e-mail digital reference services during the 1990s, later expanding into chat reference in 2000. However by the mid-2000s, the initial enthusiasm with which public libraries launched into live chat reference services had been followed by the raising of concerns in several areas. Coffman and Arret (2004a, 2004b), in a two-part series of articles, questioned whether users were asking chat questions in sufficient numbers to warrant the cost to libraries of the software and staffing, which often was supported through federal LSTA grant monies. Further, although joining statewide or regional chat consortia increased coverage hours and decreased costs, researchers such as Kwon (2005) identified problems of decreased user satisfaction when non-local librarians in collaborative services could not as effectively answer questions that required local librarians' expertise.

Chat services by their very complexity seem to be more error-prone in a variety of ways. Lupien (2006) drew attention to the many technical problems with chat virtual reference software which frustrated both librarians and users as they attempted to use advanced features such as co-browsing, and struggled with firewalls, pop-up blockers, and incompatible browser versions. Kawakami and Swartz (2003) observed that the librarians themselves also made errors due to insufficient training and proficiency with using the chat software. A Nebraska public library staff member summarized local frustrations this way: "Years of advertising and 'pushing' chat reference has resulted in near-negligible interest. 90% of chat reference sessions took over 20 minutes and could have been done by phone in less than five. Staff also found the chat reference to be an incredibly frustrating experience." While some chat question-answering library services such as Q and A NJ remain overwhelmingly popular with thousands of questions asked and answered per month (Bromberg, 2003), other services have been disappointingly underutilized.

Do users really *want* to communicate with librarians via chat software? Such questions have been spurred particularly by failures of chat reference services such as Radford and Kern's (2006) investigation of the failures of nine chat reference services for reasons such as software problems and low patron usage, and the unsuccessful launch in Morris County, New Jersey of a public library after school homework chat service from 3 to 5 pm, targeted toward schoolchildren, which only attracted one question (Weissman, 2001). Weissman concluded about choice of communication mode: "Work from what they use." It is possible that while users want to have some way of asking questions and obtaining answers quickly, it doesn't necessarily have to only be limited to communicating with librarians via call center chat software. A variety of alternative online communication choices are increasingly available to libraries including instant messaging, social networking sites, SMS text messaging from cell phones, blogging, forums, wikis, and virtual worlds.

Younger users of the virtual branch library have posed particular challenges for libraries in establishing online reference services. It is increasingly clear that young people use social networking sites such as MySpace and Facebook, and do real-time text-messaging via cell phones or instant messaging, but may be less inclined to use or to regularly check email accounts. In 2004, three-quarters of online teens used instant messaging, with nearly half saying that they preferred to use instant messaging over email; over half of all teens had a cell phone, and 64% had sent a text message (Lenhart, Madden & Hitlin, 2005, pp. 15–17, 26–27). In 2008, 65% of all teenagers had used a social net-working site (Lenhart, 2009). These findings have implications for public libra-ries, both in communicating with young patrons, as well as with their own younger library staff members. One urban public library reported that when seeking to establish ways of contacting teenaged library workers, "They said no, we don't use email." This echoes results of Pew's 2004 study in which teen focus groups spoke of email as being used when communicating with "old people" (Lenhart, Madden & Hitlin, 2005, p. ii). More recent research indicates a trend of moving away from email use by younger patrons. According to Pew Internet, the number of teenagers who use email has dropped from 89% in 2004 to 73% in 2008 (Jones & Fox, 2009).

Web 2.0 sites have fostered a cultural shift in user expectations for participa-tory involvement in online information interactions. On interactive sites such as Yahoo! Answers, users not only ask the questions but also answer them; on Wikipedia, users read entries to find answers, and can also rewrite the entries with new information. Where libraries have focused on a one-to-one process of question-answering in which users ask and librarians answer, Web 2.0 sites are fostering a one-to-many and many-to-many participatory culture of ques-tioning and answering in which anyone can ask, or answer, or even contribute toward a shared community response to a question. To better engage with users, similar participatory structures can be built right into the underpinnings of the virtual branch library through implementation of software such as wikis, discussion board forums, interactive blogs, and blogging communities.

Kajewski (2007) suggested the use of blogs not just as an information service from which the library disseminates information to readers, but also as a feed-back tool in which readers can spontaneously respond with comments and dis-cussion. For example in blogging communities, each individual blog is linked to a network of friends' blogs, and questions can be posed to an "flist" or friend list, resulting in multiple responses. Pomerantz and Stutzman (2006) advocated a "reference blogosphere" which leverages blogging community technology in expanding the traditional one-to-one questioning-and-answering interaction to a more inclusive many-to-many community conversation involving librari-ans, experts, and other patrons of the virtual branch. All participants—both librarians and patrons—are enabled to contribute answers and suggestions in response to posted questions. Lankes (2008) spoke of the reference interaction evolving into a more participatory conversation between many possible inquirers and answerers. One byproduct of the conversation would be the crea-tion of a communal answer as an online artifact in the form of a blog entry or "knowledgebase" article, which then continues to grow and evolve as it is refer-enced, annotated, revised, updated and remixed by subsequent virtual branch users.

Blogs, wikis, SMS text messaging, virtual worlds, and community forums currently are still in infancy as methods for reference interactions in the virtual branch. Many early public library adopters for SMS text messaging can be seen on the Library Success "Best Practices" wiki (http://www.libsuccess.org). For virtual worlds, Alliance Library System of Illinois has answered over 6,700 reference questions within the virtual world of Second Life (Pope et al., 2007), and has also experimented with providing services in the youth-targeted virtual world of Whyville, while the Public Library of Charlotte and Mecklenburg County has offered library services in Teen Second Life (Czarnecki, 2008). In response to growing user interest in instant messaging, many public libraries have moved to offering instant messaging reference services, and authors such as Houghton and Schmidt (2005) have started to compare chat and instant messaging services in considering the best choice for the virtual branch.

The greatest challenge for public libraries in this regard is that there is no single approach to communication that will reach all patron audiences; and in times when budgets are tight, difficult decisions may need to be made about cutting funds and staffing to some communication channels in favor of others. However, the inherent risks of cutting connections to whole groups of library patrons is that some may prefer to use one communications mode and don't use the others. The shape of reference services in the virtual branch, and the ways in which it can and should best be implemented for users today and in the future, still remains a complex open question for public libraries.

BARRIERS TO THE VIRTUAL BRANCH LIBRARY

Most people are thrilled to see that we DO 'speak' del.icio.us, Flickr, etc., and it appears to give them confidence to come back to us with other questions, technology-based or otherwise.

—from a Pennsylvania public library

While many Web 2.0 sites, and the software for building the virtual branch library, are free, what is not free is the staff time and effort needed to build and maintain the library's online presence. Providing the continuing content needed to keep the virtual branch library's blog, wiki, YouTube page or social networking pages visually appealing and up-to-date requires a great deal of staff time and expertise. Lack of time, money, and staffing were commonly cited problems among the public libraries, particularly the lack of staff with sufficient knowledge and training to work on Web 2.0 projects.

The problem of lack of Web 2.0-trained public library staff members prompted Helene Blowers at the Public Library of Charlotte Mecklenburg County to design a self-paced online training program called "Learning 2.0" (available at http://plcmcl2-things.blogspot.com/) also popularly known as "the 23 Things" (Blowers & Reed, 2007). Hundreds of libraries have since adapted and used this copyright-free training program to train their staff in Web 2.0 technologies. A California public library staff member commented: "We recently offered the 23 Things program to our staff, to encourage everyone to try new technologies and see how they might apply to what we do." The push to train existing library staff in Web 2.0 skills raises questions as well regarding technology education in library and information science graduate programs, and the extent to which current LIS graduate students are being trained in the technical skills needed to be able to participate in building the virtual branch library.

Many smaller public libraries lacked staffing, funding, and infrastructure to integrate a virtual branch presence into library services. In Missouri, a library staff member noted: "We're small and rural, so 'new technologies' to us aren't that new. We are on the cusp of offering wi-fi access. That is about as new as we have right now." However even in public libraries which had the staffing and infrastructure to implement virtual branch projects, local city or county government and local IT departments could still create barriers to library efforts. In New Mexico, a public library staff member commented about the IT department that: "They will not consider any technologies that allow for user input. Not enough bandwidth is a barrier too. We cannot have any streaming video and they even complain about online classes."

MySpace and Facebook social networking sites were often singled out by local government and IT departments to be blocked on all public library computers, either due to political concerns about child safety and social networking sites, or bandwidth issues due to high usage of the sites on library computers. Blocking the sites meant that the public library staff were likewise blocked from creating or maintaining a library MySpace or Facebook page, unless they worked on it after hours from outside the workplace. A Mississippi library staff member described efforts to maintain the library's social networking pages under these conditions: "They are currently blocked because of bandwidth issues. I check them occasionally at home but I only have dial-up there so it's tedious." Decisions to block social networking sites are all the more noteworthy when the popular use of libraries by teenagers is considered; according to a Pew Internet and American Life Project report in 2005, 54% of all online teens reported accessing the Internet from a library (Lenhart, Madden & Hitlin, 2005, p. 5). In blocking off the favored communication channel of young patrons who represent the future of the library, it is worth considering whether the public library risks marginalizing itself in the lives of these younger users.

In general, the proliferation of new technologies offers both challenges and opportunities to public libraries in redefining and positioning themselves to occupy a new role in the lives of local users. Through the online virtual branch, the public library establishes a ubiquitous presence in providing events, resources and services not only inside the physical library building, but also in reaching out via computers, laptops, handheld mobile devices, and cell phones to library users in their homes, schools and workplaces. The virtual branch has strong potential to engage community members who do not currently use the public library; however, building the foundations of the virtual branch requires thinking in new ways about public library services, resources, events, outreach, and interaction with users. Within library education, a stronger emphasis is needed as well on teaching information technology technical skills that will strengthen the public library work force of the future.

CONCLUSIONS

Survival in a world of rapidly changing technologies requires adapting new ways of delivering information resources and services. Bookselling has changed with the arrival of Amazon to include online book sales, user ratings and user-written book reviews. Radio and television stream content online and offer users downloadable video and podcasts, and newspapers provide online editions including blogs and forums for readers to post responses to the news; even the music industry is exploring new remote and online venues for doing business such as selling individual song downloads via iTunes. As the public library's users increasingly "go virtual," questions will continue to arise as to the public library's role in establishing a virtual branch library. To what extent should public libraries seek to serve local taxpayers who never physically set foot within the physical library, and how should libraries conceptualize and provide virtual branch collections and services? How might new technologies such as wikis, blogging, and social networking be appropriately integrated to build community and encourage participation in the virtual branch?

A key challenge in decision-making is that no single communication channel will reach all user audiences. Different library user groups appear to prefer different communication modes. Teenagers are more likely to be reached via instant messaging and social networking sites, while adults are users of email and chat but may not have instant messaging accounts. Seniors are least likely to use online communication channels, and more likely to visit in person or call on the telephone. Staffing only the physical library sacrifices service to many taxpaying users who may never physically visit the brick-and-mortar library, yet who potentially could become avid online users of a virtual branch library's resources and services. A public library staff member in Tennessee gave voice to this growing concern about an increasing array of technology choices by describing their main barrier faced in implementing new technologies as "deciding what would give our users the most utility."

It is no accident that the majority of the top sites on the Internet (e.g., Google, Yahoo!, YouTube, Facebook, MySpace, Blogger) offer users ways that they can publish, manage and share their own answers and creative content, as well as personalize and customize their online experience. Ultimately, building greater user involvement into the virtual library branch could move the online library away from being a one-way portal for disseminating information, and toward supporting a more inclusive sense of personal presence in a participatory online library user community.

ACKNOWLEDGMENTS

This research was supported by a grant from the Information Use Management and Policy Institute at Florida State University's College of Information. Valuable assistance was provided by Melissa Elder in conducting this research, with special thanks as well to the participants in this study throughout the public library community.

REFERENCES

Bar-Ilan, J. (2007). The use of weblogs (blogs) by librarians and libraries to disseminate information. *Information Research, 12*(4) [paper 323]. Retrieved April 29, 2009, from http://InformationR.net/ir/12-4/paper323.html.

Becker, J. (1969). Telecommunications primer. *Journal of Library Automation 2*(3), 148–156.

Blowers, H., & Reed, L. (2007). The c's of our sea change: Plans for training staff, from core competencies to learning 2.0. *Computers in Libraries, 27*(2), 10–15.

Blumenstein, L. (2007). A public library tries LibraryThing. *Library Journal*, 6/15/2007. Retrieved April 29, 2009, from http://www.libraryjournal.com/article/CA6449577.html?rssid=220.

Bromberg, P. (2003). Managing a statewide virtual reference service: How Q and A NJ works. *Computers in Libraries, 23*(4), 26–31.

Business Editors (2003). Cleveland public library to open circulating eBook collection; library web site to be first in ..." *Business Wire*, January 6, 2003. Retrieved April 29, 2009, from http://www.allbusiness.com/media-telecommunications/information-services-libraries/5669710-1.html.

Charnigo, L., & Barnett-Ellis, P. (2007). Checking out Facebook.com: The impact of a digital trend on academic libraries. *Information Technology and Libraries, 26*(1), 23–34.

Clyde, L. A. (2004). Weblogs—are you serious? *The Electronic Library, 22*(5), 390–392.

Coffman, S., & Arret, L. (2004a). To chat or not to chat—taking another look at virtual reference, part 1. *Searcher, 12*(7). Retrieved April 29, 2009, from http://www.infotoday.com/searcher/jul04/arret_coffman.shtml.

Coffman, S., & Arret, L. (2004b). To chat or not to chat—taking yet another look at virtual reference, part 2. *Searcher, 12*(8). Retrieved April 29, 2009, from http://www.infotoday.com/searcher/sep04/arret_coffman.shtml.

Crawford, W. (2006). Library 2.0 and "Library 2.0." *Cites and Insights, 6*(2), 1–32, Retrieved June 1, 2008, from http://citesandinsights.info/civ6i2.pdf.

Curran, K., Murray, M., & Christian, M. (2007). Taking the information to the public through Library 2.0. *Library Hi Tech, 25*(2), 288–297.

Czarnecki, K. (2008) Building community as a library in a 3-D environment. *Australasian Public Libraries and Information Services, 21*(1), 25–27.

Dervin, B., & Schaefer, D. J. (1998, March). Toward the communicative design of information design: A call for considering the communicating implied in the mandate for information design. Paper presented at *Vision Plus 4: The Republic of Information—an International Symposium on Design for Global Communication*, Carnegie Mellon University, University Center, PA.

District of Columbia Public Library. (2009). D.C. public library launches first free library iPhone application in nation. January 26, 2009. Retrieved April 29, 2009, from http://www.dclibrary.org/node/574.

Etches-Johnson, A. (2006). State of the library blogosphere, 2006. blogwithoutalibrary.net. Retrieved April 29, 2009, from http://www.blogwithoutalibrary.net/211.

Farkas, M. (2007). Going where patrons are: Outreach in MySpace and Facebook. *American Libraries, 38*(4), 27.

Garnett, E. (1936). Reference service by telephone. *Library Journal, 61*, 909–911.

Gartner Group. (2007). Gartner says 80% of active internet users will have a "second life" in the virtual world by the end of 2011. Retrieved April 29, 2009 from http://www.gartner.com/it/page.jsp?id=503861.

Gathright, A. (2006). Library will be first in nation to offer downloadable films, concert videos. *Rocky Mountain News*, February 17, 2006 Retrieved April 29, 2009, from http://www.rockymountainnews.com/drmn/local/article/0,1299,DRMN_15_4474821,00.html.

Gauder, B. (2007). Social networking encourages teen library usage at Denver public. *NextSpace*, 7, 12–13.

Hill, J. B., Hill, C. M., & Sherman, D. (2007). Text messaging in an academic library: Integrating SMS into digital reference. *Reference Librarian, 47*(1), 17–29.

Houghton, S., & Schmidt, A. (2005). Web-based chat vs. instant messaging. *Online, 29*(4), 26–30.

Jones, S., & Fox, S. (2009). Generations Online in 2009. Pew Internet & American Life Project. Retrieved April 29, 2009, from http://www.pewinternet.org/~/media//Files/Reports/2009/PIP_Generations_2009.pdf.

Kajewski, M. A. (2007). Emerging technologies changing our service delivery models. *The Electronic Library, 25*(4), 420–429.

Kawakami, A., & Swartz, P. (2003). Digital reference: Training and assessment for service improvement. *Reference Services Review, 31*(3), 227–236.

Kwon, N. (2005). User satisfaction with referrals at a collaborative virtual reference service. *Information Research, 11*(2) [paper 246]. Retrieved April 29, 2009, from http://InformationR.net/ir/11-2/paper246.html.

Lankes, R. D. (2008). Virtual reference to participatory librarianship: Expanding the conversation. *Bulletin of the American Society for Information Science and Technology, 34*(2), 11–14.

Lenhart, A. (2009). Adults and social network websites. [Pew Internet Project Data Memo.] Retrieved April 29, 2009, from http://www.pewinternet.org/Reports/2009/Adults-and-Social-Network-Websites.aspx.

Lenhart, A., & Madden, M. (2007). *Social networking websites and teens: An overview.* Pew Internet & American Life Project. Retrieved April 29, 2009, from http://pewresearch.org/pubs/118/social-networking-websites-and-teens.

Lenhart, A., Madden, M., & Hitlin, P. (2005). Teens and technology: Youth are leading the transition to a fully wired and mobile nation. Pew Internet & American Life Project. Retrieved April 29, 2009, from http://www.pewinternet.org/Reports/2005/Teens-and-Technology.aspx.

Library Journal Staff. (2009). And gladly teach—Michael Stephens. *Library Journal,* Retrieved April 29, 2009, from http://www.libraryjournal.com/article/CA510560.html.

Lipow, A. G. (1999). "In your face" reference service. *Library Journal, 124*(13), 50–52.

Lupien, P. (2006). Virtual reference in the age of pop-up blockers, firewalls, and service pack 2. *Online, 30*(4), 14–19, Retrieved April 29, 2009, from http://www.infotoday.com/online/jul06/Lupien.shtml.

Maness, J. (2006). Library 2.0 theory: Web 2.0 and its implications for libraries. *Webology, 3*(2), Article 25. Retrieved on March 8, 2009, from http://www.webology.ir/2006/v3n2/a25.html.

Marsteller, M. R., & Mizzy, D. (2003). Exploring the synchronous digital reference interaction for query types, question negotiation, and patron response. *Internet Reference Services Quarterly, 8*(1/2) 149–165.

Miller, P. (2005). Web 2.0: Building the new library. *Ariadne, 45.* Retrieved June 1, 2008, from http://www.ariadne.ac.uk/issue45/miller.

Mon, L., & Randeree, E. (2009). On the boundaries of reference services: Questioning and Library 2.0. *Journal of Education for Library and Information Science, 50*(3).

Montclair Public Library. (2004). A brief history of Montclair Public Library. Retrieved April 29, 2009, from http://www.montclairlibrary.org/content1055.

Norris, M. F. (1969). Strangle the machine: Experiences with a library network. *RQ, 9,* 39–44.

Oleck, J. (2007). Libraries use MySpace to attract teens. *School Library Journal, 53*(7), *16.*

Orange County Library System (2009). Podcasts & RSS. Retrieved April 29, 2009, from http://www.ocls.info/podcast/Default.asp?bhcp=1

O'Reilly, T. (2005). What is Web 2.0? Retrieved April 29, 2009, from http://www .oreillynet.com/pub/a/oreilly/tim/news/2005/09/30/what-is-web-20.html.

Pomerantz, J., & Stutzman, F. (2006). Collaborative reference work in the blogo-sphere. *Reference Services Review, 34*(2), 200–212.

Poole, H. (1966). Teletypewriters in libraries: A state of the art report. *College & Research Libraries, 27*, 283–290.

Pope, K. et al. (2007). Alliance Second Life Library end of year report 2007. Alliance Library System and Alliance Second Life Library. Retrieved April 29, 2009, from http://www.alliancelibraries.info/slendofyearreport2007.pdf.

Radford, M. L., & Kern, M. K. (2006). A multiple-case study investigation of the dis-continuation of nine chat reference services. *Library and Information Science Research, 28*(4), 24–48.

Richardson, J. V. (1999). Green, Samuel Swett. In J. A. Garrity (Ed.), *American national biography.* Retrieved April 29, 2009, from http://polaris .gseis.ucla.edu/jrichardson/dis220/ssgreen.htm.

Ryan, S. (1996). Reference service for the Internet community: A case study of the Internet Public Library reference division. *Library & Information Science Research, 18*, 241–259.

Seattle Public Library. (2004). Virtual reference 101. Retrieved April 29, 2009, from http://vrstrain.spl.org/virtual101/vrstimeline.htm.

Shaw, E. (1996). Real-time reference in a MOO: Promise and problems. Retrieved April 29, 2009, from http://www.ipl.org/div/iplhist/moo.html.

Steiner, S. K., & Long, C. M. (2007). What are we afraid of? A survey of librarian opin-ions and misconceptions regarding instant messenger. *Reference Librarian, 47*(1), 31–50.

Stephens, M. (2006). Exploring web 2.0 and libraries. *Library Technology Reports, 42*(4), 1–14.

Stormont, S. (2007). Looking to connect: Technical challenges that impede the growth of virtual reference. *Reference and User Services Quarterly, 47*(2), 116.

Swope, C. (2008). Getting in the Game. Governing. Retrieved August 19, 2010, from http://web.archive.org/web/20080607205325/http://www.governing.com/articles/0806libraryvids.htm.

Weissman, S. (2001). Know your audience. *School Library Journal, NetConnect,* April 15, 2001. Retrieved April 29, 2009, from http://www.schoollibraryjournal .com/article/CA106222.

Windham, C. (2005). The student's perspective. In D. G. Oblinger, & J. L. Oblinger (Eds.), *Educating the Net generation* (pp. 5.11–5.16). Educause. Retrieved April 29, 2009, from http://ctl.agnesscott.edu/resources/documents/EducatingtheNetGeneration.pdf.

Chapter 5

Public Library Roles in Hurricane Preparedness and Response

**Charles R. McClure, Lauren H. Mandel,
John Brobst, Charles C. Hinnant, John T. Snead,
and Joe Ryan**

INTRODUCTION

With virtually all public libraries having public access workstations connected to the Internet, numerous new applications and service roles offer opportunities for public libraries to better serve their local communities. Indeed, public libraries and Internet service roles have significantly changed the manner in which public libraries interact with their communities (McClure & Jaeger, 2009). One such set of service roles that clearly is evolving—especially in the southeastern portion of the United States and the Gulf Coast—is public library roles in community hurricane preparedness and recovery.

The purpose of this chapter is to provide an overview of the *Hurricane/Disaster Preparedness and Response by Utilizing Florida Public Libraries* study undertaken at the Information Use Management and Policy Institute (Information Institute), Florida State University. The Florida Catastrophic Storm Risk Management Center at Florida State University's College of Business awarded the grant to the Information Institute for the period August 8, 2008 through August 6, 2010. The Institute has partnered with the State Library and Archives of Florida, LYRASIS (formerly SOLINET), Florida's Multi-type Library Cooperatives, public libraries throughout the Gulf Coast region, as well as federal, state, local and community agencies concerned with Florida hurricane preparedness and response.

Public libraries, reacting to hurricane emergencies, have fulfilled a range of useful hurricane and disaster preparation and response roles. However, there has been no systematic effort to identify these roles, their associated best practices, and guidelines that might quicken widespread adoption of the roles by public libraries in the hurricane-affected region. The study described here begins to address this need.

The purpose of the study was to reduce communities' overall risk by raising the readiness level of public libraries to meet the challenges posed by these catastrophes. Study objectives included:

- Identify and then organize relevant public library hurricane-related information resources, services, roles, and best practices;
- Identify, aggregate, assess, and organize successful individual public library best practices related to hurricane preparedness and response;
- Develop model plans, standards, guidelines and recommendations—which are available via print materials and an interactive Web portal;
- Provide workshops and other training activities throughout the state of Florida and the Gulf Coast region;
- Offer strategies to assist state and regional public library and government officials with disaster coordination and organization responsibilities;
- Disseminate to public libraries, agencies, and other organizations, via print materials and the project Web portal, resources, services, experiences, best practices, plans and guidelines to coordinate Florida's public library managers and government partners to better prepare for and respond to hurricanes.

Ultimately, the project offers a significant opportunity for public libraries to better demonstrate the range of services and responses they could provide during such disasters.

EVOLVING ROLES OF PUBLIC LIBRARIES

Since 2004, researchers at the Information Institute have collected data that describe the roles and services that public libraries in Florida and along the Gulf Coast have played in hurricane/disaster preparedness and response. These data come from annual national surveys of technology use and deployment funded by the Bill & Melinda Gates Foundation and the American Library Association (Bertot, McClure, Thomas, Barton, & McGilvray, 2007; Bertot, McClure, Wright, Jensen, & Thomas, 2008, 2009), the State Library & Archives of Florida (Snead, McClure, & Bertot, 2007), as well as numerous interviews conducted by staff at the Information Institute.

These data show that:

- Public library hurricane response works best when the library is a partner with other responders in local hurricane/disaster preparedness and response teams;
- The public library contributes a range of skills and knowledge to handling information management and various communication prior to, during, and after such storms;

- The public recognizes the public library as a trusted and effective government agency in such emergencies.

These data, in conjunction with observations from the 2006 hurricane season, suggest a number of key roles in which public libraries are participating in hurricane and disaster preparedness and response.

THE 2006 HURRICANE SEASON

In the aftermath of the 2006 hurricane season, the study team found that the major areas in which libraries played a key role were the following (Bertot, Jaeger, Langa, & McClure, 2006; Jaeger, Langa, McClure, & Bertot, 2007):

1. *Helped communities prepare*—created and distributed emergency preparedness guides, both printed and Web-based; conducted disaster information workshops; and ran volunteer coordination programs.

2. *Provided emergency information*—staffed emergency operations centers and answered phone calls; answered email questions; conducted interactive chat services; handled communications in and out of the city; created community contact centers allowing community members to re-establish contact with family and friends; and addressed inquiries from other parts of the country and around the world about area conditions or particular residents.

3. *Provided shelter*—ran and staffed shelters for evacuees both in library buildings and in other buildings; provided city employees and relief workers with places to sleep; and housed city command centers for disasters (i.e., police, fire, public works).

4. *Provided physical aid*—cooked and distributed homemade meals; distributed water, ice, meals ready to eat (MREs), tarps, and bug spray; registered people with the "blue roof program"; provided hook-ups to recharge electronics and communication devices; filled water bottles; let people use library refrigerators for food and medication; and unloaded truckloads of relief supplies.

5. *Provided continuity of services, stress reduction, and normalcy restoration for community members in need*—assisted with the completion of Federal Emergency Management Administration (FEMA), insurance, and other paperwork; responded to special needs and elderly evacuees; worked as translators for evacuees; ran day camps for children when schools were closed and for children of city employees who had to work unusual hours; held programs, provided library materials to evacuees, and established temporary libraries in shelters; and sent bookmobiles and response teams to devastated areas.

6. *Worked with partner government and relief organizations*—assisted FEMA, Florida Division of Emergency Management, Red Cross, and Army Corps of Engineers personnel in their duties; provided meeting spaces for relief and rescue personnel; provided FEMA, Red Cross, National Guard, and Army Corps of Engineers personnel with a place to meet with

residents; provided relief personnel a place to use the Internet, email, and telephones; gave temporary library cards to relief workers; and helped FEMA personnel identify local areas that suffered major damage.

7. *Cleaned up the damage after the storms*—secured city buildings after storms; checked structures for damage; cleaned up debris; and restored damaged government structures.

These activities are not intended as an exhaustive list but suggest the broad areas in which public libraries were involved with hurricane preparedness and response. These services were provided by libraries throughout the Gulf Coast region, which employed their professionally trained staff, library resources, Internet access, and many other resources to assist their communities in hurricane preparedness and recovery.

In preparation for a community emergency or during a hurricane crisis, many public libraries have provided a range of useful services and activities. Yet there are no guidelines, recommendations, or best practices available to help public libraries more effectively serve in these roles. In short, those libraries that were involved in the provision of disaster services learned by doing. There has been no systematic effort to transfer what was learned at these individual libraries to all public libraries. More specifically, there has been no systematic effort to identify the activities and services provided or to better organize, coordinate, and assist public libraries to provide these hurricane/ disaster planning and response services.

There are a multitude of federal, state, and local agencies, private organizations, and other entities that prepare for and address state level emergency preparedness and response. There are so many that there is some confusion as to how public libraries might best coordinate activities with them. A clear need exists to organize and define duties, responsibilities, and resources available from each/all of these different agencies and organizations, and to inform and train library staff on the available resources and information from all of these different entities.

Virtually every community in the Gulf Coast region has access to a nearby public library. These public libraries are exceptionally well-positioned to provide hurricane/disaster preparedness and response services to their local communities. Provision of these services can be facilitated by the project's definition and organization of duties and responsibilities and identification of best practices and resources.

STUDY APPROACH

The overall goal of the study was to identify ways to reduce hurricane risk by better utilizing public libraries in community hurricane preparation and recovery. Given this goal, the study team developed some initial research questions to guide the study approach and the data collection activities, including:

- Which are the public libraries in Florida and the southeastern United States that have successfully assisted their communities to prepare for and recover from hurricane disasters?

- What role can traditional library partners play related to community hurricane preparation and recovery?
- Which are exemplar public library-agency partners?
- What information or services do citizens need related to hurricanes that public libraries might provide?
- How best can the study team transfer and communicate research results, products, and services?

Because of the exploratory nature of the study, the study team recognized that the research questions might need to be modified and refined as the study progressed. Table 5.1 in Appendix A presents the initial research questions in more detail.

Approach

A number of considerations informed the development and deployment of the study approach:

- *Exploratory*: There was no pre-conceived model available. Assumptions, research questions and study populations shifted during and after each phase, and often after each interview.
- *Pragmatic*: The conscious intent of the research was to reduce hurricane risk by better utilizing public libraries to prepare and aid their communities.
- *Iterative, phased learning*: The study operated on a continuous learning cycle—conceptualize (adjust study populations, samples and research questions as needed), collect data, synthesize/analyze data, test and re-conceptualize until saturation.
- *Opportunistic*: The study anticipated unscheduled opportunities to collect and analyze data throughout the course of the project and designed the study approach to take advantage of these opportunities.
- *Multi-method*: The study included literature review, document analysis, various qualitative techniques (e.g., individual and group interviews, focus groups, and panels conducted face-to-face, by phone and email), brief open-ended and structured surveys, and some simple social networking analysis.
- *User-based*: Wherever possible, theory development and data collection methodologies were driven by the studies' users.

Table 5.2 in Appendix A presents the Study Approach in more detail. Also in Appendix A Table 5.3 illustrates how the study's strategy was altered or refined during its course.

Data Quality

The study team made every effort to systematically reduce error due to researcher bias, incomplete or inaccurate data, and a host of other causes. The evaluators took a number of steps to reduce the threats to data quality in the present project, both during data collection and later during analysis, including (Creswell, 1994; Guba & Lincoln, 1981; Miles & Huberman, 1994; Patton, 1990; Schatzman & Strauss, 1973):

- Used pre-structured research questions and interview instruments, pre-planned fieldwork, and, where possible, a pre-planned final report format.
- Chose standard, well-regarded methods familiar to the evaluators and appropriate to the setting. Primary methods were qualitative (Miles & Huberman, 1994), including the use of documentary evidence, interviews (Spradley, 1979) and focus groups (Kruger & Casey, 2000; Morgan, 1988).
- Fully documented research design decisions in writing and in discussions among the study team.
- Actively sought disconfirming and outsider evidence and points of view. The study team attempted, within the constraints of a site visit, to interview stakeholders from multiple perspectives.
- Responded with flexibility to the new and unexpected opportunities the data offered.
- Fully documented the data collected. Evaluators conducted follow-up interviews where necessary.
- Triangulated the data collected and used multiple methods. Data collected from one source was cross-checked with another. The evaluators compared data collected using one method with answers obtained via another method. The evaluators shared drafts of factual portions of the final report with a key liaison in each region to check for accuracy.
- Pre-structured data analysis and reporting (Miles & Huberman, 1994). This approach was possible because most of the data collection was pre-structured and the intended shape of the final report was known.
- Checked the quality of the data by tracking the chain of evidence that the study team gathered to be sure it was firm enough to support statements made.

Each of these efforts and others increased the validity and reliability of the findings and provided a firm basis for making recommendations.

FINDINGS AND PRODUCTS

There are a number of findings and products that have resulted from the study thus far. These include:

- Identifying the value of building a hurricane response network;
- Synthesizing, utilizing and implementing public library hurricane service roles;
- Creating documents that help make the case for public libraries being "essential services" and better assisting residents and evacuees to prepare for and recover from hurricanes/disasters;

- Developing a Web portal to disseminate project findings and encourage social networking and collaboration among public librarians and emergency responders.

These will be briefly reviewed here; an in-depth discussion of the findings and products are available on the project Web portal at: http://hurricanes.ii .fsu.edu/.

Building a Response Network

Before disaster strikes, library managers have an opportunity to focus on what they can control and manage: preparing the library facility and staff, finding partners to help, and pre-coordinating emergency response activities, particularly with local emergency operations leaders and local government, as much as is reasonable. The team approach has proven to yield rewards greater than individual agency and independent efforts. As one library manager noted, "If I can build a relationship with directors of [local, state, and federal] agencies, it brings credibility of libraries to the table."

The first step in managing hurricane response partnerships is to gain a better awareness of what each potential partner does in community hurricane response. Discussions need to be open and frank with a range of local emergency responders and others about the resources necessary to provide services and meet partner needs. The next step is to pre-coordinate what the library can contribute, what the library needs from each partner in order to do so, and how library activities can mesh with other partners' activities.

Next, the library and its partners should prepare and test these new arrangements prior to an emergency. Working out the details in advance saves time, significantly improves response, and results in forming bonds of trust and understanding.

After a storm strikes, it is useful to assess what worked and what didn't, and then determine what else can be done to better assist the community in the future. In initiating these collaborative efforts, keep in mind that making arrangements to aid each other and to coordinate these activities takes time, and that what is possible may vary from location to location due to local situations and library-county or library-city policies.

Multi-type Library Cooperatives (MLCs), the State Libraries, large library systems, libraries adjacent to hurricane-affected libraries, library vendors, LYRASIS and others can all make significant hurricane response contributions. The key, however, is for the public library to (1) clarify relationships, responsibilities, and activities with other community, state, and federal emergency agencies prior to a hurricane; and (2) understand which of the service roles (discussed next) it has the capacity and knowledge to offer to its local community.

Public Library Hurricane Service Roles

The study team interviewed over 200 public library managers who had aided their communities to prepare for or recover from a hurricane. The project team then synthesized common service roles that were performed by hurricane-affected libraries. These roles include:

- *Get to Know Your Local EOC*: Getting to know your Emergency Operations Center (EOC) should be on the top of the list for every library so the library and EOC can work together to best provide for the community's needs.

- *Safe Haven*: The public library is the community's living room and study, before and after a storm, with safe, secure buildings, relaxing space, light, air conditioning, bathrooms and comfortable chairs.

- *Normal Service*: The community counts on normal library service before and after the storm, be it book, DVD or Internet use, reference or family programming. Normal service provides hope, re-establishes government presence, reduces stress, returns normalcy, and offers recreation and distraction.

- *Disaster Recovery Centers (DRC)*: Disaster Recovery Centers (DRCs) attempt to assemble under one roof all agencies providing disaster benefits. A DRC may be a FEMA designated DRC; a state, county or municipal DRC; a point of distribution (POD) of aid; or simply a place for neighbors to make sense and provide each other with aid.

- *Information Hub*: The community counts on the library before and after a storm to offer access to various communication equipment, to be a trusted provider of accurate, reliable information, to produce needed information aids where they do not exist, and to deliver this information using whatever technology the community uses and can afford.

- *Cultural Organizations Liaison*: Public libraries may serve as liaisons between emergency management agencies and communities' cultural organizations.

- *Evacuee Resource*: Evacuees count on the nearest public library for a safe haven, normal service, disaster recovery center, and information hub.

- *Improvise*: Should a disaster strike, the community counts on the public library to improvise and do what is needed to assist in the community's recovery. The library must be flexible, innovative, and creative to efficiently and effectively meet the needs of those impacted by this type of disaster.

Many of these key public library community hurricane response roles are further discussed on the project Web portal: http://hurricanes.ii.fsu.edu/.

Documents, Templates, and Booklets

The project team developed documents, templates, and booklets, based on study findings, that can assist public libraries make the case for being an essential service in a disaster and help residents and evacuees prepare for and recover from hurricanes (Ryan, 2009a–e):

- *Making the Case*: This document presents an extended argument for why public libraries should be viewed as an "essential service" in a community's response to hurricanes.

- *Booklets and Templates*: These resources help libraries design community-specific booklets containing essential information for hurricane/disaster preparedness and response. Booklets include: Library Recovery booklet, Resident Hurricane Preparation booklet, Evacuee and Resident Hurricane Recovery Information booklet and the Back-Home Web page template.

These resources are available on the project Web portal: http://hurricanes .ii.fsu.edu/.

Public Library Hurricane Preparedness and Response Web Portal

The project Web portal, http://hurricanes.ii.fsu.edu/summarizes and presents project findings to date. The portal has three intended phases, including:

- *Experimentation*: The Web portal went through four beta versions exploring various content and ways to present it. Of particular note was the increasing use of graphics (over text), including maps and Web 2.0 social networking.
- *Project findings*: This phase sought to summarize what the study team learned from those interviewed. Key organizing elements were the public library community hurricane response roles and their associated best practices, aids or tools promoting adoption, as well as identification of relevant resources. For example, an important role identified was the public library as Safe Haven. An associated best practice for a library playing the Safe Haven role was to have an emergency or continuity of operations (CoOP) plan. An aid to adoption of a plan is a template that outlines and provides examples of a plan.
- *Social networking*: A key early project finding was that a number of public libraries, reacting to hurricanes, had developed a series of great best practices. But often a library in the next county was unaware of these developments. There was no forum for hurricane-affected libraries, and those who might be affected at a later date, to exchange and discuss best practices. This phase focused on developing ways that public libraries could share what they have learned in this area, to encourage social networking among hurricane-affected libraries to share issues, practices, aids, news and resources.

The portal contains more detail on project findings, including descriptions of, best practices for, and related resources to each of the eight service roles.

Summary of Findings and Products

Project findings demonstrate the importance of public libraries for hurricane and disaster preparedness and response. Public libraries engage in eight disaster preparedness and response service roles, helping local communities and evacuees prepare for and recover from hurricanes and other disasters. These public library service roles may be facilitated by project products, such as the documents, templates, booklets, and Web portal.

NEXT STEPS FOR PUBLIC LIBRARIES IN THE HURRICANE ZONE

Interviews with public library managers who have experienced hurricanes suggest the follow steps to consider if a library seeks to improve service to its community in preparing for hurricane season:

- *Review the service roles, their best practices and aids as outlined on the project portal.* Decide one practice to develop this season. For example, if you want to improve your role as Safe Haven, a likely best practice to adopt is to have an emergency or CoOP plan. Decide which components of the plan to work on this year and do them. The underlying message is—do not try to do everything all at once. It is easy to get overwhelmed. Pick one small thing and do it well. There will be opportunity to do more next hurricane season.

- *Coordinate what you do with other responders in advance of a storm.* Key partners are local emergency management and government agencies, but also important are local utilities, police, fire, church groups and local businesses. Learn what these organizations intend to do and acquaint them with the roles your library intends to play. Find ways to strengthen the community's ability to respond through collaboration.

- *Prepare your staff.* Communicate with library staff what is expected of them, why their work matters to the community in emergency situations, and details of hurricane response roles and responsibilities. Reviewing this information at least once a year prior to hurricane season should become standard operating procedure.

Librarians and the library community know from experience that public libraries are essential service points in times of crisis, but they need to make the case to federal, state, and local agencies to be formally recognized as essential services in disaster recovery. This is necessary for library directors to have quick access to their facilities after a disaster strikes, not only to assess damages but also to provide access and services to the local community the library serves.

BENEFITS

The study has benefited public librarians, local communities, and local, federal, and state emergency managers by:

- *Enhancing the public library's ability to provide services, information, resources, and expertise to assist local communities and their residents.* The public library has a range of information and other services, expertise, and resources that, if properly organized and deployed, can significantly improve a community's planning for and response to hurricanes.

- *Providing a comprehensive approach for public libraries to work more effectively in their local communities and with the state for hurricane preparedness and response.* Developing a comprehensive approach for how libraries can best assist in hurricane preparedness and response will increase the library's effectiveness in serving Florida and Gulf Coast residents.

- *Improving communication and planning/response between the public library and various government and other agencies regarding hurricane preparedness and response.* Currently there are no guidelines and best practices for how libraries can collaborate with other agencies. This project will improve overall coordination and avoid duplication of efforts among agencies.

- *Educating local community members, government officials and others as to the roles public libraries can play in hurricane preparedness and response.* Previous experience among the study team suggests that many local, state, and other community members are not aware of the range of expertise and services that public libraries can contribute to hurricane preparedness and response. This project will help educate these stakeholders about the valuable roles public libraries can and do play in hurricane/disaster preparedness and response.

Ultimately, the study will improve the ability of Florida and other Gulf Coast residents to better prepare for, survive, and cope with the results of a hurricane and better leverage and coordinate the expertise of public librarians in working with other state and local government agencies for hurricane preparedness and response.

ACKNOWLEDGMENTS

The Information Institute acknowledges the generous help and support from project partners, the State Library and Archives of Florida, and LYRASIS (formerly SOLINET), as well as Florida Multi-type Library Cooperatives, librarians and state library staff who participated in the various data collection efforts, and emergency management personnel who shared their time and experiences. We are especially grateful to the Florida Catastrophic Storm Risk Management Center (http://www.stormrisk.org) at Florida State University that funded the project. The study team also acknowledges additional Institute staff for their work on this project including Susan Thomas, Mike Falcon, Bradley Wade Bishop, Lynne Hinnant, and Jordon Andrade.

REFERENCES

Bertot, J. C., Jaeger, P. T., Langa, L. A., & McClure, C. R. (2006). Public access computing and Internet access in public libraries: The role of public libraries in e-government and emergency situations. *First Monday, 11*(9). Available at http://www.firstmonday.org/issues/issue11_9/bertot/index.html.

Bertot, J. C., McClure, C. R., Thomas, S., Barton, K., & McGilvray, J. (2007). *Public libraries and the Internet 2007: Report to the American Library Association*. Tallahassee, FL: Information Use Management and Policy Institute. Available at http://www.plinternetsurvey.org.

Bertot, J. C., McClure, C. R., Wright, C. B., Jensen, E., & Thomas, S. (2008). *Public libraries and the Internet 2008: Study results and findings*. Tallahassee, FL: Information Use Management and Policy Institute. Available at http://www.plinternetsurvey.org.

Bertot, J. C., McClure, C. R., Wright, C. B., Jensen, E., & Thomas, S. (2009). *Public libraries and the Internet 2009: Study results and findings*. Tallahassee, FL: Information Use Management and Policy Institute. Available at http://www.plinternetsurvey.org.

Creswell, J. W. (1994). *Research design: Qualitative and quantitative approaches*. Thousand Oaks, CA: Sage Publications.

Guba, E. G., & Lincoln, Y. S. (1981). *Effective evaluation: Improving the usefulness of evaluation results through responsive and naturalistic approaches*. San Francisco: Jossey-Bass Publishers.

Jaeger, P. T., Langa, L. A., McClure, C. R., & Bertot, J. C. (2007). The 2004 and 2005 Gulf Coast hurricanes: Evolving roles and lessons learned for public libraries. *Public Library Quarterly, 25*, 199–214.

Kruger, R. A., & Casey, M. A. (2000). *Focus groups: A practical guide for applied research* (3rd ed.). Thousand Oaks, CA: Sage Publications.

McClure, C. R., & Jaeger, P. T. (2009). *Public libraries and Internet service roles: Measuring and maximizing Internet services*. Chicago: American Library Association.

Miles, M. B., & Huberman, A. M. (1994). *Qualitative data analysis*. Thousand Oaks, CA: Sage Publications.

Morgan, D. L. (1988). *Focus groups as qualitative research*. Newbury Park, CA: Sage Publications.

Patton, M. Q. (1990). *Qualitative evaluation and research methods*. Newbury Park, CA: Sage Publications.

Ryan, J. (2009a). *BackHome template*. Tallahassee, FL: Information Use Management & Policy Institute. Available at http://hurricanes.ii.fsu.edu/docs/04InfoHub/SlashBackHome_Initiative.doc.

Ryan, J. (2009b). *Evacuee and resident hurricane recovery information booklet*. Tallahassee, FL: Information Use Management and Policy Institute. Available at http://hurricanes.ii.fsu.edu/docs/04InfoHub/EvacueeResidentRecovery-Booklet3.27.09.doc.

Ryan, J. (2009c) *Library recovery booklet*. Tallahassee, FL: Information Use Management and Policy Institute. Available at http://hurricanes.ii.fsu.edu/libraryRecovery.html.

Ryan, J. (2009d). *Making the case*. Tallahassee, FL: Information Use Management and Policy Institute. Available at http://hurricanes.ii.fsu.edu/docs/01safeHaven/MakeTheCase3.11.09.pdf.

Ryan, J. (2009e). *Resident hurricane preparation booklet*. Tallahassee, FL: Information Use Management and Policy Institute. Available at http://hurricanes.ii.fsu.edu/docs/04InfoHub/ResidentPreparationBooklet8.3.09.doc.

Schatzman, L., & Strauss, A. L. (1973). *Field research: Strategies for a natural sociology*. Englewood Cliffs, NJ: Prentice-Hall.

Snead, J. T., McClure, C. R., & Bertot, J. C. (2007). *Florida Electronic Library five-year evaluation 2003–2007*. Tallahassee, FL: Information Use Management & Policy Institute.

Spradley, J. P. (1979). *The ethnographic interview*. New York: Holt, Rinehart and Winston.

APPENDIX A. STUDY APPROACH: FURTHER DISCUSSION

TABLE 5.1   Research Question Summary

Overall: What can the study team learn that will enable or persuade public libraries, current or potential library-agency partners and other key stakeholders to reduce hurricane risk by better utilizing public libraries in community hurricane preparation and recovery?

Specific research questions included:

- **Who are exemplar public libraries?** Who are the public libraries in Florida and the southeast U.S. that have successfully assisted *their communities* to prepare for and recover from hurricane disasters?

  - What were these libraries' hurricane *experiences* that might be of use to other public libraries?

  - Did they do any advanced *planning* or develop a hurricane plan? Did the plan include public library community hurricane preparation and recovery efforts? Was the planning effort useful, and why?

  - What *roles* did these public libraries play when assisting their communities to prepare for and recover from hurricanes?

  - What *best practices* have these libraries developed?

  - What checklists, standards, Web links, guides, forms, policies, procedures, and other *documents* have these libraries developed?

  - How did these libraries establish and maintain partnerships with other agencies related to community hurricane preparation and recovery?

  - What advice do these libraries have for other libraries?

  - What needs and issues do these libraries have related to community hurricane preparation and recovery?

- **What role can traditional library partners play related to community hurricane preparation and recovery**?

  - Traditional library partners include library systems, multi-type library consortia, state libraries, state library associations, and Lyrasis.

  - What do these library partners currently do to assist public library community hurricane preparation and recovery?

  - What do these traditional library partners believe should and can be done?

- **Who are exemplar public library-agency partners**?

  - Public library-agency partners may include units of local, state or federal government, emergency management agencies, the Red Cross and other non-governmental organizations.

  - How can public libraries establish and maintain these partnerships?

  - What opportunities are there for libraries?

- **What information or services do citizens need related to hurricanes that public libraries might provide**?

  - For example, would a model citizen hurricane desktop containing hurricane-related resources be of use to citizens?

(*Continued*)

TABLE 5.1 (Continued)

• How best can the study team transfer and communicate research results, products, and services?

    ○ How can the project team best communicate study results, products, and services to public libraries, current or potential library-agency partners, and other key stakeholders, to reduce hurricane risk by better utilizing public libraries in community hurricane preparation and recovery?

TABLE 5.2 Summary of Broad Characteristics Affecting Study Approach

Characteristic	Discussion
Exploratory	The project team was not testing a pre-conceived model, as the research literature did not suggest one. Rather, models, methods, project products and services had to be developed based on what the data suggested and what the study team learned. Assumptions, research questions and study populations shifted during and after each phase, and often after each interview.
Pragmatic	A conscious intent of this research was to use research results to persuade public library managers, their library and non-library partners, emergency management, fellow responders and other key stakeholders to reduce hurricane risk by better utilizing public libraries to prepare and aid their communities. Project results should be of immediate use for communities to better utilize public libraries in response to hurricanes.
Iterative, phased learning	This study was consciously structured to learn iteratively. In a large sense, the study's strategy and tasking were broken into research phases: ○ Get organized, ○ Identify Gulf Coast library managers experienced with hurricanes and listen, ○ Synthesize field research, ○ Identify Florida library managers experienced with hurricanes and listen, ○ Analyze and synthesize data, ○ Design and test Web portal, ○ Transfer learning through presentation and training, and ○ Have key stakeholders assess and review project products (ongoing). On a smaller scale, the exploratory research ran on a cycle of continuous learning: conceptualize (adjust study populations, samples, and research questions as needed); collect data; synthesize/analyze data; test and re-conceptualize until saturation throughout the study period.
Opportunistic	The study team anticipated informal opportunities to collect and analyze data throughout the course of the project and

TABLE 5.2 (Continued)

Characteristic	Discussion
	designed the study approach to take advantage of these opportunities (e.g., the Southern Council of State Library Agencies and the Council of State Library Agencies met in the area early in the study). The project team adjusted to collect data and brief Gulf Coast State Librarians about the project.
Multi-method	The study included literature review, document analysis, various qualitative techniques (e.g., individual and group interviews; focus groups and panels face-to-face, by phone and e-mail), brief open ended and structured surveys, and some simple social networking analysis.
User-based	Wherever possible, theory development and data collection methodologies were driven by the studies' users—the sample drawn from the study population. For example, rather than impose a model of roles that public libraries play in community hurricane preparation and recovery, the study team developed the model based on the experiences of exemplar public libraries. Therefore, rather than present a fully populated project Web portal, the project team solicited input from project participants about what was and was not useful and designed the site based on that input.

TABLE 5.3 Study Strategy Refinement

Strategy Element	Strategy Refined
Identify study population	**Public library managers with hurricane experience**: identified by project team, state libraries, MLCs and LYRASIS, prior contact, and a literature review.
	External library supporters: added to the study population.
	Emergency management: added to the study population because they coordinate local recovery efforts including the public libraries; only interviewed state, regional and county emergency managers as opportunity permitted.
	Other responders: county, state and federal agency responders and non-profits were added to the study population as potential public library partners, but only interviewed as opportunity permitted.
Listen	**Literature and Web review**: conducted review of library literature and a sample of other responder literatures. Examined Web-based Florida public library materials, hurricane preparation materials, hurricane recovery materials, and Web 2.0 hurricane materials.
	Interviews: included individual and group, phone, e-mail and in-person interviews following standard practice (e.g., pre-scripting, recording where possible, more than one observer of participants, multiple session review/synthesis, etc).

(*Continued*)

89

TABLE 5.3   (Continued)

Strategy Element	Strategy Refined
	Model testing: Regularly prepared summaries of current thinking and circulated among experts for evaluation. This included the 2/20/09 Eppes External Support Panel Discussion.
Synthesize	**Roles**: A first finding was that public library hurricane responses could be consolidated into a set of public library community hurricane response roles.
	Best practices (Activities): Each role had a set of associated activities.
	Best practices (Tools): Adoption of role activities could be aided by tools or aids.
	Basic processes: Role acceptance could be eased by certain basic processes.
	External support options: Study identified a list of potential ways to externally support hurricane affected public libraries.
	Next steps: need for understanding, advocacy, partnerships, and funding.
Transfer	**Project Web portal**: Developed capacity to offer various Web site features, in particular Web 2.0 features; tested their utility and usability; and populated site with useful content.
	Training: Presented study findings and offered training.
	Publications: Communicated findings in print and via the Web.
	E-network: Communicated ongoing study results via listservs, blogs and e-mail.

The Public Library in the Life of the Internet: How the Core Values of Librarianship Can Shape Human-Centered Computing

Kenneth R. Fleischmann

INTRODUCTION

While this book focuses primarily on the Internet in the life of the public library, this chapter considers the opposite side of this mutually constitutive relationship: the public library in the life of the Internet. This approach is based on a core concept from the field of science and technology studies—the mutual shaping of technology and society. While the Internet has certainly transformed the roles of the public libraries and the perspectives of librarians, and has significant implications for the future of public libraries, the convergence between public libraries and the Internet has also had a significant impact on the development and adoption of the Internet. The service orientation and values of librarianship continue to transform computing and, especially, research and education in the emerging interdisciplinary area of human-centered computing.

This chapter examines the influence of public libraries on the Internet in three parts. The first part explores the impact that public libraries have already had on the development and adoption of the Internet. The second part considers how the Core Values of Librarianship (American Library Association, 2004) can help to transform computing, applying the service orientation of the field of librarianship to consider how information technology can be better designed to serve the needs of users. The third part discusses the relationship between computing and information studies, arguing that the field of information studies is an ideal location for research and educational programs in human-centered computing, due to the origins of the field in librarianship and the professional orientation of librarianship as emphasizing service to users. The overall purpose of this chapter is to balance the overall emphasis on the importance of the public library for the Internet found in this book by considering the influence of public libraries on the Internet.

THE IMPACT OF PUBLIC LIBRARIES ON THE INTERNET

Public libraries have had a significant impact not only on the use of the Internet but also on the design of the Internet. This section discusses examples of the impact of public libraries on the Internet, focusing on how the role of public libraries in the provision of free Internet access for the public as well as in the development of digital libraries.

Public libraries are a primary site for public access to the Internet. Almost three quarters of public libraries responding to the *2008 Public Libraries and the Internet Survey* reported that they serve as the only site that provides free access to the Internet to the general public within their communities (Bertot, McClure, Wright, Jensen, & Thomas, 2009). Providing public access has significant implications for expanding the potential and actual user bases of the Internet, especially in terms of expanding the user base to be more diverse in terms of socioeconomic status, but also potentially in terms of ethnicity and level of education. Some users might not have access to the Internet if it were not for public libraries. Further, some users may get their first exposure to the Internet in public libraries, and then decide to purchase their own computers and/or get home Internet connections based on the benefits that they see from using the Internet in public libraries. Thus, at the very least, Internet provision by public libraries can help to spur use and adoption of the Internet.

Libraries not only provide access to the Internet, they can also provide guidance on using the Internet. Librarians are skilled in information access and user training, and can help users search for information online. Libraries often provide structured opportunities for user training, including programs targeted at specific underserved populations, such as older adults (Xie & Jaeger, 2008). True access to the Internet not only involves owning or having physical access to a computer with an Internet connection, it also requires enough education and training to use the computer, including basic skills such as literacy, and specific skills such as computer literacy (Bertot, 2003). Universal access also requires that the technology be accessible to a wide range of populations with various special needs, which is another particular strength of public access to the Internet provided by public libraries (Jaeger, 2002). Thus, public libraries not only provide computers with Internet connections, but also assistance, training, and technologies for accessibility needed to approach the overall goal of universal access to the Internet.

The access to the Internet provided by public libraries has significant implications. For example, providing universal access to the Internet in public libraries can assist with the provision of e-government (Bertot, 2010; Bertot, Jaeger, Langa, & McClure, 2006a; Jaeger, Bertot, McClure, & Langa, 2006), such that citizens can have more direct access to government forms, services, and resources. Another example is providing access to information in emergency situations (Bertot, Jaeger, Langa, & McClure, 2006b; Jaeger, Langa, McClure, & Bertot, 2007). The Internet can provide information about the safety of loved ones and the condition of property, as well as government responses to emergencies. Finally, yet another example of the impact of universal access to the Internet provided by public libraries is access to health information (Carter & Wallace, 2007; Xie & Bugg, 2009), which can improve the physical and psychological well-being of individuals and empower patients relative to practitioners (Xie, 2009).

This phenomenon is not limited to the United States, but can also be found internationally. The same trends that originated largely within the United States are also expanding to a wide range of other countries (Baltrunas, Lileikaite, & Rutkauskiene, 2008; Evans & Savard, 2008; Gordon, 2007). However, this trend is not occurring at the same rate in all locations, even within the United States (Jaeger, Bertot, McClure, & Rodriguez, 2007). Thus, although clearly the role of public libraries in providing universal access to the Internet has been impressive and influential to date, there is still room for improvement both within the United States and throughout the world, especially in the developing world.

Digital libraries have played an important role in shaping the development of the Internet. Schatz and Chen (1999) make the case that digital libraries can serve as important research initiatives, large-scale testbeds, and vehicles for semantic interoperability. Bishop, Van House, & Buttenfield (2003) provide many additional examples of the societal impact of public libraries. An argument can be made for the need to consider the role of values in the design and use of digital libraries (Fleischmann, 2007) as well as public libraries (e.g., Jaeger & Fleischmann, 2007). Thus, digital libraries provide an example of an application of the values of librarianship to the Internet and the impact that this can have.

Clearly, public libraries and digital libraries have already played an important role not only in facilitating universal access to the Internet but also in shaping the specific functionalities of the Internet. However, the potential for libraries' future impact on the development of the Internet is even greater. It is important to consider how the service orientation of public libraries can shape the growth of the Internet, especially within the overall context of the core values of librarianship.

HOW THE CORE VALUES OF LIBRARIANSHIP CAN TRANSFORM COMPUTING

The Core Values of Librarianship (American Library Association, 2004) can help to transform computing, specifically, by applying the service orientation of the field of librarianship to consider how information technology can be better designed to serve the needs of users. This section explores how each of the core values of librarianship can be used to inform and improve the design of information technology, potentially advancing both computer science and human-centered computing.

The core values of librarianship can be adapted and applied to computing as well. Table 6.1 provides each of the ALA's (2004) core values, the original

TABLE 6.1   Applying the Core Values of Librarianship to Computing

Core Values	Core Values of Librarianship (ALA, 2004)	Core Values of Computing
Access	"All information resources that are provided directly or indirectly by the library, regardless of technology, format, or methods of delivery, should be readily, equally, and equitably accessible to all library users."	All computing technologies should be designed to be readily, equally, and equitably accessible to all users.
Confidentiality/ Privacy	"Protecting user privacy and confidentiality is necessary for intellectual freedom and fundamental to the ethics and practice of librarianship."	Protecting user privacy and confidentiality is necessary to ensure public trust in computing.
Democracy	"A democracy presupposes an informed citizenry. The First Amendment mandates the right of all persons to free expression, and the corollary right to receive the constitutionally protected expression of others. The publicly supported library provides free and equal access to information for all people of the community the library serves."	Computing technologies should be designed to support the rights of all persons to free expression and the corollary right to receive the expression of others.
Diversity	"We value our nation's diversity and strive to reflect that diversity by providing a full spectrum of resources and services to the communities we serve."	Computing technologies should reflect our nation's diversity by providing a full spectrum of resources and services to all communities.
Education and Lifelong Learning	"ALA promotes the creation, maintenance, and enhancement of a learning society, encouraging its members to work with educators, government officials, and organizations in coalitions to initiate and support comprehensive efforts to ensure that school, public, academic, and special libraries in every community cooperate to provide lifelong learning services to all."	Computing professionals should promote the creation, maintenance, and enhancement of a learning society in all of the products that they build and activities in which they engage.
Intellectual Freedom	"We uphold the principles of intellectual freedom and resist all efforts to censor library resources."	Computing professionals should uphold intellectual freedom and resist censorship efforts.
Preservation	"The Association supports the preservation of information published in all media and formats. The association affirms that the preservation of information resources is central to libraries and librarianship."	Computing technologies should support the preservation of usability of information published in all computing media and file formats.

TABLE 6.1 (Continued)

Core Values	Core Values of Librarianship (ALA, 2004)	Core Values of Computing
Professionalism	"The American Library Association supports the provision of library services by professionally qualified personnel who have been educated in graduate programs within institutions of higher education. It is of vital importance that there be professional education available to meet the social needs and goals of library services."	Computing professionals should be professionally qualified personnel with appropriate education. It is of vital importance that there be education available to meet the social needs and goals of computing.
The Public Good	"ALA reaffirms the following fundamental values of libraries in the context of discussing outsourcing and privatization of library services. These values include that libraries are an essential public good and are fundamental institutions in democratic societies."	Computing technology has the potential to serve as an essential public good and a fundamental institution in democratic societies.
Service	"We provide the highest level of service to all library users . . . We strive for excellence in the profession by maintaining and enhancing our own knowledge and skills, by encouraging the professional development of co-workers, and by fostering the aspirations of potential members of the profession."	Computing professionals strive to serve the needs and values of users, and should work to enhance their own knowledge and skills, encourage the professional development of co-workers, and help to foster the aspirations of potential members of the profession.
Social Responsibility	"ALA recognizes its broad social responsibilities. The broad social responsibilities of the American Library Association are defined in terms of the contribution that librarianship can make in ameliorating or solving the critical problems of society; in supporting efforts to help inform and educate the people of the United States on these problems and to encourage them to examine the many views on and facts regarding each problem; and in the willingness of ALA to take a position on current critical issues with the relationship to libraries and library service set forth in the position statement."	Computing professionals have a broad social responsibility to participate in ameliorating or solving the critical problems of society; to support efforts to help inform and educate users on these problems and to encourage them to examine the many views on the facts regarding each problem; and to be willing to take a position on current critical issues.

definition in terms of the core values of librarianship, and a new adapted definition for the core values of computing.

For access, the modified statement for computing is: *All computing technologies should be designed to be readily, equally, and equitably accessible to all users.* Here, just as librarians put an emphasis on ensuring that all library users can have access to all information stored within (or accessible through) the library, computer professionals should also ensure access to individuals with special needs. Shneiderman's (2000) concept of universal usability is particularly relevant, as Shneiderman emphasizes the need not only to provide access to users with different physical and mental abilities but also to users with different levels of education and using different computing platforms and levels of bandwidth. However, almost a decade after the origination of this idea, reality still falls far short of this ideal. More work is necessary to ensure that all users can have equal access to the benefits that accrue from use of computing technologies. Overall, ensuring universal access (or usability) is just as important for computing professionals as it is for information professionals.

For confidentiality/privacy, the modified statement for computing is: *Protecting user privacy and confidentiality is necessary to ensure public trust in computing.* Here, it is important to note that although the ALA has consistently been a strong advocate for protecting the privacy and confidentiality of library users, and has resisted efforts that threaten library user privacy such as the USA PATRIOT Act, computing organizations have more typically caved to government demands that infringe on confidentiality and privacy of users. For example, in 2003, Yahoo! gave information to the Chinese government which was used to imprison one of their users (Dann & Haddow, 2008). Although there are a handful of organizations, most notably the Electronic Frontier Foundation and Computer Professionals for Social Responsibility, that speak out for protecting the confidentiality, privacy, and other rights of users (Bennett, 2008), none of these organizations individually carry the weight within the computing community that the ALA carries in the library community. Thus, additional attention needs to be focused on efforts to protect the confidentiality and privacy of computer users, especially in a society where search engines control so much of users' information behavior and behavior in general.

For democracy, the modified statement for computing is: *Computing technologies should be designed to support the rights of all persons to free expression and the corollary right to receive the expression of others.* Here, computing organizations tend to fall far short of this value. For example, companies such as Google, Microsoft, and Yahoo! all comply with the censorship demands of the Chinese government (Dann & Haddow, 2008). Much like in the case of confidentiality/privacy, computing organizations typically fall well short in regard to this value. Thus, it is important to consider the potential for computing technologies to play a role as a democratizing influence in society.

For diversity, the modified statement for computing is: *Computing technologies should reflect our nation's diversity by providing a full spectrum of resources and services to all communities.* One important way for computing technologies to reflect our nation's diversity is for computing professionals themselves to reflect our nation's diversity. Currently, computing professionals in the United States do not come close to reflecting the ethnic or gender balance of the United States (Trajkovski, 2006). In addition to the same problem of ethnic imbalance found in the library professions, there is also an underrepresentation of women in computing that is not found in the field of librarianship. The ethnic and gender imbalance in the computing field, which is even further skewed in mass media depictions of computing, discourages individuals from underrepresented groups from pursuing careers in computing. Further, an imbalance in computing professionals has the potential to skew the usefulness of computing technology for various communities, since individuals by default most typically tend to design for people like themselves (Keates & Clarkson, 2003). Thus, to ensure that computing technologies can reflect our nation's diversity, it is important that computing professionals are a diverse group of individuals. While many efforts for broadening participation in computing are currently ongoing, further emphasis on this important issue would help to ensure diversity not only in the computing field, but also in the communities that benefit from computing technologies.

For education and lifelong learning, the modified statement for computing is: *Computing professionals should promote the creation, maintenance, and enhancement of a learning society in all of the products that they build and activities in which they engage.* It is important to keep in mind that computing technologies typically require some specific skills from their users. While individuals who have been exposed to computing technologies throughout their lives and who constantly keep up with the latest trends in computing may feel that computing technology is completely intuitive, the same may not be the case for individuals with limited exposure to computing technology (e.g., Reed, 2008). In cases where computing technology is designed to be highly usable, computing technology may help to reduce educational inequalities. However, in cases of inequalities in educational background, computing technology may serve to increase disparities in education (Cronjé & Fouché, 2008) as well as other areas that depend on computer technology use, such as health information (Carey, Wade, & Wolfe, 2008). Thus, it is critical that computing professionals consider the role of computing technology on education and lifelong learning.

For intellectual freedom, the modified statement for computing is: *Computing professionals should uphold intellectual freedom and resist censorship efforts.* Here, it is especially compelling to see the impact that computing technologies have played in the coverage of the protests following the 2009 elections in Iran. However, as discussed above, computing technologies can also play a role in assisting government censorship efforts (Dann & Haddow, 2008). Here, computing professionals can learn from the long tradition of upholding intellectual freedom found in the profession of librarianship (Dresang, 2006). While there are differences of opinion on this issue within the library community, at least it is a major topic of discussion (Dresang, 2006); this stands in contrast to the computing field, which places less emphasis on intellectual freedom. Thus, intellectual freedom is another important issue where computing professionals can learn from the field of librarianship.

For preservation, the modified statement for computing is: *Computing technologies should support the preservation of usability of information published in all computing media and file formats.* Digital preservation is an important issue for computing professionals, as different file formats have different long-term prospects in terms of their potential to be universally and perpetually accessible (Rauch, Krottmaier, & Tochtermann, 2007). Constant vigilance is required to ensure that information stored in computing systems remains accessible to users (Strodl, Becker, Neumayer, & Rauber, 2007). Just as the field of librarianship focuses on the preservation of all information, computing should focus on ensuring future access to past applications and data.

For professionalism, the modified statement for computing is: *Computing professionals should be professionally qualified personnel with appropriate education. It is of vital importance that there be education available to meet the social needs and goals of computing.* Computing professionals should receive complete educational experiences that prepare them for all aspects of their future jobs and careers. In particular, it is important that computing professionals have sufficient educational opportunities in computing ethics to prepare them to face computing ethics challenges in the workplace (Robbins, Fleischmann, & Wallace, 2009). Here, insights from information ethics education can be applied to computing ethics education.

For the public good, the modified statement for computing is: *Computing technology has the potential to serve as an essential public good and a fundamental institution in democratic societies.* Today, we are becoming increasingly reliant on computing technology for many different aspects of life. Increasingly, e-government use is necessary to fill out government forms and hence to receive many essential government services (Jaeger & Fleischmann, 2007). Job applicants now are expected to provide e-mail addresses where they can be reached, along with or instead of telephone numbers. Given the increasingly important role of computers in society, it is critical that computing professionals are aware of and strive to fulfill their societal obligation to serve the public good.

For service, the modified statement for computing is: *Computing professionals strive to serve the needs and values of users, and should work to enhance their own knowledge and skills, encourage the professional development of co-workers, and help to foster the aspirations of potential members of the profession.* Librarianship has a long tradition of service to users, as well as respecting users' values (Fleischmann, 2007; Jaeger & Fleischmann, 2007). It is important that computing professionals also understand the importance of serving users and of designing for their values (e.g., Fleischmann & Wallace, 2006; Friedman & Kahn, 2008; Friedman, Kahn, & Borning, 2006).

For social responsibility, the modified statement for computing is: *Computing professionals have a broad social responsibility to participate in ameliorating or solving the critical problems of society; to support efforts to help inform and educate users on these problems; to encourage users to examine the many views on the facts regarding each problem; and to advance the willingness to take a position on current critical issues.* Librarianship has always focused significantly on its social responsibility, which has as a result generated a tremendous degree of public trust in libraries as an institution (Jaeger & Fleischmann, 2007). It is important that computing professionals also act in socially responsible ways, such as designing systems to be transparent so that users can understand how systems work and anticipate and cope with computer errors (Fleischmann & Wallace, 2005, 2009). Thus, as in all of the other cases above, computing professionals can learn much from the history and traditions of librarianship.

Thus, the core values of librarianship can indeed be valuable in informing and even transforming computing. In particular, the highly human-centered values of the field of librarianship make librarianship a useful model for the emerging field of human-centered computing. The final section of this chapter explores the implications of this relationship for research and education in human-centered computing.

THE ROLE OF INFORMATION STUDIES IN HUMAN-CENTERED COMPUTING

Recently, the field of information studies has emerged as a cutting-edge, interdisciplinary field that carries much of the history and tradition of librarianship into the twenty-first century and beyond. Information studies as a field is closely connected to librarianship, including granting of Master of Library Science or equivalent degrees accredited by the American Library Association. Due to the interdisciplinary nature of information studies, the field involves a wide range of degree programs, and researchers in the field are involved in a large number of research projects. However, given the convergence between the human-centered values of librarianship and the origins of information studies in librarianship, information studies is an ideal site for research and educational programs in the emerging field of human-centered computing.

The field of information studies is an ideal site for research on human-centered computing. It is important for human-centered computing researchers to consider the broad societal impacts of computing, similar to the understanding that the field of librarianship demonstrates to its own societal significance. Exciting research programs are emerging in within the field of information studies. For example, the College of Information Studies at the University of Maryland has a number of interdisciplinary centers that focus on various aspects of human-centered computing, including the Human-Computer Interaction Lab, the Center for Advanced Studies of Communities and Information, the Center for Library and Information Innovation, and the Center for Information Policy and Electronic Government. Many information studies researchers have already received funding from the National Science Foundation's Human-Centered Computing Program, as well as related programs. Thus, the field of information studies is an ideal home for research on human-centered computing.

The field of information studies is also an ideal site for educational programs in the area of human-centered computing. Many units that focus on information studies are currently offering educational programs at all levels in fields such as human-computer interaction, informatics, software engineering, information management, and information technology. Thus, given the human-centered values of librarianship and, by extension, information studies, the field of information studies is an ideal site for human-centered computing education.

While libraries have benefited greatly from advances in computing technology that have provided them with a new and critical service role as well as improving existing library services, libraries also have made and can make contributions to computing. Specifically, the human-centered nature of the core values of librarianship can serve as a compelling example for computing in general, and human-centered computing in particular, to follow. Thus, public libraries and the Internet (or librarianship and computing, on a broader scale) are clearly involved in a mutually constitutive and highly beneficial relationship that is currently transforming both libraries and computing.

REFERENCES

American Library Association. (2004). Core values of librarianship. Available at http://www.ala.org/ala/aboutala/offices/oif/statementspols/corevaluesstatement/corevalues.cfm.

Baltrunas, E., Lileikaite, A., & Rutkauskiene, U. (2008). The role of public libraries in e-inclusion. Proceedings of the BOBCATSSS Symposium, *16*, 249–255.

Bennett, C. J. (2008). *The privacy advocates: Resisting the spread of surveillance.* Cambridge, MA: MIT Press.

Bertot, J. C. (2003). The multiple dimensions of the digital divide: more than the technology "haves" and "have nots." *Government Information Quarterly, 20*(2), 185–191.

Bertot, J. C. (2010). Community-based e-government: Libraries as e-government partners and providers. Proceedings of the IFIPS EGOV 2010 conference.

Bertot, J. C., Jaeger, P. T., Langa, L. A., & McClure, C. R. (2006a). Drafted: I want you to deliver e-government. *Library Journal, 131*(13), 34–37.

Bertot, J. C., Jaeger, P. T., Langa, L. A., & McClure, C. R. (2006b). Public access computing and Internet access in public libraries: The role of public libraries in e-government and emergency situations. *First Monday, 11*(9).

Bertot, J. C., McClure, C. R., & Jaeger, P. T. (2008). Public libraries and the Internet 2007: Issues, implications, and expectations. *Library and Information Science Research, 30*, 175–184.

Bertot, J. C., McClure, C. R., Wright, C.B, Jensen, E., & Thomas, S. (2009). *Public Libraries and the Internet 2009: Survey results and findings.* College Park, MD: Center for Library & Information Innovation. Available at http://www.plinte\rnetsurvey.org.

Bishop, A. P., Van House, N. A., & Buttenfield, B. P. (Eds.). (2003). *Digital library use: Social practice in design and evaluation.* Cambridge, MA: MIT Press.

Carey, J. C., Wade, S. L., & Wolfe, C. R. (2008). Lessons learned: The effect of prior technology use on Web-based interventions. *CyberPsychology and Behavior, 11*(2), 188–195.

Carter, N. J., & Wallace, R. L. (2007). Collaborating with public libraries, public health departments, and rural hospitals to provide consumer health information services. *Journal of Consumer Health on the Internet, 11*(4), 1–14.

Cronjé, J. C., & Fouché, J. (2008). Alternatives in evaluating multimedia in secondary school science teaching. *Computers and Education, 51*(2), 559–583.

Dann, G. E., & Haddow, N. (2008). Just doing business, or doing just business: Google, Microsoft, Yahoo!, and the business of censoring China's Internet. *Journal of Business Ethics, 79*, 219–234.

Dresang, E. T. (2006). Intellectual freedom and libraries: Complexity and change in the twenty-first century digital environment. *Library Quarterly, 76*, 169–192.

Evans, G., & Savard, R. (2008). Canadian libraries on the agenda: Their accomplishments and directions. *IFLA Journal, 34*, 127–159.

Fleischmann, K. R. (2007). Digital libraries with embedded values: Combining insights from LIS and science and technology studies. *Library Quarterly, 77*, 409–427.

Fleischmann, K. R., & Wallace, W. A. (2005). A covenant with transparency: Opening the black box of models. *Communications of the ACM, 48*(5), 93–97.

Fleischmann, K. R., & Wallace, W. A. (2006). Ethical implications of values embedded in computational models: An exploratory study. *Proceedings of the 69th Annual Meeting of the American Society for Information Science and Technology*, Austin, TX.

Fleischmann, K. R., & Wallace, W. A. (2009). Ensuring transparency in computational modeling. *Communications of the ACM, 52*(3), 131–134.

Friedman, B., & Kahn, Jr., P. H. (2008). Human values, ethics, and design. In A. Sears & J. A. Jacko (Eds.), *The human-computer interaction handbook* (pp. 1241–1266). New York: Lawrence Erlbaum Associates.

Friedman, B., Kahn, Jr., P. H., & Borning, A. (2006). Value sensitive design and information systems. In P. Zhang & D. Galletta (Eds.), *Human-computer interaction and management information systems: Foundations* (pp. 348–372). Armonk, NY: M.E. Sharpe.

Gordon, B. A. (2007). Internet access management in Jamaican public libraries: The role of policy. In C. A. Peltier-Davis & S. Renwick (Eds.), *Caribbean libraries in the 21st century: Changes, challenges, and choices* (pp. 189–199). Medford, NJ: Information Today.

Jaeger, P. T. (2002). Section 508 goes to the library: Complying with federal legal standards to produce accessible electronic and information technology in libraries. *Information Technology and Disabilities, 8*(2). Available at: http://www.rit.edu/~easi/itd/itdv08n2/jaeger.html.

Jaeger, P. T., Bertot, J. C., McClure, C. R., & Langa, L. A. (2006). The policy implications of Internet connectivity in public libraries. *Government Information Quarterly, 23*, 123–141.

Jaeger, P. T., Bertot, J. C., McClure, C. R., & Rodriguez, M. (2007). Public libraries and Internet access across the United States: A comparison by state 2004–2006. *Information Technology and Libraries, 26*(2), 4–14.

Jaeger, P. T., & Fleischmann, K. R. (2007). Public libraries, values, trust, and e-government. *Information Technology and Libraries, 26*(4), 35–43.

Jaeger, P. T., Langa, L. A., McClure, C. R., & Bertot, J. C. (2007). The 2004 and 2005 Gulf Coast hurricanes: Evolving roles and lessons learned for public libraries in disaster preparedness and community services. *Public Library Quarterly, 25*, 199–214.

Jaeger, P. T., McClure, C. R., Bertot, J. C., & Snead, J. T. (2004). The USA PATRIOT Act, the Foreign Intelligence Surveillance Act, and information policy research in libraries: Issues, impacts, and questions for libraries and researchers. *Library Quarterly, 74*, 99–121.

Keates, S., & Clarkson, J. (2003). Design exclusion. In S. Clarkson, R. Coleman, S. Keates, & C. Lebbon (Eds.), *Inclusive design: Design for the whole population.* New York: Springer.

McClure, C. R., Jaeger, P. T., & Bertot, J. C. (2007). The looming infrastructure plateau? Space, funding, connection speed, and the ability of public libraries to meet the demand for free Internet access. *First Monday, 12*(12).

Rauch, C., Krottmaier, H., & Tochtermann, K. (2007). File-formats for preservation: Evaluating the long-term stability of file-formats. *Proceedings of ELPUB2007 Conference on Electronic Publishing* (pp. 101–106), Vienna, Austria.

Reed, V. (2008). How do we encourage people with limited computer experience to use online databases? *The Reference Librarian, 48*(1), 109–112.

Robbins, R. W., Fleischmann, K. R., & Wallace, W. A. (2009). Computing and information ethics education research. In R. Luppicini & R. Adell (Eds.), *Handbook of research on technoethics.* Hershey, PA: Information Science Reference.

Schatz, B., & Chen, H. (1999). Digital libraries: Technological advances and social impacts. *Computer, 32*(2), 45–50.

Shneiderman, B. (2000). Universal usability. *Communications of the ACM, 43*(5), 84–91.

Strodl, S., Becker, C., Neumayer, R., & Rauber, A. (2007). How to choose a digital preservation strategy: Evaluating a preservation planning procedure. *Proceedings of the ACM/IEEE Computer Society Joint Conference on Digital Libraries* (pp. 29–38). Vancouver, BC.

Trajkovski, G. (2006). *Diversity in information technology education: Issues and controversies.* Hershey, PA: Information Science Publishing.

Xie, B. (2009). Older adults' health information wants in the Internet age: Implications for patient-provider relationships. *Journal of Health Communication, 14*(6): 510–524.

Xie, B., & Bugg, J. M. (2009). Public library computer training for older adults to access high-quality Internet health information. *Library and Information Science Research, 31*(3), 155–162.

Xie, B., & Jaeger, P. T. (2008). Computer training programs for older adults at the public library. *Public Libraries, 47*(5), 42–49.

Assessing Florida Public Library Broadband for E-government and Emergency/Disaster Management Services

Lauren H. Mandel, Charles R. McClure, and Bradley Wade Bishop

INTRODUCTION

The extent to which public libraries can adequately provide Internet-based services and resources to their users depends, in part, on the quality and speed of their connection to the Internet. These speeds, if fast enough, are termed as "broadband" and are measured in kilobytes per second (thousands of bytes received from or uploaded to the network per second or kbps), megabytes per second (millions of bytes received from or uploaded to the network or Mbps), or gigabytes per second (billions of bytes received from or uploaded to the network or Gbps). This chapter defines "broadband" in accordance with the Broadband Technology Opportunities Program (BTOP) Notice of Funding Availability definition of at least 768 kbps downstream and 200 kbps upstream (Broadband Initiatives Program, 2009). This definition is applied *at the workstation*, not at the front door, meaning that broadband Internet requires a minimum download speed of 768 kbps *and* a minimum upload speed of 200 kbps *at the workstation*.

There has been considerable discussion in recent years regarding the need for public libraries to better leverage their knowledge and skills in the provision of e-government and emergency/disaster management services and resources

(Bertot, Jaeger, & McClure, 2008; Gibson, Bertot, & McClure, 2009; McClure, McGilvray, Barton, & Bertot, 2007). E-government (electronic government) is the use of information and communications technologies to provide government services and enable a more interactive relationship between the government and its citizens. Emergency/disaster management services include public community information hubs, disaster recovery centers, and evacuee resources, among others.

There also has been considerable discussion about the need for increased/improved public library broadband connectivity to support e-government and emergency/disaster management services and resources (Bertot, 2009b; Mandel, Bishop, McClure, Bertot, & Jaeger, 2010; McClure & Jaeger, 2009). It is also important to recognize that underserved and unserved populations may be located in urban areas (Free Press, 2009). The State Library and Archives of Florida (State Library) initiated a statewide effort in 2009 to exploit improved broadband availability and to better leverage the delivery of e-government and emergency/disaster management services and resources among Florida public libraries where increased/improved delivery of these broadband-based services and resources would benefit public libraries and Florida residents.

This chapter provides an overview of the *Needs Assessment of Florida Public Library E-Government and Emergency/Disaster Management Broadband-Enabled Services* project conducted by the Information Use Management and Policy Institute (Information Institute) of Florida State University for the State Library and Archives of Florida. The needs assessment was funded by a grant from the State Library with the goals of (1) assessing the broadband capacity and need of Florida public libraries; (2) assessing the different e-government and emergency/disaster service roles Florida public libraries provide to the local communities they serve; and (3) describing some of these roles and the public library broadband capacity needed to support these roles. The project began April 28, 2009 and ended June 15, 2009. Although this project was limited to Florida public libraries, this chapter is intended to provide an overview of the needs assessment process and findings as a guide for other states and library systems to plan and conduct similar broadband needs assessments and services.

Overall, the study finds that the existing broadband connectivity speeds to most public libraries are extremely slow and largely inadequate to support effective e-government and emergency/disaster management services—to say nothing of supporting a range of other networked and electronic services. While the connection speeds to the library "front door" are largely inadequate, the *actual* connection speeds at public library outlets' (i.e., branch libraries) public access workstations are oftentimes only moderately better than dial-up connections. The report concludes that a major upgrade of public library broadband access and computing equipment is essential if public libraries are to serve effectively in e-government and emergency/disaster management service roles.

CONTEXT OF PUBLIC LIBRARY INTERNET ACCESS AND SERVICE PROVISION

Americans need broadband Internet access in order to participate successfully in the Information Society. However, millions of Americans do not have access to broadband Internet at home and rely on public libraries for free access to computers and the Internet. To ensure that all Americans have the opportunity to participate fully in the interactive Web 2.0 environment, public library Internet access must be to the fastest possible Internet connections. In addition to this free access to the Internet and computing, public libraries serve in several Internet-enabled service roles, for example providing e-government and emergency/disaster management services. These services are affected by the libraries' connection speeds, with libraries able to provide more services as their Internet connection speeds increase. This section describes the current context in which public libraries access and use the Internet and a number of issues that affect the degree to which public libraries can successfully provide a range of broadband-based services to their users.

Importance of Free Public Internet and Computer Access

Americans who do not have home access to broadband Internet often rely on their local public library (among other public spaces) to provide free access to public high-speed Internet and computing (Communication Workers of America, American Library Association, & Speed Matters, n.d.). This is a large segment of the U.S. population—the Pew Internet and American Life Project identified 45% of American adults that lacked home broadband access in 2008 (Horrigan, 2008). Lack of home broadband access is more prevalent in rural communities (62% of rural Americans lack home broadband access) than suburban (40%) and urban (43%) communities. Microsoft has noted that the smaller populations and limited funding availability in rural and remote communities inhibit their ability to support public Internet access spots such as coffee shops, increasing their reliance on the public library for free public Internet access (Boyd & Berejka, 2009).

To best serve the Internet access needs of these communities, the public library's free public Internet and computer access needs to be provided on the largest possible bandwidth and in the fastest possible speed. Higher bandwidth and connection speeds facilitate faster and better access to the global Information Society, including e-government and emergency/disaster management services. Also, when public libraries gain access to higher connectivity speeds and greater bandwidth, that access has been brought into the community where last-mile connections can expand this high-speed Internet into private homes and businesses (Charytan, Zachary, DeVries, Sherwood, Zinman, Phillips, et al., 2009; Gupta, Berejka, Griffin, & Boyd, 2009; Hudson, 2007; Oblinger, Van Houweling, & Semer, 2009; Sheketoff, 2009). In this situation, libraries may serve as distributing hubs for improved Internet access in their communities.

Importance of Public Library Internet-Enabled Service Roles

Beyond Internet access, millions of Americans rely on public libraries for economic, educational, and social opportunities that they would not have otherwise (Golston, 2009; Kranich, 2006). Information technology and information resource training is a major component of the Internet-enabled service roles public libraries provide. Other public library Internet-enabled service roles include: providing access to and assistance with e-government services, facilitating disaster management, especially in responding to community emergencies, and promoting civic engagement through e-government services (American Library Association, 2008; Bertot, Simmons, Brogardt, McGilvray, & Clark, 2009; Goldman, 2009; Sheketoff, 2009).

Providing e-government and disaster planning and response services to American communities is one of the ways that public libraries affect the communities they serve. For people without home broadband access, public libraries may be the only way to access e-government services (Bertot, Jaeger, Langa, & McClure, 2006; Goldman, 2009). Also, public libraries provide Internet access and assistance locating friends and family, or help with Federal Emergency Management Agency and insurance forms, in the wake of disasters (Benton, Rintels, & Hudson, 2009; Bertot et al., 2006; Jaeger, Langa, McClure, & Bertot, 2007; Kranich, 2006; McClure, Ryan, Mandel, Brobst, Hinnant, Andrade, et al., 2009). Public libraries' ability to provide these Internet-enabled services rests on their Internet bandwidth and connection speeds, because Internet connections that are too slow or too limited in bandwidth hamper the libraries' ability to provide Internet-enabled services (Communication Workers of America et al., n.d.; Goldman, 2009). Increasing public library Internet connectivity speeds and bandwidth can enhance the provision of e-government, emergency/disaster management, and other Internet-enabled services.

Complexity of Factors Affecting Workstation Speeds

There are a host of factors influencing the actual speed at public (or staff) Internet workstations (Bertot, 2009a; Bertot & McClure, 2007; Charytan et al., 2009; Mandel et al., 2010; Zachem, Don, McManus, & Waz, 2009). First, there are factors related to the type and number of connection(s) and *actual* (versus advertised) bandwidth the Internet Service Provider (ISP) provides to the library (Whitt & Lampert, 2009). Further, some libraries get their connection through local government offices such as the city or county and have little direct control over the nature (i.e., bandwidth and speed) of the connection they receive or the switches and other telecommunications equipment that the city or county uses to bring the bandwidth to the library.

In addition, the configuration of the library's network, the effectiveness of library network switches and routers, cabling, workstation age, and other factors affect workstation speeds. Switching technologies, latency effects, local settings and parameters, and the connectivity path from the door to a workstation also affect speed (Bertot, 2009a; Bertot & McClure, 2007; Charytan et al., 2009). Other factors stem from the simultaneous use of multiple Internet services, age and number of workstations, and users on a shared connection (Zachem et al., 2009). For example, if the library has wireless Internet routers on the same connection as the wired Internet, connection speeds will be slowed on all workstations. In addition, if the library's Integrated Library System (ILS) runs off the same network as the Internet workstations, the type and content/applications of the ILS will affect workstation speeds. Other factors that affect workstation speeds are the number of workstations connected on the overall library network and the number of individual library networks that feed off the bandwidth coming in the front door. This is because the more users who are simultaneously running applications such as interactive videos and some gaming programs, the slower each connection is.

This discussion only begins to describe some of the factors that affect actual workstation speeds. A key issue, however, is to recognize that the bandwidth coming in the front door of the public library is *not* the bandwidth available at the workstation. Libraries need to understand how to measure the actual speed available at the workstation, as well as techniques to improve network efficiencies and other factors that can improve at-the-workstation connection speeds. For a library public access workstation to be connected to broadband Internet, that workstation must sustain a minimum download speed of 768 kbps and a minimum upload speed of 200 kbps, regardless of time of day, number of other workstations accessing the library's network, or any other factors impacting speed.

Context of Public Library Internet Access and Service Provision

With a growing number of applications requiring greater quantities of bandwidth, simply providing free public Internet access is not enough (National Telecommunications and Information Administration, 2004). Libraries now need to consider the speeds of their Internet connections as these impact the adequacy of the connectivity to meet library user and staff needs (Bertot & McClure, 2007). Libraries do not serve one user on an Internet connection at a time, limiting their ability to provide access to the maximum possible speeds that are achieved when there are few users on the same Internet connection.

This problem is more pronounced in rural public libraries that are more likely than urban and suburban public libraries to offer slower connection speeds, fewer public access workstations, and less wireless access (American Library Association, 2009). However, this does not mean that connection speeds and Internet access are sufficient in urban and suburban public libraries. Urban and suburban public libraries serve larger volumes of patrons and host more wireless access and advanced Internet-based services such as digital reference, licensed databases, audio content, and digitized collections, often on the same Internet connection, all of which slow the connection speeds available at the workstation.

To maintain and expand public Internet access, U.S. public libraries and K–12 schools may apply for E-rate discounts under the Universal Service Fund, Schools and Libraries Program, established by the Telecommunications Act of 1996 (110 Stat. 56 § 706). These discounts may be applied to selected telecommunications, Internet access, and internal connectivity. This funding is critical for public libraries' ability to sustain the provision of free public Internet access to U.S. communities.

In addition to E-rate funds, through the American Recovery and Reinvestment Act of 2009 (ARRA), the Federal government made funds available to upgrade public computer center capacity, which includes funding for broadband build-out and public computer center upgrades through the Broadband Technology Opportunities Program (BTOP), administered by the National Telecommunications and Information Administration (NTIA), and the Broadband Initiatives Program (BIP), administered by the Rural Utilities Service (RUS) (Broadband Initiative Program, 2009). The RUS-administered BIP program was specifically for broadband build-out in rural areas, but libraries might have had difficulty determining their rural status especially considering the lack of clear definitions of "rural" in ARRA and the subsequent Notice of Funding Availability (American Recovery and Reinvestment Act, 2009; Broadband Initiative Program, 2009). A more direct and targeted funding opportunity for libraries was the NTIA-administered BTOP program, which emphasized the importance of community anchor institutions in deploying and sustaining the adoption of broadband Internet. The BTOP included set-aside funds for broadband build-out, public computer center capacity expansion (including public libraries), and sustainable broadband adoption education and training programs (for more information, see http://www.broadbandusa.gov/).

Summary of Current Context

Millions of Americans rely on public libraries and other public institutions to provide high-speed Internet access to engage the global Information Society. These Americans may lack access to home broadband Internet because they live in remote, rural, or unserved locations, or because they cannot afford the higher costs of broadband connections. For these underserved and unserved Americans, public library free public Internet access is crucial. However, this access must be at the highest possible speeds and largest possible bandwidth to overcome inefficient network configurations, other factors impacting workstation speeds, and situational factors affecting each library's ability to provide different levels of broadband-enabled services. Enhanced Internet access will enable public libraries to better provide free public Internet access and associated Internet-enabled service roles, including e-government and emergency/disaster management services.

METHODOLOGICAL APPROACH TO THE NEEDS ASSESSMENT

The needs assessment described in this chapter focused on one particular state, Florida. However, the methodology employed in this study can be applied to assessing the needs of public libraries in smaller settings (e.g., counties) or other states. The methodology is described here to provide an explanation of one approach to conduct a public library broadband needs assessment.

Project Goals

The overall goals of this project were to assess the broadband capacity and need of Florida public libraries in relation to the provision of e-government and emergency/disaster service roles. Specific project goals included the following:

- Describe a number of e-government and emergency/disaster management service roles that the public library could provide its local community;
- Estimate the resource requirements necessary for public libraries to perform the e-government and emergency/disaster management service roles;
- Estimate the level of interest that different types of Florida public libraries would have in offering these various e-government and emergency/disaster management services;
- Identify and analyze Florida public libraries' Internet connectivity speeds and costs;
- Improve public library broadband connectivity and e-government and emergency/disaster management services.

Ultimately, this needs assessment was designed as a first step toward improving Florida residents' access to and use of broadband-based e-government and emergency/disaster management services, as well as assisting public libraries in obtaining better broadband connections, and better supporting these activities at the local and state levels.

Project Methodology

Research team members employed a multi-method data collection approach to conduct the needs assessment. Data-collection approaches used in this study included:

- *Literature review*: Review of the literature regarding public library technology and broadband use and deployment;
- *Interviews*: Interviews with selected public librarians, emergency management officials, and others knowledgeable about the topic to understand existing broadband connections and configurations in Florida public libraries, define levels of e-government and emergency/disaster management service roles, test and validate the service roles, estimate capacity and willingness to serve in these service roles, and obtain feedback related to the usefulness of developed maps that indicate public library Internet connectivity;
- *Public library case studies*: Selected public libraries described and collected data on current broadband connections and infrastructure, workstation connectivity speeds, and network configurations;
- *Public library site visits*: Onsite review and tests of workstation connectivity speeds and network configurations at selected public libraries;
- *Geographic Information System (GIS) analysis of public library telecommunications*: Use of GIS software to manage, analyze and map Florida

public library broadband data from the Bill & Melinda Gates Foundation Florida public library technology dataset (2009) made available from the State Library;

- *Public library national survey data analysis*: Analysis of the *Public Library Funding and Technology Access Survey* (Bertot, McClure, Wright, Jensen, & Thomas, 2009) related to technology and broadband use and deployment in Florida public libraries;

- *Connectivity costing models*: Investigation of several possible models by which to cost out library equipment and bandwidth upgrades as part of a statewide BTOP program, based on a public library's situational technology needs.

These methods were selected for their applicability to an exploratory, statewide public library technology needs assessment.

Data Quality

Libraries that conducted speed tests for the case studies and site visits utilized a free Internet-based connection speed measurement tool, available at http://www.speakeasy.net. The tool sends a signal from one of Speakeasy's servers (located around the United States) to the workstation and measures both download and upload speeds. A number of factors *outside* the library can influence speed tests, such as the connection between the workstation and Speakeasy, any sluggishness due to Speakeasy's servers, and the selection of the server from which to calculate the speed. These factors limit the reliability of the Speakeasy connection speed tests; however, these are the best tools available for libraries to test connection speeds easily and inexpensively. The speeds reported here are estimates, but they provide more detail than relying solely on ISP-advertised front door connection speeds.

The study team employed a combination of purposive and cluster sampling for the study's iterative multi-method data collection efforts. The study was exploratory and purposeful, thus limiting the generalization of the data. The data collection approaches, however, provided detailed and overlapping findings regarding broadband capacity issues associated with providing e-government and emergency/disaster management services and resources in public libraries. By using an iterative and multi-method approach, the study team identified and triangulated perspectives on broadband needs for the delivery of e-government and emergency/disaster management services and resources in public libraries from both the public library and user populations, thus ensuring reliable and valid data.

FINDINGS FROM THE NEEDS ASSESSMENT

The needs assessment used a number of data collection techniques that resulted in multiple findings. The findings presented a preliminary picture of Florida public library broadband connectivity in the summer of 2009 and the extent to which Florida public libraries had adequate broadband Internet access to provide e-government, emergency/disaster management services, and a range of other electronic and networked services. Additionally, the findings included the estimated cost to upgrade Florida public libraries' Internet connections and technology equipment through a statewide BTOP program to better provide these Internet-enabled services to Florida residents; the State Library's BTOP application subsequently went unfunded.

Overall, the findings indicated there were areas throughout the state that experienced low connectivity speeds and high connection costs. There were also a broad range of local situational factors affecting Internet speeds and connection costs for individual public library outlets. These connectivity issues hindered many librarians and libraries from adequately serving their communities, which turn to the libraries for emergency/disaster management and e-government services (see Chapter 5 on emergency and hurricane service roles elsewhere in this book), as well as free and publicly available broadband Internet access to participate in today's Information Society. However, slow Internet connectivity speeds, high Internet connection costs, and situational factors greatly impact libraries' ability to adequately support e-government and emergency/disaster management services.

This section provides an overview of the findings from the needs assessment. This is a foundation for the following section, which will provide recommendations for other libraries seeking to conduct technology needs assessments or understand public library broadband-enabled services.

Pockets of Low Connectivity and High Connection Costs

The findings from the needs assessment showed wide variation among connectivity speeds and costs across the state of Florida, and from region to region. Although public library outlets in regions with higher populations such as Southeastern Florida and the Tampa Bay area tended to have higher connectivity speeds (see Figure 7.1), there were library outlets with slower connectivity speeds in these areas as well as elsewhere in the state. When viewed aggregated by county, the public library data also showed variation in connectivity speeds (see Figure 7.2) and costs (see Figure 7.3) across the state, although rural counties (e.g., Dixie and Gilchrist) tended to show slower connectivity speeds and higher average costs.

Connection speeds impact the level of services libraries can offer the public, and in fact, over 75% of Florida public libraries reported that existing connection speeds were insufficient to meet patron and staff demand. Also, most of the librarians who participated in case studies were "shocked" at the drop-off in the connection speeds from the front door to individual workstations at the branches. Only Sarasota County public libraries averaged connectivity speeds over 50 Mbps (75.94 Mbps), the highest for the state (see Figure 7.2). The next highest average speeds were public libraries in Indian River (50 Mbps), Charlotte (45 Mbps), and Leon (33 Mbps) counties. Without these speeds, public libraries may be able to provide only minimal e-government and emergency/disaster management services such as filling out online forms, but they will not be able to support advanced applications such as large volume file transfer, digital video

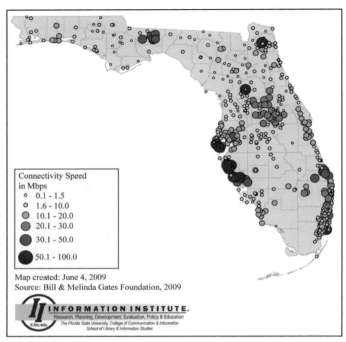

Figure 7.1 Public Libraries' Connectivity Speed: Florida 2009.

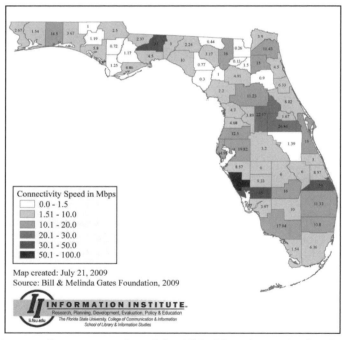

Figure 7.2 Average Connectivity Speed for All Public Library Outlets by County: Florida 2009.

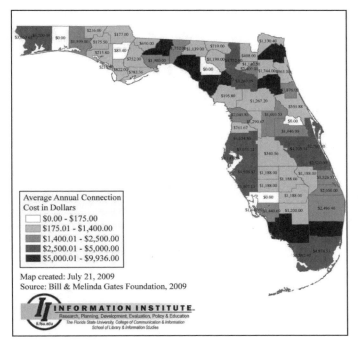

Figure 7.3 Average Annual Connection Cost for All Public Library Outlets by County: Florida 2009.

streaming, downloading, sharing, remote education, and building control and maintenance (Goldman, 2009).

Like connectivity speeds, average annual Internet connection costs for public libraries varied widely across Florida. Certain counties on average paid significantly higher rates for connectivity than others (see Figure 7.3). Rural counties tended to have higher prices, such as Dixie County, where public libraries paid an average of $7,129.00 annually. However, urban areas also showed variation among Internet connection costs. For example, libraries in Southeast Florida (Figure 7.4) fell into every range of costs used on the map, from the $0.00 to $750.00 range (i.e., the lowest) to the $5,000.01 to $9,936.00 range (i.e., the highest). In some cases, the higher costs were related to higher connectivity speeds, but this was not always the case. This preliminary data indicates further investigation might be required to detail *why* a wide disparity of Internet connection costs occurred around the state, but the data does clearly point toward a considerable assortment of costs incurred by public library outlets.

Situational Factors Affecting Broadband Internet Connectivity

The case studies and site visits indicated that myriad situational factors affect the Internet connection costs at each individual public library outlet. These factors include the number of simultaneous users on a shared network; the effectiveness of network switches, routers, and cabling; switching technologies,

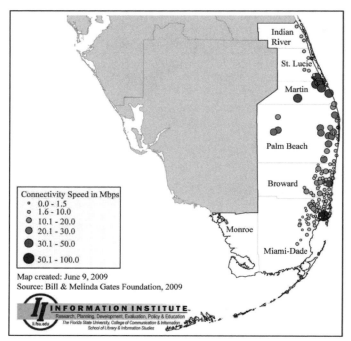

Figure 7.4 Public Libraries' Connectivity Speeds: Southeast Florida, 2009.

latency effects, local settings and parameters; and the ultimate connectivity path from the door to a workstation. The possible telecommunications network configurations are endless and can significantly affect workstation speeds, depending on the configuration and efficiency of transmissions through those networks.

Many of the libraries that participated in the case studies initially suspected that their existing broadband connections were inadequate for the various applications and demands being placed on them. A number of the libraries provided examples and anecdotes that depicted the limited bandwidth and minimal connection speeds they had. For example, libraries reported users complaining frequently that response time at the workstation was "very slow" and asking staff what was "wrong" with the workstations, as well as internal network monitoring software showing that network load (i.e., the level of traffic exerted on the network at one time) was above 95% and sometimes above 100% between 11:00 a.m. and 6:00 p.m. One librarian reported that "The DSL that our ISP provides is very unpredictable. The service is very erratic. When you have more than four patrons on the computers the bandwidth drops. Patrons get very upset when they get disconnected and lose their work." These are but a sampling of the comments and examples obtained from the case studies. Each library had extensive examples and user anecdotes depicting the inadequacy of existing broadband service to the library.

The costs that an individual public library pays for its broadband are largely dependent on which ISP is providing service to that library and the success with which that library has negotiated its service contract with the ISP. The case studies showed that while the general cost categories were similar across the various libraries, the actual amounts of the costs varied considerably from library to library. For example, the cost of a T3 (44.7 Mbps) connection to the front door at one library versus another can be quite different, network configurations may differ in size and complexity, and costs associated with technical staff can vary considerably. In addition, some library costs are embedded in costs that are charged against other organizations or in some instances provided "free" to the library. Finally, there is a need for public librarians to better understand the range of contract options for broadband services available from various ISPs.

Both the case studies and follow-up interviews asked about the libraries' network configurations. Although it is difficult to generalize findings regarding these configurations because of a range of situational factors that affect each library's network, several observations can be made. Public libraries that are dependent on a broadband connection coming through the county, municipality, a school, or other means have limited to no control over the network configuration and other management factors. Many public librarians have limited understanding of what broadband is exactly, how broadband speeds and network configurations affect applications at the workstation, why a high-speed broadband connection is necessary, what broadband speed is needed, and what can be done with connections of different speeds and bandwidths. Additionally, descriptions of network configurations from the case studies and interviews varied considerably due to local situational factors indicating that the most critical needs for upgrading a library's broadband may vary considerably from library to library. These are some of the primary observations that resulted from discussions regarding Florida public libraries' network configurations.

No matter which of these situational factors affect an individual outlet, the associated cost-related factors are large inhibitors to libraries' ability to provide public access Internet connections. However, faster Internet alone is not a sufficient solution for public libraries. As the case studies show, libraries also require funding for infrastructure upgrades, additional/newer workstations, staff, and staff training. Funding efforts such as BTOP that are geared toward increasing public library Internet access and connectivity must take into consideration these associated needs.

An important finding of this study is that libraries need to recognize that the broadband speed at the front door is not the actual speed available at the workstation. Broadband access, deployment, use, and services provided are significantly reduced by the time the connection leaves the front door of the library and before it is available at the workstation. The basic pressure points that affect the broadband speed at the workstation include the following:

- *Broadband speed at the front door:* Although an ISP may contract with the library to provide a 20 Mbps connection, for example, the actual speed coming to the library can be considerably less, so libraries need to utilize network "sniffers" that examine and monitor network traffic and other tools that can determine what speed actually is available as it comes into the library.

- *Library network and telecommunications configuration:* The manner in which the library's network is configured, deployed, moves through switches, servers, and routers, and is managed, can result in significant loss of bandwidth at the workstation.

- *Number of workstations, wireless routers, and other peripherals*: The more workstations, wireless routers, and other peripherals that are connected to the network and in use at the same time, the more this negatively impacts the speed available at a given workstation.
- *Age of workstations, wireless routers, and other peripherals*: Generally speaking, newer workstations and other peripherals require less bandwidth to run various applications, and they better use and manage the bandwidth available.
- *Type of applications in use*: Internet-accessed applications range from those requiring relatively little bandwidth use (e.g., text-only email) to bandwidth hogs (e.g., interactive high resolution videos) and the more bandwidth hogging applications that are operating on the network at any one time, the less broadband speed there will be at any given workstation.

These factors taken together affect the *load* (i.e., traffic) on the network and ultimately determine the *drop-off rate* (i.e., the decrease in connection speed between the front door and the workstation) and the broadband speed at the workstation. The experts in network management interviewed for this study said that libraries should make a goal of having a minimum of a consistent T1 connection (i.e., 1.5 Mbps) *at the workstation*.

Impacts on E-government and Emergency/Disaster Management Service Roles

The study team originally identified two levels of e-government and emergency/disaster management services, basic and advanced, with two possible models for advanced-level services—partnership and Web services. During a 2010 research project conducted for the Pasco County Public Library Cooperative, these service roles were tested as to their validity and efficacy. From the findings of that study (McClure, Bishop, Mandel, & Snead, 2010), the study team reconfigured the service roles from a 4-cell matrix to a pyramid structure (Figure 7.5). The pyramid includes four levels of public library e-government services: basic, library driven, agency driven, and collaborative.

The e-government and emergency/disaster management service levels offer challenging goals for Florida public libraries. Indeed, the vast majority of Florida public libraries are likely not to be qualified even for basic level services, given the limited broadband, internal network infrastructure, and staff to assist in e-government and emergency/disaster management services. Thus, significant efforts will need to be taken to provide the necessary broadband, internal network, workstations, other production/telecommunications equipment, and technical staff for libraries to provide the more advanced (i.e., higher up the pyramid) levels of e-government and emergency/disaster management services.

Achieving the basic level of public library broadband-enabled services in Florida will extend a basic level of e-government and emergency/disaster management services uniformly throughout the state. This service level is

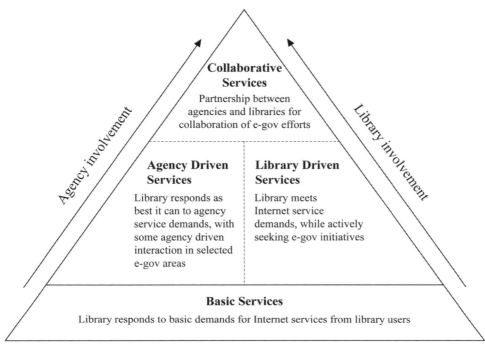

Figure 7.5 Public Library E-government Service Roles Pyramid.

important because it seeks to meet citizen demand for last resort Internet service in each Florida community in terms of broadband connection speeds, availability of workstations, and provision of adequate time to identify appropriate e-government resources and services, understand their use, and make applications to obtain government benefits. However, without stimulus or other funding to increase broadband access, public libraries across the country are struggling to provide even the basic level of these services.

The advanced levels, whether library driven, agency driven, or collaborative, expand Internet-enabled e-government and emergency/disaster management services in at least three directions: for residents and visitors, government agencies, and use of broadband technologies. Advanced level services focus on bringing public libraries beyond the basic level of broadband capacity which can support improved broadband at the community level. Provision of an advanced level of public library broadband-enabled e-government and emergency/disaster management services could enable other institutions, such as schools, hospitals, and local community businesses also to increase broadband capacity and add local broadband-enabled content to the Internet. This level can be approached via three models: library driven services, characterized by the library taking a more proactive approach to the provision of e-government services than just meeting on demand user needs; agency driven services, characterized by public libraries acting in a reactive stance to the demands of government agencies; and collaborative services, characterized by an active partnership between government agencies and public libraries.

TABLE 7.1 Critical Success Factors for Public Library Broadband-Enabled
E-government and Emergency/Disaster Management Services

Critical Success Factor	Description	Importance
Connection to the door	Bandwidth provided to the libraries' doorstep	Determines upper limit of number of workstations and users who can be supported at one time, as well as type of broadband-enabled applications available
Internal infrastructure	Routers, switches, wiring, load management, etc.	Bandwidth available at the doorstep may be lost by poor equipment and wiring, poorly designed or installed networks, and other internal infrastructure
Telecommunications staff	Assess bandwidth need, design network architecture, bid and negotiate telecommunications pricing, install and maintain equipment, and optimize bandwidth	Telecommunications experts can mitigate problems of overpaying for broadband connections or losing capacity by planning and maintaining internal telecommunications infrastructure
Workstations and peripherals	Workstations (including laptops and netbooks), broadband-enabled technologies, and peripheral equipment (e.g., printers, scanners) available for public use	Workstations are the most visible portion of a public library's broadband capacity
Computer staff	Develop a technology plan, purchase, install, and maintain information technology	Needed to negotiate, purchase, and maintain equipment according to a well-designed plan
Public service broadband assistance	Plan and deliver broadband-enabled services, including training and aid offered by the library	Public libraries can maximize broadband services if they have staff who are comfortable with the technology and familiar with how to aid the public
Availability of broadband-enabled e-government and disaster management aids	Internet services available to assist the public in e-government and disaster management	The public needs broadband-enabled aids to identify needed e-government and disaster management services, and to understand what they do and how to use them

TABLE 7.1   (Continued)

Critical Success Factor	Description	Importance
Technology capacity to produce broadband-enabled aids locally	Enabling local production of broadband-enabled content for Web distribution (e.g., Webcams and video editing software)	Broadband Internet is necessary to produce materials facilitating the use of e-government and disaster management resources, and to serve as the local center to help local businesses, agencies and the public learn how to be broadband-enabled content producers
Application staff to produce broadband-enabled aids locally	Produce broadband-enabled content	Knowledgeable personnel are necessary to create localized broadband-enabled content
Agency responsibility	Responsibility for government agency programs, benefits and services	The public library is asked to explain programs, services and benefits to residents via Web-based or other publications, but not provided with knowledgeable local or other staff to do so
Public library liability	If public library personnel, making their best effort, provide incomplete or false information, or assist a resident making an application that is later rejected	Librarians need clarification of federal, state and local liability laws as they relate to public libraries

There are numerous factors that are critical to successful deployment of the various levels of public library broadband-enabled e-government and emergency/disaster management services. Table 7.1 describes selected critical success factors and why each is important to public library broadband-enabled e-government and emergency/disaster management service deployment. For example, the lack of high speed broadband at the workstation for some libraries significantly decreases their ability to provide e-government and emergency/disaster management services. Increased bandwidth and faster connections will improve public libraries' ability to provide information technology training; educational, job-seeking, and e-government resources and services; and wireless and wired free public Internet access. A public library's ability to address some or all of these critical success factors will determine the potential level of broadband-enabled services that library can provide to the community it serves.

Cost Logic Models

The study team investigated several models for estimating costs to upgrade Florida public libraries' broadband connectivity, and therefore their ability to provide e-government and emergency/disaster management services, utilizing Broadband Technology Opportunities Program (BTOP) funding under the Public Computer Center (PCC) funding category; however, the State Library's BTOP application was not funded. The original intent was to develop a cost logic model that considered purchasing additional bandwidth through a statewide ISP contract, with libraries differentiated by population size and demographics. However, based on the National Telecommunications and Information Administration (NTIA) Notice of Funding Availability, which would not cover costs for broadband upgrades in the PCC program (Broadband Initiatives Program, 2009), the team abandoned the plan to upgrade library bandwidth.

Instead, the team developed a set of four models to upgrade internal equipment that could facilitate faster speeds at the public access workstations, including switches, routers, workstations, etc. Working with the State Library and a technology vendor, the study team developed four cost models based on library facility square footage, a measure suggested by the technology vendor as a reasonable, practical, and expedient method to approximate technology needs for public computing facilities. The four categories were as follows:

- Small libraries: outlets with less than 5,000 square feet;
- Medium libraries: outlets between 5,000 and 10,000 square feet;
- Large libraries: outlets between 10,000 and 20,000 square feet;
- Extra large libraries: outlets between 20,000 and 40,000 square feet.

These assume that library technology needs are directly related to the physical size of the facility, which may not be the case depending on situational factors such as the amount of bandwidth coming to each library, the population served, and the degree of advanced Internet applications already in use. However, given the time constraints imposed on developing cost models for use in applying for BTOP funding, the study team agreed with the technology vendor to attempt a facility size-based model as a good first effort at fitting public libraries into systematized technology upgrade cost models.

These models also assume that libraries participating in the statewide program would upgrade their bandwidth to meet the NTIA broadband definition at the workstation (768 kbps downstream and 200 kbps upstream) by utilizing the statewide ISP contract pricing and E-rate discount. In addition to developing four facility size-based models, the study team created a menu of extra equipment available for libraries, including laptops and laptop carts, designed to allow libraries to expand the number of available public access workstations without remodeling or expanding library facilities, as well as serving as a mobile training lab to expand public training options.

Although all Florida public libraries fit into the size ranges outlined above, once the State Library began soliciting libraries to participate in the program it became evident that systematized cost models would not work well for the Florida public libraries. The situational factors that impacted Florida public libraries' broadband Internet access and service provision also impacted the utility of the cost models. Each library had unique technology and service needs and the libraries could not be placed easily into a set of cost models, whether by population, facility size, or any other criterion. Instead, the study team worked with the State Library and the state certified vendor to develop a menu of equipment options from which libraries could select only the equipment they needed—regardless of their size or community context.

The equipment menu included workstations, software, laptops, switches, routers, and services such as onsite network efficiency assessment, individualized consulting time, and evaluation of program success. The State Library provided the menu to each public library to select the equipment necessary to upgrade that library's public access computing to current FCC broadband standards. In addition to the equipment options, wireless installation and upgrades and specific LAN (land area network) and server equipment were offered to libraries on an as-needed basis. The goal of this fixed-cost menu approach was to aggregate purchasing and facilitate smooth, quick upgrades for Florida public libraries, in keeping with the BTOP's goals of leveraged federal dollars and expedient deployment.

The study team's attempts to create categorized models that could be applied to public libraries based on population demographics and facility size failed to account for the unique situational factors each library faced. Ultimately, situational factors demanded an equipment menu, rather than a broader cost logic model, so that each library could select *only* the equipment necessary for *that* library to raise its public computing capacity. The majority of libraries selected workstations and mobile training labs, as well as some LAN equipment. A few of the larger libraries required unique services (e.g., wireless upgrades and system-wide LAN equipment), the costs of which were estimated on a case-by-case basis. The study team then calculated a total estimated cost for all necessary upgrade equipment for libraries participating in the State Library's BTOP grant program to increase Internet connection speeds at the workstation and the ability to provide e-government and emergency/disaster management services to Florida residents.

Summary of Key Findings

Well over half of Florida public libraries reported connection speed insufficiency at some times, and this was more pronounced in rural and suburban public libraries. Outlets all over the state reported connection speed insufficiency and the majority of Florida public libraries reported the number of public access workstations was insufficient to meet patron needs some or all of the time, to say nothing of the insufficiency of connection speeds in supporting e-government and emergency/disaster management services. Situational factors played a critical role in affecting each library's technology access and services. These factors cannot be ignored when considering how best to help libraries improve network efficiencies and computer equipment.

Pockets or not, the cost and speed of the Internet connections for Florida's public library outlets disabled many librarians and libraries from adequately serving their communities. These communities turn to their public library outlets for emergency/disaster management and e-government services, as well as free and publicly available broadband Internet access to participate in today's Information Society. However, slow Internet connectivity speeds, high Internet connection costs, and situational factors greatly impact libraries' ability to adequately support e-government and emergency/disaster management services. The cost models and statewide BTOP application were designed to help Florida public libraries upgrade computer and network equipment, improve network efficiencies, and increase workstation connection speeds so the libraries would be better poised to serve in the identified e-government and emergency/disaster management service roles.

NEXT STEPS

Recommendations for Florida Public Libraries

This study documents the significant need Florida public libraries had for increased broadband (both speeds and connections) and a range of other equipment and services related to the provision of broadband-enabled services from these libraries. Connection speeds at the front door varied considerably around the state, but overall most Florida public libraries were unable to meet existing demand and had little capacity to provide additional access to broadband services and resources. The study recommended that purchasing new workstations, routers, and switches for public libraries, as well as consulting time to assess and improve the efficiency of library networks, could upgrade connection speeds to the workstation.

The study identified numerous reasons why the actual bandwidth at the workstation can be seriously compromised from the speed at the front door. As a general statement regarding Florida public libraries' Internet connections, there were too many workstations (many of which were outdated), wireless routers, and other peripherals connected to the library network; there were not enough library networks available throughout the system; and there were too many simultaneous users of the library workstations using too many broadband-sensitive applications. Many librarians lacked the knowledge and training to manage and deploy efficient networks resulting in bandwidth that was basically "wasted" in the network. A major recommendation from this study, in addition to the significant need for obtaining drastically improved broadband connections and support services for Florida public libraries, was that simply providing these libraries with large upgrades in existing broadband, or providing additional broadband connections to the library, might not provide significant improvement of Internet connection speeds at the workstation. Many Florida public libraries will need significant technical staff in areas related to network and telecommunications management, workstation and network configuration and deployment, and broadband services planning and deployment, to ensure the design and deployment of efficient connections, internal wiring and network configuration, and upgraded workstations and related equipment.

The impact of these findings and conclusions on Florida public librarians and residents is of significant concern. As Florida libraries tried to recover from the recent vote to cut property taxes, the housing collapse, and the recession, residents were significantly handicapped by not being able to access and use effectively a range of broadband-enabled services and resources at their local public libraries. In terms of completing online job applications, interacting electronically with local, state, and federal e-government tasks, and collaborating effectively with local and state emergency/disaster management officials, Florida residents were disadvantaged in their access to quality broadband-enabled services and resources available through their public libraries. Attention should be given to remedy these issues and improve Florida public libraries' ability to provide adequate public computer and Internet access and services, including e-government and emergency/disaster management services.

Recommendations for Other Public Libraries

While the majority of the results of this needs assessment are not generalizable beyond Florida, the needs assessment process and e-government and emergency/disaster management service roles are. This study shows the value of a technology needs assessment in reviewing the current situation and recommending actions for improvements. Libraries around United States and elsewhere can employ some or all of the methods employed in this needs assessment to evaluate their own network efficiencies and e-government and emergency/disaster management services. It is crucial for individual public libraries to understand the situational context in which they provide Internet access and services, including successes, weaknesses, deficiencies, and inefficiencies, so they may seek funding through E-rate and other programs to improve their Internet connections and public access computing.

For example, libraries in other states may have access to GIS, statewide library, and other Internet connection data files and can produce maps depicting the Internet connection speeds and costs for public libraries in their state. This process may be facilitated by the nationwide broadband data-mapping project currently being undertaken by NTIA. In addition to mapping library Internet connectivity, other libraries can conduct technology and Internet case studies, site visits, and interviews to understand better the situational factors impacting public library Internet access and broadband-enabled service provision. Ultimately, this study demonstrates the critical need to consider situational factors in any public library technology needs assessment or upgrade plan. The study team strongly recommends that library technology needs assessment and upgrade plans consider situational factors rather than attempting a cookie-cutter approach that will not meet the unique needs of each public library.

Libraries need to consider that, in upgrading computing capacity, a key evaluation metric of success will be the number of workstations currently with connection speeds of less than 786 kbps down and 200 kbps up versus the number of workstations that meet or exceed these speeds *after* the upgrade. It is possible that upgrades, even with increased bandwidth at the front door, still may not meet the FCC requirements for broadband connectivity at the *workstation*. Libraries still may have poorly designed and deployed networks serving too many workstations, wireless routers, and bandwidth-hogging applications to meet the FCC standard for broadband workstation speed. This is especially true in libraries where countless users access the network at one time, many of whom rely on the library to access bandwidth-hogging applications such as file-sharing, Web 2.0 tools, and e-government forms and services. In such instances additional onsite assessment may be necessary to either re-configure the technology and telecommunications infrastructure or to obtain additional broadband at the front door.

ACKNOWLEDGMENTS

The Information Institute gratefully acknowledges the assistance received from the State Library and Archives of Florida, especially Mark Flynn, and all librarians who participated in the case studies and other data collection activities. The Institute also thanks Melinda Crowley and Maureen Githens at the Florida Department of Education for their assistance and support. We also acknowledge the work of John T. Snead, Assistant Professor at the School of Library and Information Studies, University of Oklahoma (previously of the Information Institute) and Charles C. Hinnant, Joe Ryan, Carla B. Wright, and John Brobst, all from the Information Institute, who assisted with the original report.

REFERENCES

American Library Association. (2008). *Opening the "window to a larger world": Libraries' role in changing America: Report to President-Elect Obama and Vice-President-Elect Biden transition team.* Chicago: American Library Association. Retrieved April 21, 2009, from http://www.ala.org/ala/aboutala/offices/wo/ALA%20Report%20To%20Transi.pdf.

American Recovery and Reinvestment Act of 2009, Pub. L. No. 111–5, 123 Stat. 115 (2009). Retrieved September 14, 2009, from http://www.gpo.gov/fdsys/pkg/PLAW-111publ5/pdf/PLAW-111publ5.pdf.

Benton, C., Rintels, J., & Hudson, H. E. (2009). *Comments of the Benton Foundation, Center for Creative Voices in the Media and Professor Heather E. Hudson before the Federal Communications Commission in the matter of a national broadband plan for our future.* Washington, D.C.: Benton Foundation. Retrieved June 15, 2009, from http://fjallfoss.fcc.gov/ecfs/document/view?id=7020038908.

Bertot, J. C. (2009a). Capacity planning for broadband in public libraries: Issues and strategies. *Library Technology Reports, 45*(1), 38–42.

Bertot, J. C. (2009b). *Public libraries and the Internet, 1994–2009* [Electronic resource]. College Park, MD: Center for Library & Information Innovation. Retrieved October 1, 2009, from http://www.plinternetsurvey.org.

Bertot, J. C., Jaeger, P. T., Langa, L. A., & McClure, C. R. (2006). Public access computing and Internet access in public libraries: The role of public libraries in e-government and emergency situations. *First Monday, 11*(9), n.p. Retrieved April 21, 2009, from http://www.uic.edu/htbin/cgiwrap/bin/ojs/index.php/fm/article/view/1392/1310.

Bertot, J. C., Jaeger, P. T., & McClure, C. R. (2008). Citizen-centered e-government services: Benefits, costs, and research needs. In S. A. Chun, M. Janssen, & J. R. Gil-Garcia (Eds.), *Proceedings of the 9th Annual International Digital Government*

Research Conference (pp. 137–141). Digital Government Society of North America. Retrieved June 15, 2009, from http://delivery.acm.org/10.1145/1370000/1367858/p137-bertot.pdf?key1=1367858&key2=8285535421&coll=GUIDE&dl=GUIDE&CFID=40200149&CFTOKEN=64478100.

Bertot, J. C., & McClure, C. R. (2007). Assessing sufficiency and quality of bandwidth for public libraries. *Information Technology and Libraries, 26*(1), 14–22.

Bertot, J. C., McClure, C. R., Wright, C.B, Jensen, E., & Thomas, S. (2009). *Public Libraries and the Internet 2009: Survey results and findings.* College Park, MD: Center for Library & Information Innovation. Available at http://www.plinternetsurvey.org.

Bertot, J. C., Simmons, S. N., Brogardt, D., McGilvray, J., & Clark, L. (2009). *U.S. public libraries and e-government services.* Chicago: American Library Association. Retrieved October 1, 2009, from http://www.ala.org/ala/research/initiatives/plftas/issuesbriefs/IssuesBrief-Egov.pdf.

Bill and Melinda Gates Foundation. (2009). *Florida public library technology dataset* [Electronic database]. Seattle, WA: Bill and Melinda Gates Foundation.

Boyd, P., & Berejka, M. (2009). *Consolidated comments of Microsoft Corporation before the Department of Commerce, National Telecommunications and Information Administration, Department of Agriculture, Rural Utilities Service, and the Federal Communications Commission in the matter of American Recovery and Reinvestment Act of 2009 broadband initiatives, the Commission's consultative role in the broadband provisions of the Recovery Act.* Redmond, WA: Microsoft Corporation. Retrieved April 24, 2009, from http://www.ntia.doc.gov/broadbandgrants/comments/78A.pdf.

Broadband Initiatives Program, Broadband Technology Opportunities Program notice of funding availability, 74 Fed. Reg. 33104 (2009). Retrieved July 9, 2009, from http://www.broadbandusa.gov/files/BB%20NOFA%20FINAL%2007092009.pdf.

Charytan, L. R., Zachary, H. M., DeVries, W. T., Sherwood, A. H., Zinman, J. S., Phillips, G. L., et al. (2009). *Comments of AT&T Inc. before the Federal Communications Commission in the matter of a national broadband plan for our future.* Washington, D.C.: AT&T. Retrieved June 15, 2009, from http://fjallfoss.fcc.gov/ecfs/document/view?id=7020037017.

Communication Workers of America, American Library Association, & Speed Matters. (n.d.). *High speed Internet: And libraries.* Washington, D.C.: Communication Workers of America. Retrieved June 15, 2009, from http://fjallfoss.fcc.gov/ecfs/document/view?id=7020350518.

Free Press. (2009). *Wired less: Disconnected in urban America.* Washington, D.C.: Free Press. Retrieved June 15, 2009, from http://www.freepress.net/files/Wired_Less_Disconnected_in_Urban_America.pdf.

Gibson, A. N., Bertot, J. C., & McClure, C. R. (2009). Emerging role of public librarians as e-government providers. In R. H. Sprague, Jr. (Ed.), *Proceedings of the 42nd Hawaii International Conference on System Sciences* (pp. 1–10). doi:10.1109/HICSS.2009.183.

Goldman, D. (2009). *Comments of Communication Workers of America before the Federal Communications Commission in the matter of a national broadband plan for our future.* Washington, D.C.: Communication Workers of America. Retrieved June 15, 2009, from http://fjallfoss.fcc.gov/prod/ecfs/retrieve.cgi?native-or-pdf=pdf&id=6520220214.

Golston, A. (2009). *Comments of the Bill & Melinda Gates Foundation before the United States Department of Commerce National Telecommunications and Information Administration in the matter of implementation of the Broadband Technology Opportunities Program.* Seattle, WA: Bill & Melinda Gates Foundation.

Retrieved April 15, from http://www.ntia.doc.gov/broadbandgrants/comments/7358.pdf.

Gupta, A., Berejka, M., Griffin, T., & Boyd, P. (2009). *Comments of Microsoft Corporation before the Federal Communications Commission in the matter of a national broadband plan for our future*. Redmond, WA: Microsoft. Retrieved June 15, 2009, from http://fjallfoss.fcc.gov/prod/ecfs/retrieve.cgi?native-or-pdf=pdf&id=6520220228.

Horrigan, J. B. (2008). *Home broadband adoption 2008: Adoption stalls for low-income Americans even as many broadband users opt for premium services that give them more speed*. Washington, D.C.: Pew Internet and American Life Project. Retrieved May 11, 2009, from http://www.pewinternet.org/~/media//Files/Reports/2008/PIP_Broadband_2008.pdf.

Hudson, H. E. (2007). *The future of Universal Service Fund support for organizations: Schools, libraries and rural health care providers*. San Francisco, CA: Communications Technology Management Program, University of San Francisco. Retrieved June 15, 2009, from http://fjallfoss.fcc.gov/prod/ecfs/retrieve.cgi?native-or-pdf=pdf&id=6520220174.

Jaeger, P. T., Langa, L. A., McClure, C. R., & Bertot, J. C. (2007). The 2004 and 2005 Gulf Coast hurricanes: Evolving roles and lessons learned for public libraries. *Public Library Quarterly, 25*, 199–214.

Kranich, N. (2006). *Libraries as universal service providers*. Washington, D.C.: Benton Foundation. Retrieved June 15, 2009, from http://fjallfoss.fcc.gov/prod/ecfs/retrieve.cgi?native-or-pdf=pdf&id=6520220175.

Mandel, L. H., Bishop, B. W., McClure, C. R., Bertot, J. C., & Jaeger, P. T. (2010). Broadband for public libraries: Importance, issues, and research needs, *Government Information Quarterly, 27*(3), 280–291.

McClure, C. R., Bishop, B. W., Mandel, L. H., & Snead, J. T. (2010). *Pasco County Public Library Cooperative e-government services in public libraries, 2009–2010: Final report of project activities*. Tallahassee, FL: Information Use Management and Policy Institute. Retrieved August 12, 2010, from http://ii.fsu.edu/content/download/38777/244546.

McClure, C. R., & Jaeger, P. T. (2009). *Public libraries and Internet service roles: Measuring and maximizing Internet services*. Chicago: American Library Association.

McClure, C. R., McGilvray, J., Barton, K. M., & Bertot, J. C. (2007). *E-government and public libraries: Current status, meeting report, findings, and next steps*. Tallahassee, FL: Information Use Management and Policy Institute. Retrieved June 15, 2009, from http://www.ii.fsu.edu/announcements/e-gov2006/egov_report.pdf.

McClure, C. R., Ryan, J., Mandel, L. H., Brobst, J., Hinnant, C. C., Andrade, J., et al. (2009). Hurricane preparedness and response for Florida public libraries: best practices and strategies. *Florida Libraries, 52*(1), 4–7.

National Telecommunications and Information Administration. (2004). *A nation online: Entering the broadband age*. Washington, D.C.: U.S. Department of Commerce. Retrieved April 10, 2009, from http://www.ntia.doc.gov/reports/anol/nationonlinebroadband04.pdf.

Oblinger, D. Van Houweling, D., & Semer, J. (2009). *Comments by EDUCAUSE, Internet2 and ACUTA before the Federal Communications Commission in the matter of a national broadband plan for our future*. Washington, D.C.: EDUCAUSE. Retrieved June 15, 2009, from http://net.educause.edu/ir/library/pdf/EPO0917.pdf.

Sheketoff, E. (2009). *Comments of the American Library Association before the Federal Communications Commission in the matter of a national broadband plan for our future.* Washington, D.C.: American Library Association Washington Office. Retrieved June 10, 2009, from http://www.wo.ala.org/districtdispatch/wp-content/uploads/2009/06/alanoi6-8.pdf.

Telecommunications Act of 1996. (1996). 110 Stat. 56 § 706. Retrieved June 15, 2009, from http://frwebgate.access.gpo.gov/cgi-bin/getdoc.cgi?dbname=104_cong_bills&docid=f:s652enr.txt.pdf.

Whitt, R. S., & Lampert, D. N. (2009). *Comments of Google Inc. before the Federal Communications Commission in the matter of a national broadband plan for our future.* Washington, D.C.: Google. Retrieved June 15, 2009, from http://fjallfoss.fcc.gov/prod/ecfs/retrieve.cgi?native-or-pdf=pdf&id=6520220241.

Zachem, K. A., Don, D. M., McManus, M. P., & Waz, J. W., Jr. (2009). *Comments of Comcast Corporation before the Federal Communications Commission in the matter of a national broadband plan for our future.* Washington, D.C.: Comcast Corporation. Retrieved June 15, 2009, from http://fjallfoss.fcc.gov/prod/ecfs/retrieve.cgi?native-or-pdf=pdf&id=6520219851.

Part

Populations

Providing Services for the Underserved in Public Libraries through an Understanding of Information Poverty and Access

Kim M. Thompson

INTRODUCTION

Information poverty is an issue discussed by journalists, government and non-governmental organizations, and academics from various social science disciplines. Terms such as "information inequality," "information barrier," "information gap," "knowledge gap," "information disadvantage," "cyberpoor," "digital divide," and "virtual inequality" are also used in the literature to describe a worrisome gap that sometimes exists between people and the information they need. Literature from communication, library and information science, political science, economics, sociology, social anthropology, psychology, education, and other social science fields contribute to the body of literature on information poverty.

The concept of information poverty was coined in the early 1970s, not long after the United States declared "war against poverty" (Johnson, 1964a, p. 375). Information and library scientists, among others, began examining the effects of economic poverty on information access within the context of what we now consider to be the early days of the *information age*. This chapter provides background on how both economic and information poverty have been conceptualized and measured in the United States using similar lenses.

There are no distinct trends in the literature. For example, communication literature doesn't exclusively discuss information poverty as a problem related to information and communication tools, library and information science (LIS) doesn't only discuss information poverty in light of libraries and information systems, education doesn't only suggest educational solutions for problems associated with the information poor, and so forth. Likewise, the poverty paradigms discussed in the next section are not exclusively used in one body of literature or another. There seem to be no patterns, in fact, for how information poverty is addressed within any one field. Even political science research varies on whether policy should focus more on universal access or social services related to training and education.

The recommendations suggested in much of the literature focus largely on providing a more egalitarian national infrastructure—not only in relation to the provision of information, but also in relation to education and training, socioeconomic opportunities, and employment. This chapter will neither evaluate nor discuss all of the suggestions provided in the literature reviewed. However, a historical review of the concept of information poverty makes it very clear that the issue is still very much an issue 40 years after the first published mention of the problem. This work and any research that builds upon it will only help improve our understanding of the problem and will lend to solution structures that may reduce the impacts of information poverty on individuals and society, should such aid be possible. The chapter concludes with recommendations for how public libraries might use both lenses to create better information service for all user groups.

POVERTY PARADIGMS

Traditionally, poverty has been studied using two paradigms, namely: (1) the structural/economic paradigm; and (2) the cultural/behavioral paradigm (Jordan, 2004; Rodgers, 2000). Through the structural/economic lens, poverty is seen as a result of a lack of equal opportunities. The cultural/behavioral view is that poverty is a consequence of "the behavior, values, and cultures of the poor" (Rodgers, 2000, p. 69). This is not to say that all poverty research falls cleanly within the scope solely of either one or the other. Some structural/economic discussions include behavioral components, and cultural/behavioral research often cites lack of opportunity as leading to cultural marginalization and anti-social behaviors. Still, poverty research since the 1960s in particular has aligned rather closely with either one of these two paradigms.

In the early 1960s the United States was already one of the richest and most powerful nations in the world. The United States and Soviet Union were the notable superpowers of the world, with global cultural, economic, military, and political influence (Fox, 1944). As communist antagonism grew, the United States appeared to be a shining example of the prosperity of democracy. Unemployment was low and around 62% of Americans were homeowners, an increase from 55% in 1950 and about 44% in 1940 (U.S. Census Bureau, 2009). In the midst of financial prosperity, American sociologist Daniel Bell foresaw an economic trend of decreased dependence on production and industry in the United States and an increased reliance on service relationships and communication between individuals. He called this the *post-industrial society*. According to Bell (1960), the post-industrial society relied quite heavily on information, and this information was one of the factors that helped decrease disparity in Western society. As information and communication technologies (ICTs) advanced, information was increasingly available at the push of a button.

Within the U.S. democratic ideology, ease of access to and availability of information among the populace is fundamental (Hacker, 1996; Jaeger & Burnett, 2005; Smolla, 1992). The federal government historically has strong interest in the global spread of democracy, information, and continued American prosperity. During the 1960 presidential campaign, both Republican candidate Richard Nixon and Democratic candidate John F. Kennedy promised policies that would foster continued national economic progress (Farber & Bailey, 2001). Upon election, Kennedy promptly outlined federal economic plans that would provide tax cuts and additional economic opportunities for Americans.

Within a few years, however, a book by social activist Michael Harrington (1962) reportedly "jarred the country" (Miringoff, Miringoff, & Opdycke, 2006, p. 1). Harrington's book revealed that during this time of unprecedented prosperity and focus on democracy nearly one quarter of Americans were living in poverty. Harrington's poverty calculations were similar to the typical government poverty instruments, derived by setting dollar figures "with greater or lesser amounts of supporting details and rationales" (Fisher, 1994, n.p.). Harrington's dollar figure for poverty was "somewhere between $3000 and $3500 for an urban family of four" based on a calculation in which he took a recent U.S. Bureau of Labor Statistics "adequate" budget for urban family of four living ($6,147) and then halved it (1962, pp. 181–182). This poverty measurement may seem somewhat arbitrary, but it was no more arbitrary than the standards the government used at the time. Harrington wrote of his poverty line, "If some statistician should find an error in technical approach, if he could say, there are 10,000,000 less poor, that would not really be important. Give or take 10,000,000, the American poor are one of the greatest scandals of a society that has the ability to provide a decent life for every man, woman, and child" (pp. 172–173).

Harrington's discussion of poverty in America was one of the major catalysts for serious government consideration of the poverty problem as well as the impetus for creating a more carefully designed poverty threshold (Fisher, 1994; U.S. Department of Labor, 2006). Harrington called upon the federal government to offer "real opportunities to these people by changing the social reality that gives rise to their sense of hopelessness," creating an extended welfare package, and ensuring the longevity of social security (p. 167). He also recommended that the federal government oversee "the political, economic, and social integration of the poor with the rest of society," noting that slums and other low-income housing isolate communities of poor individuals, disconnecting them from the rest of society and making it easy to ignore the poverty problem (p. 168). Finally, Harrington pointed out that the racial prejudices of the day were stifling opportunity and creating an extra set of barriers to economic integration (pp. 169–170).

Poverty through a Structural/Economic Lens

What is most significant about Harrington's book is that the federal government actually responded to it, implementing policies that attempted to provide at least the basic tools a person might need in order to succeed in modern America. Kennedy increased the federal focus on combating American poverty with a plan that would include policy reform and social services similar to those of the New Deal era. Before he could implement his plan, Kennedy was assassinated (in 1963) and his Vice President, Lyndon B. Johnson, was sworn into office and continued the federal fight against American poverty.

Another force in fighting poverty was Martin Luther King Jr.'s leadership in the civil rights movement. King helped turn the nation's attention to the grave disparities in economic and social status between white American citizens and minority groups. With the increased focus on intercultural understanding, race relations also slowly improved. The same year that King won the Nobel Peace Prize for his leadership in methods of non-violent protest, President Johnson signed the *Civil Rights Act of 1964* (P.L. 88–352), targeting segregated schools and discrimination in the workplace that had been taking a toll on the employment opportunities of racial minorities.

The *Economic Opportunity Act of 1964* officially began the push for "The Great Society," a place of "abundance and liberty for all" (Johnson, 1964b, p. 704). The Act created Kennedy's designed Office of Economic Opportunity and provided free training and temporary financial subsidies for unskilled workers so they could "break out of the pattern of poverty" and "strike away the barriers to full participation in our society" (Johnson, 1964a, pp. 377–378). The Act included support for policy that would include all members of the American public to "participate in the workings of . . . society" by offering opportunities for "education and training, the opportunity to work, and the opportunity to live in decency and dignity" (P.L. 88–352, Introduction).

Poverty through a Cultural/Behavioral Lens

While Harrington's recommendations for federal reform are generally structural/economic based (i.e., the government should provide more opportunities), his book is composed of a series of anecdotes and cultural descriptions that point to cultural/behavioral problems that do not overtly tie directly to the solutions he names. Harrington's call for government-directed integration and welfare support are counterpoised with descriptions of, among others, the "urban hillbillies," who come from rural areas to try to survive in an urban environment without adopting the urban lifestyle, inevitably leading a very marginalized social existence (p. 96), and the "intellectual poor," who choose a lifestyle of economic poverty, "fleeing a spiritual poverty in the Affluent Society," often experimenting with drugs and social rebellion (p. 86). Harrington cites what was at that time a recently framed *culture of poverty* theory to describe what he saw among America's poor.

The idea of a culture of poverty was first presented in social anthropologist Oscar Lewis' (1959) book, *Five Families: Mexican Case Studies in the Culture of Poverty.* Lewis had spent years engaging in ethnographic observation among the poor in Latin America, Canada, Spain, and India. He had noticed a trend of poverty lifestyle "which transcend[s] regional, rural-urban, and even national differences" (1961, p. xxv). According to Lewis (1961), a culture is "a design for living which is passed down from generation to generation" (p. xxiv), and within the lower-class settlements he had observed that there seemed to be a common culture, based on "similarities in family structure, interpersonal relations, time orientations, value systems, spending patterns, and the sense of community" (Lewis, 1961, p. xxv).

Lewis's and then Harrington's writings spurred a new wave of social research that focused less on the system or infrastructure and more on the culture or behavior of marginalized groups of individuals. Lack of motivation to change is a common theme in this culture of poverty research. Much of Harrington's discussion, for example, centers on the routine of poverty. Harrington (1962) noted a "common sense of hopelessness" among the poor that creates a situation in which "even when there are programs designed to help [them], the poor are held back by their own pessimism . . . the impoverished American tends to see life as a fate, an endless cycle from which there is no deliverance" (p. 161). Harrington referred to the commonly proffered solution of education as "less and less meaningful," since "a person has to feel that education will do something for him if he is to gain from it" (p. 161). He continues:

> Placing a magnificent school with a fine faculty in the middle of a slum is, I suppose, better than having a run-down building staffed by incompetents. But it will not really make a difference so long as the environment of the tenement, the family, and the street counsels the children to leave as soon as they can and to disregard schooling. (pp. 161–162)

Thus, even though Harrington's recommendations were for government intervention, the government action he recommended was specific: focus on redefining the poverty culture.

Not long after Lewis and Harrington popularized the culture of poverty theory, the government funded a report entitled *The Negro Family: A Case for National Action* (Moynihan, 1965). This report, often referred to as "The Moynihan Report," proposed that the "disorganization" of Black family life was a result of a dysfunctional subculture of poverty (Moynihan, 1965, chapter 1, n.p.). The report, like the overall culture of poverty theory, was vehemently criticized as reinforcing negative racial and low-income group stereotypes. That is, the culture of poverty theory seemed to blame the victims of social disparity rather than work to ameliorate unequal socioeconomic opportunities (e.g., Coward, Feagin, & Williams, 1974; Irelan, Moles, & O'Shea, 1969; Miller, 1976; Roach & Gursslin, 1967).

Thus, proponents of the two different approaches to assessing poverty were engaged in lively debate in the 1960s and early 1970s. Is American poverty caused by government neglect or sociocultural failing? Is poverty only ameliorated through federal intervention, or are grassroot efforts more effective in addressing poverty concerns? These questions and others were on the minds of social researchers trying to understand the poverty problem. The structural/economic and cultural/behavioral paradigms both seemed to apply to different aspects of poverty. The difficulty was deciding which paradigm was the best fit overall. As we will see, the limitations of these two poverty paradigms are ech-oed by similar limitations in conceptualizations of information poverty.

CONCEPTUALIZING INFORMATION POVERTY AND THE INFORMATION POOR

In the early 1970s, the terms *information poor* and *information poverty* began appearing in scholarly discussions regarding the social implications of infra-structural poverty within the context of the information society. Information scientist Edwin B. Parker (1970) may have been the first to use the term "information-poor" (p. 53) in a conference report entitled "Information Utilities and Mass Communication." In this work, Parker suggests that new information utilities or technologies would exacerbate the information divide between tech-nology haves and have-nots.

"Information poverty" and "information poor" appear next a few years later in *Psychology Today* article by sociologist James S. Coleman (1972) that describes a structural difference between the modern information environment and the information environment of 100 years prior. Coleman describes the differences in American information infrastructure resulting from mass electronic dissemi-nation of information (i.e., via radio, television). He notes that these changes in the way individuals (particularly children) access information consequently also change many other aspects of society, including the lessening of adult authority and a shift in the overall structure of the education system from a focus on information dissemination to a focus on teaching critical thinking skills and moral judgment. In the Coleman article, the environment 100 years ago was "information-poor" in comparison to today's "information-rich" infra-structure (1972, p. 72).

Another article published that same year by the aforementioned Parker and his colleague Donald A. Dunn (1972) about the distribution of information and communication technologies (ICTs) throughout society also used the term information poor, this time to describe people. They posit that "if access to . . . information services is not universally available throughout society, then those already 'information-rich' may reap the benefits while the 'information-poor' get relatively poorer" (p. 1396). Contrary to Bell's (1960) earlier statement that ease of physical access to information via modern information technologies would lead to greater social equality, Parker and Dunn suggest that information dis-crepancies potentially create "social tensions" because information gaps, they say, contribute to gaps "in economic and political power" (1972, p. 1396).

The term information poor appears in several other articles published in the early 1970s, describing the need for Black communities to begin focusing on becoming "information-rich" (Martin, 1973, p. 586; 1974, p. 263), discussing the social implications of unequal ICT dispersion throughout American society (Katzman, 1974; Parker, 1973/1974), and noting the lack of information avail-able to individuals with visual disabilities (Suppes, 1974). After this there was relatively little produced regarding information poverty until the mid-1980s, when personal computers and other information technologies began to take center stage in American society.

Information Access through a Structural/Economic Lens

In the 1980s, as personal computers grew in popularity, appearing in homes, offices, and schools, information poverty was discussed in terms of the information processing potential within the context of the information society, particularly in relation to the disadvantages Americans without ready access to computers might face (Buckley, 1987; Mason, 1986; Scherer, 1989). Also in the 1980s, researchers began exploring information poverty in terms of the global information society, comparing the advantages the information- and technology-rich United States and other developed countries had over less developed, technology-poor nations (Dubey, 1985; Gannett Center, 1987; Lang, 1988; Menou, 1983).

Throughout the 1970s and 1980s, the concept of information poverty was usually tied closely to economic poverty, and information poverty research in the 1990s continued much along the lines of economic-poverty-begets-information-poverty with few exceptions. After 1990 information poverty publications rose markedly; this may be a result of the heavy focus the Clinton/Gore administration (from 1993 to 2000) placed on the role of information technology as contributor to the American information society.

In the mid-1990s the United Nations formally defined poverty as "a condition characterised by severe deprivation of basic human needs, including … education and information" depending "not only on income but also on access to services" (United Nations, 1995). Around this same time the Internet was becoming a part of the American popular culture. It was quickly evident that access or lack of access to the Internet had the potential to either provide individuals with or divide them from choices and opportunities. The U.S. National Telecommunications and Information Administration (NTIA) began a series of studies charting American Internet adoption and use. The NTIA studies identified the information poor as "those who are younger, those with lower incomes and education levels, certain minorities, and those in rural areas or central cities" who do not own computers or have in-home Internet access (1999, Executive Summary). This gap between these Internet haves and have nots was termed the *digital divide* (Cisler, 2000). According to Cisler, the term digital divide was originally used in a story by journalist Amy Harmon in 1996 to describe the social problem that arises when a person uses digital technology at the expense of his or her real-life interpersonal relationships. The term was quickly adopted by NTIA when talking about the issues related to unequal ownership of computational technology. It is through NTIA documents that the term gained its popularity when discussing Internet haves and have-nots. The digital divide literature often blurred with information poverty literature; however, the digital divide only accounted for one slice of the larger information poverty problem.

Information Access through a Cultural/Behavioral Lens

One of the strongest exceptions to the economic-poverty-begets-information-poverty equation was advanced by Chatman's (1992, 1996; Chatman & Pendleton, 1995) ethnographic studies of the "impoverished information world" of non-poor demographic groups (Chatman, 1992, p. 137). Within the context of the prevailing structural/economic digital divide literature, Chatman returned attention to the cultural/behavioral aspects of information poverty. Rather than focus on information technology ownership, she proposed instead that it is "our membership within a particular social group [that] contributes to information poverty" (Chatman, 1996, p. 197). She searched for established social theories that might explain the information problems she observed. She found that the extant theories clarified some, but not all, aspects of information poverty. In 1996 she published her own theory of information poverty, one with a heavy cultural/behavioral focus. She described this theory as middle range, as it was based on a limited amount of ethnographic observation among a limited number of American subcultures.

While Chatman's theory has been a launching point for a new wave of cultural/behavioral information poverty research (e.g., Fisher, Marcoux, Miller, Sánchez, & Cunningham, 2004; Hersberger, 2002; Jaeger & Thompson, 2004; James, 2000; Pollock, 2002; Sligo & Williams, 2001; Thompson, 2006), there are still questions about information poverty left unanswered. Chatman's research, although she does expand our understanding of the information poverty phenomenon, shows no evidence that she took the structural/economic information poverty approach into account.

LIMITATIONS OF THE POVERTY LENSES

The approaches to information poverty summarized here, when viewed in conjunction, create a richer understanding of how the concept of information poverty has been used in the literature to attempt to describe problems of information access. Within the parameters of the structural/economic approach, the most common argument today is that the growing amount of digital information that is produced every day creates a digital divide, or lack of access to digital information, because of lack of access to digital information technologies. When we use the narrow focus of the digital divide to measure information access, however, we overlook very fundamental questions such as: What are the desired outcomes tied to lessening the digital divide (i.e., democratic participation? economic stability or prosperity? social inclusion)? What types of information are necessary to achieve the desired outcomes? How does the speed of information delivery affect the value of the information delivered? Is the current information infrastructure helping the United States and other countries achieve these outcomes or is it hindering this cause?

The second approach to information poverty focuses on the influence of culture and behavior on information access. However, research using the social/behavioral lens overlooks other important aspects of the information poverty phenomenon and, like the structural/economic approach, leaves many questions unanswered. For example, what criteria might be used to ensure that the "right" information is being delivered to meet an individual or group's information needs? Are there information literacy proficiencies that might help researchers suggest policy and develop education curricula that would provide appropriate training for all Americans? Is it possible to measure how much information an individual needs to have in order to not be considered information poor? Is it possible to fashion an information poverty line that can help measure the information poverty phenomenon?

Rather than thinking in terms of which of these two poverty lenses is better suited or more important when addressing information poverty, a *both/and* approach allows us to consider them simultaneously. For example, a side-by-side analysis of national/community information infrastructures and social information networks is useful for teasing out the role of each of these contributors to information access. In addition, focusing on information access rather than information poverty can help reduce the confusion that information poverty is tied specifically to economic poverty.

APPLICATION TO PUBLIC LIBRARIES AND THE INTERNET: USER-CENTERED DESIGN

Since 1994 the American Library Association, the U.S. National Commission on Libraries and Information Science, the U.S. Institute of Museum and Library Services, the Bill & Melinda Gates Foundation, the AARP, Benton Foundation, and other interested parties have funded research tracking public library Internet adoption. The resulting reports have been invaluable for providing a broad-brush image of how the Internet has been incorporated into the American public library system over the past 15 years. Findings show that today almost all public libraries provide free public computer access to the Internet (e.g., Bertot, McClure, Wright, Jensen, & Thomas, 2009). The issues explored with these studies have primarily focused on structural and infrastructural aspects of connectivity—for example: How many work stations are available? What bandwidth is in use? What databases are available? Is there training provided?—but some have also examined the prevalence of skills needed to access the information available through the Internet (e.g., Bill & Melinda Gates Foundation, 2004).

While provision of Internet access and training for computer use are excellent first steps for libraries to take in light of the structural/economic approach to information access, the social/behavioral approach to information access must not be overlooked. The Internet has changed the way some library services are offered. Catalogs, reference services, even library collections are more and more frequently provided online. This is done in part as a means to provide information service to individuals who cannot or do not come to the library building itself. This does not lessen the need for libraries.

Studies show that users are typically pleased with and use libraries (Emery, 2008; Martell, 2007; University College London, UCL, 2008) and that these electronic resources and services libraries provide are commonly used (American Library Association, 2007; Dickenson, 2006). Still, library portals and Web sites are not the first place users typically think of when looking for information. Rather, users indicate that they find commercial search engines to be "almost perfect" (UCL, 2008, n.p.) and tend to use Google or other search engines first, before trying a digital library to meet their information needs (Griffiths & Brophy, 2005; Head, 2007), even when commercial search engines may not actually help them retrieve the information they need (Emery, 2008).

This last behavior seems to illustrate Mooers' Law, which states that "an information retrieval system will tend not to be used whenever it is more painful and troublesome for a customer [*sic*] to have information than for him [*sic*] not to have it" (Mooers, 1960, p. i). In other words, if a commercial search engine is easier to use (even if the search results in a failure to meet information needs), it will be tried before the more difficult system—for example, a public library Web site—is accessed. The more difficult system will be used only as a last effort if all else fails and the information need is of sufficient importance to the user. Indeed, commercial search engines do have their place in meeting information needs; however, when library users are not able to meet their information needs because of over-reliance on commercial search engines and lack of understanding of digital library structures (UCL, 2008), this is a problem that libraries need to address.

As information infrastructures continue to develop, designing systems that take into account the social/behavioral aspect of Internet and library use is becoming more and more important. A more usable library Web interface will allow more users more access to the information therein contained (Bertot, Snead, Jaeger, & McClure, 2006). One objective of user studies in relation to information seeking is to determine user behavior and user satisfaction in light of information systems used to meet information needs (Hernandez, 2008). The greater the usability of an information system, the better it can be used to meet these information needs.

Viewing information access at the macro-level, Information Studies researcher Reijo Savolainen (2008) notes that even everyday information, or that which is "regular, repeated, familiar, quotidian, banal, and even boring" "once probed in detail" becomes "ambiguous and elusive" (p. 2). Individuals typify information as a way to reduce the amount of information we must consciously assess in a day. In other words, we classify information as being of lesser or greater quality. This information typing is similar to social typing. Social typing is the classification of individuals based on a common worldview. Social typing creates "a commonsense system in which to create a typology of persons based on predictable behavior" (Chatman, 2000, p. 12). This typology is used to maintain control over one's social interactions. Likewise, information typing is a way to manage one's dealings with information. In the effort to create some agreeable level of met expectation in the world around him/her, the same lens that colors his/her view of the social world colors his/her view of the information environment.

As social typing is based on social norms (i.e., ideas of how individuals *should* act, react, and interact) the acceptance of information as useful or relevant is similarly normative. Standards or information tastes are passed on to others within the same social group whether explicitly or by example and nuance. Similar to social typing, this classification of information is not easily changed. Thus, identifying the type of information that satisfies one's needs is based upon the same worldview that affects all other parts of his/her small world existence. This sense of taste in information also affects the judgment of quality of information or information resources. In-house studies that help libraries determine the worldview of their own users will allow libraries to design services and online interfaces that provide the most usable information access possible.

CONCLUSION

Understanding both the structural/economic and the social/behavioral approaches to information access is vital for provision of usable information services and resources, both online and within the walls of the library. While a main objective of libraries is to meet user information needs, the librarians and the users may have differing ideas of what services and project details will best meet those needs. Library policy should reflect a systemic understanding of both infrastructural and user-centered elements related to information access.

REFERENCES

American Library Association. (2007). New data shows increased library usage. *American Libraries, 38*(6), 17.

Bell, D. (1960). *The end of ideology: On the exhaustion of political ideas in the Fifties.* Glencoe, IL: Free Press.

Bertot, J. C., McClure, C. R., Wright, C. B., Jensen, E., & Thomas, S. (2009). *Public Libraries and the Internet 2008: Study results and findings.* Tallahassee, FL: Information Use Management and Policy Institute. Retrieved April 27, 2009, from http://www.plinternetsurvey.org.

Bertot, J. C., Snead, J. T., Jaeger, P. T., & McClure, C. R. (2006). Functionality, usability, and accessibility. *Performance Measurement and Metrics, 7*(1), 17–28.

Bill & Melinda Gates Foundation. (2004). *Toward equality of access: The role of public libraries in addressing the digital divide.* Retrieved April 27, 2009, from http://www.imls.gov/pdf/Equality.pdf.

Buckley, F. J. (1987). Knowledge-access issues. *The Information Society, 5*(1), 45–50.

Chatman, E. A. (1992). *The information world of retired women.* Westport, CT: Greenwood Press.

Chatman, E. A. (1996). The impoverished world of outsiders. *Journal of the American Society for Information Science, 47,* 193–206.

Chatman, E. A. (2000). Framing social life in theory and research. *New Review of Information Behaviour Research, 1,* 3–17.

Chatman, E. A., & Pendleton, V. (1995). Knowledge gap, information-seeking and the poor. *Reference Librarian, 49–50,* 135–145.

Cisler, S. (2000). Subtract the "digital divide." *San Jose Mercury News,* January 16, 2000. Retrieved April 27, 2009, from: http://www.athenaalliance.org/rpapers/cisler.html.

Civil Rights Act of 1964. P.L. 88–352.

Coleman, J. S. (1972). The children have outgrown the schools. *Psychology Today, 5,* 72–75, 82.

Coward, B. E., Feagin, J. R., & Williams, J. A. (1974). The culture of poverty debate: Some additional data. *Social Problems, 21,* 621–634.

Dickenson, D. (2006). How students and faculty use academic libraries differently. *Library Research Service.* Colorado State Library. Colorado Department of Education. Retrieved April 27, 2009, from http://www.lrs.org/documents/fastfacts/242_ALIS_2_KL.pdf.

Dubey, Y. P. (1985). Information poverty: A third-world perspective. ERIC document ED 314051.

Economic Opportunity Act of 1964, P.L. 88–452. Retrieved April 27, 2009, from http://www.etsu.edu/cas/history/docs/eoa.htm.

Emery, B. (April 2008). Undergrads' research habits, motivators and attitudes. What studies tell us. *Library Connect Newsletter*, 5.

Farber, D., & Bailey, B. (2001). *The Columbia guide to the 1960s*. New York: Columbia University Press.

Fisher, G. (1992). The development and history of the poverty thresholds. *Social Security Bulletin, 55*(4). Retrieved April 27, 2009, from http://aspe.hhs.gov/poverty/papers/HPTGSSIV.htm.

Fisher, G. (1994). *From Hunter to Orshansky: An overview of the (unofficial) poverty lines in the United States from 1904 to 1965*. Washington, D.C.: U.S. Department of Health and Human Services. Retrieved April 27, 2009, from http://aspe.hhs.gov/poverty/papers/htrssmiv.htm.

Fisher, K. E., Marcoux, E., Miller, L. S., Sánchez, A., & Cunningham, E. R. (2004). Information behaviour of migrant Hispanic farm workers and their families in the Pacific Northwest. *Information Research, 10*(1). Retrieved April 27, 2009, from http://informationr.net/ir/10-1/paper199.html.

Fox, W. T. R. (1944). *The superpowers*. New York: Harcourt Brace.

Gannett Center for Media Studies. (1987). *The cost of technology: Information prosperity and information poverty*. New York: Columbia University.

Griffiths, J., & Brophy, P. (2005). Student searching behavior and the Web: Use of academic resources and Google. *Library Trends, 53*(4), 539–554.

Hacker, K. L. (1996). Missing links in the evolution of electronic democratization. *Media, Culture, and Society, 18*(2), 213–232.

Harrington, M. (1962). *The other America: Poverty in the United States*. New York: Macmillan.

Head, A. J. (2007). Beyond Google: How do students conduct academic research? *First Monday, 12*(8). Retrieved April 24, 2008, from http://firstmonday.org/htbin/cgiwrap/bin/ojs/index.php/fm/article/view/1998/1873.

Hernández Salazar, P. (2008). Métodos cualitativos para estudiar a los usuarios de la información. *Cuadernos de Investigación 5*. Ciudad de México: Universidad Nacional Autónoma de México.

Hersberger, J. (2002/2003). Are the economically poor information poor? Does the digital divide affect the homeless and access to information? *Canadian Journal of Information and Library Science, 27*(3), 45–63.

Irelan, L. M., Moles, O. C., & O'Shea, R. M. (1969). Ethnicity, poverty, and selected attitudes: A test of the "culture of poverty" hypothesis. *Social Forces, 47*, 405–413.

Jaeger, P. T., & Burnett, G. (2005). Information access and exchange among small worlds in a democratic society: The role of policy in redefining information behavior in the post-9/11 United States. *Library Quarterly, 75*(4), 464–495.

Jaeger, P. T., & Thompson, K. M. (2004). Social information behavior and the democratic process: Information poverty, normative behavior, and electronic government in the United States. *Library and Information Science Research, 26*, 92–107.

James, L. C. (2000). Living with information poverty: A study of the information behavior of homeless parents. Unpublished thesis, University of Washington.

Johnson, L. B. (1964a). Proposal for a nationwide war on the sources of poverty. *Modern history sourcebook*. Retrieved April 27, 2009, from http://www.fordham.edu/halsall/mod/1964johnson-warpoverty.html.

Johnson, L. B. (1964b). Great Society speech. *Public Papers of the Presidents of the United States: Lyndon B. Johnson, Book I (1963–1964)*. Retrieved April 27, 2009, from http://coursesa.matrix.msu.edu/~hst306/documents/great.html.

Jordan, G. (2004). The causes of poverty—cultural vs. structural: Can there be a synthesis? *Perspectives in Public Affairs, 1*, 18–34.

Katzman, N. (1974). The impact of communication technology: Some theoretical premises and their implications. *Ekistics, 225*, 125–130.

Lang, J. P. (Ed.). (1988). *Unequal access to information resources: Problems and needs of the world's information poor.* Ann Arbor, MI: Pierian Press.

Lewis, O. (1959). *Five families: Mexican case studies in the culture of poverty.* New York: Basic Books.

Lewis, O. (1961). *The children of Sánchez: Autobiography of a Mexican family.* New York: Random House.

Martell, C. (2007). The elusive user: .Changing use patterns in academic libraries, 1995 to 2004. *College and Research Libraries, 68*(5), 435–444.

Martin, C. A. (1973). "There's more than one way to skin a cat" (The issue of heredity and anti-egalitarian research). *Journal of Negro Education, 42*(4), 559–569.

Martin, C. A. (1974). Editorial comment: Black English and Black history—continuing themes. *Journal of Negro Education, 43*(3), 263–264.

Mason. R. O. (1986). Four ethical issues of the information age. *MIS Quarterly, 10*(1), 5–12.

Menou, M. J. (1983). Mini- and micro-computers and the eradication of information poverty in the less developed countries. In C. Keren & L. Perlmutter (Eds.). *The application of mini- and micro-computers in information, documentation and libraries.* (pp. 359–366). North Holland: Elsevier.

Miller, D. B. (1976). A partial test of Oscar Lewis' culture of poverty in rural America. *Current Anthropology, 17*(4), 720–723.

Miringoff, M. L. Miringoff, M. L., & Opdycke, S. (2006). *Social indicators: What we need to make them count.* U.S. Government Accounting Office. Retrieved April 27, 2009, from http://www.gao.gov/npi/sicount.pdf.

Mooers, C. N. (1960). Mooers' Law: Or why some information retrieval systems are used and others are not. *American Documentation, 11*(3), i–ii.

Moynihan, D. P. (1965). *The Negro family: A case for national action.* Washington D.C.: U.S. Department of Labor.

NTIA. (1999). *Falling through the Net: Defining the digital divide.* U.S. Department of Commerce: National Telecommunications and Information Administration. Retrieved April 27, 2009, from http://www.ntia.doc.gov/reports/anol/index.html.

Parker, E. B. (1970). Information utilities and mass communication. In H. Sackman & N. Nie (Eds.). *Information utility and social choice: Papers prepared for a conference sponsored jointly by the University of Chicago, Encyclopedia Britannica and the American Federation of Information Processing Societies.* (pp. 51–70). Montvale, NJ: AFIPS Press.

Parker, E. B. (1973/1974). Implications of the new information technology. *Public Opinion Quarterly, 37*(4), 590–600.

Parker, E. B., & Dunn, D. A. (1972). Information technology: Its social potential. *Science, 176*(4042), 1392–1399.

Pollock, N. (2002). Conceptualising the information poor: An assessment of the contribution of Elfreda Chatman towards an understanding of behaviour within the context of information poverty. *Information Science.* Retrieved April 27, 2009, from http://npollock.id.au/info_science/chatman.html.

Roach, J. L., & Gursslin, O. R. (1967). An evaluation of the concept "culture of poverty." *Social Forces, 45*, 383–392.

Rodgers, H. R. (2000). *American poverty in a new era of reform.* Armonk, NY: ME Sharpe, Inc.

Savolainen, R. (2008). *Everyday information practices: A social phenomenological perspective.* Lanham, MD: Rowan & Littlefield.

Scherer, C. W. (1989). The videocassette recorder and information inequity. *Journal of Communication, 39*(3), 94–103.

Sligo, F., & Williams, J. (2001). Investigating information poverty and its implications for community development. National Social Policy Conference, University of NSW. Retrieved April 27, 2009, from http://www.sprc1.sprc.unsw.edu.au/nspc2001/abstract.asp?PaperID=196.

Smolla, R. A. (1992). *Free speech in an open society.* New York: Alfred A. Knopf.

Suppes, P. (1974). A survey of cognition in handicapped children. *Review of Educational Research, 44*(2), 145–176.

Thompson, K. M. (2006). Multidisciplinary approaches to information poverty and their implications for information access. Unpublished dissertation. The Florida State University, Tallahassee.

United Nations. (1995). World Summit for Social Development at Copenhagen. Retrieved April 27, 2009, from http://www.un.org/esa/socdev/wssd/.

University College London (UCL). (January 11, 2008). *Information behaviour of the researcher of the future.* Retrieved April 27, 2009, from http://www.bl.uk/news/pdf/googlegen.pdf.

U.S. Census Bureau. (2009). *Historical census of housing tables.* U.S. Census Bureau, Washington, D.C. Retrieved April 27, 2009, from http://www.census.gov/hhes/www/housing/census/historic/owner.html.

U.S. Department of Labor. (2006). Eras of the New Frontier and the Great Society: 1961–1969. *A Brief History: The U.S. Department of Labor.* U.S. Department of Labor, Washington D.C. Retrieved April 27, 2009, from http://www.dol.gov/oasam/programs/history/dolchp06.htm.

Chapter 9

Serving Older Adult Health Information Seekers in the Internet Age: The Role of Public Libraries

Bo Xie, Amy Cooper White, Chadwick B. Stark, David Piper, and Elizabeth Norton

INTRODUCTION

A number of recent societal and technological trends have created a need for providing age-appropriate training to help older adults learn to navigate, evaluate, and use the wide range of reliable health information available on the Internet. Public libraries, as one of the key access points to information and education, can play an important role in meeting this need.

In this chapter, we first address the three major societal and technological trends that have created this emerging need. We then provide a detailed discussion about an innovative public library program currently underway in suburban Maryland that aims to meet this need. This discussion covers the history and development of this program, challenges encountered, and lessons learned. Finally, we provide a number of recommendations for public library administrators and staff who may be interested in developing a similar program to meet the health information needs of the older adult patrons in their own communities.

RECENT TRENDS

The American population is aging rapidly. By mid-2008, almost 39 million U.S. residents were 65 years or older (U.S. Census Bureau, 2009). In 2011, the "Baby Boom" generation will begin to turn 65. It is projected that in 2030 nearly one in five U.S. residents will be 65 years or older; in 2050, the number of U.S. residents in this age group is projected to increase to 88.5 million, more than doubling the 2008 number (U.S. Census Bureau, 2008). The aging of the population presents serious challenges for public libraries in that older adults often have diverse information needs, preferences, and behaviors that tend to be different from those of their younger counterparts (Asla, Williamson, & Mills, 2006; Bundy, 2005; Chatman, 1991; Curzon, Wilson, & Whitney, 2005; Dunn, 2005; Gollop, 1997; Jones, Morrow, Morris, Rites, & Wekstein, 1992; Moore & Young, 1985; Sit, 1998; Van Fleet, 1989; Wicks, 2004). In particular, older adults typically have a greater need than younger adults for health and medical information; yet, they often have difficulties acquiring such information through conventional sources such as face-to-face interactions with health care professionals (Xie, in press).

Another trend is towards shared medical decision-making. Before the late 1970s, the dominant paradigm in medical decision-making had been the paternalistic model where doctors were expected to make all the decisions on behalf of their patients. During the past few decades, the expectations for doctor-patient relationships have changed substantially (Brody, 1980; Jones & Phillips, 1988). With the shared medical decision-making model increasingly becoming the preferred model in medical encounters, patients are now encouraged to stay well informed and to play a more active role in their own medical care decision-making (Ballard-Reisch, 1990; McNutt, 2004). For the older generations who grew up under the paternalistic model, this paradigm shift can be challenging, as older patients are not used to being so involved in the medical decision-making process (Xie, in press).

This challenge is further amplified given that making medical decisions requires adequate health literacy, which the older population as a whole does not possess. Health literacy, or "the degree to which individuals have the capacity to obtain, process, and understand basic health information and services needed to make appropriate health decisions" (U.S. Department of Health and Human Services, 2000), has become a major concern in this country (Andrus & Roth, 2002). The vast majority of American adults have lower than proficient level of health literacy: The majority of American adults (53%) had only *Intermediate* health literacy; 22% of American adults had *Basic* health literacy, and 14% had *Below Basic* health literacy. Only 12% of American adults had *Proficient* health literacy. The health "illiteracy" problem is even more severe among older adults who have the lowest level of health literacy among all adult age groups: only 3% of American adults in this age group had *Proficient* health literacy (Kutner, Greenberg, Jin, & Paulsen, 2006). Thus, improving health literacy is an especially challenging task for our rapidly aging population.

The rise of the Internet is a further trend. The Internet has the potential to meet older adults' needs for a diverse range of health information (Xie, 2008, in press). As government agencies like the National Institutes of Health (NIH), non-profit organizations (e.g., medical associations), and for-profit companies (e.g., WebMD) are increasingly putting health information and services online, the Internet has already become an important source of health information (Bylund, Sabee, Imes, & Sanford, 2007; Fox, 2007). Unfortunately, older adults are at risk of being left behind because, due to age-related declines in cognitive, sensory, and physical abilities and a lack of age-appropriate training to help to compensate for age-related declines (Xie, 2003), their general adoption of the Internet, particularly use of the Internet for health information, lags behind other age groups (Fox, 2006; Kaiser Family Foundation, 2005). Although some older adults have already begun to make use of the Internet in meeting their health information needs (Fox, 2006; Kaiser Family Foundation, 2005), still, the overall percentage of older adults using the Internet for health-related purposes lags far behind younger age groups (Bundorf, Wagner, Singer, & Baker, 2006; Fox, 2006). Even among the small number of older adults who are beginning to use the Internet for health information, the majority lack sophisticated skills and are thus unable to take full advantage of online resources (Fox, 2006; Xie, 2008).

The convergence of these three trends points to a need for effective interventions that can help older adults learn necessary skills so that they can take full advantage of the rich—and rapidly growing—online health information resources. By improving older adults' e-health literacy, or "the ability to seek, find, understand, and appraise health information from electronic sources and apply the knowledge gained to addressing or solving a health problem" (Norman & Skinner, 2006), these interventions can have a positive impact on the lives of older adults, their families, and society in general (e.g., through improved health, reduced health care costs).

Since September 2007, the faculty and students of the College of Information Studies at the University of Maryland have been working with public libraries in Maryland to develop such an intervention for older adults. The rest of this chapter provides detailed descriptions of this intervention program, focusing more on the practical issues to help other public libraries adopt this program to meet the needs of older adults in their own communities. The more research-oriented issues can be found in Xie & Bugg (2009).

HISTORY AND DEVELOPMENT OF THE PROGRAM (SEPTEMBER 2007–JUNE 2009)

The development of this program to date can be roughly divided into three major phases: preparation (spring–August 2007), initial offering (at one public library in fall 2007), and expansion and continuation (the program expands to and has been continuously offered at two public libraries from spring 2008–June 2009).

Preparation (Spring–August 2007)

In spring 2007, a faculty member of the College of Information Studies at the University of Maryland (the first author), talked with the then Director of the Prince George's County Memorial Library System (PGCMLS) in Maryland about the possibilities of working together to provide a computer training program for older adults that would improve their e-health literacy. The training would focus on finding reliable health information online, and use a series of pre-written lessons designed especially for older adults by the National Institute on Aging (NIA), part of the National Institutes of Health (NIH). Such a program would allow an academic institute and a local organization to combine their resources to better serve the community. Students in the Master of Library Science (MLS) program of the college would provide the instructional staff for the training course while public libraries would provide the physical space and networked computers. In this way, the MLS students could gain valuable experience working in a public library setting and with older adult patrons while older adults in the community could have the opportunity to learn to use computers and the Internet to meet their health information needs.

After receiving full support from Ms. Freeny, this faculty member prepared and submitted grant proposals and subsequently received funding from the National Library of Medicine of the National Institutes of Health (through the National Network of Libraries of Medicine) and complementary funding from the Community Partners Program of the University of Maryland to carry out this project. These funds allowed the hiring of a semester-long full-time Graduate Assistant (GA), an MLS student with an interest in pursuing a career as a public librarian and a professional background in adult education, to work on the project in the fall 2007 semester. Meanwhile, the Hyattsville branch library of the PGCMLS, due to its convenient geographic location near the university and its readily available facility and staff, was identified as the first branch library to offer the computer classes.

In late August, we designed the recruitment flyer, in which we deliberately chose to use the images that would represent diversity, hoping that, in doing so, we could send a strong message to our potential participants that this would be a program for every older adult, regardless of their gender or ethnicity. Once the flyer was ready, we began focusing on the promotion of this project on two fronts that went side-by-side. On the library side, two librarians of the Hyattsville branch library sent copies of the flyer to each of the branch libraries of the PGCMLS and posted many more at the Hyattsville branch library. Perhaps more importantly, these librarians also spent a great deal of time making personal phone calls as well as writing personal emails to the mangers of other branch libraries to secure their full support in promoting this project among their patrons.

On the non-library side, the GA made multiple phone calls and physical trips to local senior-oriented organizations (e.g., senior centers, community centers, nutrition centers, churches, and pharmacies) to ask for permission to hang our flyers at their facilities and then began distributing flyers to their various locations. We also contacted and sent our announcement to several local newspapers. During our initial contact with these organizations, the OASIS senior center, located very near the Hyattsville Library, expressed exceptionally strong interest in and support for our project (see *Collaborations/Partnerships* below for more details on our interactions and collaborations with the OASIS senior center).

Initial Offering (Fall 2007)

Originally, the flyers asked interested individuals to come to an information session in early September to sign up for classes. However, due to lack of lead time between when the flyers were distributed and when the information session was held, this strategy was not very successful. Although we had initially hoped to have 40–50 older adults come to this session, the actual attendance turned out to be extremely disappointing: only five older adults—two men and three women. Unfortunately, after we explained in more detail what this project was about, both men decided to not take our classes—one man who lived in Virginia said that it would be too much driving for him to come to Hyattsville, Maryland twice a week for four weeks, and the other man felt that the training classes would be "too basic" for him given his current computer skills. Fortunately, all three women who came to the information session showed strong interest in taking our training classes.

The enthusiasm we felt from these three women gave us enough confidence to start our first training session the following week. Between the time of the information session and the first class began, two other women called the library to take the class. Thus, we were able to have a total of five students in our first class.

At this point, we decided to change our recruitment strategy. We sent out new flyers but this time we asked those who were interested to call the adult services desk at the Hyattsville library. The librarians logged all of the calls and referred each interested older adult to the Project Manager (the first author), who passed the information on to the GA. The GA—and later, a volunteer MLS student from the College of Information Studies—called each patron, answered questions about the class, and scheduled him or her for an upcoming session.

Once we started the first round of classes, we began getting phone calls from interested patrons on a regular basis. In addition to the new system of enrolling students, word-of-mouth from these first five students helped boost interest in the course. In addition, many library patrons saw the class in action when they went to the library for other purposes, and then decided to sign up for the class. *We found that the best advertising is the product itself!*

A second group of students began two weeks later. This class was held on Mondays and Wednesdays and because classes were now being offered four days a week, a greater number of library patrons were exposed to the program, and this generated more interest in the classes. The October/November sessions filled quickly, as did the November/December sessions. Our waiting list was growing rapidly. To address some of this demand, an afternoon session was added in late October, increasing the offering to two morning classes and one afternoon class.

Even with this newly added afternoon class, all interested patrons could not be accommodated in a timely fashion. By the end of October, we ceased actively promoting this project at all branch libraries of the PGCMLS. All branch libraries were asked to tell any interested patrons that no class would be available until late January; however, if the patron was still willing to leave his or her name and contact information, the libraries would place him or her on the waiting list. Even with these adjustments, more patrons signed up and our waiting list continued to expand.

Our training classes at the Hyattsville branch library continued until mid-December. By this point we had trained more than 50 older adults in the computer classes.

Expansion and Continuation (Spring 2008–June 2009)

Due to the holidays, the University's winter break, and cold weather, we did not hold any class sessions from mid-December to late January. Starting at the end of January 2008, we resumed our training classes at the Hyattsville branch library as planned. We also began planning and preparing for classes at a second training site: the New Carrollton branch library of the PGCMLS. Recruitment flyers were distributed through senior centers and community centers in New Carrollton, and we offered the first training class at New Carrollton, which began in mid-February of 2008. Since then, we have been continuously offering computer classes at both the Hyattsville and New Carrollton libraries. By the end of June 2009, we had trained more than 200 older adults at these two public libraries. The waiting list for the class continues to grow and enthusiasm for the training remains high. Our trainees have shown tremendous excitement for the program through personal comments to the instructor and library staff, class evaluations, and their dedicated attendance of classes for the entire program. Many have even requested to take the class again because they found it to be so useful (detailed data on our trainees' perceptions of the computer classes can be found in Xie & Bugg, 2009).

BENEFITS OF THE PROGRAM

There are a number of benefits to library customers and the library: first, older adults become more confident because they are able to use computers to find materials and access information through library databases and the Internet; second, as older adults become more proficient and less dependent upon library staff for service, library staff will have more time to help other customers; and third, many older adults see the value of the public library and they may, in the future, contribute to the library.

In addition to the benefits received by our older adult trainees, this program also benefits the MLS students who serve as instructors of the computer training classes. These students gain important instructional and class preparation experience and a strong subject background in consumer health informatics. Students interested in working in a public library setting gain a skill that is becoming increasingly important in this type of setting—the ability to get patrons in the door for useful and engaging public programs. Student instructors also find that the experience is fulfilling because the older adults are so appreciative for the help in learning to use a computer. Many of the older adults described how family members were usually "too busy" to teach them. The MLS students also have the opportunity to see older adults outside the stereotypes portrayed in the mainstream media, which often show them as reluctant to learn new technology. The students have found that the older adults who participated in the computer training classes were an attentive and highly appreciative audience who were motivated to take on new challenges and participate in the electronic world.

COLLABORATIONS AND PARTNERSHIPS: MAJOR FACTORS BEHIND OUR SUCCESS

During the course of this project, we have developed multiple extremely productive partnerships, which have greatly contributed to the success of this project. First, we formed—and strengthened—a strong, active, enthusiastic, dedicated, on-going partnership between the College of Information Studies of the University of Maryland and the PGCMLS. This partnership has not only allowed this project to have a site—and since Spring 2008, two sites—for the training classes, but also facilitated the development of a new mechanism: that is, an academic unit that trains future librarians collaborating with public libraries to better serve the community, which can optimize both the short-term success and long-term impact and sustainability of this project.

To date thirteen MLS students have already been involved in this project in various ways: as the course instructor, as the assistant course instructor, or as the scheduler who makes phone calls to schedule interested patrons into a class. Their involvement in this project has been made possible through a diverse range of mechanisms. Some students have worked on the project through full-time or part-time graduate assistantships funded through the grants, others have received course credit for participation in the project by enrolling in a field study or independent study course, and others have simply chosen to volunteer in order to gain more professional experience. On the library side, seven librarians at different hierarchical levels—the director of the PGCMLS, managers of the Hyattsville and New Carrollton branch libraries, the heads of adult services at these two branch libraries, and library staff—have been deeply involved in and making significant contributions to this project. This highly qualified and dedicated team with complementary expertise has been one of the most important contributing factors to the success of this project.

The success of this project is to a large extent due to the ability of all parties involved to work well together enthusiastically and collaboratively. For instance, there is daily communication between the Project Manager, the MLS students involved in this project, and the library staff though emails, phone calls, and in-person meetings. This open and regular communication has allowed all potential problems to be tackled collaboratively and for solutions to be implemented quickly. There has also been a strong willingness on the part of all parties involved to be flexible in adjusting the schedule in order to better accommodate as many students as possible and as fast as resources allow.

Secondly, we have formed important partnerships with senior centers in Prince George's County, especially the OASIS senior center, who expressed exceptionally strong interest in and support for our project. After initial discussions about ways for collaboration, we have come to the agreement that, given the circumstances (that the OASIS senior center did not have the ideal facility to be a site for this project because all of its six computers were crowded into a very small room back to back that would not have any space for the instructors or a computer projector, but the center was geographically very close to the Hyattsville library), the best approach to a productive partnership would be for the OASIS senior center to help promote this project among its members and send its members to the Hyattsville library to take the training classes. This arrangement turned out to be very fruitful because many of our trainees were sent by the OASIS senior center. The strong and continuing partnership with the OASIS senior center in Hyattsville has also greatly contributed to the success of this project.

Thirdly, we have formed a partnership with the National Institute on Aging (NIA) of the National Institutes of Health. During prior interactions with the NIA, Dr. Xie learned that the NIA had already developed a Toolkit—"Helping Older Adults Search for Health Information Online"—to help trainers train older adults to use the NIHSeniorHealth and MedlinePlus Web sites for health and medical information. This Toolkit at the time was not yet publicly available; luckily, Dr. Xie was able to convince the NIA that our project would be a great opportunity to try out their material at a real site. Thus, the NIA has provided us with the entire Toolkit to use for this project.

This NIA Toolkit teaches trainers how to train beginning, intermediate, and more advanced students by providing easy to follow instructions for the trainers and also in-class and take-home exercise handouts for the students. It provided us with several step-by-step lessons designed specifically for teaching older adults how to find health information on the NIHSeniorHealth and MedlinePlus Web sites. Having these well-designed lesson plans greatly aids in having effective instruction and minimizes planning time for the trainer. Without this ready-to-use Toolkit of lessons, it would have been much harder to recruit students to deliver the instruction. It also would have taken much longer to start the project, and required additional monetary resources if we had had to design the lesson plans from scratch. The feedback we have received from our students and also the instructors suggests that the NIA curriculum, which made the lessons extraordinarily pedagogically sound and well-paced, has been another major reason for the success of our project.

A fourth major factor contributing to the success of this project is need. Despite the prevalence of computers in our society, many individuals still do not have the computer skills necessary to perform basic tasks or the economic resources to acquire the skills in other settings. The public library offers the classes at no charge, and older adults see the library as an accessible, trusted and valued institution where their needs for learning can be met.

CHALLENGES ENCOUNTERED, LESSONS LEARNED, AND POTENTIAL SOLUTIONS

Though this project has been, by and large, incredibly successful, it has not been without challenges. These challenges, which will be described below along with lessons learned and potential solutions, fall into four general categories:

classroom/facility challenges, computer reservation challenges, resource limitations, and teaching challenges.

Classroom/Facility Challenges

Teaching in a non-traditional classroom environment such as a public library can raise a number of issues. Because our class occupies several library computers—all located in a public area of the library—for two-hour periods of time, patrons have occasionally become upset when they are not able to use the computers during these times. There have also been a few complaints about the noise generated from the class in a space that is normally supposed to be quiet. However, as patrons have gotten used to our presence and seen what an important service we were providing, the complaints have gone away. Some initially upset patrons even signed up to take the class themselves!

Use of a public area has sometimes caused other problems. Our computer classes typically begin at 9:00 a.m., with the library opening to the public at 10:00 a.m. Therefore, each two-hour class overlaps with public computer reservations for one hour. An electronic computer reservation system sometimes closes down terminals during class and gives them to other library customers. When this happens, library staff are forced to explain to the other customer that this reservation is a system error, and he/she then moves the customer to another terminal. Very seldom, a customer refuses to surrender the terminal and he/she uses the computer sitting in the middle of the class during learning activities.

The physical arrangement of the computers within the libraries also created a few obstacles in the beginning. At one library, the computers are lined up facing a cement block wall. Using a projector to demonstrate points in the lessons added no value as it was difficult for class members to see the projected images in the brightly lit room and they needed to turn on a 90-degree angle for viewing. We eventually abandoned the use of the projector and instead now walk back and forth behind the participants, demonstrating points on their computers as necessary. This also makes the class feel informal and participatory rather than like a prescribed lecture.

The physical layout of the computers also limits how many students we can accept per class. At the same branch library mentioned above, there are 10 computers set up in a row at the area where we provide the training classes. We initially planned to use all the computers and enroll 10 students in each class. However, we learned that one of the 10 computers cannot be used for our training classes because it is a library catalog computer that does not provide generalized access to the Internet. This computer divides the row of Internet accessible computers, which makes it impractical to use the computers to one side, limiting the class to seven spaces.

A further classroom/facility challenge is that the computers at some libraries have multiple versions of Internet Explorer. This presents a major challenge when instructing students to use features that vary by color or location depending on version of the browser. Version control by the library would be helpful to both the new learners and to the instructor.

Computer Reservation Challenges

Another major lesson we have learned is that we need to be very patient with the computer reservation system at the library sites. Most public libraries use an electronic reservation or queuing system to allocate computer time to public users. The branch libraries of the PGCMLS use a reservation system, which allows more flexibility than would a queuing system; however, it still involves some manipulation by library staff in order to ensure uninterrupted two hour sessions for our students, within the context of a computer use policy that offers 30 minute sessions to the general public. When the classes start before the library is open to the public, staff must merely override the preset session time after each user logs in, extending the user's 30 minutes to 120 minutes.

More complex and uncertain is blocking out two hour sessions for classes that begin after the library is open (e.g., for the afternoon classes that we offered from late October to mid-December 2007). For each computer, staff must create a series of four reservations, 30 minutes apart. To avoid interruptions by an automatic reboot after each 30 minutes, staff must cancel the three remaining reservations on each computer after each user has logged in to extend the first reserved session to 120 minutes. When the library is open, there is a risk that during the short gap when the reservations are adjusted, the reservation will be assigned to a library patron. The staff must then negotiate with the library patron to return the computer to the class member.

Teaching Challenges

The instructors of the program have had some challenges learning to work with the older adult population. While some of our instructors have had some experience teaching adult education classes, none have had experience working with a class exclusively for older adults.

For one, instructors have to be cognizant of age-related disabilities such as hearing loss, low vision, and arthritic hands. These physical challenges require special attention and some adjustments. For hearing difficulties, instructors may need to speak louder and use strategies to ensure information is communicated in other ways, such as through handouts. Also helpful is using a teaching assistant who can assist students individually if they miss some of the instruction. For arthritic hands, an alternative to using the mouse—which can be the primary difficulty for these students—is to show students the up/down arrow keys. For low vision, the students may need to increase the font size of the screen text. More suggestions for teaching older adults in a program such as this can be found in the "Recommendations for public libraries Interested in starting similar programs" section.

Another challenge is getting participants to arrive on time and to come consistently. Because participation is voluntary and the classes are free of charge, participants are willing to miss class to attend to other commitments. This disrupts the continuity of learning and requires that the instructor or assistant take extra time to get students caught up with the lessons. A possible solution would be to have one or two "make-up" classes after each session is over. The instructor could repeat lessons that students may have missed without disturbing the flow of the class. It is also important to emphasize to class members the importance of coming to class on time and consistently.

Resource Limitations

Resource limitations, in terms of both time and money, have presented further challenges. For one, we quickly learned that non-teaching related activities (e.g., setting up the equipment, scheduling)—are a lot more time consuming than we had previously anticipated (fortunately, we were able to find a volunteer from the college to help with the scheduling, which helped greatly).

We also learned that handouts—especially color copies—cost a lot more money than we originally calculated. Originally, we were planning to make color copies of the training materials—as recommended by the developers of the materials, the NIA—for our students. However, we quickly realized that providing color handouts would be too costly: The lowest estimate we could get was over $1000 for just 25 copies of the training handouts. We found this to be cost-prohibitive and settled for black and white copies of the student handouts. Fortunately, we were able to obtain two complete sets of color copies of the training materials for the instructors directly from the NIA. However, we still are using black and white copies for the student handouts. We hope to find a way in the future to be able to provide color copies of the handouts to students, as the color version is easier to read—the students who have taken the class treasure the handouts and want them even when they miss a class. Their only suggestion was that they could get color copies so that they could see the information on the handouts more clearly.

Because the classes have become really popular and the waiting list has been getting longer, the biggest resource-related challenge in the future will be trying to accommodate the number of students who are interested. This will require funding to pay for the instructor(s) and enough copies of the handouts.

RECOMMENDATIONS FOR PUBLIC LIBRARIES INTERESTED IN STARTING SIMILAR PROGRAMS

To help public libraries nationwide to adopt this model and start similar programs in their own communities, we offer the following recommendations:

Tips for Program Administrators

1. Seek funding and establish partnerships early, particularly if you do not have a facility at which to offer the class. Find partners who have a similar mission so that the collaboration will be mutually beneficial.

2. Market the plan through both flyers and community announcements as soon as possible, preferably at least two weeks before you hope to have the first class. Ask directors at senior centers to make actual announcements to their members about the class and to provide the

flyers to their members. As classes start, invite potential students to stop by and observe if they are interested. Also, ask current students to spread the word.

3. Once classes have begun, make sure that there is regular and honest communication between all parties. Daily emails are one way to accomplish this. With regular, open communication all parties can work effectively together to quickly solve issues as they arise. Also, this avoids any parties having the feeling of being "left out" of the decision making process.

4. Embrace volunteers who would like to help with the class. Volunteer work can save a lot of time and frustration.

5. Regular communication between the teacher, the volunteers, the library staff, and the program administrator also proved to be very useful. It is especially important for the teacher and any teaching assistants to communicate what goes on in the classroom so that the administrator and library staff can deal with any potential issues before they become problems. Regular communication also ensures that all stake holders know what is going well in the class so that those aspects can be capitalized on.

6. Allocate resources to establish a computer lab if at all possible.

7. Find instructors who have experience and are interested in working with older adults.

8. If a private room (e.g., a computer lab in a separate room) is not available, it might be helpful to place a sign over the computers to notify the regular patrons that a class is in session.

9. Provide headphones. The class was held at least partially during public hours and headphones were essential for listening to the audio portions of the lessons.

10. Support of the library staff. Without the support and assistance of the staff at the library, this class could not be successful. Extra effort was required to schedule the computers, organize the equipment and assist with the classes.

11. Offer a class for Spanish-speaking older adults if the demographics indicate a need. MedlinePlus has a Spanish-language version.

Tips for Teachers

1. Begin each class by repeating tasks or reviewing vocabulary or concepts learned from previous class sessions. For example, the instructor can always make a point to ask the students before each class to show the instructor where such things as the hard drive was located physically, or what terms like the "World Wide Web" mean.

2. Make sure that students get practice using the computers by asking them to log on to the Internet in order to prepare for that day's lesson. This allows the students to get as much hands-on experience as possible with the computers.

3. As an instructor you want to try to talk as little as possible. This way the students stay fresh mentally and do not get bored with the lesson plan.

4. Provide individual assistance. Walking back and forth behind the class members and stopping to point things out on the computer screen is very effective in keeping everyone focused and ensuring that every participant is following along.

5. Giving the students a 10-minute break at the halfway point of the class is important because it allows them to use the restroom, get a drink of water or just get up and stretch their muscles.

6. Always provide handouts to help reinforce the learning.

7. Engage trainees in collaborative learning activities. In the NIH SeniorHealth lesson plan, there is a script that provides opportunities for students to engage in collaborative learning. Students would step away from the computers and read aloud a script, learning about health conditions and then applying that knowledge using the SeniorHealth homepage. Instructors who used these scripts and methods were rewarded with better class participation and enthusiasm on the part of their students. There was a wide variation in the level of understanding and experience with computers within each group—rarely was there a group with a homogeneous skill set. Because of the instructional design, all participants had to proceed at the same pace, a pace that included a great deal of repetition and very basic steps. While this was very well suited to those without much experience with computers, it could also mean losing the interest of the ones who had already mastered the basics. Engaging the more experienced participants in helping the less experienced kept everyone focused. Class members were delighted to share tips with those sitting next to them.

8. Have an assistant instructor help the less experienced users. Otherwise, it may be difficult to maintain the pace of the lessons, particularly the earlier ones in the session. The assistant should be engaged with each participant and watchful of those falling behind or needing extra assistance.

9. Expect that many students will not have an understanding of basic computer concepts. These concepts often interfered with successful completion of the lesson. When explained, however, these concepts helped our trainees complete the lessons successfully. Examples include (but are not limited to): the nature of the Internet, the definition of a Web address/URL, hyperlinks and the semantics of multi-layered Web pages, navigational tips/tricks, the role of an Internet browser, and the difference between a database and a Web page.

10. Incorporate personal examples into lessons. The class members enjoyed sharing and hearing personal examples that were relevant to the class topics. These should be integrated into the instruction as much as possible.

11. Be aware that double-clicking to open a page or program is a difficult skill for some. Offer an alternative to those individuals by clicking once with the mouse and hitting enter.

12. Be flexible. The lessons in some cases could be accelerated and in others, slowed down. The instructor needs to use his or her judgment to gauge the abilities of the class and find ways to keep all class members engaged while not losing those with less advanced skills. Going off the lesson plan was necessary at times to keep things moving.

13. Never assume students understand. Instead, constantly check their comprehension by verbally quizzing students throughout the class on the material we have covered and providing hands-on activities in each class session so students demonstrate their understanding. The "comprehension checks" worked well with the older adult population.

14. Encourage the participants to supplement the skills that they learn in the class with additional computer training, and provide them with the information they need to follow up. Often computer skills classes are offered at the library or a local community center. As with any newly learned skill, practice is required to maintain a comfort level.

15. Instruct the class participants in how to identify quality information on the Internet early in the curriculum and repeat this regularly with examples throughout the set of lessons. Have the class members make comparisons of Web sites that contain health information and have them point out the clues that indicate whether the sites are trustworthy. Knowing what to look for to evaluate a Web site is an essential skill and should be part of every lesson.

16. Ensure that every participant understands that the class is about learning to use the computer to find quality health information, not about email or learning how to shop on the Internet. The skills they learn in the class will transfer to these other activities, however.

17. Allow time for conversations among the participants, even if it reduces the amount of time for the formal lessons. Forming bonds and sharing information about health and personal issues enhanced the learning environment and provided a form of socialization that many seemed to enjoy.

18. Other successful teaching factors include: using a slow, loud tone; repeating when necessary; creating a welcoming environment; encouraging questions; keeping the class on schedule; stopping to help struggling students; having a sense of humor; and utilizing creative/inventive teaching methods to create interest.

CONCLUSION

Though many public libraries are providing free Internet, free WiFi and computer equipment, the public now expects computer instruction from its local libraries. Many public systems are already pursuing these endeavors. Older adults are generally neglected in the realm of computer adoption, but the public library is a trusted institution where they feel comfortable taking computer classes. In the county where the classes were hosted, the Parks and Recreation Department currently offers a number of computer classes, yet patrons walk through the doors of the public library daily, asking for help with computers. They expect the public library to offer classes, likely due to the nature of information itself that causes this expectation: County residents understand that computers deliver information that is crucial to their learning and personal or professional goals. They do not expect the Parks and Recreation Department to offer such services, since libraries offer information services. Parks and Recreation refers to leisure activities, and computers are not leisure devices: in truth, they are crucial tools of survival in today's world. This is why many seniors turn to the public library when they need help with information access. Quite often, an older adult has suffered technostress in the chasm of the digital divide. He or she has functioned for many years without learning computer skills, and a moment arises where avoidance of the computer is no longer possible.

Librarians are the "missing link" between the library users and the information technology professional. We have the unique privilege of connecting a customer to his/her desired information. Many older adults struggle in a state of denial regarding the ubiquity of computers in human culture today. While some of our youngest computer users are uploading photographs to their facebook accounts, navigating complex databases and exercising advanced searching skills, many computer "have-nots" are walking into the public library for the first time to confront the computer. We have the opportunity to show them that the computer is not the enemy, but a useful tool that empowers them to perform tasks quickly and efficiently. The Internet and Web open a new world that becomes accessible through their fingertips. Combined with the valuable print collection of the public library, this kind of information access redefines the public library in the mind of the older adult. He/she already values the library as a repository of history and culture, but a new kind of respect develops for the library as a true information center. The older adult's crucial shift in mental paradigm is invaluable, since he/she understands the true empowerment that comes from the public library.

Teaching older adults how to use computers can be challenging and rewarding at the same time, particularly because while many of the class participants could identify the computer mouse, using one for the first time was quite an adventure for some. An instructor could be unprepared for the difficulty with manual dexterity that many had while learning to use the mouse, including the inability to "double-click." However, an instructor could also be unprepared for other things, such as the excitement the class participants exhibited at finally knowing how to get information that is ubiquitously advertised with a "w-w-w-dot...," the surprise and delight the participants expressed that the public library was offering these services and use of the computers for free, and how friendships between class participants invariably bloomed during the four-week sessions.

ACKNOWLEDGMENTS

This project has been funded in whole or in part with federal funds from the National Library of Medicine, National Institutes of Health, under Contract No NO1-LM-6-3502. The University of Maryland's Community Partners Program (CPP) provided complementary funding for this project. We thank the PG

County public library administrators and staff and MLS students in the College of Information Studies at the University of Maryland who generously and enthusiastically helped to carry out this project.

REFERENCES

Andrus, M. R., & Roth, M. T. (2002). Health literacy: A review. *Pharmacotherapy, 22* (3), 282–302.

Asla, T., Williamson, K., & Mills, J. (2006). The role of information in successful aging: The case for a research focus on the oldest old. *Library and Information Science Research, 28*, 49–63.

Ballard-Reisch, D. S. (1990). A model of participative decision making for physician-patient interaction. *Health Communication, 2*, 91–104.

Brody, D. S. (1980). The patient's role in clinical decision-making. *Annals of Internal Medicine, 93*, 718–722.

Bundorf, M. K., Wagner, T. H., Singer, S. J., & Baker, L. C. (2006). Who searches the Internet for health information? *Health Research and Educational Trust, 41* (3), 819–836.

Bundy, A. (2005). Community critical: Australian public libraries serving seniors. *Aplis, 18*(4), 158–169.

Bylund, C. L., Sabee, C. M., Imes, R. S., & Sanford, A. A. (2007). Exploration of the construct of reliance among patients who talk with their providers about Internet information. *Journal of Health Communication, 12*(1), 17–28.

Chatman, E. A. (1991). Channels to a larger social world: Older women staying in contact with the great society. *Library and Information Science Research, 13*, 281–300.

Curzon, P., Wilson, J., & Whitney, G. (2005). Successful strategies of older people for finding information. *Interacting with Computers, 17*, 660–671.

Dunn, L. (2005). The fairfield seniors survey project. *Aplis, 18*(2), 76–78.

Fox, S. (2006). *Online Health Search*. Washington D.C.: PEW Internet & American Life. Available at http://www.pewinternet.org/pdfs/PIP_Online_Health_2006.pdf.

Fox, S. (2007). *E-patients with a disability or chronic disease*. Washington D.C.: PEW Internet & American Life. Available at http://www.pewinternet.org/pdfs/EPatients_Chronic_Conditions_2007.pdf.

Gollop, C. J. (1997). Health information-seeking behavior and older African American women. *Bulletin of the Medical Library Association, 85*(2), 141–146.

Jones, R. A., Morrow, G. D., Morris, B. R., Rites, J. B., & Wekstein, D. R. (1992). Self-perceived information needs and concerns of elderly persons. *Perceptual and Motor Skills, 74*, 227–238.

Jones, J. A., & Phillips, G. M. (1988). *Communicating with your doctor: Rx for good medical care*. Carbondale: Southern Illinois University Press.

Kaiser Family Foundation. (2005). *e-Health and the elderly: How seniors use the Internet for health information*. Available at http://www.kff.org/entmedia/upload/e-Health-and-the-Elderly-How-Seniors-Use-the-Internet-for-Health-Information-Key-Findings-From-a-National-Survey-of-Older-Americans-Survey-Report.pdf.

Kutner, M., Greenberg, E., Jin, Y., & Paulsen, C. (2006). *The Health Literacy of America's Adults: Results from the 2003 National Assessment of Adult Literacy (NCES 2006–483)*. U.S. Department of Education. Washington D.C.:

National Center for Education Statistics. Available at http://nces.ed.gov/pubs2006/2006483.pdf.

McNutt, R. A. (2004). Shared medical decision making: problems, process, progress. *JAMA, 292*, 2516–2518.

Moore, B. B., & Young, C. C. (1985). Library/Information services and the nation's elderly. *Journal of the American Society for Information Science, 36*(6), 364–368.

Norman, C. D., & Skinner, H. A. (2006). eHealth literacy: essential skills for consumer health in a networked world. *Journal of Medical Internet Research, 8*(2), e9.

Sit, R. A. (1998). Online library catalog search performance by older adult users. *Library and Information Science Research, 20*(2), 115–131.

U.S. Census Bureau. (2008). *An older and more diverse nation by midcentury.* Available at http://www.census.gov/Press-Release/www/releases/archives/population/012496.html.

U.S. Census Bureau. (2009). *Annual estimates of the resident population by sex and selected age groups for the United States: April 1, 2000 to July 1, 2008 (NC-EST2008-02).* Available at http://www.census.gov/popest/national/asrh/NC-EST2008/NC-EST2008-02.xls.

U.S. Department of Health and Human Services. (2000). *Healthy People 2010: Understanding and Improving Health (Chapter 11: Health Communication).* Washington, D.C.: Author. Available at http://www.healthypeople.gov/Document/HTML/Volume1/11HealthCom.htm.

Van Fleet, C. (1989). Public library service to older adults: Survey findings and implications. *Public Libraries, 28*(March/April), 107–113.

Wicks, D. A. (2004). Older adults and their information-seeking. *Behavioral and Social Sciences Librarian, 22*(2), 1–26.

Xie, B. (2003). Older adults, computers, and the Internet: Future directions. *Gerontechnology, 2*(4), 289–305.

Xie, B. (2008). Older adults, health information, and the Internet. *ACM Interactions, 15*(4), 44–46.

Xie, B. (in press). Older adults' health information wants in the Internet age: Implications for patient-provider relationships. *Journal of Health Communication.*

Xie, B., & Bugg, J. M. (2009). Public library computer training for older adults to access high-quality Internet health information. *Library and Information Science Research, 31*(3), 155–162.

Chapter 10

Plugging into Youth: Youth Library Services in the Digital Age/Era

Erin V. Helmrich and Erin Downey Howerton

INTRODUCTION

The Internet age has been an exciting yet tumultuous time for youth services in public libraries. In the Internet's infancy, libraries grappled with new issues of ensuring access and the explosion of information, only to suddenly face filtering constraints. Legislation on the federal, state, and local levels as well as lawsuits soon followed. The continued growth of information and the multiple ways to digitally access it mean that public libraries services have been in flux ever since.

Online access has had an enormous impact on services to youth, but after observation and research, librarians and researchers began to identify a growing digital divide in access to the Internet. While librarians have taken strides to harness the Internet in order to teach young people how to survive in the information age, public libraries have played a significant role in helping young people bridge the digital divide and expanding access to those who have only limited experiences online at home or in school.

The Internet access offered by public libraries has changed librarians' relationship with both information and our young patrons. The Internet has become an indispensable part of library services, both as a tool for reference and circulation and as a content delivery device for remote users. No longer are youth obligated to enter a library building to make use of resources; with the Internet, public librarians now have many means by which they can connect with young people and provide them with information experiences far from the library buildings. This constant access has only increased in importance with the advent of mobile Internet-capable devices such as cell phones and other personal electronic devices. Convenient, user-led communication with public libraries may allow these traditional institutions to morph from content warehouses to content factories, where youth manipulate information in new and exciting ways.

In this chapter, we will survey the history and current state of Internet access for and access by youth in public libraries. Through an exploration of legislation and legal decisions relating to Internet filtering and safety in public libraries, we will trace the development of the implementation infrastructure in which digitally mediated library programming for youth has occurred. We will illustrate Internet-mediated approaches that foster information literacy, reading, and leisure-focused activities that demonstrate that public libraries have found creative and innovative ways to engage young users and build lifelong library patrons.

LEGISLATIVE AND LEGAL CONCERNS FOR YOUTH IN THE INTERNET'S INFANCY

On October 24, 1995, the Federal Networking Council (FNC) unanimously passed a resolution defining the term Internet. They resolved that:

Internet refers to the global information system that—

(i) is logically linked together by a globally unique address space based on the Internet Protocol (IP) or its subsequent extensions/ follow-ons;

(ii) is able to support communications using the Transmission Control Protocol/Internet Protocol (TCP/IP) suite or its subsequent extensions/follow-ons, and/or other IP-compatible protocols; and

(iii) provides, uses or makes accessible, either publicly or privately, high level services layered on the communications and related infrastructure described herein. (Federal Networking Council [FNC], 1995, p. 13)

At nearly the same time, Yahoo! incorporated in 1995, and the Internet revolution was underway. In the years since 1995, the Internet has become a vital tool for daily life. Young people today did not experience a time when they did not have access to digital information and librarians must respond to their unique needs in order for public libraries to stay relevant into their adult years. When the generally quiet walls of the public library were suddenly torn down and access to and from the "real world" was not only very easy but also very threatening, the early years of Internet in public libraries by children and teens was marked by a preoccupation with access control and content filtering. Public librarians were concerned about the material young people could see and hear, and spent a great deal of time and energy on filtering Internet content, adhering to ever-expanding legislation and government intervention to protect children online, creating Internet usage polices, and, in some cases, requiring parental permission to access the Internet. For youth librarians who believed strongly in freedom of information, this time was fraught with anxieties about denying access and protecting the freedom to read online.

FILTERING, LEGISLATION, AND SAFETY

While many librarians were still taking tentative steps into digital communication, young people immersed themselves in the Internet. The growing interest in and use of the Internet by youth engendered their first encounters with government involvement in their information access. Fear of the new Internet frontier caused federal, state, and local governments to respond with many attempts to constrain this new information world with legislation.

The first of these legislative responses was the Communications Decency Act (CDA) passed by Congress in 1996. The CDA contributed two important ideas to considerations of Internet use. First, Title V of CDA affected Internet content providers by attempting to define and regulate indecency and obscenity based on standards used for television and print material. Second, Section 230 of CDA allowed for Internet service providers to not be considered publishers, thus not holding them liable for the indecent and obscene content they might transmit (U.S. Congress, 1995). Amidst contradiction, confusion, and numerous legal challenges, just a year later, the U.S. Supreme Court struck down the new law. The Court ruled that the Internet was entitled to the highest degree of free speech protection. In relating the decision of the Court, Justice Stevens noted that "the content on the Internet is as diverse as human thought," and that there is "no basis for qualifying the level of First Amendment scrutiny that should be applied to this medium" (*Reno v. ACLU*, 1997). The CDA's attempts to shield young people from obscene online communication was found to limit both children's and adult's access to a wide range of material and was deemed unconstitutional. Supporters of the CDA tried to rework its principles into new laws and proposed rating systems, but ultimately local librarians made decisions for their own communities. They diligently devised standards and policies that would work locally and preemptively before more legislative challenges could be presented.

Content filtering software, which allows only select Web sites to be viewed, seemed to be the tool that made lawmakers, communities, and parents feel "safe" with the Internet. Yet, youth librarians and other professionals with first hand knowledge of these blocking-based approaches knew what an inadequate solution filtering provided and that filters were not replacements for parental involvement in children's Internet use. Many public librarians knew that filtering measures were not effective because the filters were easy to work around and often blocked educational information and failed to block all objectionable content. For example, it was well known that words like "breast" were considered obscene and some filtering software would prevent a young person from conducting a search for "breast cancer." Researchers confirmed these real world experiences and studies were done to determine if filters provided reliable content control. For example, one study reported that a search engine which advertised itself as providing access only to safe sites, rendered more than

90% of non-obscene online content invisible (Electronic Privacy Information Center [EPIC], 1997). Bolstered with reports like those published by EPIC, the library community worked tirelessly to expose filters for the faulty tools they were.

The American Library Association (ALA), which had joined the court challenge to the CDA, passed a resolution on the use of filtering software in libraries in July 1997. ALA spokespeople stated that "the use in libraries of software filters which block constitutionally protected speech is inconsistent with the United States Constitution and federal law" (ALA, 1997, n.p.).

In contrast, immediately following the ALA resolution, President Clinton sided with the concept of voluntary filtering and proposed the "Strategy for a Family Friendly Internet" (Clinton, 1997). The goal was self-regulation and Netscape and Microsoft (the major Web browser companies at the time), declared that they would include filtering technology in their products so that parents could "choose from a variety of ratings systems to block sites that are inappropriate for children" (1997, n.p.). For youth librarians, the discussion of vendor-led filtering left them in a censorship conflict (Sobel, 2003). Suddenly freedom of information and access was threatened and librarians found themselves having to defend the work they were doing in trying to protect the rights of young people.

Despite ALA's objections, legislators worked to affirm President Clinton's support for content filtering. In 1998, Congress passed the Children's Internet Protection Act (CIPA), which made it a crime for commercial Web sites to display material that was deemed harmful to minors. Many of the plaintiffs who had succeeded in striking down the CDA challenged CIPA as unconstitutional and were affirmed by a federal judge in Philadelphia in February 1999 (*ACLU v. Reno*, 1999). Yet, a few years later, in June 2003, the U.S. Supreme Court declared the CIPA constitutional (*United States v. American Library Association*, 2003). The Court concluded that even though the filters may block access to necessary information, CIPA does not violate patrons' First Amendment rights, and that any organization that received federal funds must install filtering software blocks to information that can be defined as obscene, child pornography, or harmful to minors (Jaeger, Bertot, & McClure, 2004).

The Herrick District Library in Holland, Michigan found itself caught in the middle of the filtering mandate issue. In February 2000, voters in Holland rejected a ballot measure that would have required the city to withhold funding from the Herrick District Library unless it installed filters on all its public Internet workstations (Oder, 2000). Although filters were ultimately rejected at the Herrick District Library, similar challenges were taking place across the country. Local media published reports that groups like the Family Friendly Libraries (FFL) group, whose mission is to combat "the growing problem of Internet pornography and age-inappropriate materials in school and public libraries" (2007, n.p.), and the American Family Association, financed many of the efforts to enforce filtering rules (Sobel, 2003). Many public librarians resented the financial intrusion of national groups into local affairs.

Still, a positive outcome of the early years of the Internet was the proactive approach to Internet safety for young people. Librarians embraced the familiar role of helping their patrons navigate information seeking by providing resources, tips and advice for parents and young people. The focus on safety put the control of Internet use back in parents' hands and served as reminder that they are their child's best teacher. By focusing on safety and awareness, librarians and parents enabled young people with guidance to make their own decisions rather than controlling their online choices so tightly that they were denied the freedom of intellectual exploration and customary mistake-making.

One of the first exemplary public library programs that fused parental concern over their child's online activity with education and engagement was the Cyberkids Club program at the Canton Public Library, in Canton, Michigan. Launched in the summer of 1996, the program received the 1997 *Today Library of the Future* award from ALA. The program was an Internet orientation that included both parent and child signing a consent form; for the parents, their signatures meant they understood that the library cannot act in loco parentis. For children, signing the form meant that they must agree to follow the policies of the Cyberkids Room and to treat others with respect. Once both parties sign the form, the library gives the child a Cyberkids sticker.

While in some ways this program may sound restrictive or even dated in its approach, those of us on the front lines would not mind taking a little bit more control in educating young people and their parents to what's available, reliable, and safe. The Internet is now so ubiquitous that most libraries have taken a more hands-off role in how they engage young people with the Internet. Interestingly Cyberkids was referenced to during testimony for CIPA since it was such a positive example of how libraries could and should manage Internet usage without federal mandates (Schneider, 1997).

This proactive approach was supported by the efforts of groups like The National Center for Missing and Exploited Children, an early advocate for Internet safety. The Center developed informational material for public librarians to distribute to community members and established a program called *NetSmartz* that included education components designed for parents, educators, law enforcement officials, and, of course, young children and teens. *NetSmartz* has continued to evolve along with the Internet and now has modules to educate teens about using common sense and being aware while using social networking sites, as well as about the consequences of cyberbullying.

Promoting Internet safety and providing guidance was a natural progression for librarians. With the help of ALA, librarians developed policies, safety tips, and computer classes to help promote the positive and important experiences that could be had online when using the proper precautions.

DIGITAL PRESENCE: LIBRARY WEB SITES, HUMAN MEDIATION, AND INFORMATION QUALITY

The next step for most libraries in the early days of the Internet was to create their own online presences with Web sites. In September 1996, for example, there were 413 public library Web pages in 18 countries that could be accessed by using the directory of *Public Libraries with Gopher/World Wide Web Services* (Clyde, 1996). By March 2000, the number of public libraries accessible through his site had increased by approximately 48% to a total of 614.

During the early years, many librarians began their discussions of the Internet with youth by focusing on dissecting and defining Web addresses. The easiest patterns to teach young people were the differences between .com, .edu, .org, etc. While the perception is that young people are Internet- and technology-savvy, the reality is quite different. Though many young people are nimble with technology and online information, some of these young people do not know how to discern between good and bad sources of information (Dresang, 2005). Many public librarians also know that there are many young people who do not get as much time with computers as other children and they are not as nimble with their skills (Agosto, 2005; Hughes-Hassell & Agosto, 2006).

Again, librarians embraced their roles as information educators and selectors of the high quality sites. Youth librarians created classes and tools to teach young people about searching for quality information. They dedicated portions of their library Web sites to lists of recommended sites selected for young people's educational, recreational, informational, health-related, and developmental needs and interests. One study detailed the number of libraries that had Web sites for children, their content recommendations, and the roles these Web sites played in guiding children (Gillespie, 2000). One of the main conclusions of the study was that the majority of the library Web sites surveyed had the main goal of encouraging reading. However, the goal of promoting reading is no longer the primary focus of many library Web sites.

In 1995 the School of Information at the University of Michigan created the Internet Public Library (IPL). A few months after its launch, the IPL team debuted a dedicated children's section called KidSpace. The IPL was one of the first digital libraries and served as a model for how to build and maintain a selected directory of online information. The IPL served as a positive place for youth librarians to start the important conversation about the quality of information available online and how to discern what is inaccurate, commercially motivated, or unreliable.

MAINTAINING THE HUMAN PRESENCE WITH DIGITAL REFERENCE

Because the number of children seeking homework help online continued to grow, librarians provided more remotely accessible reference databases on their Web sites. While databases remain one of the most content-rich options for offering quality information in an online format, librarians struggle with how to market these products in a way that differentiates them from the Internet at large. To this end, human mediation in the form of online reference services was clearly still needed to guide children's navigation and information retrieval.

When remote reference first started in the mid-1990s it was typically an email-based service. While some young people may have used email reference, the later development of chat-based reference has engaged more young people. The chat interface is a much more familiar and comfortable platform for many young people to connect with librarians. These sorts of digital reference services are also helpful in bridging the discomfort and potential for a negative experience that many young people have when asking face-to-face reference questions (Gross, 2005). In fact, teen use of digital reference services has a great potential to improve them. In an interesting study published in 2005, researchers studied the transactions between young people and librarians answering questions on the subscription-based online service *tutor.com* and concluded that:

> Unfortunately, the librarians we studied seem to have grafted inferior versions of the communication styles and protocols of face-to-face reference onto some rather clunky software. It would be interesting to see what would happen if the designers of such online reference services followed the principles of good young adult library practice and involved the teens as active participants in both the planning and the delivery of the services. At the moment, teens are from Neptune, librarians are from Pluto. Better services would result if they could meet somewhere closer together in cyberspace. (Walter & Mediavilla, 2005, p. 10)

In order to engage young people, librarians who have adapted to, but were not born in, a digital world must understand the complex ways that teens use and feel about the Internet. In 2003, the Pew Internet and American Life Project commissioned a qualitative study of the attitudes and behaviors of Internet-using students in middle and high schools across the country (Levin & Arafeh, 2002). Five metaphors that describe how children use and think about the Internet emerged from the study:

> Metaphor 1. The Internet as virtual textbook and reference library. "Students think of the Internet as the place to find primary and secondary source material for their reports, presentations, and projects. This is perhaps the most commonly employed metaphor" Metaphor 2. The Internet as virtual tutor and study shortcut. "Students think of the Internet as one way to receive instruction about material they are interested in or about which they are confused or unclear" (Levin & Arafeh, 2002, p. 6). Metaphor 3. The Internet as virtual study group. This metaphor is aptly summed up by the following student comment: "So it's not just the paradigm where the Internet is the library. It's not the library, it's a chat room. . . . You talk with people from somewhere else, compare notes, or whatever." Metaphor 4. The Internet as virtual guidance counselor. As one explanation of this use of the Internet, consider these remarks: "I can find out what I expect in the next grades up, or, if I think a little further, what college I might attend. If someone recommends a university online and I'm interested, I can just pull up another window and search for that on the Web and find out more." Metaphor 5. The Internet as virtual locker, backpack, and notebook. This is one of the more intriguing uses of the Internet and shows just how very savvy these students are: The great thing about the Internet from my point of view is that it saves me having to carry two hundred pounds worth of books, my binders, my work, my whatever paper I'm working on. . . . I have all my stuff. I have a hotmail account. I e-mail myself every paper I am working on. . . . So, wherever I am, if I have a couple of free minutes, I get whatever paper I'm working on, go with it, and when I'm done, I e-mail it back to myself. (Levin & Arafeh, 2002, pp. 11–13)

Seeing the flexible, and in many ways trusting, ways youths interact with the Internet is eye-opening. The Pew study demonstrated that the services for teens must be consistent, familiar, and easy to access. It is important for librarians to

revisit their services for teens on a regular basis to ensure that they are continuing to meet the needs of their young patrons.

POLICIES CREATE DIGITAL DIVIDES

The digital divide is a major concern for youth-serving librarians. Even when
youth have access to equipment to use the Internet, they are often subject to a
variety of policies and restrictions that regulate what and when they can access
information online.

Public libraries that accept the federal E-rate subsidy are required to use
content filters on their computers. This filtering obligation pushed public
librarians into the roles of censors rather than selectors. Many commercial
filtering solutions use site classification and allow for the filtering of entire
categories of material online. For librarians, these designations may also mean
manually maintaining lists of sites that have been judged to be harmless and
lists of sites that are blocked. While some state libraries and consortia have
provided filtering software to their public libraries so that they can benefit from
the E-rate subsidy, many public libraries have had to purchase commercial
products (Sobel, 2003). Some of these commercially available filtering programs actually record user's actions online, and have been recently discovered
to have created a new income stream by disclosing young people's online
searches and chat logs to marketing agencies. These logs create an ethical
dilemma for public librarians who either do not have access to other filtering
programs or who lack staff with sufficient technical expertise to run a free or
open source filter (Yao, 2009).

Many public libraries also prohibit young people from using computers from
having the filter turned off or a particular site unblocked for access. When
young users are deprived of the right to access information, inequality of service
is institutionalized. While most public librarians would never deny a young user
access to a medical journal or anatomy book, some of the same content online is
being filtered through software that cannot discern between hardcore pornography and medical terminology (Goodes, 2003).

Beyond the well-known flaws in content filters, many public libraries have
policies that restrict access to social networking sites. Social networking sites
like MySpace, Facebook, and Twitter are common methods of communicating
with family, friends, and even business contacts. Despite the failure of the
Deleting Online Predators Act (DOPA), which would have legislated the filtering
of all sites classified as social networking for organizations that receive E-rate
subsidies, to pass in the House of Representatives in 2006, some public libraries have elected to use their filters to block these sites or simply forbid their
use altogether. These libraries' policies justify blocking access to social
networking sites based on claims that the sites waste bandwidth and encourage
patrons to tie up computers with activities other than business or research.
Young users are especially affected when public library computers are the only
ones they have to communicate with other people online (Tapscott, 2009).
Thus, the bias against social networking enforces two classes of patrons—those
who are engaging in sanctioned activities that restrict users to a narrowly
defined concept of what is productive in the library and on the Internet, and

those who are using unsanctioned new tools to collaborate and stay in touch (Lenhart, 2009a).

Young people are able to engage in more productive learning activities online when they have more freedom and access to the Internet. *Technology Review* columnist Wade Roush quoted Henry Jenkins, director of the Comparative Media Studies Program at MIT, on restricting young people's access to the Internet:

> The impact on youth from economically disadvantaged families is what Jenkins worries about most. "Already, you have a gap between kids who have 10 minutes of Internet access a day at the public library and kids who have 24-hour-a-day access at home," he says. "Already, we have filters in libraries [required under the Child Internet Protection Act of 2001] blocking access to much of the Internet. Now we're talking about adding even more restrictions. It exaggerates the participation gap—not a technology gap, but a difference in access to the defining cultural experiences that take place around technology today." (Roush, 2006, n.p.)

Freedom to access the Internet without content or time restrictions is much more valuable than tightly limited experiences that allow little room for experimentation. Free access is an especially major benefit for youth who lack adequate access elsewhere. Additionally, the Internet can serve as a "third space" in the community for those young people who lack a place other than home and school to which they belong and where they can fully participate. Danah Boyd asserts that these interstitial spaces are ones that youth have always had to create for themselves, and that these spaces are increasingly online and increasingly mobile:

> Given the structures of their lives, teens have often had very little control over their social context. In school, at home, at church . . . there are always adults listening in. Forever more, there have been pressures to find interstitial spaces to assert control over communications. Note passing, whispering, putting notes in lockers, arranging simultaneous bathroom visits, pig latin, neighbor to neighbor string communication . . . all of these have been about trying to find ways to communicate outside of the watchful eyes of adults, an attempt to assert privacy while stuck in a fundamentally public context. The mobile phone is the next in line of a long line of efforts to communicate in the spaces between. (Boyd, 2008, n.p.)

To enable this teen-controlled space, public librarians need to develop policies that treat mobile users with equity. Although the gap is closing, there remains a large divide between different socioeconomic and racial groups of both adults and youth who primarily use their cell phones to access to the Internet. Urban, minority youth tend to access the Internet via cell phones while suburban teens have Internet access via home connections and pricey laptops (Horrigan, 2009; Lenhart, 2009b). When public libraries privilege desktop or laptop computer use over the use of mobile technology, they may be cutting off a whole swath of young people from utilizing library resources. Also, making library resources accessible from mobile devices is increasingly important as the number of mobile users increases. If public libraries do not offer their resources in the modes of information experiences familiar to young users, they will be less likely to spontaneously use them.

WHERE DO WE GO FROM HERE?

To provide youth with optimal online access and content, public librarians must continually assess how and why this user group is making use of the Internet. Librarians should be able to identify the programs, services, and information that their key constituencies need to access, whether this means tweaking the user interfaces for databases aimed at young people; reassessing policies and procedures to make sure that youth are able to make use of the library's wireless access with their Internet-capable devices; or providing a way for young people to upload content.

For example, some devices have little use to young people unless they are used in concert with Internet access. Small hand-held video cameras are within the budget of many youths who might not be able to afford a computer. Editing and uploading video content online with free Web-based software is possible but requires the use of an unrestricted computer with a reliable Internet connection. The explosion of small Internet-ready devices, including mobile phones that can connect to computers using Bluetooth, and gaming devices that can take pictures and upload them to the Internet, means that many young people need access to desktop computers to manipulate their content intermittently, but access to connectivity constantly.

Today's youth live in a culture in which they are actively engaged in participating with content as much as they are engaged in consuming content. Their digital culture of creation and experimentation is one where text, pictures, video, and music can be easily threaded together to create something new. Lawrence Lessig, founder of Stanford Law School's Center for Internet and Society, says that we live "in a world in which technology begs all of us to create and spread creative work differently from how it was created and spread before ... " (Lessig, 2008, p. xviii). And nowhere is Lessig's contention more evident than in a public library, designed specifically to collect and distribute creative work. Libraries are expanding beyond the concept of simple information warehouses and librarians must work together to create a new perception of the public library in the digital world.

School Library Journal blogger Joyce Valenza and columnist Doug Johnson asserted that librarians must embrace a new idea of what young people should be able to accomplish in a library:

> Libraries need to change from places just to get stuff to places to make stuff, do stuff, and share stuff. Our libraries should not be grocery stores. We need to use those groceries, to open the boxes, pour the milk, mix the batter, make a mess ... We need production space. We need to serve up our creations in presentation or story space. We need to inspire masterpieces of all sorts. And we need to guide members of our communities through new library metaphors. (Valenza & Johnson, 2009, n.p.)

Although they are talking about school libraries, their insights definitely also apply to public libraries. No matter how wonderfully equipped a school library, the fact remains that when school is out, the public library meets young people's information needs.

As the Internet has become ubiquitous in our society, some public libraries have responded by making different equipment and devices available to youth. The Darien Library of Connecticut has a "Creation Station" in a suitcase that includes a laptop (with various free and commercial software), a video camera, a voice recorder, a digital camera, and a tri-pod. The Creation Station enables young people (or people of any age) to quickly, easily, and affordably get the tools they need to create content at the library. The Public Library of Charlotte and Mecklenburg County in North Carolina also provides Internet-ready creation equipment. Their youth-centric ImaginOn facility houses a multimedia production space with all the equipment to allow patrons to dabble in various types of animation, music production, and filming. Their facility also boasts a sound recording booth. Other libraries in their system can use a portable animation studio that allows for a full multimedia production experience complete with video editing, animation, and sound creation software. These libraries have made Internet-ready creation space and tools a priority for youth, and all signs indicate they will keep innovating in order to stay relevant to young patrons as technology evolves and changes (Public Library Association, 2009; Public Library of Charlotte & Mecklenburg County, 2009).

As more materials such as e-books, downloadable audiobooks, and other media are offered via the Internet, the question of equity becomes even more urgent. Young people may be solely dependent on a reliable Internet connection at a public library to access these materials. While nearly all public libraries offer open access to the Internet in their buildings, use policies vary from library branch to library branch, from workstation to workstation, and from user group to user group. In some instances, young people must rely on adults in their families to provide the access that they need to use digital library materials, and so often cannot choose whether or when the resources are available. In order to promote the highest equity of access, public librarians should provide ways for children and teens to upload and download content at library locations, using library resources.

Providing youth-tailored access means that librarians must make connectivity a primary concern for their services. Offering multiple ways to access information and materials is the future of library services; being able to reach users wherever they are is paramount. The ability to provide information access experiences through a variety of devices not only helps patrons become more informed about their preferences for using devices, but it also promotes the use of library collections and resources.

Public libraries have the duty to look forward in order to meet the needs of youth in a digital age. Youth can benefit from exposure to developing technology and exposure to the Internet. The Internet's power to connect young people is second only to the similar power of books. Public librarians have the opportunity to embrace this role and shape our libraries to meet this growing need. The ability to create and share their own stories is an important mode of self-expression for young people, and if they have the means to do this in the library, their lives can be forever changed. The ability to access library resources through the Internet can help young people shape those stories in different and unexpected ways, empowering youth to make use of all the information that is available to them instead of only what is sitting on our physical shelves. By working to eliminate the inequities of access that currently exist, public libraries are poised to help young people build an informed and empowered future.

REFERENCES

ACLU v. Reno, 31 F.Supp.2d.473 (U.S. District Court, Eastern District of Pennsylvania 1999).

Agosto, D. E. (2005). The digital divide & public libraries: A first-hand view. *Progressive Librarian, 25*, 23–27.

American Library Association. (1997, July 2). *Resolution on the use of filtering software in libraries.* Available at http://www.ala.org/Template.cfm?Section =ifresolutions&Template=/ContentManagement/ContentDisplay.cfm &ContentID=78171.

Boyd, D. (2008, November 11). How youth find privacy in interstitial spaces. Available at http://www.zephoria.org/thoughts/archives/2008/03/09/how _youth_find.html.

Clinton, W. (1997, July 16). Remarks by the President at an event on the E-Chip for the Internet. Available at http://clinton3.nara.gov/WH/New/Ratings/ 19970716-6738.html.

Clyde, L. A. (1996). The library as information provider: The home page. *Electronic Library, 14*, 549–558.

Dresang, E. (2005). The information-seeking behavior of youth in the digital environment. *Library Trends, 54*(2), 178–196.

Electronic Privacy Information Center. (1997). *Faulty filters: How content filters block access to kid-friendly information on the Internet.* Available at http://epic .org/reports/filter_report.html.

Family Friendly Libraries. (2007). About us. Available at http://www.fflibraries.org/ About_Us_1.html.

Federal Networking Council. (1995). *FNC resolution: Definition of "Internet" 10/24/95.* Available at http://www.nitrd.gov/fnc/Internet_res.html.

Gillespie, M. P. (2000). *Public library Web pages for children: A content analysis.* MLS Master's Thesis, University of North Carolina, Chapel Hill.

Goodes, P. A. (2003). Kaiser study: Filters impede health research. *American Libraries, 34*(1), 20.

Gross, M. (2005). *Studying children's questions: Imposed and self-generated information.* Lanham, MD: Rowman & Littlefield Publishers, Inc.

Horrigan, J. (2009). *Wireless Internet use.* Washington, DC: Pew Internet & American Life Project.

Hughes-Hassell, S., & Agosto, D. E. (2006). Planning library services for inner-city teens: Implications from research. *Public Libraries, 45*(6), 57–63.

Jaeger, P. T., Bertot, J. C., & McClure, C. R. (2004). The effects of the Children's Internet Protection Act (CIPA) in public libraries and its implications for research: A statistical, policy, and legal analysis. *Journal of the American Society for Information Science and Technology, 55*(13), 1131–1139.

Lenhart, A. (2009a). *The democratization of online social networks.* Washington, D.C.: Pew Internet and American Life Project.

Lenhart, A. (2009b). *Teens and mobile phones over the past five years: Pew Internet looks back.* Washington, D.C.: Pew Internet & American Life Project.

Lessig, L. (2008). *Remix: Making art and commerce thrive in the hybrid economy*. New York: Penguin.

Levin, D., & Arafeh, S. (2002). *The digital disconnect: The widening gap between Internet-savvy students and their schools*. Available at http://www.pewinternet.org/reports/.

Oder, N. (2000). Michigan town rejects filters. *Library Journal, 125*(5), 12–13.

Public Library Association. (2009, November 11). Shepard Fairey, Lawrence Lessig, Steven Johnson REMIX it up at NYPL. Available at http://plablog.org/2009/02/shepard-fairey-lawrence-lessig-steven-johnson-remix-it-up-at-nypl.html.

Public Library of Charlotte & Mecklenburg County. (2009). Imaginon: Programs and events. Available at http://www.imaginon.org/programs_&_events/default.asp#tech.

Reno v. ACLU, 521 U.S. 844 (Supreme Court of the United States 1997).

Roush, W. (2006). The moral panic over social-networking sites. *Technology Review*. Available at from http://www.technologyreview.com/communications/17266/?a=f.

Schneider, K. G. (1997). Cyber Kids: A recipe for success. *American Libraries, 28*(8), 80.

Sobel, D. L. (2003). Internet filters and public libraries. *First Reports*. Nashville, TN: First Amendment Center.

Tapscott, D. (2009). *Grown up digital: How the net generation is changing your world*. New York: McGraw-Hill.

United States v. American Library Association, 539 194 (Supreme Court of the United States 2003).

U.S. Congress. (1995). *Telecommunications Act of 1996*. Available at http://www.fcc.gov/Reports/tcom1996.txt.

Valenza, J. K., & Johnson, D. (2009, November 11). Things that keep us up at night.

Walter, V. A., & Mediavilla, C. (2005). Teens are from Neptune, librarians are from Pluto: An analysis of online reference transactions. *Library Trends, 54*(2), 209–227.

White House. (1997, July 17). *A family friendly Internet*. Available at http://clinton3.nara.gov/WH/New/Ratings/.

Yao, D. (2009). Web-monitoring software gathers data on kid chats: Web-monitoring software reads kids' private messages and sells data to advertisers. Available at http://www.abcnews.go.com/print?id=8494258.

Chapter 11

Persons with Disabilities and Physical and Virtual Public Library Settings

Jonathan Lazar, Paul T. Jaeger, and John Carlo Bertot

INTRODUCTION

Public libraries have long sought to meet the information needs of patrons with disabilities and include them in library activities. Prior to the rise of the Internet in libraries, primary concerns for meeting the needs of patrons with disabilities focused the provision of materials in alternate formats and designing buildings to allow access for all members of the community. The Internet and related technologies, however, present many more complicated problems in ensuring equal access, ranging from the lack of availability of accessible resources, to the fact that many electronic resources are not controlled by the library, to the interactive nature of Web 2.0 technologies. These issues will grow more pronounced as the population continues to age and more patrons develop age-related disabilities. This chapter provides an overview of the history of accessibility in libraries, approaches to creating and implementing accessible and usable library Web sites and electronic resources, and strategies for meeting the challenges of accessibility in the Internet age to ensure equal access for all patrons.

THE EVOLUTION OF PUBLIC LIBRARY ACCESSIBILITY

In the United States, 54 million people have a disability, while the number of persons with disabilities worldwide is more than 550 million (Albrecht & Verbugge, 2000; Metts, 2000). The number of Americans age 55 or older is increasing rapidly as a percentage of the total population (U.S. Census Bureau, 2000). As a result, the number of persons with disabilities will grow significantly in the next few years as the baby boom generation ages, since the majority of persons with disabilities are over the age of 55 (Jaeger & Bowman, 2005). While the percentage of the population with disabilities is sizeable and increasing, the Internet has become an essential platform for information, communication, and interaction in contemporary societies (Fox, 2006; Fox & Madden, 2005).

As the primary social access point for the Internet and as the guarantors of digital library resources, public libraries clearly have need to ensure that the electronic services that they provide meet the needs of patrons with disabilities. The Internet and electronic resources, however, present new challenges for public libraries in terms of equal access. For example, one of the major challenges in providing equal access to social networking and other Web 2.0 services is that these new services are based in communication rather than information provision, requiring different conceptions of what equal access entails (Jaeger & Xie, 2009). The public library legacy of meeting the information needs of person with disabilities, though, dates back to a century before the Internet.

Providing equal access for persons with disabilities was a commitment among public libraries many decades before it was a commitment among other social and government institutions. The first library services specifically for persons with disabilities were tactile print book libraries for the blind at state schools for the blind in the mid-1800s (Lovejoy, 1983). By the beginning of the 1900s, many larger public libraries had their own collections of materials in alternate formats (Brown, 1971). In sharp contrast, the federal law guaranteeing a public elementary and secondary education to persons with disabilities was not passed until the 1970s. Prior to the Internet age, the struggles of equal access focused primarily on physical issues—buildings, transportation, communication systems, and public environments (Barnartt & Scotch, 2001). In libraries, the main issues were providing materials in alternate formats for patrons with a range of different disabilities and ensuring that patrons with mobility impairments could get into and navigate the buildings.

The majority of public libraries now have mission statements explicitly asserting that the library provides equal access and services to all patrons, including persons with disabilities, in both physical and electronic contexts (Jaeger, 2002). Public libraries have traditionally incorporated new information-related assistive technologies as they have become available for acquisition—Braille, large print, talking books, reading machines, video enlargement, electronic texts, screen readers, and screen magnifiers, among others (McNulty, 2004).

Public libraries are also central to national and state efforts to disseminate materials in alternate formats to persons with disabilities. Since the founding of the Library of Congress's National Library Service (NLS) for persons with disabilities that distributes materials in alternate formats such as Braille, cassette, and disc in 1931, public libraries have served as the backbone of the NLS (Dziedzic, 1983). Public libraries comprise many of the regional and sub-regional libraries in the system, while many public libraries not officially part of the system house demonstration collections and refer patrons to the NLS (Dziedzic, 1983). Further, many public libraries have developed their own parallel programs tailored to the needs of the persons with disabilities in their communities. In addition, the Library Services and Construction Act (LSCA) was amended in the mid-1960s to provide funding to state libraries to enhance services to patrons with disabilities, particularly through public libraries.

Along with individual public libraries, the American Library Association (ALA) has a history of outreach to persons with disabilities. The ALA created its first set of standards for patrons with disabilities in 1961. It now has a statement on "Access to Electronic Information, Services, and Networks" (2000) and a "Library Services for People with Disabilities Policy" (2001). The preamble of the later includes the firm assertion the ALA "is dedicated to eradicating inequalities and improving attitudes toward and services and opportunities for people with disabilities" (2001, p. 1). As a result, public libraries must consider the accessibility not only of buildings and tangible resources, but of computers, software, digital libraries, and other electronic resources.

The need to provide equal access to electronic resources for persons with disabilities not only results from the values of librarianship, it also has roots in federal law. The United States has a range of laws—including Section 504 of the Rehabilitation Act, Section 508 of the Rehabilitation Act, the Americans with Disabilities Act, the E-government Act, and the Telecommunications Act—that require accessibility for electronic information and services for entities receiving federal funds, with a number of these laws relating to public libraries (Jaeger, 2004; Jaeger & Bowman, 2005).

The challenges of inclusive access to electronic resources have received attention in the professional literature. Recent literature on the practice of providing inclusive services to patrons with disabilities has included papers focusing on: specific Internet-related contexts of library Web sites (Ballas, 2005; Jaeger, 2002; Yu, 2002), online resources (Schmetzke, 2005; Stewart, 2005), digital libraries (Bell & Peters, 2005), and assistive technologies (Vaccarella, 2001). Other papers have included accessibility of electronic resources as part of more general discussions of inclusion of patrons with disabilities in library practice (Auld & Hilyard, 2005; Hawthorne, Denge, & Coombs, 1997; Holt & Hole, 2003; Mendle, 1995; Oliver, 1997; Will, 2005). In spite of the attention these issues have received, they merit greater focus by individual libraries and coordination between libraries. To help facilitate an increased understanding of these issues and ways to effectively address them, this chapter will next present a detailed exploration of the development, testing, and implementation of library Web sites and other electronic resources that are accessible and usable.

As many library services are now being offered online, one of the greatest challenges is ensuring that these networked information services are accessible for people with disabilities. There are multiple aspects to accessible online library services—not only the library Web sites with information available for all users, but also services available only to registered patrons, the registration processes (such as signing up for and/or logging into a library account) for those library patrons, as well as the digital libraries which library patrons have access to through their logins (Bertot, Snead, Jaeger, & McClure, 2006). These digital libraries and other services, since they are typically provided by outside firms, are sometimes the hardest to manage in terms of accessibility (Byerley & Chambers, 2002). While it would be ideal if accessibility requirements are noted in the original contract when the library acquires access to these digital libraries, what happens if the digital libraries start out accessible, but over time, as the digital library changes, the services become inaccessible? This is actually a quite common phenomenon, where natural modifications to a Web site over time lead to increased problems with accessibility (Hackett, Parmento, & Zeng, 2004; Lazar & Greenidge, 2006).

What does it mean to make an accessible Web site? In theory, it means that people with all types of disabilities can technically access all portions of the Web site. People with various impairments may use different types of assistive technologies, such as screen readers, refreshable Braille displays, alternative keyboards, alternative pointing devices, and speech recognition. For these individuals to be able to use a site, it must be flexible enough to work with all of these assistive technology devices. That does not mean a text-only Web site; in fact, the visual appearance of the Web site does not need to change in any way to become accessible (Lazar, 2006). Rather, additional features are built into the back-end code, so for instance, there are textual descriptions of images and graphs, navigation is not only provided by a clickable image map but also by textual links (which can be reached via a keyboard), and videos have transcripts of the audio portion (Lazar, Allen, Kleinman, & Malarkey, 2007). These are just a few of the examples of what specific features make a Web site accessible.

The reality is that it is not sufficient to simply tell developers to "make your site accessible." Therefore, an accessible Web site often is defined as a Web site that follows a set of design guidelines. While design guidelines are never perfect, they are the best tool in ensuring accessible Web sites. There are multiple sources for design guidelines—the research community, non-governmental organizations, and both federal and state-level laws. Often, these various sets of design guidelines are intertwined. Even with design guidelines (which are discussed below in more detail), accessibility does not happen overnight. Nor does it happen without careful planning. In the case of library Web sites, most public libraries in the United States already have existing sites. While Web sites might be modified on an almost daily basis, a full redesign of a site may happen once every year or two. It is therefore important to include accessibility as a goal for the next redesign of the Web site (Lazar, 2006). Even if a Web site already is accessible, the redesign process is more efficient and effective if accessibility is a design goal in a project—when accessibility features are easy to add, rather than as a retrofitting after-the-fact. While existing Web sites can be retro-fitted for accessibility, it is more challenging to retrofit than to include accessibility features in the first place.

WEB ACCESSIBILITY GUIDELINES

The World Wide Web Consortium (www.w3.org) sponsors the Web Accessibility Initiative (www.w3.org/wai), which has a number of sets of guidelines. The set of guidelines that is most relevant for web designers is the Web Content

Accessibility Guidelines, known as WCAG. Other guideline sets include those for user agents, rich Internet applications, and authoring tools. The WCAG provides guidance on how to build web pages that are accessible to people with disabilities. WCAG 1.0 originally was approved in 1999 (http://www.w3.org/TR/WCAG10/). Those guidelines were then used in creating the web guidelines for Section 508 in the United States. Section 508 is the set of rules that addresses people with disabilities in the procurement and development of information technology by the U.S. federal government (http://www.section508.gov/).

The specific section of Section 508 that deals with web pages is section 1194.22, "Web-based intranet and internet information and applications." Those rules were approved by the U.S. Access Board (http://www.access-board.gov) at the end of 2000, to go into effect in mid-2001. The Section 508 rules for web pages were based on the WCAG 1.0, and the law even clearly provides a comparison table that shows how Section 508 was based on WCAG. Those Section 508 laws then influenced state-level laws, which generally came into place a few years after Section 508. For instance, in the State of Maryland, the new web accessibility laws required all state government Web sites to be accessible by 2005, using the exact same set of guidelines as Section 508 (http://doit.maryland.gov/policies/Pages/nva.aspx). These different sources (NGO, federal-level, state-level) each provide similar, but not exactly the same, guidelines.

Currently, the web accessibility guidelines are undergoing revision. The newest version of the WCAG, version 2.0, was approved in December 2008 (http://www.w3.org/TR/WCAG20/). All Section 508 guidelines are undergoing revision (known informally as the "508 refresh"). TEITAC (the Telecommunications and Electronic and Information Technology Advisory Committee) made recommendations to the U.S. Access Board on how to implement the 508 refresh (see http://www.access-board.gov/sec508/refresh/report/) in April 2008, and the accessibility community is now awaiting action from the Access Board. The suggestions from TEITAC clearly reference both the current Section 508 guidelines, as well as the WCAG 2.0.

Whether or not they realize it, the Section 508 guidelines apply to most public libraries in the United States. The federal government makes complying with Section 508 standards a requirement of the receipt of many types of federal funds, including a large number of funds distributed as "pass through dollars," funds that are given to states to award to public agencies within the state. As a result, almost every public library receives funding—directly or indirectly—that is attached to Section 508 compliance (Jaeger, 2002). In addition, public libraries are covered by and expected to comply with several other key federal disability rights laws, such as the Americans with Disabilities Act, that include equal access to technology among the general components of equal rights for persons with disabilities (Jaeger, 2004). A number of states have their own legal requirements for libraries to provide equal access to technology for persons with disabilities (Fagan & Fagan, 2004). While public libraries typically are not checked for compliance with guidelines for accessible technology by federal and state government agencies, compliance with Section 508 guidelines and the provision of equal access to technology is clearly an expectation of public libraries.

Guidelines are often considered to be the final word on accessibility, although the guidelines generally aren't perfect. For instance, accessibility guidelines often focus on perceptual (visual and hearing) impairments and motor impairments, but leave out cognitive impairments (Lazar, 2007). There are multiple reasons for this. There is not enough research done yet on the human-computer interaction needs of people with various cognitive impairments (such as Down Syndrome, Autism, Amnesia, and Dementia, which are each incredibly different from one another). Whereas there is generally a very good understanding of how people with perceptual or motor impairments utilize computers, we really don't have a full understanding yet of how people with cognitive impairments use computers (Jaeger & Bowman, 2005). Furthermore, people with perceptual or motor impairments generally want to achieve the same task goals as someone without impairments, and they just utilize different input or output devices. Someone with a cognitive impairment often may have different task goals (Lazar, 2007). Even the 2008 TEITAC report with recommendations to the U.S. Access Board did not come to any consensus on guidelines for cognitive impairment, noting that any such guidelines couldn't be specific, couldn't be measured, and therefore would be impossible to achieve.

DIFFERENCES BETWEEN ACCESSIBILITY AND USABILITY FOR PEOPLE WITH DISABILITIES

In addition to the needs of people with cognitive impairments not being met, there is often another challenge with web accessibility guidelines. Accessibility is not the same as usability (Theofanos & Redish, 2003). Accessibility means that a Web site, software application, or operating system can technically be accessed by someone using an assistive technology input or output device. Technical accessibility, however, does not necessarily equate to an interface that is easy to use. There is a big gap between accessibility and usability of interfaces for people with disabilities (Theofanos & Redish, 2003). A perfect example of the gap between accessibility and usability is in the form of web-based human-interaction proofs (known as HIPS or CAPTCHAs). A HIP is a test to determine whether someone is a human or a computer, to help avoid bots and viruses from automatically signing up for thousands of accounts and logins. The most common HIP is text that appears twisted or garbled, where the human user has to decipher the text, but the idea (in theory, at least), is that a computer bot could not decipher the text. Figure 11.1 shows an example of a visual CAPTCHA. Clearly, someone with a visual impairment could not use this CAPTCHA, as it would be technically impossible. Some Web sites now offer audio CAPTCHAs, which offer the same idea, except that the words read are provided in garbled audio. Again, the idea (in theory, at least) is that a human could listen to the sounds and decipher the text, but a computer bot could not. ·

Figure 11.1 Sample CAPTCHA.

The reality is that multiple studies have shown that blind users are only successful with audio CAPTCHAs less than 50% of task attempts (Bigham & Cavender, 2009; Sauer, Holman, Lazar, Hochheiser, & Feng, 2009). This is an example of an interface that may be technically accessible, but with a task success rate below 50%, is simply not usable (Lazar, 2006). This is something to be aware of when digital library vendors claim that their sites are accessible: ask if they have done any type of user testing, and ask how easily users were able to perform the tasks. User-based testing, where representative users attempt to perform representative tasks, is the best way to determine the usability of the Web sites. While automated usability software tools (such as Bobby, WebXact, Watchfire, InFocus, Deque RAMP, etc.) claim to replace the need for both usability testing and expert inspections, these claims fall short, as the software tends to give misleading results (Jaeger, 2006, 2008; Mankoff, Fait, & Tran, 2005). Automated usability software often misses true problems, while simultaneously flagging other interface features as poor when in fact they are both accessible and usable for people with disabilities (Lazar, Feng, & Hochheiser, in press).

ACCESSIBILITY OF LIBRARY WEB SITES

Generally, since a large majority of libraries receive both state and federal government funding in the United States, they usually are covered by either state or federal rules relating to web accessibility for people with disabilities. The focus of this chapter is on public libraries, not specialized libraries or library services, such as the National Library Service for the Blind and Physically Handicapped, sponsored by the Library of Congress. As mentioned earlier in this chapter, there are at least two major foci on web accessibility in the public library world: the library Web sites themselves, and the web-based digital libraries which public library patrons access. Unfortunately, it's impossible to get a clear picture of exactly what accessibility levels are today, since many of the published studies on this topic are a few years old. However, the following review will present some historical context from this decade on the topic of library Web site accessibility.

Early in this decade, accessibility problems were reported with many of the commercial digital libraries and commercial databases offered to library patrons (Byerley & Chambers, 2002). In a study from 2005, it appeared that improvements had been made in many digital libraries; however, only the basic search features tended to be accessible, and while technically accessible, were still not easy to use (Stewart, Narendra, & Schmetzke, 2005).

One study examined the accessibility of public library Web sites. A study of the most popular public libraries in the United States, during the year 2000, found that only 18.9% (14/74) of public library home pages were fully accessible (Lilly & Van Fleet, 2000). It's important to note that originally 100 library Web sites were selected for the study, but in 2000, an earlier time in web design, 26 of those libraries did not even have a Web site (Lilly & Van Fleet, 2000). Another study of research libraries in 2008 found that 16.5% (20/121) of libraries studied offered a separate text-only version of the home page (Hazard, 2008). This is not considered to be good accessibility practice, as having a separate text-only home page often leads to an accessible home page which is out of date and does not provide current content (Hazard, 2008).

In a 2002 study, Spindler evaluated a cross-section of university library Web sites across the United States for accessibility. Of the university library home pages studied, 42% (79/188) were found to be accessible (Spindler, 2002). More specifically, the Web sites for library schools, and the corresponding university libraries, have also been evaluated for accessibility. In data collected in 2006, Comeaux and Schmetzke examined the accessibility of 56 university library science colleges/schools (49 in the United States, 7 in Canada) and found that 41% of the home pages of library schools in the United States were found to be accessible, without any recognizable accessibility violations (Comeaux & Schmetzke, 2007). The home pages of the campus libraries themselves were also examined, and 55% of the home pages (for the U.S. universities) were found to be accessible. It's important to note that some top-level pages on the respective Web sites were also examined. For both library schools and campus libraries, the accessibility percentages were a bit higher in Canada; however, there was a very small number sampled. In addition, it was shown that between 2002 and 2006, both library school web pages and campus library web pages showed an improvement in regards to accessibility (Comeaux & Schmetzke, 2007). In other studies of non-library Web sites, accessibility was shown to decrease over time (Hackett, Parmanto, & Zeng, 2004; Lazar & Greenidge, 2006), so this is certainly a good sign for the library schools.

It's important to note that most of the previous studies examined only the home page of a Web site. Some recent research indicates that often, lower-level pages of a Web site may actually be more accessible than the home page, so that analysis of pages below the home page may be useful (Hackett & Parmanto, 2009). At the same time, other research indicates that using automated software tools for testing can provide misleading results and human evaluation is far more accurate (Jaeger, 2006, 2008; Mankoff, Fait, & Tran, 2005). All of the previously mentioned studies of library web accessibility use automated software evaluation of accessibility. However, it's impractical to do both human evaluation and evaluation of multiple levels (potentially thousands) of pages within a site (Hackett & Parmento, 2009). Some trade-offs are involved, and a middle ground (e.g. human evaluation of the home page, and a maximum of 5 top-level pages) may need to be reached.

In addition to the research discussed above, a wide range of studies have attempted to measure the accessibility of various kinds of Web sites. As a result of the Section 508 guidelines and other government requirements, a particular focus of investigations has been the accessibility of e-government Web sites (e.g., Ellison, 2004; Marincu & McMullin, 2004; Stowers, 2002; World Markets Research Centre, 2001). More broadly, studies of the accessibility of Web sites have also focused on education, employment, academic, retail, tourism, airline, distance learning, and popular Web sites, among others (e.g., Coonin, 2002; Gutierrez, Loucopoulos, & Reinsch, 2005; Jackson-Sanborn, Odess-Harmish, & Warren, 2002; King, Ma, Zaphiris, Petrie, & Hamilton, 2004; Klein, Myhill, Hansen, Asby, Michaelson, & Blanck, 2003; Milliman, 2003; Ritchie & Blanck, 2003; Schmetzke, 2003; Shi, 2006; Sloan, Gregor, Booth, & Gibson, 2002; Thompson, Burgstahler, & Comden, 2003; Witt & McDermott, 2004). While the quality and depth of these studies varies considerably, many of these studies offer different approaches to the study of accessibility that can provide lessons for public libraries that wish to determine the best ways to conduct accessibility testing.

ACCESSIBILITY OF ONLINE INFORMATION

Information content produced by governments, health organizations, publishers, corporations, libraries, aggregators, researchers, and others is increasingly produced in digital formats—often only in digital format. These digital contents can take a variety for forms and hold a range of media formats such as text, images, voice, streaming video, and more. Though these formats can enhance the user's experience with information, each of these modes of information, and the ways in which providers present this content to users, presents both opportunities and challenges in terms of accessibility.

As discussed earlier in this chapter, technology clearly offers substantial potential to make digital content accessible to individuals with any number of disabilities. Indeed, through diligent design, libraries can provide persons with disabilities a range of tools that facilitate access to digital content, both inside the library as well as through a library's digital presence—thus better serving those individuals who are unable to come to the public library. By using a combination of adaptive technologies and accessible design, the public library can enhance greatly its service to users.

The challenge remains, however, that much digital content of interest to persons with disabilities is not content provided directly by the public library. For example, libraries license a range of resources from vendors, publishers, and aggregators. In this scenario, the library serves only as a gateway to content stored and accessed elsewhere, and thus in essence is simply a passive participant in the information exchange. Governments almost exclusively provide their resources and services electronically through e-government services—and increasingly require users to interact with government through these means. Though public libraries do not control these services, they do often serve as the primary point of contact between users and the service and/or resource. It is therefore critical that libraries consider accessibility in the larger context of all library-provided—either indirect or direct—services and create partnerships with a range of information service and resource providers (e.g., governments, state library agencies, vendors, health organizations) so that persons with disabilities can access content.

CONCLUSION

Technology offers substantial opportunities for the public library community to enhance its services to persons with disabilities. And yet technology also presents challenges as information content is created, combined, and presented in new and different ways. This complexity is also magnified by the range of information providers, many of whom only make available their services and resources in digital formats. Accessibility and service to persons with disabilities increasingly is not the lone purview of the public library, however. There are simply too many providers for libraries to not seek and enhance partnerships in order to better serve persons with disabilities in a comprehensive manner.

One key component of such partnerships are the many specialized libraries (i.e., libraries for the blind) that have substantial expertise in serving populations with disabilities. By working collaboratively, special and public libraries can demonstrate leadership and commitment to service to persons with disabilities—an increasingly growing segment of our population.

"Information is power, and a healthy democracy must guarantee access to this information and power equally for all of its citizens" (Hawthorne, Denge, & Coombs, 1997, n.p.). Public libraries have long recognized the potential of equal services to patrons with disabilities to increase community awareness and acceptance of persons with disabilities (Dziedzic, 1983). As libraries continue this commitment and further extend it into the online environment, libraries will serve critical roles in ensuring equitable access for all.

REFERENCES

Albrecht, G. L., & Verbugge, L. M. (2000). The global emergence of disability. In G. L. Albrecht, R. Fitzptraick, & S. C. Scrimschaw (Eds.), *The handbook of social studies in health and medicine* (pp. 293–307). London: Sage.

American Library Association (ALA). (2000). *Access to electronic information, services, and networks*. Chicago: Author.

American Library Association (ALA). (2001). *Library services for people with disabilities policy*. Chicago: Author.

Auld, H., & Hilyard, N. B. (2005). "That all may read . . ." *Public Libraries, 44*(2), 69–76.

Ballas, J. L. (2005). Does your library's website pass the usability test? *Computers in Libraries, 25*(9), 36–39.

Barnartt, S. & Scotch, R. (2001). *Disability protests: Contentious politics 1970–1999*. Washington, D.C.: Gallaudet University Press.

Bell, L., & Peters, T. (2005). Digital library services for all. *American Libraries, 36*(8), 46–49.

Bertot, J., Snead, J., Jaeger, P., & McClure, C. (2006). Functionality, usability, and accessibility: Iterative user-centered evaluation strategies for digital libraries. *Performance Measurement and Metrics, 7*(1), 17–28.

Bigham, J., & Cavender, A. (2009). Evaluating existing audio CAPTCHAs and an interface optimized for non-visual use. *Proceedings of the ACM Conference on Human Factors in Computing Systems (CHI)*, 1829–1838.

Brown, E. F. (1971). *Library services to the disadvantaged*. Metuchen, NJ: Scarecrow.

Byerley, S., & Chambers, M. (2002). Web-based library databases for non-visual users. *Library Hi-Tech, 20*(2), 169–178.

Comeaux, D. and Schmetzke, A. (2007). Web accessibility trends in university libraries and library schools. *Library Hi-Tech, 25*(4), 457–477.

Coonin, B. (2002). Establishing accessibility for e-journals: A suggested approach. *Library Hi Tech, 20*(2), 207–213.

Dziedzic, D. (1983). Public libraries. In F. K. Cykle (Ed.), *That all may read: Library service for blind and physically handicapped people* (pp. 309–326). Washington, D.C.: Library of Congress.

Ellison, J. (2004). Accessing the accessibility of fifty United States government Web pages: Using Bobby to check on Uncle Sam. *First Monday, 9*(7). Available at http://www.firstmonday.org/issues/issue9_7/ellison/index.html.

Fagan, J. C., & Fagan, B. (2004). An accessibility study of state legislative web sites. *Government Information Quarterly, 21*, 65–85.

Fox, S. (2006). *Online health search.* Washington, D.C.: Pew Internet and American Life Project. Available at http://www.pewinternet.org.

Fox, S., & Madden, M. (2005). *Generations online.* Washington, D.C.: Pew Internet and American Life Project. Available at http://www.pewinternet.org.

Gutierrez, C. F., Loucopoulos, C., & Reinsch, R. W. (2005). Disability-accessibiltiy of airlines' Web sites for U.S. reservations online. *Journal of Air Transport Management, 11*, 239–247.

Hackett, S., & Parmanto, B. (2009). Homepage not enough when evaluating web site accessibility. *Internet Research, 19*(1), 78–87.

Hackett, S., Parmanto, B., & Zeng, X. (2004). Accessibility of Internet Websites through Time. *Proceedings of the ACM Conference on Assistive Technology (ASSETS)*, 32–39.

Hawthorne, S., Denge, J., & Coombs, N. (1997). The law and library access for persons with disabilities. *Information Technology and Disabilities, 4*(1). Available at www.rit.edu/~easi/itd.htm.

Hazard, B. (2008). Separate but equal? A comparison of content on library web pages and their text versions. *Journal of Web Librarianship, 2*(2/3), 417–428.

Holt, C., & Hole, W. (2003). Training rewards and challenges of serving library users with disabilities. *Library Media Connection, 23*(6), 17–19.

Jackson-Sanborn, E., Odess-Hamish, K., & Warren, N. (2002). Web site accessibility: A study of six genres. *Library Hi Tech, 20*(3), 308–317.

Jaeger, P. T. (2002). Section 508 goes to the library: Complying with federal legal standards to produce accessible electronic and information technology in libraries. *Information Technology and Disabilities, 8*(2). Available at www.rit.edu/~easi/itd.htm.

Jaeger, P. T. (2004). Beyond Section 508: The spectrum of legal requirements for accessible e-government websites in the United States. *Journal of Government Information, 30*(4), 518–533.

Jaeger, P. (2006). Assessing Section 508 compliance on federal e-government websites: A multi-method, user-centered evaluation of accessibility for persons with disabilities. *Government Information Quarterly, 23*(2), 169–190.

Jaeger, P. T., & Bowman, C. A. (2005). *Understanding disability: Inclusion, access, diversity, & civil rights.* Westport, CT: Praeger.

Jaeger, P. T., & Xie, B. (2009). Developing online community accessibility guidelines for persons with disabilities and older adults. *Journal of Disability Policy Studies, 20*, 55–63.

King, N., Ma, T. H-Y., Zaphris, P., Petrie, H., & Hamilton, F. (2004). An incremental usability and accessibility evaluation framework for digital libraries. In P. Brophy, S. Fisher, & J. Craven (Eds.), *Libraries without walls 5: The distributed delivery of librarian ad information services* (pp. 123–131). London: Facet.

Klein, D., Myhill, W., Hansen, L., Asby, G., Michaelson, S., & Blanck, P. (2003). Electronic doors to education: Study of high school website accessibility in Iowa. *Behavioral Sciences and the Law, 21*, 27–49.

Lazar, J. (2006). *Web usability: A user-centered design approach.* Boston: Addison-Wesley.

Lazar, J. (2007). Introduction to Universal Usability. In *Universal usability: Designing computer interfaces for diverse user populations* (pp. 1–12). Chichester, UK: John Wiley & Sons.

Lazar, J., Allen, A., Kleinman, J., & Malarkey, C. (2007). What frustrates screen reader users on the web: A study of 100 blind users. *International Journal of Human-Computer Interaction, 22*(3), 247–269.

Lazar, J., Feng, J., & Hochheiser, H. (in press). *Research methods in human-computer interaction.* Chichester, UK: John Wiley and Sons.

Lazar, J., & Greenidge, K. (2006). One year older, but not necessarily wiser: An evaluation of homepage accessibility problems over time. *Universal Access in the Information Society, 4*(4), 285–291.

Lilly, E., & Van Fleet, C. (2000). Measuring the accessibility of public library home pages. *Reference and User Services Quarterly, 40*(2),156–165.

Lovejoy, E. (1983). History and standards. In F. K. Cykle (Ed.), *That all may read: Library service for blind and physically handicapped people* (pp. 1–24). Washington, D.C.: Library of Congress.

Mankoff, J., Fait, H., & Tran, T. (2005). Is your web page accessible? A comparative study of methods for assessing web page accessibility for the blind. *Proceedings of the ACM Conference on Human Factors in Computing Systems (CHI),* 41–50.

Marincu, C., & McMullin, B. (2004). A comparative analysis of Web accessibility and technical standards conformance in four EU states. *First Monday, 9*(7). Available at http://www.firstmonday.org/issues/issue9_7/marincu/index.html.

McNulty, T. (2004). Libraries, media centers, online resources, and the research process. In C. A. Bowman & P. T. Jaeger (Eds.), *A guide to high school success for students with disabilities* (pp. 117–131). Westport, CT: Greenwood.

Mendle, J. (1995). Library services for persons with disabilities. *Reference Librarian, 49/50,* 105–121.

Metts, R. L. (2000). *Disability issues, trends, and recommendations for the World Bank.* Washington, D.C.: World Bank.

Milliman, R. E. (2002). Website accessibility and the private sector: Disability stakeholders cannot tolerate 2% access! *Information Technology and Disabilities, 8*(2). Available at www.rit.edu/~easi/itd.htm.

Oliver, K. (1997). The spirit of the law: When ADA compliance means overall excellence in service to patrons with disabilities. *Public Libraries, 36*(5), 294–298.

Ritchie, H., & Blanck, P. (2003). The promise of the Internet for disability: A study of online services and website accessibility at centers for independent living. *Behavioral Sciences and the Law, 21,* 5–26.

Sauer, G., Holman, J., Lazar, J., Hochheiser, H., & Feng, J. (in press). Accessible privacy and security: A universally usable human-interaction proof. *Universal Access in the Information Society.*

Schmetzke, A. (2003). Web accessibility at university libraries and library schools: 2002 follow-up study. In M. Hricko (Ed.), *Design and implementation of web-enabled teaching tools* (pp. 145–189). Hershey, PA: Idea Group.

Schmetzke, A. (2005). Access to online library resources for all: Role of policy and policy change. *Interface, 27*(4), 4–11.

Shi, Y. (2006). The accessibility of Queensland visitor information centres' websites. *Tourism Management, 27,* 829–841.

Sloan, D., Gregor, P., Booth, P., & Gibson, L. (2002). Auditing accessibility of UK higher education websites. *Interacting with Computers, 14,* 313–325.

Spindler, T. (2002). The accessibility of web pages for mid-sized college and university libraries. *Reference and User Services Quarterly, 42*(2), 149–154.

Stewart, A. (2005). Accessibility and usability of online library databases. *Library Hi Tech, 23*(2), 265–286.

Stewart, R., Narendra, V., & Schmetzke, A. (2005). Accessibility and usability of online library databases. *Library Hi-Tech, 23*(2), 265–286.

Stowers, G. N. L. (2002). *The state of federal Websites: The pursuit of excellence.* Washington, D.C.: IBM Endowment for the Business of Government.

Theofanos, M., & Redish, J. (2003). Bridging the gap: Between accessibility and usability. *Interactions, 10*(6), 36–51.

Thompson, T., Burgstahler, S., & Comden, D. (2003). Research on Web accessibility in higher education. *Journal of Information Technology and Disabilities, 9*(2). Available at www.rit.edu/~easi/itd.htm.

U.S. Census Bureau. (2000). *Profile of General Demographic characteristics: 2000 Census of Population and Housing.*

Vaccarella, B. (2001). Finding our way through the maze of adaptive technology. *Computers in Libraries, 21*(9), 44–47.

Will, B. H. (2005). Library services for all. *Library Journal, 130*(19), 47.

Witt, N., & McDermott, A. (2004). Web site accessibility: What logo will we use today? *British Journal of Educational Technology, 35,* 45–56.

World Markets Research Centre. (2001). *Global e-government survey.* Providence, RI: Author.

Yu, H. (2002). Web accessibility and the law: Recommendation for implementation. *Library Hi Tech, 20*(4), 406–419.

Part **IV**

Institutions and Support

Public Library Funding: An Overview and Discussion

Denise M. Davis

INTRODUCTION

To understand public libraries, it is important to have an overview of their organization, funding, and operations models. Libraries are organized in a variety of ways, operating within legal geographic boundaries and within set governance structures. Sometimes one dictates the other. A library may provide service from a single building or through one or more outlets or bookmobiles. Often public libraries are referred to as "systems" whether they operate from a single building or more.

In Fiscal Year (FY) 2005 there were 9,198 public library systems in the United States providing services through 16,543 outlets and bookmobiles (National Center for Education Statistics, 2008). Fiscal year 2005 is the most current year for which comprehensive, national data were available at the time this chapter was written.

Of the 9,198 library systems, only 1,544 (16.8%) had more than one outlet (or building), and 700 (7.6%) had bookmobiles. The predominant national model of library service is through a single library outlet. The majority of public libraries serve smaller communities—78% of public libraries serve communities under 25,000 residents. Figure 12.1 presents the distribution of libraries by population served range.

Legal basis reflects the state or local law that authorizes the library to be funded, hire staff, and provide services to communities. The predominant legal basis in the United States—the type of local government structure within which the library functions—is municipal government. There are seven legal basis structures that are most common:

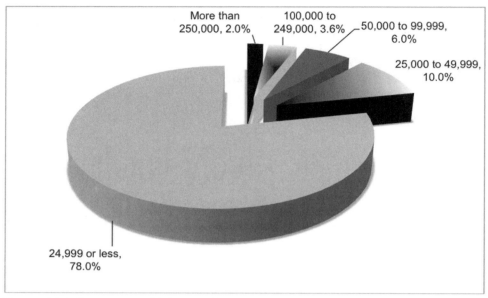

Figure 12.1 Percentage of Libraries by Population Served Range, Fiscal Year 2005.

- Municipal government (53%),
- City/parish or city/county (11.2%),
- Multi-jurisdictional (3.4%),
- Non-profit association or agency (14.8%),
- School districts (0.2%),
- Library districts (14%), and
- Other (e.g., Indian reservation, etc.) (1.4%).

For descriptions of each type of legal basis, please consult Appendix A at the end of this chapter.

The variation in hours of operation, collections and services provided by public libraries is daunting. Tables 12.1–12.5 present national averages and medians as reported in *Public Libraries in the United States: Fiscal Year 2005* for core metrics of library operations (National Center for Education Statistics, 2008).

TABLE 12.1   Library Outlets and Service Hours, FY 2005

	Average Number of Weekly Public Service Hours Per Outlet	**Number of Outlets**	**Total Staff**
National average	39	2	16
National median	40	1	4

Source: Used with permission from the American Library Association.

TABLE 12.2   Library Funding (Revenue), FY 2005

	Local Revenue Per Capita	**State Revenue Per Capita**	**Total Revenue Per Capita**
National average	$28.48	$3.27	$37.16
National median	$21.65	$0.86	$28.04

Source: Used with permission from the American Library Association.

TABLE 12.3   Library Expenditures, FY 2005

	Total Collection Expenditures Per Capita	**Total Staff Expenditures as % of Total Expenditures**	**Total Operating Expenditures Per Capita**
National average	$5.01	64.8	$34.56
National median	$3.72	65.4	$26.52

Source: Used with permission from the American Library Association.

TABLE 12.4   Library Collections and Use, FY 2005

	Print Materials Per Capita	**Users of Electronic Resources Per Capita**	**Total Circulation Per Capita**	**Circulation of Children's Materials as % of Total Circulation**
National average	6.51	1.42	8.39	35.6
National median	4.38	.9	6.59	36.7

Source: Used with permission from the American Library Association.

TABLE 12.5   Library Program Attendance, FY 2005

	Total Program Attendance	**Children's Program Attendance**
National average	8,401	6,374
National median	2,093	1,591

Source: Used with permission from the American Library Association.

ABOUT PUBLIC LIBRARY FUNDING

Funding of public libraries is extremely complex and much of the complexity results from where and how libraries operate within government or as independent (non-governmental) entities. There is no single funding protocol for public libraries, nor is there a single "best practice" model for operations.

Models of library funding include:

- *Direct tax model*—this is the most typical form of public library funding. The tax revenue comes directly from the community the library serves.
- *Indirect tax model*—a tax applied to a good or service to support the cost of a governmental service. An example of this may be fuel taxes, lottery funds or fees (dog registration fee) being collected and redirected to the library.

Most libraries operate under a "*plural*" model—multiple revenue sources. Nationally, public library funding is derived from three primary sources (National Center for Education Statistics, 2008):

- Local (81.4%);
- State (9.6%); and
- Federal (0.6%).

A fourth source, "other," represents about 8.4% nationally and is derived from a variety of sources such as telecommunications discounts (E-rate), private and governmentally (federal) funded competitive grants (NEA, IMLS, etc.), or fund raising and donations.

In fiscal year 2005 only one state did not operate using local tax revenue, Hawaii, and Ohio had proportionally less local tax support and higher state tax support (65% state and 28% local) than other states. Pennsylvania and West Virginia also reported high levels of state support compared with other states (about 22% and 30%, respectively).

An element of governance that addresses more the fiscal autonomy of the library is its independent taxing authority. The *2008 Public Library Data Service Statistical Report* (PLDS) included supplemental questions on library finance and reported that only 208 (about 23.8%) of responding libraries had independent taxing authority (Public Library Association, 2008). Although not a representative response of libraries in smaller communities, if applied to the nation about 2,189 public libraries may have independent taxing authority.

Longitudinal Review of Public Library Funding

Annual "snapshots" of library funding are useful in understanding the fiscal climate of a particular point in time, usually a fiscal year. However, a longer view of the data exposes trends not otherwise evident in yearly review.

Although libraries have experienced an average annual increase of 4% in operating funds from 1996 to 2005 (Table 12.7) (National Center for Education Statistics, multiple years), the national public library data collection (IMLS) for fiscal year 2006, although unedited, indicates that individual states are experiencing a shift of expenditures away from (print) collections and staff to other expenditures (e.g., technology, utilities, building maintenance) (Institute of Museum and Library Services, 2009). And, reporting for fiscal year 2008 in

TABLE 12.6 Fiscal Year 1996–2005 Average Percentage Change in Public Library Operating Expenditures by Type and Population Served Range (NCES/IMLS)

Population Served	Average % Change Staff Expenditures	Average % Change Collections Expenditures	Average % Change Other Expenditures	Net Annualized % Change All Expenditures
1,000,000 or more	6.9	8.5	11.4	8.9
500,000–999,999	6.0	3.7	5.4	5.0
250,000–499,999	7.0	4.2	5.9	5.7
100,000–249,999	6.5	4.3	5.5	5.4
50,000–99,999	7.5	4.9	6.3	6.2
25,000–49,999	7.1	3.7	6.9	5.9
10,000–24,999	6.3	2.8	5.9	5.0
5,000–9,999	6.1	2.5	5.1	4.6
2,500–4,999	7.4	3.6	6.1	5.7
1,000–2,499	7.6	2.6	7.5	5.9
Less than 1,000	7.6	3.4	7.0	6.0

Source: Used with permission from the American Library Association.

the PLFTAS report indicate decreases in both library expenditures and the redistribution of expenditures during fiscal year 2008 (American Library Association, 2008).

As Table 12.6 shows, collection expenditures increased more than 200% during the 1996–2005 period, yet funding did not keep pace (see http://www.arl.org/sc/marketplace/journals/serials.shtml and Bowker Annual price indices).

Modest growth in operating budgets of public libraries was eroded by increasing salary/benefits expenses and utilities, which libraries must pay. Overall, operating revenue from all sources barely kept pace with expenditures (see Table 12.7).

Making Ends Meet: Mid-Year Operating Reductions

The American Library Association (ALA) regularly monitors library funding. In 2006, the ALA conducted a survey of a sample of public libraries to confirm the extent of mid-year operating budget cuts that had been surfacing in the media. The results were disturbing both in the extent of multi-year flat operating budgets, but also in the depth and the localization of the reductions (e.g., urban and rural libraries more so than suburban). Reductions were not modest—an average of 16.9% of libraries responding indicated mid-year revenue reductions for the fiscal years studied. Concerns about funding reductions were reflected in the responses from public libraries serving populations below 25,000 and above 500,000. There clearly were differences in funding changes,

TABLE 12.7   Net Annualized Percentage Change, Operating Revenue and Expenditures, FY 1996–FY 2005

Population Served	Operating Revenue (%)	Operating Expenditures (%)	Difference, Revenue to Expenditures (%)
1,000,000 or more	5.3	8.9	−3.7
500,000–999,999	6.5	5.0	1.4
250,000–499,999	6.1	5.7	0.4
100,000–249,999	6.2	5.4	0.8
50,000–99,999	5.9	6.2	−0.3
25,000–49,999	6.0	5.9	0.2
10,000–24,999	6.5	5.0	1.5
5,000–9,999	6.7	4.6	2.1
2,500–4,999	6.2	5.7	0.5
1,000–2,499	6.0	5.9	0.1
Less than 1,000	6.3	6.0	0.3

Source: Used with permission from the American Library Association.

with little relief anticipated for our smallest public libraries in the West and Midwest—48% experienced reductions in fiscal year 2003, 35.8% in fiscal year 2004, and 34.5% in fiscal year 2005. Nearly 20% of Northeast libraries indicated budget reductions in fiscal year 2004, up from 12% in fiscal year 2003. The findings of that "quick and dirty" survey are presented in Tables 12.8 and 12.9 (American Library Association, 2006a).

Less than one-fourth of libraries reported increases, and those reported were modest. Libraries serving more than 500,000 and those serving fewer than 25,000 people saw the greatest midyear funding cuts. The study also found that libraries in the West and Midwest sustained greater cuts than their counterparts in the South and East.

High numbers of public libraries reported level (flat) funding for multiple fiscal years (FY 2003–2005). An equal number of respondents reported level funding for all fiscal years—between 77% and 82% of all libraries responding—resulting in a net decrease in local revenue for these libraries. The result of level funding over so many years was that a vast majority of U.S. public libraries had stilted buying power as a result of the level funding during these fiscal years. Given this reality it should not be surprising that libraries have been slow to incorporate technology expenditures into normal operating budgets—they were trying to keep the doors open and maintain services as best they could.

State librarians were asked in November 2007 about the fiscal climate for public libraries (Table 12.10) as part of the *Libraries Connect Communities: Public Library Funding & Technology Access Study 2007–2008* (American Library Association, 2008, pp. 16–17). Although 21 states reported overall funding improvement in FY2007, 18 states reported no change in overall funding—flat funding continues. Four states reported overall funding reductions (one Midwest state reporting an 11% reduction).

TABLE 12.8   Operating Revenue Increases Experienced by U.S. Public Libraries, FY 2003–05

Size of Revenue Increase	Fiscal Year		
	FY 2003	FY 2004	FY 2005
1–2%	51	46	52
Percent of libraries	11.0%	9.8%	11.2%
3–4%	31	41	33
Percent of libraries	6.7%	8.8%	7.0%
5–6%	14	18	25
Percent of libraries	3.1%	3.9%	5.4%
7–8%	5	8	8
Percent of libraries	1.2%	1.7%	1.6%
9–10%	12	12	13
Percent of libraries	2.5%	2.6%	2.8%
11% or more	10	17	24
Percent of libraries	2.1%	3.6%	5.2%

N = 468 (100%).
Source: Used with permission from the American Library Association.

TABLE 12.9   Operating Revenue Reductions Experienced by U.S. Public Libraries, FY 2003–05

Size of Revenue Reduction	Fiscal Year		
	FY 2003	FY 2004	FY 2005
1–2%	28	28	28
Percent of libraries	6.1%	6.0%	5.9
3–4%	11	14	11
Percent of libraries	2.4%	2.9%	2.3%
5–6%	13	14	10
Percent of libraries	2.7%	3.0%	2.1%
7–8%	2	4	2
Percent of libraries	0.4%	0.8%	0.5%
9–10%	10	2	8
Percent of libraries	2.1%	0.4%	1.8%
11% or more	19	29	16
Percent of libraries	4.1%	6.2%	3.4%

N = 468 libraries (100%).
Source: Used with permission from the American Library Association.

TABLE 12.10 State Libraries Reporting Overall Funding Change for Public Libraries by Percent, FY 2007

	Percent Decrease (n = 3)			No Change	Percent Increase (n = 21)				Totals
	1–2%	3–4%	5–10%	11%+	(n = 18)	1–2%	3–4%	5–10%	11%+	
Midwest	0	0	0	1	6	2	1	1	1	12
Northeast	0	0	0	0	3	0	0	1	0	4
South	0	1	0	0	6	1	1	3	1	13
West	0	0	1	0	3	0	2	7	0	13
Totals	0	1	1	1	18	3	4	12	2	42

N = 42 state libraries (84%)
Source: PLFTAS 2007–2008, http://www.ala.org/ala/ors/plftas/pullibfunandtechaccstudy.cfm

Funding Allocations Are Changing

Not only were budgets flat or declining for many public libraries, estimated imbalances in budgeted operating revenue by source were apparent as early as fall 2007. Between 2006–2007 and 2007–2008, overall budgets remained level for most libraries. By way of example, libraries reported in fiscal years 2005 and 2007 the following proportion of funding by source:

NCES FY 2005

- 81.4% local/county;
- 9.5% state;
- 0.5% federal; and
- 8.4% other sources.

PLFTAS 2007–2008

- 74.7% local/county;
- 12.4% state;
- 0.7% federal; and
- 12.3% other sources.

It is evident from the funding proportions reported by libraries in fiscal year 2005 and what they actually spent in 2007–2008 that funding sources are shifting away from local revenue. Many libraries experienced increased usage while operating with decreasing operating budgets (American Library Association, 2009). In fact, mid-year operating budget reductions were again reported across the United States and became more pronounced during the 2008 national economic downturn.

Preliminary data available in the *Compare Libraries* tool for fiscal year 2006 (IMLS) suggest that shifts in historic patterns of expenditure distributions away from collections to other expenditures continue (Institute of Museum and Library Services, 2009). An anticipated increase of more than 6% in other expenditures, compared with about 3% for salaries and collections, may indicate a "greater than inflation rate" expense increase in this area. This is compounded by an anticipated decline in capital expenditures for building repair or improvement that are not part of the general operating budget of a library. Capital expenditures declined slightly between fiscal years 2004 and 2005, and continued decreases may be expected in FY 2006 reporting by public libraries.[1]

When comparing anticipated FY 2007 operating expenditures reported in the 2006–2007 PLFTAS study libraries with the actual expenditures reported in this year's study, it quickly became apparent that anticipated expenditures were not realized. Overall operating expenditures fell short by 15.5%, and they varied by specific expenditure type from those anticipated by as much 20%:

- 20% below anticipated expenditures for salaries;
- 0.8% below anticipated expenditures for collections; and
- 12.5% above anticipated expenditures in other areas.

When considered by source of funding, average expenditures missed or exceeded anticipated levels as follows:

- Local/county missed anticipated levels by –22.2%;
- State exceeded anticipated levels by +0.8%;
- Federal exceeded anticipated levels by +28.6%;
- Fines/fees missed anticipated levels by –22.5%;
- Donations/local fundraising exceeded anticipated levels by +136%; and
- Grants, including private grants, exceeded anticipated levels by +19.9%.

A smaller percentage of overall expenditures have been attributed to salaries and more to collections and other expenditures than anticipated. Considerably more funding came from soft, non-tax sources than not. The most notable shifts occurred with reported local/county support for salaries, donations and local fundraising for other expenditures, and the unexpected increase in federal funding directed to support salaries and collections (see Figure 12.2). The increase in federal support may be a result of specific Library Services and Technology Act (LSTA) sub-grants to libraries for specific projects and could be expected to readjust in future years.

The national average for funding operating expenditures from other sources of revenue (non-tax sources) was 8.4%, as reported in the Institute of Museum and Library Services (IMLS) *Public Libraries in the United States: Fiscal Year 2005* study (Institute of Museum and Library Services, 2008). However, libraries reporting in the 2007–2008 PLFTAS study have indicated using non-tax sources for operating expenditures at 12% in FY2007, with 10% anticipated in FY 2008—as much as 3.6% higher than the national average. The increased reliance on

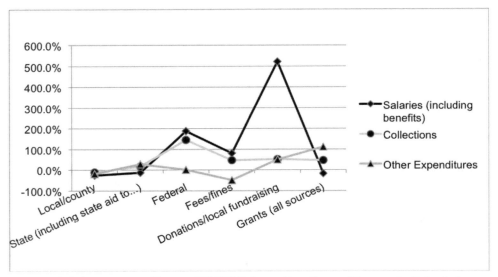

Figure 12.2 Percentage Change FY 2007 Operating Expenditures, Anticipated vs. Reported.

non-tax revenue reported in the PLFTAS studies may be an indicator of what national IMLS data will show when FY 2006 and newer data are published.

Overall, the uses of non-tax revenue reported in the 2007–2008 PLFTAS study were:

- About 37% was used to pay for staff salaries in FY 2007; about 33% is anticipated in FY 2008.
- About 20% was used to fund collections in FY 2007; 23% is anticipated in FY 2008.
- About 42% was used to support other expenditures in FY 2007; 44% is anticipated in FY 2008.

Rural libraries were more likely than urban libraries to report the use of non-tax revenue to pay for other expenditures in both FY 2007, as well during the anticipated FY 2008. Rural libraries reported that they rely fairly equally upon all sources of tax revenue (local, state, federal) to pay for staff salaries in FY 2007 (51–61%), and they anticipated this would also be the case in FY 2008 (46–61%).

Suburban libraries, like their counterparts in rural communities, reported directing a greater proportion of fines/fees, donations/local fundraising, and private foundation grants toward other expenditures in FY 2007, and anticipate this trend will continue in FY 2008. Local, state and national grant program revenue was more heavily directed toward paying for staff salaries in FY 2007 than is anticipated for FY 2008—64% versus 17%. Suburban libraries also anticipate that they will direct a greater proportion of federal funding sources to staff salary expenditures in FY 2008 than in FY 2007—32% compared with 11% in FY 2007. Much more could be learned from these data as indicated from the highlights.

PAYING FOR PUBLIC ACCESS COMPUTING

Technology-related expenditures reported in the 2007–2008 PLFTAS survey indicate as a type of expenditure they have not benefited from stable local funding as have long-standing expenditures such as collections. In addition, libraries have demonstrated increased dependence on "soft" money (fees/fine, donations and grants) to pay for staff salaries. This is alarming because these sources of support are more volatile and, therefore, undependable and can distort the true cost of library operations.

Suburban libraries—a segment of the library community that has historically had strong and stable local funding—anticipated continued declines in overall local/county support into FY 2008, as well as declines in donations and grants directed to technology expenditures.

The smaller the community, the less funding is available for telecommunications and outside vendors, and the more goes to IT salaries as a proportion of overall technology-related expenditures. This is not dissimilar from the distribution of overall library expenditures—65.9% staff, 13.2% collections, and 20.9% other expenditures (Institute of Museum and Library Services, 2008).

TABLE 12.11   Average Percent Change Comparing Technology-Related Expenditures by Source, FY 2006–2007

Sources of Funding	% Change
Local/county	–0.2
State (all)	–10.8
Federal	26.3
Fees/fines	–0.8
Donations/local fundraising	–28.7
Grants (all)	–40.7
Net change	**–3.9**

Note: Data are determined from the 2006–07 and 2007–08 PLFTAS study results.
Source: Used with permission from the American Library Association.

There was considerable improvement in libraries' ability to report technology-related expenditure data in the 2007–2008 PLFTAS study. Building on the data first collected in 2006–2007, library systems were asked to estimate expenditures for FY 2008 in four categories—salaries, outside vendors, hardware/software, and telecommunications. The 2007–2008 study added the category of outside vendors and merged hardware and software into a single category. Tables 12.11 and 12.12 outline these results.

Estimated expenditures for technology-related expenditures declined slightly between FY 2006 and FY 2007, approximately –3.9% overall (see Table 12.12). Declines in expenditures from local/county and state sources were about 11%, and about 26.3% more than anticipated was spent from federal sources. Expenditures from soft funding sources (fees/fines, etc.) declined most noticeably from FY 2006 in donations and grant funding categories. For FY 2007–2008, overall anticipated expenditures were expected to decline by less than 1% (–0.3%). Although local/county funding sources were anticipated to continue declining, notable increases were anticipated from state

TABLE 12.12   Average Percent Anticipated Change Technology-Related Expenditures by Source, FY 2007–2008

Sources of Funding	% Change
Local/county	–6.4
State (all)	58.0
Federal	37.0
Fees/fines	80.3
Donations/local fundraising	–29.5
Grants (all)	–22.2
Net change	**–0.3**

Note: Data are from the 2007–08 PLFTAS study only.
Source: Used with permission from the American Library Association.

and federal sources. Also, more fees/fines support was being directed to technology-related expenditures, with less reliance on donations and grants.

It is important to remember that, although salaries for technology staff may be supported heavily from soft-funding sources, those salaries are a small proportion of overall salary expenditures for libraries. Technology expenditures, such as hardware/software, outside vendors, and telecommunications, may be a significant proportion of "other expenditures" as a category. As such, it may be that libraries continue to use local tax support to pay traditional and ongoing expenses, such as programs, utilities and transportation. Reliance on non-tax revenue to support basic technology hardware and telecommunications expenditures is a reflection of creating a revenue stream from soft-funding sources to build new services and their continued support. This was especially evident in suburban and rural libraries.

Tables 12.13 and 12.14 present the estimated changes reported by public libraries for technology-related expenditures by funding source and type of expenditure for FY2006–2008. Although there were declines in the use of certain funding sources to pay for technology, these tables show the item-level variations with overall expenditures. For instance, although use of local/county funding sources to pay for technology declined by –0.2%, expenditures increased for software and telecommunications and declined for salaries and hardware. Further, even though overall use of donations to pay for technology declined, libraries reported spending 135.5% more on software from this funding source in FY 2007 over FY 2006. In FY 2007–2008 considerably more funds in all categories are anticipated to be directed to software expenditures, and more state and federal funds and fee/fines are expected to be used to pay technology staff salaries.

The unknown impact of a shift of local/county revenue away from funding telecommunications costs, together with a growing reliance on soft sources—fees/fines and donations—and state and federal support for these expenditures, is worrisome. It will be interesting to see if this shift continues across types of funding sources, even though overall expenditures have fluctuated very

TABLE 12.13   Average Percent Change in Technology-Related Expenditures, by Type and Funding Source, FY 2006–2007

Sources of Funding	Salaries (including benefits) (%)	Hardware (%)	Software (%)	Telecommu- nications (%)
Local/county	–6.1	–5.5	22.6	12.8
State (all)	–2.9	–27.3	6.3	–16.1
Federal	16.2	–68.8	–50.7	66.9
Fees/fines	–22.1	–18.6	53.1	–25.7
Donations/ local fundraising	4.4	–49.0	135.5	–14.2
Grants (all)	–62.3	–32.4	–9.4	–46.8

Source: Used with permission from the American Library Association.

TABLE 12.14   Average Percent Anticipated Change in Technology-Related Expenditures, by Type and Funding Source, FY 2007–2008

Sources of Funding	Salaries (including benefits) (%)	Hardware (%)	Software (%)	Telecommunications (%)
Local/county	−13.7	−5.2	53.8	−35.2
State (all)	46.5	44.5	141.2	8.3
Federal	26.4	119.7	291.1	25.2
Fees/fines	94.2	6.9	109.5	147.8
Donations/ local fundraising	−41.5	−48.7	1.9	58.9
Grants (all)	−72.4	−91.6	387.7	−13.5

Source: Used with permission from the American Library Association.

little during the last three fiscal years. Discovering the impact of the 2008 economic downturn also will be valuable in understanding how libraries maintain core technology infrastructures.

A View of Technology Funding by Population Served Ranges

Greater variations were observed when expenditures were analyzed by metropolitan status. Presenting library finance data in parallel with other findings reported in this study—by metropolitan status (rural, suburban, and urban) and poverty ranges—provides a useful context for understanding public access computing services. However, the finance data tell a somewhat different story when viewed through the lens of community size.

Table 12.15 presents the average anticipated FY 2008 technology-related expenditures from all revenue sources by population served ranges. These ranges are used by the ALA Public Library Association in its annual study of public libraries (PLDS) (Public Library Association, 2008) and by other studies of public libraries conducted by the ALA.

TABLE 12.15   Average Anticipated Percentage FY 2008 Technology-Related Expenditures for All Revenue Sources by Population Served

	Salaries (%)	Outside Vendors (%)	Hardware/ Software (%)	Telecommunications (%)
Less than 10,000	47.08	15.50	24.42	13.00
10,000–24,999	45.69	15.07	28.21	11.03
25,000–99,999	44.55	17.85	26.55	11.05
100,000–499,999	38.45	20.19	25.92	15.44
500,000 or more	26.37	23.12	29.53	20.98

Source: Used with permission from the American Library Association.

One of the more surprising findings from this recalculation was the nearly equal distribution of expenditures across all technology categories for public libraries in the largest communities. The smaller the community, the more expenditure distributions shift toward salaries away from telecommunications and outside vendor expenditures as a proportion of overall technology-related expenditures.

Rural libraries anticipated the most improvement in all funding categories for technology expenditures between FY 2007 and FY 2008. Interestingly, suburban libraries—a segment of the library community that has historically had strong and stable local funding—anticipated continued declines in overall local/county support into FY 2008, as well as declines in donations and grants directed to technology expenditures. Suburban libraries did, however, anticipated improvement in state and federal funding directed to technology expenditures.

Urban libraries continued to show fairly steady improvement in local/county support for technology, and anticipated improvements in their use of state and federal funding for these expenditures. Urban libraries anticipated a significant increase in the use of fees/fines for technology, and a decline or very modest improvement in using other soft funding—donations and grants—to pay for these expenditures.

Expenditures by specific funding sources, type of expenditure, and population served ranges present even greater detail:

- Libraries serving more than 500,000 residents reported 45% of telecommunications costs were paid from local tax revenue and 55% from federal. Libraries reporting in this population served range reported no state tax support and no use of soft revenue sources (e.g., fee/fines, grants, etc.) to pay for telecommunications costs.

- Libraries serving 100,000–499,999 residents reported telecommunications costs paid 55.7% from local tax revenue, 21.7% from state and about 16% from federal sources. The remaining 22.6% of costs were paid from soft revenue sources.

- Libraries serving 25,000–99,999 residents reported telecommunications costs paid 73.4% from local tax revenue, 13.9% from state and 8% from federal sources. The remaining 12.7% of costs were paid from soft revenue sources.

- Libraries serving 10,000–24,999 residents reported telecommunications costs paid 68.5% from local tax revenue, 10.9% from state and 8.9% from federal sources. The remaining 20.6% of costs were paid from soft revenue sources.

- Libraries serving fewer than 10,000 resident reported telecommunications costs paid 55.7% from local tax revenue, 12.7% from state and 9.8% from federal sources. The remaining 31.6% of costs were paid from soft revenue sources.

When libraries were asked specifically about technology-related expenditures anticipated in FY 2008, reliance on specific types of funding sources skewed from those estimates reported for salaries and "other expenditures." Specifically, the larger the library service area, the more likely libraries were to report that technology expenditures were paid from local or state revenue sources rather than from soft revenue sources (e.g., fee/fines, grants, etc.), even though libraries reported relying on soft funds for "other expenditures."

Technology Support from Non-tax Revenue

Table 12.16 presents these distributions of non-tax revenue sources. The first two columns present what libraries reported for anticipated FY 2008 operating expenditures that would include the detailed technology-related expenditures, and the next four columns present anticipated FY 2008 operating expenditures for some specific technology-related expenditures.

Public libraries serving smaller communities were far more likely to rely on soft revenue sources to acquire and pay for outside vendors than larger libraries. Except for the anomaly of telecommunications expenditures, which were well-supported with E-rate discounts and local tax support, this pattern also was true for the other technology-related expenditures categories. Some good news was visible in the population served analysis—for libraries with technology staff, a significant proportion of financial support was from local, state, or federal tax revenue. This was not particularly surprising since these libraries were more likely to report not having dedicated IT staff. However, for libraries serving 100,000–499,999 the striking level of support from non-tax revenue was surprising.

Hardware/software and telecommunications expenditures were the most likely to rely on non-tax revenue. Very few libraries reported grants as a source of support for either hardware/software or telecommunications expenditures, but did report reliance on fee/fines, donations/local fund raising, and private foundation support for these particular expenditure categories. The smaller the population served range, the greater the reliance on private foundation support for hardware/software (30.9% versus 8%). This can be attributed to private foundation hardware strategies targeting high poverty and rural communities (Bill & Melinda Gates Foundation, 2009). Libraries serving 100,000–499,999 reported the lowest level of private foundation support, about 5%.

Libraries in the smallest communities also reported a higher proportion of donations being directed toward hardware/software and telecommunications costs than did other population served ranged. Although the funding amounts were considerably less than other population served ranges, libraries serving fewer than 10,000 residents reported 21.6% of support coming from donations. Libraries serving 100,000–499,999 reported relying on about 6% of donations to fund hardware/software and telecommunication expenditures.

IMPACTS OF UNSTABLE LIBRARY FUNDING

It may seem, to some, that the failure to support core library services with steady and predictable funding is simply the luck of the fiscal draw. Libraries are faced with difficult service planning, budgeting, and management decisions, just as any local government or non-profit community agency is. What makes matters even more difficult for libraries is their broad, "serve all" philosophy—even mandate.

TABLE 12.16 Average Anticipated Percentage Technology-Related Expenditures from FY 2008 Non-tax Revenue Sources by Type and Population Served

	Operating Expenditures		Technology-Related Expenditures by Type			
	All Salaries Expenditures (%)	Other Expenditures (%)	Salaries (%)	Outside Vendors (%)	Hardware/ Software (%)	Telecommunications (%)
Less than 10,000	10.69	30.82	4.59	17.71	45.54	21.82
10,000–24,999	4.94	18.91	4.27	4.52	25.80	11.72
25,000–99,999	2.69	15.17	1.87	8.95	20.64	4.67
100,000–499,999	3.71	13.89	3.47	16.70	13.51	6.57
500,000 or more	15.49	25.62	0.00	0.17	8.60	0.00

Source: Used with permission from the American Library Association.

When the economy is strong and library funding is stable, service decisions are creative and responsive to the community. When economies lag or decline and library funding is unstable, service decisions become challenging, as exemplified by this statement: "Law enforcement and other county departments seem to be a higher priority to our County Commissioners. We have eliminated our outreach services and the person responsible for them. We have reduced our weekly hours by four" (American Library Association, 2006a, n.p.).

The 2006 ALA funding study showed that libraries behave predictably when faced with budget increases and reductions. And, there is a reason for this. The following list of areas where reductions are made reflects the pliability of each category—the order in which the reductions are easiest to make. It could be argued that reducing staff and hours are equally difficult due to policy or employment requirements.

Libraries reported reductions in services fairly consistently regardless of the severity of the reduction. Reductions were ranked as follows:

1. Materials (average of 68.3% of libraries responding)
2. Staffing (average of 41.6% of libraries responding)
3. Hours open (average of 24.6% of libraries responding)
4. Electronic access (12.6% of libraries responding)

Electronic access is difficult to reduce because it underlies much of the services libraries provide, and service plans are negotiated in advance and sometimes for specific contract periods. A library may be in a position to reduce access to databases, but not to reduce the telecommunications services required to maintain basic library services, such as materials check-out and online catalog searching.

USES OF PUBLIC LIBRARIES AND LOCAL GOVERNMENT SERVICES

Household surveys sponsored by the American Library Association reveal interesting trends in library usage. The number of households with library cards remained fairly consistent across two decades. However, between the start of 2008 and late summer, American households reported a sharp increase in library card ownership.[2]

- 1990   59% of adults in household with a library card
- 2002   62% of adults in household with a library card
- 2006   63% of adults in household with a library card
- January 2008   59% of adults in household with a library card
- August 2008   68% of adults in household with a library card

Of those with library cards, library use increased since 2006. In-person visits increased to 76% in 2008 from a reported 65.7% in 2006 (up 10.3 percentage

points, or about 30.9 million visits). "By computer" visits increased 17.4 percentage points between 2006 and 2008—41% in 2008 from a reported 23.6%
in 2006 (about 52.2 million "by computer" visits). Even more interesting was
the increase of computer use by those ages 63+ in the two-year period between
2006 and 2008—computer use increased from 12.4% to 17% during this period
(about 7.7 million users) (U.S. Census Bureau, 2009).

Perceptions of Library Value Remain High

Also investigated by ALA household surveys conducted by KRC in 2002 and
2006 were satisfaction with and perceptions of the benefit of libraries for the
money spent (tax support) (American Library Association, 2006b). Overall,
Americans are very satisfied with and have positive perceptions of their public
libraries. Almost 9 in 10 Americans (89%) report being satisfied with their
public libraries. Fully 7 out of 10 Americans say they are either extremely or
very satisfied (70%) with their public library, which is a 10 percentage point
increase since 2002.

Regarding the ways in which public libraries may be valuable to residents,
four characteristics or services stand out:

- 79% say it is very important that "the services are free"
- 71% say it is very important that it "is a place where I can learn for a
  lifetime"
- 65% say it is very important that it "enhances my education"
- 65% say it is very important that it "provides information for school and
  work"

Moreover, three-quarters of households (75%) say they strongly agree the public library plays an important role in giving everyone a chance to succeed
because libraries provide free access to materials and resources. About 2 in 3
Americans (68%) strongly agree that the library improves the quality of life in
their community.

When asked how they would rank (top, middle, bottom) the benefits of the
public library compared to the benefits of other tax-supported services, such
as schools, parks and roads, households reported:

	2002	2006
• At the **top** of the list	30%	36%
• In the **middle**	58%	53%
• At the **bottom**	8%	8%

When asked to rank the value of librarians in public libraries compared to
the value of other professionals in the community households reported:

In both cases, the value of the library and its employees gained value in the view of American households between 2002 and 2006.

	2002	2006
• At the **top** of the list	22%	32%
• In the **middle**	63%	57%
• At the **bottom**	10%	8%

National economies effect local government and local economies, and patron perception of the value of libraries. A 2002 American Library Association study found increased library use during the recession in the earlier part of this decade. "Circulation is 8% above trend in March 2001, the date when the recession officially began. It stayed well above trends, an average of 9.1% above, for the rest of the year" (Lynch, 2002, pp. 62–63). Libraries across the United States reported increased use in the double-digits during the economic downturn in 2008. Hundreds of news articles in publications ranging from NPR to the Washington Post to Fremont News Messenger have been published and broadcast about the critical roles libraries have played for communities in the wake of the current economic downturn (American Library Association, 2009). The Chicago Public Library reported circulation increases of 28% over 2007, and reported more than 1 million visits monthly to its main library and 1.1 million visitors monthly to its 79 Chicago branches (Swartz, 2008). They also reported providing more than 3.8 million free one-hour Internet sessions in the previous year. With recent automation improvements usage will rise with the introduction of an online (remote) reservation system for public access computers online.

CONCLUSION

Libraries perform complex balancing acts meeting patron demand and spending within their economic means. The funding patterns discussed in this chapter demonstrate the volatility of library funding and position library technology expenditures within that context. Meeting patron needs means more and more that services are provided electronically while maintaining "traditional" library services. The costs are high and libraries have been doing more with less for many years. It is critical that libraries be successful in providing these needed, and now expected, core services. Those most successful have developed technology planning strategies, have technology staff available to support them, and have strong local funding for core library services, of which public access computing is a part. Libraries with deficits in any of these categories struggle to maintain and improve services.

NOTES

1. Individual state annual reports indicate a continued decline (see COSLA individual state Web pages http://www.cosla.org).

2. Household surveys sponsored by the American Library Association. See "Surveys & Research" at http://www.ala.org/ala/aboutala/offices/ors/reports/reports.cfm.

REFERENCES

American Library Association. (2006a). *Funding issues in U.S. public libraries, fiscal years 2003–2006*. Chicago: American Library Association. Available at http://www.ala.org/ala/research/librarystats/public/fundingissuesinuspls.pdf.

American Library Association (2006b). *2006 KRC @ your library household survey.* Available at http://www.ala.org/ala/research/librarystats/public/index.cfm.

American Library Association. (2008). *Libraries connect communities: Public Library Funding and Technology Access study: 2007–2008*. Chicago, IL: American Library Association.

American Library Association. (2009). *Funding news @ your library®*. Available at http://www.ala.org/ala/issuesadvocacy/libfunding/public/index.cfm.

Bill & Melinda Gates Foundation. (2009). *U.S. Libraries Program.* Available at http://www.gatesfoundation.org/libraries/Pages/default.aspx.

Chief Officers of State Library Agencies. (2009). Individual state annual reports indicate a continued decline (see COSLA individual state Web pages http://www.cosla.org).

Institute of Museum and Library Services. (2008). *Public libraries in the United States: Fiscal Year 2005*. Available at http://harvester.census.gov/imls/pubs/pls/index.asp.

Institute of Museum and Library Services. (2009). Compare public libraries, Fiscal Year 2006 [online search tool of public library data]. Available at http://harvester.census.gov/imls/compare/index.asp.

Lynch, M. J. (2002). Economic hard times and public library use revisited. *American Libraries, 33*(August): 62–63. Available at http://www.ala.org/ala/aboutala/offices/ors/reports/economichard.cfm.

National Center for Education Statistics. (2008). *First look. Public libraries in the United States: Fiscal Year 2005*. Appendix B (NCES 2008-301). Available at http://harvester.census.gov/imls/pubs/pls/pub_detail.asp?id=116.

National Center for Education Statistics. *Public libraries in the United States* (Various years). Available at http://harvester.census.gov/imls/pubs/pls/index.asp.

Public Library Association (2008). *2008 Public library data service statistical report.* Available at http://www.ala.org/ala/mgrps/divs/pla/plapublications/pldsstatreport/index.cfm.

Swartz, T. (2008, September 26). "Libraries making a big return." *RedEye*. Available at http://articles.chicagotribune.com/2008-09-26/news/0809260292_1_library-marketing-director-reservation-chicago-public-libraries.

U.S. Census Bureau. (2009). *American FactFinder*. DP-1. General Demographic Characteristics. Available at http://factfinder.census.gov.

APPENDIX A: LEGAL BASIS DEFINITIONS, PUBLIC LIBRARIES

Established by the National Center for Education Statistics. Federal State Cooperative System of Public Library Data. 1988. Available at: http://harvester.census.gov/imls/publib.asp.

1. City/County. A multi-jurisdictional entity that is operated jointly by a county and a city.
2. Municipal Government (city, town, or village). A municipal government is an organized local government authorized in a state's constitution

and statutes and established to provide general government for a specific concentration of population in a defined area.

3. County/Parish. An organized local government authorized in a state's constitution and statutes and established to provide general government.

4. Library District. A library district is a local entity other than a county, municipality, township, or school district that is authorized by state law to establish and operate a public library as defined by FSCS. It has sufficient administrative and fiscal autonomy to qualify as a separate government. Fiscal autonomy requires support from local taxation dedicated to library purposes (e.g., a library tax).

5. Multi-jurisdictional. An entity operated jointly by two or more units of local government under an intergovernmental agreement which creates a jointly appointed board or similar means of joint governance; to be distinguished from a library which contracts to serve other jurisdictions and from special library districts.

6. Native American Tribal Government. An organized local government authorized and established to provide general government to residents of a Native American reservation. Note: Include native Alaskan villages in this category.

7. Non-profit Association or Agency. An entity privately controlled but meeting the statutory definition of a public library in a given state; includes association libraries.

8. School District. An organized local entity providing public elementary, secondary, and/or higher education which, under state law, has sufficient administrative and fiscal autonomy to qualify as a separate government. Excludes "dependent public school systems" of county, municipal, township, or state governments.

The Role of State Library Agencies in Public Library Internet Development

Robert Bocher

INTRODUCTION

This chapter describes a number of activities and initiatives typically provided by State Library Agencies (SLAs) as they have assisted in and supported the development of public library Internet services. These activities are significant and, for many SLAs, have provided both direct and indirect support since the inception and adoption of Internet services in public libraries. Much of this support originated from: (1) the Library Services and Construction Act (LSCA) and later the Library Services and Technology Act (LSTA); (2) individual state aid to public libraries; and (3) regional library consortia (RLC). This support, in many cases, played an instrumental role in improving significantly Internet-based resources and services offered by public libraries to the communities that they serve.

AN OVERVIEW OF STATE LIBRARY AGENCIES

Over the past several decades, the assistance and support that State Library Agencies (SLAs) provide to enhancing public library services has been increasingly focused on technology, particularly the Internet. For many SLAs, Library Services and Technology Act (LSTA) funding was, and continues to be, an important funding source to help support technology infrastructure in the state's public libraries. Nationwide, 54% of LSTA funds allocated to states in

FY 2007 were spent on technology and Internet-related services (Henderson et al., 2008). Also, some SLAs provide funding directly to public libraries or to regional library cooperatives. And some of this funding is commonly used to support a variety of Internet-related services.

For example, the Wisconsin state library agency administers $16.9 million annually to fund the state's 17 regional library cooperatives (RLCs). The RLCs use these funds for a variety of purposes including paying for their member libraries' Internet access and library broadband costs. A survey the Wisconsin state library did in February 2009 showed that RLCs spend 62% of their state funding on supporting technology—in all its varied facets—for their member libraries.

All 50 states have an SLA. It is the agency that is often responsible for the development and enhancement of public library services. It is also the agency that administers the funding provided via the federal LSTA, which in FY 2009 distributed some $171.5 million to SLAs for library development (Manjarrez, Langa, & Miller, 2009, p. 24). However, beyond these commonalties, there are differences in how SLAs support their public libraries and in other services and responsibilities they have. For example, some SLAs manage large libraries with collections that number in the millions of items and some do not mange any type of library. SLAs are most often located within the framework of state government, as these numbers illustrate (Henderson et al., 2008):

- In 19 states the SLA is a separate, independent state agency that reports to a state library board, the legislative or governor;
- In 13 states the SLA is a part of the state's public education agency; and
- In 18 states the SLA is part of another state agency.

These categories are similar to how SLAs have been organized historically (Asp, 1986; Wiegand, 1986).

State Library Agency support for public library technology long predates more specific support for Internet access. Many SLAs began providing technology assistance dating as far back as the early 1980s. This often included use of state or LSCA/LSTA funds allocated to local public libraries to enable them to purchase the first generation of desktop PCs and the first automated circulation systems (a precursor to today's integrated library systems). Some states also provided funding for public libraries to join their state or regional OCLC network. In the area of support for technology innovation (or other innovations in library services), the SLAs often served an important role as promoters and advocates of early adaptation. Without this support from the state library, public libraries may not have had the local resources needed to initiate innovative projects or start new services. This role has continued to the present.

As will be seen throughout this chapter, SLAs play a very important role in providing both direct and indirect support to public libraries to help them become connected to the Internet and support the networked needs of their community's residents. Regardless of whether this support comes from LSTA funds, state aid, or other sources, public libraries have benefited considerably (as have the community members they serve) by this ongoing involvement and support by the SLA.

INTERNET ACCESS AND THE STATE LIBRARY: AN HISTORICAL PERSPECTIVE

From its development in the 1970s until the mid-1990s, Internet access was mostly found in academic and research institutions. In these formative years the National Science Foundation (NSF) had overall responsibility for the Internet backbone (the NSFNET), and it exerted some degree of control on who or what organizations had access. By the early 1990s most academic institutions had access, but most public libraries and SLAs did not. This changed several years later when the NSF ended its control of the Internet backbone network (Gaston, 1995). In brief, this decision opened access beyond the academic and research communities to public libraries and ultimately the general public. Thus access to, and use of, the Internet began to permeate the consciousness of the public library community in the mid-1990s. It was in this time frame that many SLAs started serious efforts to assist their public libraries in getting Internet access and using this new information and communications medium.

This early effort manifested itself in a variety of ways. For example, a role that many SLAs undertook was one of advocacy in promoting and encouraging Internet access. Many SLAs also sponsored Internet workshops and provided consulting services that addressed such basic issues as how to establish a dial-up account and how to configure modem settings. Some SLAs provided a list of local Internet service providers to ensure that their public libraries were only a local call from the Internet. LSTA was often an important source of funding for these early connectivity efforts.

The great majority of libraries that moved quickly to join the nascent Internet Age often did so by dial-up access to local Internet service providers, which were starting to proliferate especially in urban areas. Limitations on dial-up access—often just a single PC connected at slow modem speeds—are well known now but they were not always recognized as limitations in the context of the time. For example, much of the content then available was text only and even with a modem connection the text appeared on the screen much faster than one could read it. Since the Internet was a new experience for many library staff and patrons, they had nothing against which to judge the limitations of the library's connection. Increased modem speeds throughout the 1990s also had the impact of delivering textual content at ever faster rates.

In 1994, the first nationwide public library Internet survey was conducted (McClure, Bertot, & Zweizig). The results showed that just 12.7% of the nation's 8,900 public libraries offered Internet access to their patrons and that less than 1% offered direct (broadband) access (McClure, Bertot, & Zweizig, 1994, p. 20). Within just three years the percentage offering patron access increased dramatically to 60.4%. Yet even the 1997 survey showed that a large majority of libraries with Internet access (73.6%) still had dial-up access (Bertot & McClure, 1998, p. 5).

STATE LIBRARY SUPPORT OF CONNECTIVITY IN PUBLIC LIBRARIES

Support from the state library continues to be important in helping sustain public access computing. This was documented in the results of the 2006 annual American Library Association (ALA) public library technology survey which showed that many successfully networked libraries had good working relationships with their state library. As the survey notes, the state library plays "A significant, often primary, external role in enabling public libraries to become successfully networked" (Bertot, McClure, & Jaeger, 2006, p. 127). The survey further stated that some of the services and resources the state library provides include advocacy, providing consulting services, offering continuing education, and the funding of demonstration projects. Below is a more detailed exploration of the many Internet-related programs, services and assistance that are commonly offered by SLAs.

Internet connectivity has obviously changed dramatically over the past 15 years. In fact, with 99% of the nation's public libraries now having Internet access, basic connectivity is no longer an issue (Bertot, McClure, & Jaeger, 2007). Yet there is still a certain "connectivity continuum" that has remained fairly constant since the time of the early Internet adaptors. And that common thread is one of seeking to ensure that our public libraries have adequate, high quality Internet connectivity. For example, the current bandwidth issues that many libraries are experiencing can be viewed as just part of this "connectivity continuum" dating back to the mid-1990s. That is, a single workstation with a 28.8 Kbps modem dial-up connection was inadequate in 1995. And in the current environment of multiple networked workstations, many libraries still have inadequate access because of insufficient bandwidth. As many SLAs allocated resources for initial Internet connectivity in the 1990s, so many SLAs continue to advocate for and support projects and programs that address current Internet connectivity issues. And most of these issues over the past several years have focused on bandwidth needs.

The close of the twentieth century saw an increasing number of libraries moving from limited dial access to faster, direct access. As reported above, in 1997 dial-up was still the means of access for 73.6% of the nation's public libraries. But this changed dramatically by 2002 when only 6.5% of libraries reported that they still relied only on dial access (Bertot, McClure, & Thompson, 2002). As SLAs assisted many public libraries with their initial dial access, many SLAs also assisted their local libraries to move to faster broadband access. For some libraries the impediment to moving to broadband was lack of a local area network (LAN) in the library. If the library had no LAN then broadband was often limited to just a single workstation. SLAs often assisted their public libraries in getting the necessary local network infrastructure in place to facilitate the move to broadband Internet connectivity. Another major impediment in moving to broadband was cost. The need to pay for the initial installation and ongoing costs for a dedicated telecommunications circuit, related network expenses (e.g., router), and additional Internet Service Provider costs required a substantial investment, far more than the typical $30/month cost of dial-up service. Again, like its support for LANs, SLAs often assisted their libraries with state or LSTA funds to offset the increased costs for broadband connectivity.

Library bandwidth continued to increase throughout the first decade of the twenty-first century. However, the annual ALA public library technology surveys also continued to show that libraries were still having problems attaining adequate bandwidth. In other words, the increased demands of the medium— the Web 2.0 world of multi-media and graphics-rich content—was outpacing the libraries' increases in bandwidth. In an attempt to get a better understanding of the bandwidth conundrum, in 2007 ALA's Office for Information Technology Policy (OITP) conducted a study that reviewed the library bandwidth landscape in 13 states (Bard, Bolt, Weingarten, & Windhausen, 2007). The study was done with the cooperation and participation of the respective SLAs.

This study included interviews with SLA staff, and the SLAs also helped organize focus groups representative of the state's public library community. Some of the states highlighted were quite successful in addressing the bandwidth issue and were viewed as role models for other states which were encountering more problems in this area. In reviewing the broadband landscape on a state-by-state basis the study showed differences in a number of critical areas including commitment, collaboration, funding, political structure, and the nature of the state's telecommunications environment. The results of the study showed that public libraries reported fewer problems or issues with bandwidth in states with statewide or regional telecommunication networks. In relation to this, the following are two critical findings from the study highlighting the key role of SLAs.

- In states which were successful in developing state or regional networks, collaboration works. In many of these states the state library was part of the early planning efforts and it was often a critical voice in advocating for the inclusion of public libraries. As the report indicates, "Where there was a strong library coalition or where libraries could combine their needs with other entities . . . they were more likely to be included in network development" (Bard, Bolt, Weingarten, & Windhausen, 2007, p. 22).

- From an ongoing perspective, in states with state or regional networks, SLAs were—and still are—active players in ensuring that public libraries receive adequate broadband. SLAs often participate in the operation or overall governance of their state's network. Giving the state library a permanent "seat at the table" helps to ensure that issues like adequate library bandwidth are addressed and that future network enhancements are made to benefit public libraries.

These are critical roles that the state library plays in support of broadband and network development.

There are a number of significant factors that often determine at what level or to what degree SLAs are involved with broadband. In some states the demand for action comes from the library community itself. This "bottom up" approach often drives the priorities the state library places on how it allocates its limited resources. Like any priority setting process, placing an emphasis on addressing broadband issues requires deemphasizing other services, and there are winners and losers accordingly. Priority setting can be especially difficult when budgets are being reduced and SLAs are being downsized.

SLAs that, for whatever reason, choose to not address this demand place their libraries in the often frustrating position of having to address the broadband issue on their own. This is exactly the position that the above ALA study found often times simply does not work, especially in smaller libraries. In some states the SLA has taken the lead in addressing broadband needs ("top down" approach). Regardless of who or what process places broadband on the "high priority list," it is essential to have the firm commitment from the state librarian that the SLA will do as much as reasonably possible to address this priority.

For some states that have not previously made broadband a priority, a major factor in jump-starting a statewide broadband planning process has been the American Recovery and Reinvestment Act (ARRA). The ARRA has $7.2 billion allocated for broadband grants and loans. To again emphasize, SLAs have to be aggressive and make sure they are included in any state sponsored broadband task force or committee that is seeking to take advantage of ARRA broadband funding. But where a statewide network does not exist, and there appears no realistic expectation that ARRA funding or any other incentives will start the process in a reasonable (1–2 year) timeframe, the state library should focus on developing regional networks in close cooperation with regional library consortia (RLC).

Below are examples of several states where the state library has been a partner—often working with other entities (e.g., state government network office, state university system)—to develop statewide telecommunication networks that include public libraries.

- Missouri: Many public libraries in the state have Internet access through MOREnet, the statewide network managed by the state's public university system. The network provides broadband Internet connectivity, training, and technical support to member organizations, including public libraries. The Missouri legislature provides substantial support for MOREnet, which also includes content in the form of periodical and other informational databases for public libraries and the K–20 education community. The state library manages the appropriation for public library Internet access and databases. When a library experiences bandwidth issues, MOREnet staff assists the library in evaluating its condition and increases the bandwidth if it is warranted. As a consortium, MOREnet is governed by a council which includes permanent seats for the state librarian and two public library representatives. For more information, see the MoreNet Web site http://www.more.net.

- Mississippi: The state library, in cooperation with the Mississippi Information Network (Missin3), offers many Internet-related services to the state's public libraries. These services include basic Internet connectivity to all public library outlets, help desk support, technical consultation email accounts and Web site hosting. More information is at their Web site http://www.mlc.lib.ms.us/ServicesToLibraries/MS_IN.htm.

- Wisconsin: Wisconsin had a distance education, full-motion (45 Mbps) video network available in much of the state in the 1970s. And by the early 1990s there were more than 8,000 miles of fiber in the state. In 1993, then-governor Tommy Thompson established a Blue Ribbon Telecommunications Task Force to investigate the establishment of a statewide network for libraries, K–20 educational institutions and government agencies. The outgrowth of the task force report was legislation passed in 1995 creating BadgerNet. More information is available at their Web site http://www.doa.state.wi.us/badgernet. BadgerNet covers all of the state, and the network provides backbone, middle, and last-mile connectivity. Ninety-five percent of the state's public libraries use BadgerNet to link to their shared integrated library system (ILS), and for Internet access. Over $13 million annually in state universal service funds heavily subsidize BadgerNet connectivity for both public libraries and K–12 school districts. BadgerNet is governed by an Advisory Council which includes permanent representatives from the state library and the state's regional library cooperatives.

Such statewide networks require considerable planning and direct involvement by the state library.

The development of statewide telecommunication networks can entail a long planning and implementation process involving multiple parties (e.g., state and local governments, K–12 schools, higher education) each with its own agenda. And the process has to be cognizant of the budget timeframes of the various parties. It is not unusual for it to take several years to develop, from the initial planning stages, an actual working network. Because the bandwidth needs of libraries are increasing at such a rapid pace, libraries may not have the luxury of waiting several years while a statewide network is developed. And for a variety of reasons some states will simply not develop such networks.

Where state networks are not an option, a viable alternative may be building regional networks managed by regional library cooperatives or other organizations. In this regard, ALA issued a report titled *Regional Library Cooperatives and the Future of Broadband* (2008). Like the role that SLAs have in some states in helping develop statewide networks, the regional cooperative report demonstrated that SLAs can also serve as advocates for addressing bandwidth issues on a regional level, too. Yet another option that SLAs can support is the development of community area networks (CANs). These networks often include the local K–12 schools, community colleges, municipal government, and the public library.

The above ALA/OITP studies clearly document the problems that many public libraries have with attaining adequate broadband and the various roles that SLAs have in helping address these problems. Partly in response to the issues that these studies documented, in late 2008, OITP was awarded a grant from the Bill & Melinda Gates Foundation to focus on states where bandwidth issues were most pronounced. Initially, the OITP's *Broadband Strategy Advisor Project* will provide information and consulting services to seven SLAs to support their efforts to develop viable broadband connectivity and sustainability plans (ALA, 2009). OITP will help participating SLAs review and evaluate possible solutions, and develop strategies to overcome potential barriers. The SLAs will then submit proposals to the foundation for funding to help ensure that every public library will have a minimum of 1.5 Mbps connectivity. Grant funds will also be allocated for technical support, training, and for E-rate support. The project may be expanded to additional states.

In addressing broadband issues, the state library agency provides assistance in a number of ways. Table 13.1 shows the most common actions that SLAs have taken over the past several years to support high-speed, broadband Internet access for their public libraries (Davis, Bertot, & McClure, 2009). Advocacy remains the most common activity in most states. This often means informing and educating funding or legislative bodies on why public libraries need high

TABLE 13.1   State Library's Support for High-Speed Internet Access

State Library Support for High-Speed Internet Access	Percent Agree
Advocate for improved broadband through legislative process	59
Offer some degree of financial support for broadband	30
Build broadband networks with other public/private agencies	26
Broker broadband access and negotiate telecom costs on behalf of public libraries	26
Advocate for improved broadband through outreach to Internet service providers	24
Train library staff to broker broadband access and negotiate telecom costs	13
Build broadband networks independently	11

speed access. Advocacy can also mean educating key stakeholders to counter the assumption held by some that the Internet will render libraries obsolete.

In addition to advocacy, 30% of SLAs report that they offer funding to the public libraries in their states to help pay broadband costs (Davis, Bertot, & McClure, 2009, p. 122). Only 11% of SLAs said they had no role or provided no services in the area of broadband access or support. More recent survey data show that the broadband issue is assuming an ever more important role. For example, findings from the December 2008 SLA Chief Officers' Qualitative Questionnaire revealed that 39% of states said there was a statewide broadband task force currently in place and 9% said one was planned for the near future (Davis, Bertot, & McClure, 2009, p. 130). Other actions reported by state librarians in the December survey included rebidding of the state's existing telecommunications network and conducting a statewide assessment on library broadband needs.

STATE LIBRARY SUPPORT FOR ACCESS TO CONTENT

Most SLAs have—and will continue to have—important roles in assisting their public libraries in addressing issues related to Internet connectivity and use. Yet, to focus only on the technical issues of access and broadband connectivity presents an incomplete picture. Such a narrow focus misses another key role that SLAs have as supporters of access to content. In fact, access to electronic content is the most common Internet-related service provided by SLAs. Below is a selection of the types of content to which SLAs support public libraries access.

Periodical/Reference Databases

Forty-seven SLAs offer some type of access to full-text databases (Henderson et al., 2008, p. 15). The databases are often provided via commercial vendors and include Web access to thousands of full-text periodicals and other reference resources. This content is almost always offered at no direct cost to libraries because the state library is supporting the service using state funds, federal (LSTA) funds, or a combination thereof. In fact, SLAs report that by far the most common technology-related expenditure the state library makes on behalf of its public libraries is for licensed databases, including e-books (Davis, Bertot, & McClure, 2009, p. 122). The economies of scale such statewide licensing offers are substantial. The service not only saves the local public library a considerable amount, but offers the library's staff and patrons access to thousands of periodicals the library could not afford to subscribe to.

The types of databases, the degree of coverage and the extent of access (e.g., in the public library only, available to other libraries, available in private households too, etc.) varies considerably from state to state:

- Alaska: Via a commercial vendor, the Alaska State Library offers access to almost 6,000 magazines and scholarly publications. Most of these are available both in the library, and by state residents in their households, too. Like many states, the state library also offers access to electronic resources that focus on information pertinent to that particular state or region. PolarPac, a database of publications covering materials from Alaska and Arctic regions, is a good example.

- New York: The New York State Library offers over 6,000 periodicals and various other reference resources free to every resident of the state through their local public, academic or school library. In addition, the databases in the New York Online Virtual Electronic Library (NOVEL) can be accessed outside the library using a library card or a state driver's license for verification. The service also offers access to various newspapers from communities in the states. The licensing by the state library saves local libraries in the state more than $87 million annually. More information may be found at their Web site http://www.nysl.nysed.gov/libdev/stackup.pdf.

These are only two such examples, as many other states have some type of a "Digital Library" oftentimes supported all or in part with federal LSTA money (e.g., the Florida Electronic Library http://www.flelibrary.org/.

Digitization

Another area related to the provision of access to content includes state library management or support for digitization projects. In 2007 at least 34 SLAs reported that they supported digital programs of some type (Henderson et al., 2008). Its statewide perspective and oftentimes staff expertise in digital organization (e.g., metataging) places SLAs in the ideal position to help initiate or coordinate statewide digital library programs. This effort is often done in cooperation with other partner organizations like state archive offices, higher education, and museums. Digitization projects often focus on the conversion of content related to each state's unique history and character:

- Illinois: In 2000 the Illinois State Library announced the opening of the Illinois Digital Archives http://www.idaillinois.org. This site provides access to primary source materials from a variety of sources including libraries in the state, museums, local historical societies, and other cultural institutions.

- Colorado: The Colorado State Library worked with the Colorado Historical Society and other organizations on a Colorado Historic Newspapers Collection. The collection currently includes 477,000 digitized pages from 147 newspapers published in the state from 1859 to 1923 (The time period for which publications are in the public domain) http://www .coloradohistoricnewspapers.org/Default/Skins/Colorado/Client .asp?Skin=Colorado&AW=1243715815150&AppName=2. The Colorado State Library has placed digitization as one of its objectives in its long range plan, stating that "a sustainable statewide coordinated digitization and preservation effort of intellectual holdings will be expanded, funded, and implemented" (Colorado Library Advisory Board, 2005, p. 1).

A related digitization role for SLAs is serving as the electronic depository or records manger for publications from state government agencies. Eleven SLAs have this responsibility (Henderson et al., 2008).

Shared Integrated Library Systems and Resource Sharing

In the age of ubiquitous library Internet access, it is often easy to overlook one of the core missions that public libraries still have—that of ensuring their patrons have access to print resources. In this regard the Internet has greatly facilitated access to traditional print collections. This has been accomplished primarily via statewide or regional online union catalogs, shared integrated library systems, and interlibrary loan programs. Forty-eight SLAs report supporting one or all of these methods to help enhance access to individual library collections (Henderson et al., 2008). Support for shared integrated library systems and resource sharing again highlights the role of the state library as the logical—and sometimes only—organization that has the authority and wherewithal to support statewide resource sharing programs and initiatives:

- Georgia: The Georgia State Library is an example of a comprehensive approach in assisting its public libraries in this area via the Georgia Library Public Information Network for Electronic Services (PINES). It is a shared integrated library system used by about 70% of the state's public libraries. It allows patrons access to the collections of participating libraries that total over 8.8 million books and other materials (Georgia Public Library Service, 2007). The state library is also recognized for its decision to go with an open source (Evergreen) ILS, and it was instrumental in the initial development of Evergreen. When PINES went "live" in September 2006, it was the largest implementation of an open source, shared integrated library system in the country (Georgia Public Library Service, 2009).
- Ohio: Some SLAs support statewide resource sharing programs that link other types of libraries or link to libraries that have different ILS.

The Ohio state library supports statewide resources sharing via its MORE program. As the library states, "The day has dawned in Ohio where any library user can request an item from any Ohio library and check it out from the user's home library—whether that home library is a public, school, academic, or special library" (State Library of Ohio, 2009, para. 1). Support for shared integrative library systems and resource sharing allows the state library to leverage scarce funding statewide.

E-rate

The E-rate program continues to be important in providing the public library community with discounts on Internet and telecommunications costs, including discounts for increased bandwidth. Yet the program also continues to be plagued by a Byzantine application process and an often onerous follow-up review process. As a result, libraries often fail to maximize the discounts they are entitled to, or in some instances they do not bother to even apply. This is another area where SLAs have been instrumental in providing their public libraries with E-rate support and assistance to help local library staff overcome some of the program's obstacles.

A review of the results from the 2008 ALA public library funding and technology survey shows that the library community is not maximizing its E-rate discounts (Davis, Bertot, & McClure, 2008). Forty-four percent of public libraries did not apply for the E-rate. And the most common reason cited for not doing so (40.4%) was the complex application process. As a result of E-rate money being "left on the table," OITP has received funding from the Bill & Melinda Gates Foundation to hold a series of workshops for state library E-rate coordinators. The purpose of the workshops is to provide in-depth information to state library staff so that they are more knowledgeable about the program's idiosyncratic rules and regulations. On average, over 40 SLAs have sent staff to these workshops, which have been held in the spring and fall of each year since 2007. State library E-rate coordinators then use their increased knowledge to hold workshops in their respective states and provide some level of consultation to public library staff in completing the E-rate application process. State library E-rate coordinators are also invited to participate in regular conference calls that OITP has with the Schools and Libraries Division (SLD) that administers the E-rate program. In addition, many SLAs sponsor E-rate Web sites and email lists to help facilitate communications with their public library community.

Except for discounts on plain voice telephone service, libraries must have a certified technology plan to obtain E-rate discounts on Internet access and other telecommunication services. In over 90% of the states, the state library is recognized by the SLD as the official technology plan certification agency (Henderson et al., 2008). State library staff often assist their public libraries with advice on revising technology plans, and help to ensure that the plan meets the requirements and timelines established by the SLD. It is not unusual for state library staff to review hundreds of technology plans, and there is no financial support for this from the SLD.

Technology Maintenance and Troubleshooting

One of the essential aspects of Internet access is ensuring that all the requisite hardware and network components are operating in an acceptable fashion. The on-site library hardware (e.g., desktop PCs) and local area network are often the responsibility of the local library. But several SLAs have assumed some degree of responsibility in this area. Other SLAs do not offer direct IT support but do provide their public libraries with access to online subscription resources, like WebJunction. The SLA also often serves an informational role, such as keeping the library community informed of statewide contracts from which libraries can purchase. Below are highlights from several SLAs that offer technology support to the public libraries in their states:

- Texas: Since 1999 the Texas State Library has used $700,000–$800,000 annually in LSTA funds to supported TANG—Technical Assistance Negotiated Grants. The program offers public libraries a variety of services including onsite and remote assistance for desktop workstations, servers, integrated library systems, and troubleshooting Internet connectivity. As the state library's LSTA five-year plan (2003–2007) evaluation states, "Clearly, TANG is a lifeline for libraries, especially rural, isolated, and poorly funded libraries in maintaining, upgrading, and making technology, and a rich array of information resources, available to their patrons" (Texas State Library and Archives Commission, 2007, p. 57).

- West Virginia: The public libraries in West Virginia not only have a statewide telecommunications network managed by their state library, the SLA also provides considerable support down to the library's local area network and staff and patron workstations. This comprehensive support is accomplished by 11 technicians; each assigned to a specific region in the state. These staff are on the road constantly doing site visits to the libraries in their service area. In FY 2007/08 the technicians traveled over 55,000 miles and made 722 library visits. (The state has 174 public libraries.) To facilitate this degree of support the SLA maintains documentation for each public library that includes the floor plan, number and make/model of each PC, router location, etc. Most of this support is paid for by out of state funds. In addition, the SLA will host a library's Web site, and provide library staff with email accounts.

This type of support from SLAs is especially important for the smaller and rural public libraries.

Continuing Education

The ever-changing Internet landscape makes it difficult for library staff to keep up-to-date as new services and applications are being continuously developed and brought online every day. This makes continuing education a critical, ongoing process. To address this need many SLAs sponsor or offer to financially support workshops and other continuing educational (CE) opportunities

targeted at a wide variety of Internet-related services. This state library responsibility is often done in partnership with regional library cooperatives (RLC). In
states that certify their public library directors or other staff, continuing education (CE) is often required as part of maintaining one's certification.

SLAs that are members of WebJunction can offer their public library staff
access to hundreds of online CE opportunities on both technology and a wide
variety of other subjects, too. These courses are done via the Internet, as are
an increasing number of CE courses from other organizations. In the 2007
ALA technology study, SLAs also identified a training and continuing education
need on technology issues, like the value of broadband (Davis, Bertot, &
McClure, 2008, p. 126). Here is an example from one state on how the state
library assists its public libraries in this area.

- California: The California State Library offers the state's public libraries
  a wide variety of CE activities (technology and other topics) via a contract with Infopeople http://infopeople.org. The CE venues vary from
  face-to-face to Web-based asynchronous workshops and programs.
  Funding comes from a combination of LSTA and workshop revenue.
  A sample of the Internet-related CE opportunities includes Podcasting,
  and using Web 2.0 tools.

Virtually every state library agency has some type of continuing education program or services that support public libraries on a range of broadband, telecommunications, network deployment and configuration, E-rate, and other
technology-oriented training.

Other Services

There are many other services and programs that SLAs provide related to
Internet access and networking, including the following:

- *Advocacy:* SLAs serve as an important advocate for library services
  related to technology and Internet use. Of the SLAs that offer CE opportunities, 37 of them report that workshops related to advocacy and
  marketing are the most common type of workshops provided (Davis,
  Bertot, & McClure, 2008). Advocacy can also be tied to the public relations efforts conducted by SLAs to better inform the public on the
  importance of adequate Internet access, which in turn can influence
  decision makers. Many SLAs also provide information for library staff
  to use with their boards and local funding bodies. The SLA's advocacy
  efforts are often done in coordination with other interested parties like
  the state's library association. At the federal level, the Chief Officers of
  SLAs (COSLA) is the official state library organization that advocates
  for public libraries. COLSA works closely with ALA's Washington D.C.
  office on many issues of a national scope impacting public libraries.
- *Communications:* Many SLAs use the Internet to provide a variety of resources to help foster easy and rapid communication and information

sharing with the state's public library community. Typical examples include: Searchable library directories, e-newsletters, email lists, blogs, wikis and RSS feeds. An increasing number of SLAs also have established accounts on social networks (e.g., Facebook) and use Twitter.

- *Technology/Internet standards:* Some SLAs have standards or less stringent "guidelines" related to technology and Internet access. Common examples include the number of Internet connected public access PCs or the minimal bandwidth a library should have. Obviously setting such benchmarks is done with good intentions and libraries that are below the standards often use them in their local advocacy efforts. But standards are sometimes criticized because there are not always the resources (e.g., funding, technical support) allocated from the state library to enable the local library to meet the standards. In a 2000 study by the National Information Standards Organization (NISO), 93% of SLAs cited cost as the most common barrier to adopting standards (NISO, 2000). Thus in most states compliance is voluntary. Nonetheless, setting even informal guidelines can be useful as an indication of how far a local library must go (or how far to has come) in meeting the basic needs of Internet access and connectivity.

- *E-government:* There are several different aspects of e-government services in which SLAs are important players. For example, in 41 states the SLA is an official depository for state government publications. As an ever-increasing number of these documents are born digital, many SLAs are taking the lead role to help ensure that the documents are properly cataloged (e.g., use of metatags) for digital retrieval. Another rapidly growing e-government service is the provision of government services via the Internet. Several typical and popular services that have made this transition include the electronic availability of government permits, forms, and licenses. For example, citizens in 35 states can now renew their vehicle registration online and in 39 states allow the filing of taxes online (Davis, Bertot, & McClure, 2009). The public library serves as a key enabler for e-government because it provides *access* to the ever increasing number of services that have migrated to the Web. And SLAs often serve as intermediaries or coordinators between the state agencies that sponsor the e-government services and the local public library.

- *Bill & Melinda Gates Foundation Grants:* In addition to targeting some states for broadband funding as referenced above, SLAs have worked with the foundation for over a decade on grants related to Internet use in public libraries. The first grant, the State Partnership Grant, allocated over 45,000 PCs to libraries throughout the country. As a requirement of the grant, the PCs had to be connected to the Internet. SLAs helped to coordinate this grant effort and others that followed, including grants focused on sustaining technology and staff development, and training efforts focused on enhancing technology skill sets.

- *SLAs and regional library cooperatives:* Many SLAs do not have the staff resources to provide the services or the degree of help and technical support their public libraries need related to sustaining Internet access and use. To address this issue the SLAs often rely on the services provided by regional library consortia. The relationship between the RLCs and the state library differs in each state but some states provide the majority of the RLCs' budgets. The regional cooperative then usually has a directive from the state library to provide various services like ensuring that their member libraries have acceptable Internet access and the needed support to sustain such access.

- *Statewide studies and needs assessment.* An important activity that a number of SLAs provide is conducting studies, needs assessments, services evaluation, etc. that assist public libraries better plan for and provide a range of services. This type of needs assessment and evaluation has been especially significant in planning for and implementation of public library Internet-based services. State library agencies also work closely with ALA in encouraging their public libraries to complete the annual ALA funding and technology survey.

These other types of support are only examples of a broad array of roles that SLAs play in supporting pubic libraries in their access to and use of the Internet and networked services.

IMPORTANT ROLES AND A DEMANDING FUTURE

This chapter offers numerous areas and activities in which SLAs support public libraries and Internet resources, services, and programs. In summary, these include the following:

- Placing broadband at the top of the state library's service priorities;
- Advocating for library broadband at the local and state levels and especially in state legislative efforts;
- Being aggressive to ensure SLA participation in any state broadband planning process, especially if any process is initiated as a result of the ARRA broadband funding—if state efforts are not forthcoming, work with regional library consortia to address broadband issues at the regional level;
- Opening lines of communication and collaborate with key stakeholders like the K–12 and higher education communities, the state network office, state utility commission, and broadband providers;
- Working with municipal government to develop community area networks (CANs) that connect community anchor institutions. (Many public libraries are part of a local government [e.g., city, county]);
- Being proactive in continuing to offer statewide access to periodical, reference and other Web-based information resources; and
- Filing for federal broadband stimulus grants from the American Recovery and Reinvestment Act of 2009 or assisting regional library cooperatives in filing grant applications for enhancing broadband or public access computing. (The federal agencies that administer the broadband

funding encourage cooperative and collaboration applications, and SLAs are in an excellent position to foster such applications).

Since the mid-1990s SLAs have provided support and advocacy for Internet access and related services to their state's public libraries. The state library has often provided critical initial funding and support to enable public libraries to offer new Internet services and applications. And the state library serves an important advocacy role by informing key stakeholders and the public at large about why our libraries need reliable and robust Internet connectivity. The commitment by the state library to maintain such support and advocacy will very likely continue for the foreseeable future.

However, that future is likely to be a demanding one. As this chapter is written in the fall 2009, many SLAs are under siege with significant funding cuts already received and the likelihood of more such cuts in the future. For example, in the 2008–2009 Florida legislative session, some $20 million in state aid to public libraries was eliminated until a massive public outcry took place and the state aid (although reduced) was restored. The 2009–2010 legislative sessions for most SLAs are likely to be both demanding and challenging as SLAs continue advocating to maintain funding support for public libraries. Indeed, in a recent report describing the role of LSTA and SLAs, IMLS concluded "current economic conditions will present new challenges for State Library Administrative Agencies as they strive to meet the public's growing library service expectation in the face of constrained state budgets" (Manjarrez, Langa, & Miller, 2009, p. 33).

Another demand on SLAs will be staying current with new network, broadband, and telecommunications technologies. Increasingly the state library will play an important role in assisting public libraries plan for, deploy, manage, and assess their Internet services and broadband connections. Many SLAs participate in statewide technology planning for libraries and as new technologies and applications become available and deployed so too will these need to be incorporated into public library services, resources, and programs.

And finally, the impact of the National Telecommunications and Information Administration (NTIA) Broadband Technology Opportunity Program (BTOP) and the Department of Agriculture Rural Utilities Services (RUS) stimulus programs from the American Recovery and Reinvestment Act of 2009 will certainly place new demands on the roles of SLAs (U.S. Department of Commerce, 2009). In Wave 1 of the BTOP funding, many SLAs submitted proposals related to broadband deployment, upgrades, and sustainability. How these broadband stimulus programs support SLAs and individual public libraries has yet to be determined.

These are but a few of the current topics/issues currently facing SLAs as well as the demands they will be facing in the future. To some degree, state library staff are unsung heroes in their efforts to assist public librarians improve services in general and Internet-based resources, services, and programs more specifically. Despite the current funding crises confronting public libraries and SLAs, state library staff members continue to make significant strides in assisting public libraries improve a range of Internet and network-based services. Their roles in continuing such support, while likely to change, are equally likely to continue to be essential as public libraries move forward in using the Internet.

REFERENCES

American Library Association, Office of Information Technology Policy. (2008). *Regional library cooperatives and the future of broadband.* Chicago: American Library Association. Available at http://www.ala.org/ala/aboutala/offices/oitp/publications/booksstudies/rlc.pdf.

American Library Association, Office of Information Technology Policy. (2009). Broadband strategy advisor project. Chicago: American Library Association. Available at www.ala.org/ala/issuesadvocacy/telecom/broadband/bsap/index.cfm.

Asp, W. G. (1986). The state of state library agencies. In C. R. McClure (Ed.), *State library services and issues.* Norwood, NJ: Ablex.

Bard, M., Bolt, N., Weingarten, R., & Windhausen, J. (2007). *Public library connectivity study—findings and recommendations.* Chicago: American Library Association. Available at http://www.ala.org/ala/aboutala/offices/oitp/publications/booksstudies/index.cfm.

Bertot, J. C., & McClure, C. R. (1998). *Moving toward more effective public Internet access: The 1998 national survey of public library outlet Internet connectivity.* Washington, D.C.: U.S. National Commission on Libraries and Information Science. Available at http://www.plinternetsurvey.org.

Bertot, J. C., McClure, C. R., Jaeger, P. T., & Ryan, J. (2006). *Public libraries and the Internet 2006: Survey results and findings.* Tallahassee, FL: Information Use Management and Policy Institute. Available at http://www.plinternetsurvey.org.

Bertot, J. C., McClure, C. R., & Jaeger, P. T. (2007). *Public libraries and the Internet 2007: Report to the American Library Association.* Tallahassee, FL: Information Use Management and Policy Institute. Available at http://www.plinternetsurvey.org.

Bertot, J. C., McClure, C. R., & Thompson, K. (2002). *Public libraries and the Internet 2002: Internet connectivity and networked services.* Tallahassee, FL: Information Use Management and Policy Institute. Available at http://www.plinternetsurvey.org.

Colorado Library Advisory Board. (2005). *Strategic plan for library development in Colorado.* Available at http://www.cde.state.co.us/cdelib/download/pdf/4.9StrategicPlanGoalsandObjectives.doc.

Davis, D., Bertot, J. C., & McClure, C. R. (2008). *Libraries connect communities: Public Library Funding & Technology Access Study 2008–2009.* Chicago: American Library Association. Available at http://www.ala.org/ala/research/initiatives/plftas/2008_2009/librariesconnectcommunities3.pdf.

Gaston, B. (1995). *NSF-MCI—background information on the Internet/NSFNet.* Available at http://www.stewart.cs.sdsu.edu/nsf-internet.faq.

Georgia Public Library Service. (2007). *Library Services and Technology Act: Five-year plan for Georgia's Libraries, 2008–2012.* Available at http://www.imls.gov/pdf/5yrplans/GAplan2012.pdf.

Georgia Public Library Service. (2009). *About us.* Available at http://www.georgialibraries.org/gpls/about_us.pdf.

Henderson, E., Manjarrez, C., Miller, K., Dorinski, S., Freeman, M., Music, C., O'Shea, P., & Sheckells, C. (2008). *State library agency survey: Fiscal Year 2007 (IMLS-2008–StLA-02).* Washington D.C.: Institute of Museum and Library Services. Available at http://harvester.census.gov/imls/pubs/Publications/StLA2007.pdf.

Manjarrez, C., Langa, L. A., & Miller, K. (2009). *A catalyst for change: LSTA grants to states program activities and the transformation of library services to the public (IMLS-2009-RES-01)*. Washington, D.C.: Institute of Museum and Library Services. Available at www.imls.gov/pdf/CatalystForChange.pdf.

McClure, C. R., Bertot, J. C., & Zweizig, D. (1994). *Public libraries and the Internet: Study results, policy issues, and recommendations. Final report*, June, 1994. Washington, D.C.: U.S. National Commission on Libraries and Information Science. Available at http://www.plinternetsurvey.org.

National Information Standards Organization. (2000). *A study of State Library Agencies' information technology standards policies and practices*. Available at http://www.unt.edu/wmoen/projects/StateLibraryStandardsStudy/TitlePage.htm.

State Library of Ohio. (2009). *Ohio libraries share: MORE*. Available at http://library.ohio.gov/IT/MORE.

Texas State Library and Archives Commission. (2007). *Evaluation of LSTA five-year plan for Texas, 2003–2007*. Available at http://www.tsl.state.tx.us/ld/pubs/lstaplan/2003/report.pdf.

U.S. Department of Commerce. (2009). *Broadband USA: The portal to apply for broadband funding under the American Recovery and Reinvestment Act of 2009*. Available at http://www.broadbandusa.gov/.

Wiegand, W. A. (1986). The historical development of state library agencies. In McClure, C. R., (Ed.), *State Library Services and Issues*. Norwood, NJ: Ablex.

14

Public Libraries and the Internet: A View from the Trenches

Larra M. Clark

INTRODUCTION

As most library advocates will affirm, communicating the value of public library services requires a combination of statistics and stories. This also is the case for better understanding the state of technology access and funding in U.S. public libraries. Input from hundreds of library directors, staff, trustees, and patrons over two years has greatly informed the Public Library Funding & Technology Access Study and suggested new lines of inquiry (American Library Association, 2007–2009).

This chapter is not about the leading edge of technology, but rather about the daily challenges and successes public libraries experience in meeting patron technology needs. It is about:

- How libraries struggle to balance traditional library services with ever-growing demand for technology services with roughly the same number of staff;

- How ill-equipped most library buildings are to provide twenty-first century technology connections to their communities;

- A widespread need for trained information technology staff that will allow libraries to "push to the next level while keeping things running on the floor"; and

- How library directors and trustees are advocating to sustain and grow library services.

Computers and the Internet are now as fundamental to providing valuable access to information and entertainment as the books that preceded and now co-exist with them at the public library. Library staff members are even more actively engaged in teaching new skills and connecting patrons with vital resources—including employment, education, and e-government. Technology also has made library collections and many services available around the clock, further proving that the Internet has not put the public library in decline, but rather fostered new growth and need of a range of Internet-enabled services and resources.

BACKGROUND

As part of the Public Library Funding & Technology Access Study, a small team of researchers visited more than 60 libraries in nine states eligible for "Opportunity Online" hardware grants from the Bill & Melinda Gates Foundation. Site visits and focus groups were conducted between March 2007 and December 2008 in Delaware, Indiana, Maryland, North Carolina, Nevada, New York, Pennsylvania, Utah, and Virginia.

Site visit research objectives were to:

- Elucidate trends suggested by the quantitative data;
- Explore quantitative data anomalies;
- Deepen understanding of certain aspects of U.S. public library advocacy, funding, and sustainability; and
- Focus attention on current U.S. public library funding hot topics of interest.

The site visit planning and execution employed several methods to achieve its goals. These included:

- Reviewing previous studies and reports and state-level data regarding Internet connectivity, technology-based services provided by libraries, and stability of funding;
- Engaging in discussions with a range of individuals familiar with library funding, governance, and telecommunications issues;
- Conducting state site visits to more fully explore factors influencing public libraries providing stable and sufficient funding, staffing, and technology; and
- Conducting follow-up phone interviews with selected state and public library staff as required or appropriate.

The use of environmental scan techniques, secondary data analysis, focus groups, and telephone follow-up enables the project team to support the detailed data reported by individual libraries by "grounding" those data in governance and funding realities of a library community.

The research team worked with staff in each of the nine state libraries to identify public library directors to participate in small focus groups. The research team requested that these library directors reflect a range of libraries of varying population sizes, budgets, and governance structures. The team also sought representation of libraries that had experienced a high degree of success in creating and sustaining technology access, as well as those more financially vulnerable and/or challenged in deploying technology services.

KEY FINDINGS

Providing technology access does not represent a one-time investment of funds or staff training. Speed of change in hardware, software, and Internet services demand updates and upgrades. The unique complexity of library technology—which combines intense public computer use with back-end operating systems for staff—further complicates what already is a challenging environment. In addition to nearly ubiquitous online catalogs, libraries are building impressive suites of online services—including audio, video, and digital collections—and managing public access to computer resources via reservation, time, and print management systems.

As part of the study's site visits and focus groups, questions were asked in three key areas: use of public access computing and related services; technology infrastructure (including staff and funding); and challenges for sustaining technology services into the future. Several broad themes emerged as a result:

- Most libraries report flat public funding and increased fundraising efforts;
- Technology has brought more—not less—library use;
- Library infrastructure (including physical space and staffing) is being pushed to capacity; and
- Successful library advocacy demands strategic, frequent outreach to key stakeholders.

Funding

It is rare to visit a library where the staff believes its financial resources are adequate to provide the level of service they would like to provide members of their communities. Even in states like Maryland—where library advocates in 2006 successfully secured an increase in state aid (Baykan, 2006) or in New York, which ranks third in the nation for per capita operating revenue (National Center for Education Statistics, 2007)—library staff reported difficulties in maintaining or growing local funding to support increased technology demands. The majority of libraries visited reported flat funding, sometimes going without increases for a decade or longer despite increased cost of living. Where cuts had been made, materials budgets were usually the first target area for reductions.

The issue of flat or declining funding appears to be particularly onerous for rural libraries. "The issue is, they really don't have a lot of money. So when it comes to fixing a bridge or funding a library, it's hard to be out there in front," reports one rural library director. As a non-profit or government agency in a city or county not seeing any revenue growth, competition is fierce for extremely limited resources. Public safety and education are generally the last services to be cut, with libraries often less of a priority.

Leading up to the recession beginning in December 2007 (National Bureau of Economic Research), library directors expressed growing concerns over property tax caps and voter resistance to bond measures. Tax caps mean population growth doesn't pay for itself, thus increasing the burden on public services, including libraries. The state of Nevada, for instance, only taxes on 35% of a property's assessed value (Nevada Revised Statute 361.225). The state legislature also voted to cap recurring revenue from assessments so that it can be no more than 2% per year for residential property or 8% for commercial property. The Virginia General Assembly also was considering an amendment to the state constitution that would allow localities to lower property taxes by 20%, but it failed to pass.

In fact, a 2005 article in *Library Journal* looking back over the previous decade of referenda for building projects and operating budgets showed significant declines from a high mark of 91% for building projects and 92% passage of referenda for operating budgets in 2000 (Gold, 2006). In 2005, less than 58% passed, before rebounding in 2007 to a 69% operating, and 74% building, referenda passing (Freeman, 2008).

Where tax funding has been mostly flat, many libraries have stepped up private fundraising efforts. Almost all public libraries have Friends groups that do some fundraising, but more libraries of all sizes report that they have established library foundations and/or endowments that fundraise to assist with maintaining or growing services. At least a few libraries are beginning to leverage these discretionary funds to pilot technology projects. "We want to be able to prototype and help justify (projects) to the county," one North Carolina foundation board member said. "This allows the library to stay on the vanguard." This shift to "other" revenue sources is further discussed by Davis in Chapter 12 of this book.

Physical Infrastructure

Another challenge for many libraries is the age of their buildings. Technology requires space for computers and electrical and cabling infrastructure unimagined 20 years ago. According to a 2007 survey by the Chief Officers of State Library Agencies, a majority of library buildings are 25 to 50 years old, and 40% of library buildings are estimated to be in fair or poor condition (COSLA, 2007).

A 2002 Utah study found that 63% of libraries in the state were constructed before 1980 (Utah State Library Division, 2002). This created a substantial issue for libraries, as the report indicated—libraries reported having new computers and/or funds to purchase computers, but the buildings were unable to accommodate the computers due to space and power constraints.

The most obvious manifestation of the space crunch is the limited space available for desktops, which may be grouped in a small island, spread along and hugging a wall or crammed into what once might have been a staff office. But it also is evident in the jumble of cables below staff desks, servers in public areas or staff bathrooms, and the increased role of laptops in meeting computing needs. The lack of space for a computer lab or other dedicated space for library computers is frequently cited as a barrier to offering information technology training to patrons.

An effective workaround that many libraries have developed is a mobile laptop lab. Libraries develop and use these labs in branches with meeting rooms and wi-fi to provide training for both staff and patrons. In some cases, the mobile lab also is used in schools, senior centers, or other outreach locations where there is a demand for training.

At least one new library building visited included a "finished basement" that currently is used for storage but was built to allow the building to accommodate expanding library services and change over the next 20 years. The building was built with few interior load-bearing walls, and there is no place in which CAT5 cable is more than 10 feet away.

"I was comfortable we could get the bond, but also was sure that we couldn't do it again," the Nevada library director explained. "If you'd asked me 25 years ago what we'd be doing, I couldn't have predicted. I just know it'll be different!"

Patron Technology Needs

Public libraries reported hosting more than 376.5 million uses of electronic resources, including the Internet, the online catalog, computer software and more in fiscal year 2005 (National Center for Education Statistics, 2008). During our site visits we frequently saw lines of people waiting to get into library in the morning, and most public access computers were in use most of the day. The hours after school until close were the busiest in the majority of libraries visited. "We're busy every moment we're open, and they're actually outside with their laptops before we open," said one New York library director.

Over time, the research team identified six main groupings of patron technology use reported both by staff and by library computer users:

- Employment (e.g., job seeking, resume preparation, entrepreneurship);
- Education/information (e.g., online classes, homework, genealogy, news);
- E-government (e.g., unemployment applications, tax forms, licenses, and fees);
- Communication (e.g., email, chat, and social networking);
- Entertainment (e.g., downloadable books and movies, games); and
- Routine tasks (e.g., bill paying, shopping, banking, travel).

As is the case with traditional library services, library technology users represent a spectrum. At one end are those who bring their own technology—including USB drives, laptops, MP3 players, and digital cameras—to the library and expect it to work seamlessly. At the other end are first-timers who have never touched a mouse or keyboard and who completely depend on their public library to provide technology access and teach them how to use it.

A library director in one Maryland county reported that 85% of residents in the library's legal service area had home computers, and 93% of those residents also have Internet access at home. "And we're asking ourselves, how come we're so busy?" The answer from many patrons interviewed ranged from faster access speeds at the library (broadband versus dial-up) to a need for assistance from library staff, to competition among family members for a single home computer.

Employment

In every library visited, directors, staff, and patrons talked about the critical role library technology plays in supporting job seeking and small businesses in communities. Most aspects of seeking and applying for employment now require Internet access and basic computer skills, even if the job itself does not require the use of a computer, such as housekeeping in casinos or stocking shelves in grocery stores. For many job seekers, a library computer was the first one he or she had used. Not only did they need to fill out an online job application, they also needed to establish an email account and check back frequently to see if they were a candidate for employment. In addition to low technology skills, many of these new library patrons had low literacy rates and/or spoke English as a second language.

Seventy percent of the top 100 U.S. retailers (including Wal-Mart, Home Depot, and Kroger) accepted online applications for hourly positions, up from 41% in 2004, and 16% *only* accepted online applications, according to a 2006 study from Taleo Research, which analyzes best practices and economics of human resources management (Taleo Research, 2006). The numbers have doubtless climbed in more recent years.

Entrepreneurs also are frequent users of library computers. These library patrons told us they use the computers and Internet access to research grants, stay in touch with professional contacts, update business Web pages, read online business publications, prepare invoices and more.

With millions of jobs lost between December 2007, when the most recent recession is said to have begun, and December 2008, library technology is more vital than ever for community residents, particularly as some government agencies also are closing satellite unemployment offices as part of cost-cutting measures.

E-government

Library staff in all states also said more library patrons are interacting with government agencies online. As with job seeking, many of these patrons are the least equipped to manage complex online forms and applications—such as those required to schedule an appointment with the Immigration and Naturalization Service or apply for unemployment.

Virginia library directors reported the Virginia Employment Services recently had closed several satellite offices with public access computers and posted notices on their doors directing people to their local libraries with no advance notice of their closures. The state department of revenue also has stopped print-ing tax forms.

Another Indiana library director said she has patrons in her library every day applying for unemployment benefits. "They could also go to the unemployment office, but the lines are long there, and there is no one to help them navigate." She added that the library's hours also are more conducive since they can look for work all day, then come to the library at night.

Communication and Social Networking

Library computers and Internet access are used as frequently to connect peo-ple with one another as to connect them with online information and resources. Staying in touch with friends, family, and potential employers via email or social networking sites is a highly valued use of public access computers. In addition to community residents, business travelers and tourists frequently find public libraries a convenient and affordable access site. Many libraries now offer "express" computers with 15-minute time limits that allow people to quickly check email (or print boarding passes) rather than wait for a public access com-puter with a longer time limit. This tiered access balances different patron needs and allows more users to access the Internet in a timely fashion.

Particularly for younger technology users, however, instant messaging (IM) or chat and social networking are replacing email as the preferred way to stay connected with peers. Young people expect to use library computers to check Facebook, upload videos *and* work on homework—often all at the same time. Along with gaming and recreational uses of computers, some library staff mem-bers reported conflicting feelings about "frivolous" uses of computers (often raised by adult patrons wanting more time online) and the desire to provide access to the online services teenagers prefer.

Summary findings from a November 2008 report funded by The John D. and Catherine T. MacArthur Foundation, in fact, support this view and admonish adults to facilitate young people's engagement with digital media. "It might sur-prise parents to learn that it is not a waste of time for their teens to hang out on-line," said Mizuko Ito, University of California, Irvine researcher and lead author of the study *Living and Learning with New Media.* "We found that spend-ing time online is essential for young people to pick up the social and technical skills they need to be competent citizens in the digital age" (The John D. and Catherine T. MacArthur Foundation, 2008, n.p.).

With all the various uses and diversity of users, it should be no surprise that demand continues to outstrip supply, despite an 86% increase in the number of computers available in libraries between 2000 and 2005 (National Center for Education Statistics, 2008b). Library staff members work to provide public access to computers and the Internet to the greatest number of people in their communities by limiting the amount of time available online and, increasingly, by providing tiered public access.

"It's a real contradiction that needs to come through. We're really not allowing people enough time to fill out an application, to do homework . . . Thirty minutes is nothing," said one Utah library director, leading the research team to add a ques-tion to its national survey to learn more about time limits. The 2007–2008 survey findings confirmed site visit impressions: three-quarters of public libraries have time limits, and 60 minutes is the most common limit per session (45.7%), followed by 30-minute limits (35%). Nearly half of libraries allow patrons to take as many sessions as they desire in a day—as long as no one else is waiting (American Library Association, 2008).

The impact of time limits, however, appears to be reflected in a 2008 study funded by the Institute for Museum and Library Services, which found that the average time spent per in-person online visit was 29 minutes, compared with an average 63 minutes for remote online visits (Institute of Museum and Library Services, 2008). Only 4% of in-person online visits lasted more than one hour.

Staffing

One finding from the 2007–2008 Public Library Funding & Technology Access Study that may surprise some people is that a majority of libraries (59%) identified staff issues as the most significant challenge to maintaining public access workstations and Internet access. Financial concerns followed closely (57%), but were not the chief barrier (American Library Association, 2008). Of course, these two concerns are intertwined as overall staffing levels and the ability to hire or expand information technology staff have a direct relationship to financial resources.

Since non-IT building-based staff constitute the most common IT support (39.6% overall and 44% in rural and 40% in urban libraries) for public library branches, it may not be surprising how many of the site visits found that one, often self-taught, staffer carried the burden of all staff and patron technology needs. This makes sense given that almost 60% of U.S. public libraries have fewer than five full-time equivalent staff (National Center for Education Statistics, 2007) and nearly 100% of all libraries provide public access to computers and the Internet (American Library Association, 2008).

With limited resources and time, it is likely one staff member may "bulk up" in one area of expertise and allow for a more efficient triaging of patron requests. Unfortunately, this paradigm often gets distorted to become ANY technology question immediately getting referred to a formal or informal "techie"—including simple activities like how to download media from the library Web site, upload a digital photo, or print a document. This provides a disservice to everyone in the library setting. The library patron is sometimes kept waiting in a queue for the attention of a single staff member—or even told to come back another day if the "techie" is off that day. Staff members continue to fear "breaking" something and fall further behind in their abilities to engage technology for core services and patron assistance. The "techie" is constantly distracted and diverted from higher-level projects such as technology planning, evaluation, and formal IT training for staff and patrons.

In the March/April 2007 issue of *Library Technology Reports*, Sarah Houghton-Jan (2008) points to a lack of technology competencies among library staff and the impacts of this lack:

> In the year 2007, we all still have staff members who are not comfortable operating in a Windows environment, who do not know how to change font

size in Microsoft Word, or who do not know how to attach a document to an email message. This is unacceptable, but it points to our own failings—that we have not clearly outlined expectations, and that we have not trained to those expectations in a satisfactory way . . . hoping against hope that our staff would simply magically pick these skills up along the way.

In interviews, library staff frequently voiced their frustrations with both a lack of technology training and/or a speed of change that outpaces what training they may be able to acquire—formally or informally.

Investing in staff development is a vital component of improving library services overall and technology access in particular. Libraries use a variety of approaches to keep staff engaged with technology and better equipped to assist patrons:

- Require technology training and testing as part of new hire practices;
- IT staff provide weekly or monthly talk-back sessions with library staff based on staff-identified needs;
- Libraries invite staff to participate with patrons in training sessions and/or videotape and edit training sessions to make them available to library staff via the intranet;
- Libraries take advantage of online learning opportunities to reduce staff travel and coverage costs;
- Libraries close two or four times a year to provide staff development; and
- Require and fund continuing education for staff.

Advocacy

A key area of interest for the focus groups and site visits was around advocacy—who are libraries collaborating with to achieve their mission? How have they mobilized support for the library? How are library directors and trustees illustrating the value of the library and its technology to decision-makers?

With term limits and frequent turnover of government officials, library directors report advocacy efforts can feel a little like a hamster wheel of proving and proving again the value of libraries and the changing roles libraries are playing in their communities. The library "brand" is still closely tied to books, even though most people now are aware libraries offer free access to the computers and the Internet. Many elected officials, however, are unaware of the high volume and critical nature of public use of library computers. "It was a big surprise to a number of county officials that we're doing the volume of computer use and support that we do, and that so many people come to us. They live in this bubble that people have home computing," said one Utah library director.

Library directors employ a variety of techniques to increase awareness and support of library technology, including:

- Arranging and providing a tour of the library for newly elected officials—particularly at a time when the library is at its busiest. This tour may be the first time many of these men and women have been to the library. Many libraries also host annual luncheons for elected officials to thank them for their support and alert them to library developments.

- Treating local government agencies as library customers. Look for ways to help solve problems for a sister agency; encourage library staff to serve on city or county taskforces; host the town government's Web site; invite elected leaders to participate in strategic planning.
- Regular networking. Several directors commented that the only contact with government funders can't be only once a year at budget time if the library is going to be successful in positioning itself. Share library successes, as well as funding needs.
- Leveraging library trustees, friends, and patrons. Community members (and voters!) can often make a stronger case for the library than can staff employed by the library.

Often, however, directors only mobilize these human resources to pass the budget or raise votes for referenda. Advocacy specifically around technology and technology services was rare. In some cases, trustees are reluctant to take on additional responsibilities or fear that lobbying for increased funding would represent a conflict of interest if employed by the government.

Most trustees interviewed as part of site visits report that they see their role as assisting with fundraising, including grant writing and passing library bond or millage, followed by promoting the library and serving as a liaison to local government. Perhaps because of their vital roles in funding library services, trustees most often cited Friends of the Library groups and city or county councils as key partners for the library in the community. Schools also were mentioned, but business groups, service clubs, and other nonprofits were seldom referenced. This may be due in part to the fact that trustees were usually not involved in ongoing outreach with these community organizations. If the library was a member of the Chamber of Commerce or involved with similar community groups, it was usually the library director or senior manager that represented the library.

Trustees were more split on what technology services were most valued by members of the community. Simple access to computers and to the range of on-line services available through the library (including homework help, databases, e-government, and resources for small businesses) were mentioned the most often, but staff assistance, high-speed Internet access, and wireless availability also were referenced. The means of promoting technology access included:

- Media outreach;
- Community presentations and outreach, including demonstrating new technology offerings; and
- The library Web site and newsletters.

And the messages included highlighting digital divide concerns and talking about return on investment for local tax dollars. Several trustees, though, thought it was not necessary to promote technology access because it already is so well-known and taken for granted in the community.

Board membership can make a significant difference for the visibility and standing of the library in the community. Regardless of whether the board is advisory or governing and whether it is appointed or elected, the library director and trustees must take an active role in recruiting for and developing a diverse board with the connections and experiences necessary to plan for the future of libraries. A Utah trustee with an IT background helped jumpstart the library's technology plan by moving technology funding from grants and gifts to an operating budget line item. Library trustees who also serve on city or county councils serve as regular liaisons between the agencies. One board president focused on recruiting an accountant and local business people to help improve fiscal systems. An Indiana library director put it this way: "We used to take what we got (from appointments). But when we got a few lemons, we began making recommendations."

CONCLUSION

Public administrators always are faced with the challenge to make decisions about how to best invest limited financial and staff resources. "Public things are usually funded to mediocrity but you don't have to accept mediocrity," said Dr. Ron Anderson, CEO of a Dallas public hospital, in an August 2008 *Governing* magazine article. "There are public institutions and public universities that are world-class outstanding. How do they get that way? With philanthropy, with management and with leadership" (Buntin, 2008, n.p.).

The same may be said of library services, which, as many directors mentioned, are not considered "essential" services de jure (state statute) or de facto. When faced with limited funding, space, and bandwidth, library leaders described long-term plans for ameliorating these issues, often in partnership with other government or nonprofit agencies. Many described how building projects mobilized community support and engagement with the library that could be leveraged for ongoing improvements. Others developed consortia that allowed for a volume discount on electronic subscriptions or contractual IT support services.

Fortunately, there is an amazing wealth of experience and effective practices to be shared in the profession—along with an infusion of new librarians and paraprofessionals excited by how technology can be used to extend the reach of library services. Just as our patrons use technology to stay connected, library staff in even the most geographically remote locations can use it to connect to listservs and communities of practice to gain practical and strategic advice on concerns. But we must make time for these conversations, as well as opportunities to explore and "play" if we are to continue personal growth and remain relevant in the future.

REFERENCES

American Library Association. (2007). *Libraries connect communities: Public Library Funding and Technology Access study: 2006–2007*. Chicago, IL: American Library Association.

American Library Association. (2008). *Libraries connect communities: Public Library Funding and Technology Access study: 2007–2008.* Chicago, IL: American Library Association.

American Library Association. (2009). *Libraries connect communities 3: Public Library Funding and Technology Access study: 2008–2009.* Chicago, IL: American Library Association.

Baykan, M. (2006). Maryland's successful campaign to increase library funding. *InfoToday,* September. Available at http://www.infotoday.com/cilmag/sep06/Baykan.shtml.

Buntin, J. (2008). Lifeline. *Governing Magazine,* August. Available at http://www.governing.com/articles/0808hospital.htm.

Chief Officers of State Library Agencies (COSLA) (2008). Legislative Committee, National Construction Survey, 2007. Prepared by the New Jersey State Library for COSLA.

Freeman, C. (2008). Library referenda 2007: A mixed ballot bag. *Library Journal,* March 15.

Gold, A. M. (2006). Library referenda 2005: By the people. *Library Journal,* March 15.

Houghton-Jan, S. (2007). Technology competencies and training for libraries. *Library Technology Reports, 43*(2).

Institute of Museum and Library Services. (2008). *Interconnections: The IMLS national study on the use of libraries, museums and the Internet.* Available at http://interconnectionsreport.org/.

The John D. and Catherine T. MacArthur Foundation. (2008). *Living and learning with new media.* Available at http://www.macfound.org/site/c.lkLXJ8MQKrH/b.4773437/.

National Bureau of Economic Research. (2008). *Determination of the December 2007 peak in economic activity.* Available at http://www.nber.org/cycles/dec2008.html.

National Center for Education Statistics (2007). *Public libraries in the United States (FY 2000–2005).* Available at http://www.nces.ed.gov/pubsearch/getpubcats.asp?sid=041#.

Nevada Revised Statute 361.225

Taleo Research. (2006). *Trends in hourly job application methods.* Available at http://www.taleo.com.

Utah State Library Division. (2002). *21st Century library needs assessment.* Salt Lake City: Utah State Library Division.

Part

V

Moving Forward

Chapter

15

Shaping the Debate: The Present and Future Impacts of Policy on the Internet and Library Services

Paul T. Jaeger and John Carlo Bertot

INTRODUCTION

The provision of Internet access and training presents public libraries with significant challenges in meeting the needs of individuals, communities, and governments. The ways in which libraries can meet the needs of these stakeholder groups, however, is shaped by the impacts that public policies often have in the provision and management of Internet services. While each state and many local governments have policies of their own that affect libraries, this chapter focuses on the federal policies that shape the provision of Internet access and training in public libraries, given that federal laws impact all libraries.

Policy at any level is the collection of government directives intended to shape decisions and actions of individuals, organizations, and government agencies in a society. Policy can be established by legislation, executive orders, judicial rulings, guidelines and regulations, rulemaking, agency memos, signing statements, agency circulars, and other types of official statements (Relyea, 2008). As such, different agencies often create incompatible, redundant, or conflicting policies. Once implemented, these policies directly affect actions of individuals, organizations, and governments, and issues related to them tend to be the subject of ongoing debate and long-term discussion (McClure, 1999).

Public libraries are most often affected by a kind of policy known as information policy. "Information policy can best be understood as the set of specific goals created by governments to shape the creation, access, usage, management, exchange, security, display, collection, and other uses of information" (McClure & Jaeger, 2008, p. 257). As a result, information policy includes issues related to privacy; secrecy and security of government records; information access, retrieval, and use; freedom of information legislation and government transparency; intellectual property, e-government, veracity of government information, ICTs, and information management. "As printed and electronic information has become the lifeblood of government, commerce, education, and many other daily activities, information policy has come to influence most interactions in society" (Jaeger, 2007, p. 842). Information policy affects the everyday use of information in myriad ways, including the access, management, content, and training issues in the provision of Internet access and training in public libraries.

KEY POLICIES CURRENTLY AFFECTING LIBRARIES

There are numerous laws and other policy instruments related to the technology and Internet access provided by libraries, including such major laws as the Telecommunications Act of 1996 (47 U.S.C. § 225), the Digital Millennium Copyright Act (P.L. 105–304), the USA PATRIOT Act of 2001 (P.L. 107–56), the Homeland Security Act of 2002 (P.L. 107–295), the E-government Act of 2002 (P.L. 107–347), and the Children's Internet Protection Act (P.L. 106–554). The legal landscape "has become filled with laws and regulations dealing with information and communication," as more than "600 bills dealing with the Internet alone were on the table during the 107th Congress" (Braman, 2004, p. 153). Information issues now consume more time in congressional hearings than do many other issues (Mueller, Page, & Kuerbis, 2004).

The policy instruments have created many considerations and obligations in information provision and access in libraries, from mandating filtering of Internet access to creating new guidelines for what electronic information can be requested from libraries in investigations (Jaeger, Bertot, & McClure 2004; Jaeger & Burnett, 2005; Jaeger, Bertot, McClure, & Langa, 2006; McClure & Jaeger, 2008). While a complete overview of all federal policies that have any impact on public libraries and Internet access could be the size of a book unto itself, the following are the main areas where policy has a major influence on the provision of Internet access and training in public libraries.

Telecommunications

There are several telecommunications issues related to access, quality, cost, and availability (rural vs. urban areas) that affect the success with which public libraries can engage in meeting expectations for Internet-enabled services. At the most basic level, the ability of public libraries to provide Internet access and resources is dependant on the quality and sufficiency of the bandwidth available in the library (Bertot & McClure, 2007).

Overall, the policy and technological environments surrounding broadband are extremely complicated in the United States (Weiser, 2008). In recent years, there have been significant disputes about the U.S. broadband policy environment and the degree to which federal telecommunications and broadband policy does (National Telecommunications and Information Administration, 2008) or does not (Center for Creative Voices in Media, 2007) promote increased access to broadband with higher quality and reduced cost. Further, there are still significant areas of the country where broadband access—and in the most extreme cases any level of Internet access—is not available (Grubesic, 2008a, 2008b).

Public libraries that have lower levels of broadband access often also have limitations on the range of Internet-enabled services and resources they can provide (American Library Association, 2007; Bertot & McClure, 2007). Such is especially true in the provision of large data sources and many of the Web 2.0 technologies that require large amounts of bandwidth for video, audio, interactive, and other social networking capacities.

Through the American Recovery and Reinvestment Act of 2009 (ARRA), the Federal government is making funds available to upgrade public computer center capacity, middle mile, sustainable broadband, and broadband infrastructure throughout the United States through the Broadband Technology Opportunities Program (BTOP), administered by the National Telecommunications and Information Administration (NTIA), and the Broadband Initiatives Program (BIP), administered by the Rural Utilities Service (RUS) (Broadband Initiative Program, 2009). NTIA BTOP grants are competitively based, while the RUS BIP program is essentially a loan-based program specifically for broadband build-out in rural areas. As of December 2009, the NTIA began announcing the first recipients of these funds, and libraries were among the recipients. It is unclear at this time: (1) how many libraries will benefit from the ARRA broadband stimulus funds; (2) what the impact on library broadband will be; and (3) the extent to which public library broadband will be upgraded significantly enough to build adequate and future-looking broadband infrastructure for public library Internet-enabled service provision.

E-rate and Universal Service

Within the broad topic of telecommunications is the information policy issue of E-rate and universal service, which shapes the quality and sufficiency of public library provision of Internet access through the distribution of economic resources. The Telecommunications Act of 1996 established a Universal Service Fund administered by the Universal Service Administrative Company to oversee the Schools and Libraries Program (www.usac.org/about/universal-service). Under this program, public libraries, schools, and hospitals can apply for E-rate support to obtain discounts for selected telecommunications, Internet access, and internal connectivity.

These discounts are sizeable, ranging from 20% to 90% for total costs. The procedures for requesting these discounts have been criticized for a range of reasons, including the complexity of the application process, the delay in the release of the funds awarded, and the propensity of certain states to receive disproportionate amounts of the funds awarded (Jaeger, Bertot, McClure, & Rodriguez, 2007; Jaeger, McClure, & Bertot, 2005). Libraries receive only 4% of total E-rate funds, yet this amount is quite substantial, with public libraries receiving more than $250 million between 2000 and 2003; in contrast, E-rate provided $12 billion to public schools in the same period (Jaeger, McClure, & Bertot, 2005).

The American Library Association (2002) has noted that the E-rate program has been particularly significant in its role of expanding online access to library patrons in both rural and underserved communities. In addition to the impact on libraries, E-rate and LSTA funds have affected the lives of individuals and communities in a significant way. Goldstein (2002) has estimated that approximately 11 million low-income individuals rely on public libraries to access online information. Many libraries do not need to apply for E-rate funds or do not meet the requirements for receiving funding. However, many other libraries rely on the E-rate program to be able to afford the provision of Internet access. Ultimately, the success with which many public libraries can work through the E-rate application procedures has a direct bearing on the quality of these libraries' information infrastructure and degree to which that infrastructure can support the provision of Internet access.

Filtering Access

The Children's Internet Protection Act (CIPA) established requirements for public libraries that receive many types of E-rate or Library Services & Technology Act (LSTA) funding to place filters on all computers to protect children from online content deemed potentially harmful. Under CIPA, public schools and public libraries receiving certain kinds of federal funds are required to use filtering programs to protect children under age 17 from harmful visual depictions on the Internet and to provide public notices and public hearings to increase public awareness of Internet safety. Since the implementation of CIPA, adoption of filtering has reached 100% on public school computers and approximately 50% on public library computers (Jaeger & Yan, 2009).

Many libraries fought against the filtering requirements of CIPA, which are perceived to violate the principle of librarianship to provide equal access to information, along with objections to the requirements to filter access by adult patrons and staff as well as minors (Cabe, 2002; Goldstein, 2002; Horowitz, 2000; Minow, 1997; Peltz, 2002). Filters are also widely acknowledged to block more materials than they are intended to, limiting access to information about personal health, government, environment, and politics, among other areas; in many cases, filters incorrectly block more information than they correctly block (Jaeger, Bertot, & McClure, 2004; Jaeger, McClure, Bertot, & Langa, 2005). Filters also do not account for different ages among users, treating the social, physical, and cognitive processing abilities, developmental processes, and technical knowledge of all children—and all adults—as if there are no differences (Yan, 2005, 2006, 2008).

Influenced by such concerns, approximately one-third of public libraries refused to apply for E-rate or LSTA funds in 2007 specifically to avoid CIPA requirements, a substantial increase from the 15.3% of libraries that did not apply for E-rate as a result of CIPA in 2006 (Bertot, McClure, & Jaeger, 2008). As a result of defending patrons' rights to free access, the libraries that are not applying for E-rate funds because of CIPA requirements are being forced to turn down the chance for funding to help pay for Internet access in order to preserve full community access to the Internet. Because many libraries feel that they cannot apply for E-rate funds, different levels of Internet access are available to patrons of public libraries in different parts of the country (Jaeger, Bertot, McClure, & Rodriguez, 2007).

Public Access

One of the significant concerns about the impact of CIPA on the quality and quantity of information available on library computers is the fact that many people rely on public libraries for Internet access, and public policy encourages this reliance. While about three-quarters of Americans are Internet users, 27% of Americans live in a household that has no Internet connection and 58% of Americans live in a household that lacks broadband access (Fox & Madden, 2006). As a result, many people rely on public libraries for any access or for sufficient speed of access (e.g., broadband). As a result, youths, especially children from unrepresented populations, are more likely to be adversely affected by these gaps in access (Pastor & Fairlie, 2006). In three-quarters of communities in the United States, the public library provides the only public place in the community where free Internet access is provided (Bertot, McClure, & Jaeger, 2008).

Government agencies are furthering this reliance on public libraries for Internet access by sending people to the public library to access e-government. Federal, state, and local government agencies now rely on public libraries to provide citizens with access to and guidance in using e-government Web sites, forms, and services (Bertot, Jaeger, Langa, & McClure, 2006a, 2006b). Many government agencies now direct citizens to the nearest public library for access and help in applying for permits, scheduling appointments, paying fees and taxes, and completing numerous other local government functions online.

Public policies can also present challenges to libraries attempting to provide specific information and services through the Internet. Consider government information itself. The U.S. Code outlines a range of laws related to public access to and the role of the depository library program in the provision of government information (especially Title 44). Because many of the sections of the code have not been updated for the electronic, networked environment and the provision of e-government services, existing policies administered by the Government Printing Office (GPO) may complicate public library provision of e-government resources and services. Indeed, some GPO policies are so outdated in the age of the Internet that one of the requirements for the head of the GPO is to be well-skilled in the art of book binding.

There are provisions of the E-Government Act, especially Chapter 36 (Management and Promotion of Electronic Government Services), that appear to bypass a range of information policies and regulations regarding public access that traditionally have been under the jurisdiction of the GPO. In addition, numerous federal and state agencies either require or recommend use of public libraries in agency regulations. However, most citizens appear to have different ideas about how they wish to access government information. A 2008 study of library patrons found 77.4% regularly used Google or another commercial search engine to find government information, but only 16.5% used the www.usa.gov portal, only 9.3% used GPO Access and only 5.5% used the print collection (Burroughs, 2009).

Intellectual Property

Libraries must also be cognizant of policies related to the ownership of information in both the provision of Internet access and services and the use of the Internet by patrons. The extension of copyright protection in the Digital Millennium Copyright Act (DMCA) to the life of the author plus 80 years creates many questions of ownership. Such conflicts are magnified by the increase in access to information brought about by the Internet and electronic files. The exceptions created to try to address these issues, such as the fair use exemption and the exemptions for use in distance education, only serve to make the issues murkier and leave many libraries confused (Butler, 2003; Travis, 2006). Orphan works—older works for which the copyright owner is untraceable—are considered virtually unusable by many libraries, even by the libraries that own the items themselves (Brito & Dooling, 2006; Carlson, 2005). Libraries must also struggle with the implications of new means for storing and disseminating texts that may be covered by intellectual property rights, such as the Google Books database, to which many libraries contributed (Hanratty, 2005; Thompson, 2006).

Libraries have to work hard to avoid infringing on the intellectual property rights of many parties, including the vendors that provide digital content. Libraries struggle mightily with what previously were clearer issues of interlibrary loan, electronic resources, and services to distance patrons (Allner, 2004; Carrico & Smalldon, 2004; Ferullo, 2004; Gasaway, 2000). At the same time, libraries must also struggle with the implications of electronic files and the ability of patrons to share files for music, movies, books, and other content formats (Strickland, 2003, 2004). The rise of the use of social networking and other Web 2.0 technologies in libraries create further complications about the sharing of protected materials through library computers by library patrons (Lankes, Silverstein, & Nicholson, 2007).

Privacy

Policies related to privacy can be critical to the usage and trust of Internet access provided by public libraries. Privacy raises many concerns for protecting patrons and library staff, and these concerns have been complicated by many laws and policies that place expectations on libraries to provide access to certain types of information or to preserve certain records should the government wish to see them (Adams, Bocher, Gordon, & Barry-Kessler, 2005). At the heart of many privacy concerns are the privacy of patron records, both records of physical activities—like books checked out—and of electronic activities—like

Internet usage (Bowers, 2006). In terms of Internet usage, these include the sites a patron visits and their actions on those sites. Libraries have taken a range of approaches to limit access to patron records or limit retention of those records to as short a period as possible to try to protect patron privacy (Bowers, 2006; Coombs, 2004; Johnston, 2000; Shuler, 2004). Embedded in this issue is that given the range of patron information that a library can capture regarding a patron's library usage (e.g., circulation, workstation/wi-fi usage since libraries increasingly require patron barcodes to use these, licensed resource usage, to name a few), it is possible to develop a substantial profile of patron information seeking and technology usage.

The assistance that librarians provide to patrons in using the Internet can lead to many difficult privacy questions. As the librarians assist patrons to complete forms or engage other services to get information about sensitive personal health issues, apply for jobs, seek benefits, fill out tax and other government forms, e-mail, chat, and countless other activities, a range of personal information may become visible to the librarians. These situations raise practical questions such as: How can librarians shield themselves from this information? To what degree (if any) do librarians infringe on privacy policies by assisting patrons in this manner? To what degree are librarians liable should such information be released to third parties? This one example is replicated countless times as patrons rely on assistance from librarians.

Libraries must also balance privacy and other community interests. This problem was exemplified by a situation in 2008 where a library found itself criticized for not releasing the Internet activities of a teenage patron who had just gone missing; the library believed it had to protect patron privacy while the police believed those records might help to identify where the girl was (Associated Press, 2008). Situations such as these reveal the depth and ramifications of privacy issues raised by the provision of Internet access and training in public libraries.

Homeland Security

The degree to which public libraries can successfully deliver the full range of government information and services that they are expected to provide has been aggravated by national security policies that resulted from the terrorist attacks of September 11, 2001. Since the attacks, federal, state, and local government information has been much more carefully scrutinized for perceived national security information to ensure that such information is not released to the public. The tighter controls over access to public information involve government information that has been removed from government Web sites (scrubbing), restrictions on the release and availability of "sensitive" government information, and increased difficulty for public libraries to identify and access certain types of government or other types of information requested by patrons (Jaeger, 2007, 2009).

Numerous information policy areas, many of which are outlined in the USA PATRIOT Act, have a direct impact on public library provision of e-government services and resources (Gorham-Oscilowski & Jaeger, 2008; Jaeger & Burnett, 2005; Jaeger, McClure, Bertot, & Snead, 2004). For example, libraries may restrict access to the records they keep and to whom they provide services under the fear that federal agents will demand access to user logs and other personal information regarding the use of electronic government services from their particular library. Federal agents may engage in wiretaps of selected tele-communications going into or out of the library to obtain information on sus-pected terrorists. A National Security Letter requesting access to library files can compel a library to turn over patron records without informing the patron.

These and other information policy issues have a significant impact on the degree to which patrons may feel comfortable seeking information through elec-tronic means, ultimately creating a chilling effect on patron information activ-ities. Even if the information being sought by the government is harmless and innocent, patrons may worry that what they are seeking may be misinterpreted, or they simply may want to preserve their privacy.

INTERACTIONS BETWEEN INFORMATION POLICY AND PUBLIC LIBRARY INTERNET ACCESS

As the areas noted above reveal, information policies shaping the provision of Internet access by public libraries are often interconnected. In conjunc-tion, public policies can also have significant impacts on the ways in which libraries provide Internet access and training. Only a small portion of public libraries used filters prior to the passage of CIPA, which tied the receipt of federal funds to filtering of Internet access (McCarthy, 2004). Since the advent of com-puters in libraries, librarians had typically used informal monitoring practices to ensure that nothing age-inappropriate or morally offense was publicly visible, with some state library systems, such as Kansas and Indiana, even developing formal or informal statewide approaches (Comer, 2005; Estabrook & Lakner, 2000; Reddick, 2004). However, CIPA changed many of these practices.

The Supreme Court's holding regarding CIPA reflected several misconcep-tions about libraries, adopting an attitude that "we know what is best for you" (Gathegi, 2005, p. 12). The Court assumed that libraries select printed materi-als out of a desire to protect and censor rather than recognizing the basic reality that only a small number of print materials can be afforded by any library. Though the Internet frees libraries from many of the costs associated with print materials, the Court assumed that libraries should censor the Internet as well, ultimately upholding the same level of access to information for adult patrons and librarians in public libraries as students in school libraries. Further, since filtering software companies make the decisions about how their products work, content and collection decisions for electronic resources in public libra-ries were taken out of the hands of librarians and local communities and placed in the trust of proprietary software products (McCarthy, 2004).

These types of misunderstandings of the capacities and social roles of libraries, especially the importance of Internet-enabled roles and expectations for libraries, are reflected in public policy. There are significant gaps between public policy and technology, which are only growing as the United States continues to make laws reactively and based on a pre-electronic age menta-lity (Braman, 2006; Grimes, Jaeger, & Fleischmann, 2008; Jaeger, Lin, & Grimes, 2008). The gaps between policies and technological realities are becoming so significant that arguments can be made that information policies may have to be completely rethought (Travis, 2006). However, if libraries are to help shape the information policies that impact the provision of Internet access to better represent the realities of library principles, situations, and services, they must be actively working to have their views represented in the relevant policy discussions.

As information technology becomes increasingly ingrained into all everyday activities, people will rely on the public library to an increasing extent for access to, training for, and help using Internet information and services. For example, in times of economic distress, the demand for library computing to fill out job applications and communicate with potential employers increases significantly (Carlton, 2009). And as e-government becomes more and more central to the delivery of government information and services, libraries will be relied upon by greater numbers of citizens and government agencies for access and assistance.

Due to this significant and increasing reliance on public libraries for Internet access and training, future developments in information policy will have significant ramifications for public libraries, particularly in the provision of Internet access and training. Public libraries do not have the option of ignoring or being insufficiently involved in the policy process. It is imperative they actively work to shape the policy process to better reflect and support the true nature and roles of public libraries and to better help libraries effectively manage the increasing demands for Internet access and training.

SHAPING THE FUTURE OF INFORMATION POLICY

Public libraries are at the center of many of the debates regarding these information policy issues. Yet, for all the difficulties associated with ensuring Internet access, training, and services, they have given public libraries the opportunity to take on increased importance to their communities in new ways. By the late 1990s, the public library's role in most communities was being redefined by its provision of Internet access and training (Bertot, McClure, & Jaeger, 2008). Internet access and training are now central components of public library services and societal expectations for the public library, yet public policy does not seem to fully recognize this reality.

From its initial appearance, the Internet has suffered gaps in access related to income, education, language and literacy, geography, social groups, and other factors, leading to a large number of residents being unable to access Internet services except through the public library (Burnett & Jaeger, 2008; Burnett, Jaeger, & Thompson, 2008; Jaeger & Thompson, 2003, 2004). To ensure equal access to information, public libraries have embraced a new social role as a guarantor of public access to Internet service to all and then subsequently adapted to roles like e-government provider and emergency response and recovery center (Bertot, Jaeger, Langa, & McClure, 2006a, 2006b). For public libraries to be given a greater role in the development of public policy, libraries must better articulate these vital benefits they provide to society.

To confront challenges posed by public policy most effectively, all members of the public library community need to acknowledge the vital importance of

Internet-related roles and expectations to the societal meaning of public libraries. If strategic plans, library activities, and library advocacy have a consistent message about the need for support, the Internet access and training roles can make a compelling argument for increases in funding, support, and social standing of public libraries. The most obvious source of further support for these activities would be the federal government. Amazingly, federal government support accounts for only about 1% of public library funding (Bertot, Jaeger, Langa, & McClure, 2006a, 2006b). Given that federal government agencies are already relying on public libraries to ensure Internet access and training, to ensure access to e-government, and to foster community response and recovery in times of emergencies, federal support for these social roles of the public library clearly can and should be increased significantly.

A unified front in evaluating, assessing, studying, and describing the Internet access and training will greatly help libraries positively impact the policy process and educate the public and policymakers of libraries' significant value to society. Regardless of what approaches are taken to finding greater support, however, public libraries must do a better job of communicating their key roles in the provision of Internet access and training to governments and private organizations in order to increase support. Such communications will need to be part of a larger strategy to define a place within public policy that gives public libraries a voice in e-government issues. To increase their support and their standing in policy discourse, libraries must not be hesitant in reminding the public and government officials of their successes in ensuring Internet access and training for all members of the community, in assisting in the response to and recovery from disasters, and in providing the social infrastructure for e-filing of taxes and enrolling in Medicare prescription drug plans, and myriad other routine Internet activities.

REFERENCES

Adams, H. R., Bocher, R. F., Gordon, C. A., & Barry-Kessler, E. (2005). *Privacy in the 21st century: Issues for public, school, and academic libraries.* Westport, CT: Libraries Unlimited.

Allner, I. (2004). Copyright and the delivery of library services to distance learners. *Internet Reference Services Quarterly, 9,* 179–192.

American Library Association. (2002). *U.S. Supreme Court arguments on CIPA expected in late winter or early spring.* Available at http://www.ala.org.

American Library Association. (2007). *Libraries connect communities: Public library Funding and Technology Access Study 2006–2007.* Chicago: American Library Association.

Associated Press. (2008). Girl's case had library, cops in privacy standoff. Available at http://www.msnbc.msn.com/id/25751801/.

Bertot, J. C., Jaeger, P. T., Langa, L. A., & McClure, C. R. (2006a). Public access computing and Internet access in public libraries: The role of public libraries in e-government and emergency situations. *First Monday, 11*(9). Retrieved February 28, 2007 from http://www.firstmonday.org/issues/issue11_9/bertot/index.html.

Bertot, J. C., Jaeger, P. T., Langa, L. A., & McClure, C. R. (2006b). Drafted: I want you to deliver e-government. *Library Journal, 131*(13), 34–39.

Bertot, J. C., & McClure, C. R. (2007). Assessing the sufficiency and quality of bandwidth for public libraries. *Information Technology and Libraries, 26*(1), 14–22.

Bertot, J. C., McClure, C. R., & Jaeger, P. T. (2008). The impacts of free public Internet access on public library patrons and communities. *Library Quarterly, 78*, 285–301.

Bertot, J. C., McClure, C. R., Wright, C. B, Jensen, E., & Thomas, S. (2008). *Public Libraries and the Internet 2008: Survey results and findings.* Tallahassee, FL: Information Use Management and Policy Institute. Available at http://www.plinternetsurvey.org.

Bowers, S. L. (2006). Privacy and library records. *Journal of Academic Librarianship, 32*(4), 377–383.

Braman, S. (2004). Where has media policy gone? Defining the field in the 21st century. *Communication Law and Policy, 9*, 153–182.

Braman, S. (2006). *Change of state: Information, policy, and power.* Cambridge, MA: MIT Press.

Brito, J., & Dooling, B. (2006, March 25). Who's your daddy? *Wall Street Journal,* A(9).

Burnett, G. B., & Jaeger, P. T. (2008). Small worlds, lifeworlds, and information: The ramifications of the information behaviors of social groups in public policy and the public sphere. *Information Research, 13*(2) paper 346. Available at http://InformationR.net/ir/13-2/paper346.html.

Burnett, G., Jaeger, P. T., & Thompson, K. M. (2008). The social aspects of information access: The viewpoint of normative theory of information behavior. *Library and Information Science Research, 30*, 56–66.

Burroughs, J. M. (2009). What users want: Assessing government information preferences to drive information services. *Government Information Quarterly, 26*, 203–218.

Butler, R. P. (2003). Copyright law and organizing the Internet. *Library Trends, 52*, 307–317.

Cabe, T. (2002). Regulation of speech on the Internet: Fourth time's the charm? *Media Law and Policy, 11*, 50–61.

Carlson, S. (2005). Whose work is it, anyway? *Chronicle of Higher Education, 51*(47), A33–A35.

Carlton, J. (2009, January 15). Folks are flocking to the library, a cozy place to look for a job. *Wall Street Journal,* A1.

Carrico, J. C., & Smalldon, K. L. (2004). Licensed to ILL: A beginning guide to negotiating e-resources licenses to permit resource sharing. *Journal of Library Administration, 40*(1/2), 41–54.

Center for Creative Voices in Media (2007). *The case for universal broadband in America: Now.* Keswick, VA: Author.

Comer, A. D. (2005). Studying Indiana public libraries' usage of Internet filters. *Computers in Libraries,* June, 10–15.

Coombs, K. A. (2004). Walking a tightrope: Academic libraries and privacy. *Journal of Academic Librarianship, 30*(6), 493–498.

Estabrook, L., & Lakner, E. (2000). Managing Internet access: Results of a national survey. *American Libraries, 31*, 60–62.

Ferullo, D. L. (2004). Major copyright issues in academic libraries: Legal implications of a digital environment. *Journal of Library Administration, 40*(1/2), 23–40.

Fox, S., & Madden, M. (2006). *Generations online.* Washington, D.C.: Pew Internet and the American Life Project.

Gasaway, L. (Fall 2000). Values conflict in the digital environment: Librarians versus copyright holders. *Columbia—VLA Journal of Law & the Arts,* 115–161.

Gathegi, J. N. (2005). The public library and the (de)evolution of a legal doctrine. *Library Quarterly, 75*, 1–19.

Goldstein, A. (2002). Like a sieve: The Children's Internet Protection Act and ineffective filters in libraries. *Fordham Intellectual Property, Media and Entertainment Journal, 12*, 1187–1202.

Gorham-Oscilowski, U., & Jaeger, P. T. (2008). National Security Letters, the USA PATRIOT Act, and the Constitution: The tensions between national security and civil rights. *Government Information Quarterly, 25*(4), 625–644.

Grimes, J. M., Jaeger, P. T., & Fleischmann, K. R. (2008). Obfuscatocracy: Contractual frameworks in the governance of virtual worlds. *First Monday.* Available at http://www.uic.edu/htbin/cgiwrap/bin/ojs/index.php/fm/article/view/2153/2029.

Grubesic, T. H. (2008a). The spatial distribution of broadband providers in the United States: 1999–2004. *Telecommunications Policy, 32*, 212–233.

Grubesic, T. H. (2008b). Spatial data constraints: Implications for measuring broadband. *Telecommunications Policy, 32*, 490–502.

Hanratty, E. (2005). Google library: Beyond fair use? *Duke Law and Technology Review, 10.*

Horowitz, A. (2000). The constitutionality of the Children's Internet Protection Act. *St. Thomas Law Review, 13*, 425–444.

Jaeger, P. T. (2007). Information policy, information access, and democratic participation: The national and international implications of the Bush administration's information politics. *Government Information Quarterly, 24*, 840–859.

Jaeger, P. T. (2009). The fourth branch of government and the historical legacy of the Bush administration's information policies. *Government Information Quarterly, 26*, 311–313.

Jaeger, P. T., Bertot, J. C., & McClure, C. R. (2004). The effects of the Children's Internet Protection Act (CIPA) in public libraries and its implications for research: A statistical, policy, and legal analysis. *Journal of the American Society for Information Science and Technology, 55*(13), 1131–1139.

Jaeger, P. T., Bertot, J. C., McClure, C. R., & Langa, L. A. (2006). The policy implications of Internet connectivity in public libraries. *Government Information Quarterly, 23*(1), 123–141.

Jaeger, P. T., Bertot, J. C., McClure, C. R., & Rodriguez, M. (2007). Public libraries and Internet access across the United States: A comparison by state from 2004 to 2006. *Information Technology and Libraries, 26*(2), 4–14.

Jaeger, P. T., & Burnett, G. (2005). Information access and exchange among small worlds in a democratic society: The role of policy in redefining information behavior in the post-9/11 United States. *Library Quarterly, 75*(4), 464–495.

Jaeger, P. T., Lin, J., & Grimes, J. (2008). Cloud computing and information policy: Computing in a policy cloud? *Journal of Information Technology and Politics, 5*(3), 269–283.

Jaeger, P. T., McClure, C. R., & Bertot, J. C. (2005). The E-rate program and libraries and library consortia, 2000–2004: Trends and issues. *Information Technology and Libraries, 24*(2), 57–67.

Jaeger, P. T., McClure, C. R., Bertot, J. C., & Langa, L. A. (2005). CIPA: Decisions, implementation, and impacts. *Public Libraries, 44*(2), 105–109.

Jaeger, P. T., McClure, C. R., Bertot, J. C., & Snead, J. T. (2004). The USA PATRIOT Act, the Foreign Intelligence Surveillance Act, and information policy research in libraries: Issues, impacts, and questions for library researchers. *Library Quarterly, 74*(2), 99–121.

Jaeger, P. T., & Thompson, K. M. (2003). E-government around the world: Lessons, challenges, and new directions. *Government Information Quarterly, 20*(4), 389–394.

Jaeger, P. T., & Thompson, K. M. (2004). Social information behavior and the democratic process: Information poverty, normative behavior, and electronic government in the United States. *Library and Information Science Research, 26*(1), 94–107.

Jaeger, P. T., & Yan, Z. (2009). One law with two outcomes: Comparing the implementation of the Children's Internet Protection Act in public libraries and public schools. *Information Technology and Libraries, 28*(1), 8–16.

Johnston, S. D. (2000). Rethinking privacy in the public library. *International Information and Library Review, 32*(3–4), 509–517.

Lankes, R. D., Silverstein, J., & Nicholson, S. (2007). Participatory networks: The library as conversation. *Information Technology and Libraries, 26*(4), 17–33.

McCarthy, M. M. (2004). Filtering the Internet: The Children's Internet Protection Act. *Educational Horizons*, Winter, 108–113.

McClure, C. R. (1999). Information policy. In A. Kent (Ed.), *The encyclopedia of library and information science* (pp. 306–314). New York: Marcel Dekker.

McClure, C. R., & Jaeger, P. T. (2008). Government information policy research: Importance, approaches, and realities. *Library and Information Science Research, 30*, 257–264.

McClure, C. R., Jaeger, P. T., & Bertot, J. C. (2007). The looming infrastructure plateau?: Space, funding, connection speed, and the ability of public libraries to meet the demand for free Internet access. *First Monday, 12*(12). Available at http://www.uic.edu/htbin/cgiwrap/bin/ojs/index.php/fm/article/view/2017/1907.

Minow, M. (1997). Filters and the public library: A legal and policy analysis. *First Monday, 2*(12). Available at www.firstmonday.org/issues/issue2_12/minow/.

Mueller, M., Page, C., & Kuerbis, B. (2004). Civil society and the shaping of communication-information policy: Four decades of advocacy. *Information Society, 20*, 169–185.

National Technical Information Administration (2008). *Networked nation: Broadband in American 2007*. Washington, D.C.: U.S. Department of Commerce.

Pastor, M., & Farilie, R. (2006). *Race, youth, and the digital divide*. New York: William T. Grant Foundation.

Peltz, R. J. (2002). Use "the filter you were born with": The unconstitutionality of mandatory Internet filtering for adult patrons of public libraries. *Washington Law Review, 77*, 397–479.

Reddick, T. M. (2004). Building and running a collaborative Internet filter is akin to a Kansas barn raising. *Computers in Libraries*, April, 10–14.

Reylea, H. C. (2008). Federal government information policy and public policy analysis: A brief overview. *Library and Information Science Research, 30*, 2–21.

Shuler, J. A. (2004). Privacy and academic libraries: Widening the frame of discussion. *Journal of Academic Librarianship, 30*(2), 157–159.

Strickland, L. S. (2003). Copyright's digital dilemma today: Fair use or unfair constraints? Part 1: The battle over file sharing. *Bulletin of the American Society for Information Science and Technology*, October/November, 7–11.

Strickland, L. S. (2004). Copyright's digital dilemma today: Fair use or unfair constraints? Part 2: The DCMA, the TEACH Act, and e-copying restrictions. *Bulletin of the American Society for Information Science and Technology*, December/January, 18–23.

Thompson, B. (2006). Search me? Google wants to digitize every book, publishers say read the fine print first. *Washington Post*, August 13, 2006, D1 & D7.

Travis, H. (2006). Building universal digital libraries: An agenda for copyright reform. *Pepperdine Law Review, 33,* 761–833.

Weiser, P. J. (2008). *A framework for national broadband policy: Report of the 2007 Aspen Institute Conferences on Telecommunications and Spectrum Policy.* Washington, D.C.: Aspen Institute.

Yan, Z. (2005). Age differences in children's understanding of the complexity of the Internet. *Journal of Applied Developmental Psychology, 26,* 385–396.

Yan, Z. (2006). What influences children's and adolescents' understanding of the complexity of the Internet? *Developmental Psychology, 42,* 418–428.

Yan, Z. (2008). Differences in high school and college students' basic knowledge and perceived education of Internet safety: Do high school students really benefit from the Children's Internet Protection Act? *Journal of Applied Developmental Psychology.* doi:10.1016/j.appdev.2008.10.007.

The Ever Changing Impacts of Internet Access on Libraries and Their Communities

Charles R. McClure, John Carlo Bertot, and Paul T. Jaeger

INTRODUCTION

Public libraries are confronted with increased demands for a range of public access computing services and resources, while simultaneously facing diminished capacity to provide such services and resources. A number of economic, social, technological, and governmental factors contribute to this situation. This paper explores the implications of increased demand and diminished capacity for providing public access computing services on both the library and the community, offering a number of possible strategies that public librarians might consider to mitigate this situation and better provide public access computing services in the future.

The data from the 2007–2009 *Public Library Funding & Technology Access Study* (PLFTAS) (American Library Association, 2007, 2008, 2009) offer a perspective on public libraries' deployment and use of public access computing that raises a number of issues regarding the degree to which public libraries can continue to provide simultaneously many of their traditional and Internet-enabled services and activities. While the data suggest that some libraries continue to strengthen their technological capacity and involvement in public access technologies, other libraries find the current environment and increasing service demands to be significant challenges.

CONTINUING CONTEXT

Much of the data show a continuation of trends from earlier PLFTAS studies. These include increased deployment of wireless, some limited increases in connectivity speeds, increased demands for and use of various Internet-enabled services, limitations with existing physical facilities to support new or more technology, lack of staff with technology skills, and stagnant technology budgets. These issues are more accentuated in rural and small library settings. Overall, the 2008–2009 data continue to support the theme that public libraries are stretched to (and sometimes beyond) their capacity to provide a range of public access technologies, services, and resources (American Library Association, 2009; Bertot et al., 2009). Specific findings include:

- Almost 72% of libraries report that they are the only source of free access to computers and the Internet in their community, basically the same as in 2008;
- The vast majority of libraries (75%) report their wireless and desktop computers share the same network, thus diminishing the effective speed of access to the Internet at the workstation. This percentage has increased sharply since 2007 when only 44.5% reported that their wireless shared the same network as the desktop computers. Further, libraries are not moving above the 3.0 Mbps speed as quickly as had been anticipated;
- Funding remains flat for many public libraries while grappling with declining purchasing power;
- Staffing is at a standstill. The ratio of full time public library staff to the numbers of computers is declining, that is, there are increasingly fewer staff available to help patrons on more computers;
- Internet services show double digit growth in areas of homework resources, audio content, video content, E-books, etc. Some of the largest areas of growth can be seen in E-books, from 38.3% of outlets reporting providing E-books in 2007 to 55.4% in 2009. In addition, audio content significantly increased from 38.9% in 2007 to 72.9% in 2009; and
- More than three-quarters of libraries reported that space limitations are a key factor when considering adding public access computers. This finding has been consistently in the 75–77% range between 2007 and 2009.

These are but a few of the key findings reported in the 2009 PLFTAS study and begin to paint the picture of too much demand and not enough capacity.

In addition, traditional public library social and service roles have changed dramatically to providing a broad range of Internet-based social and service roles. Social roles are large societal purposes for which libraries exist and which communities, individuals, and governments expect the library to serve certain societal purposes. Service roles are the responses that libraries make to address society's expectations. Societal expectations of libraries have resulted in the public library responding with a large increase in both the scope and amount of Internet-based services, resources, capacity, and undertakings.

And yet, when public access technology is studied in context and service, public libraries face external pressures to expand their public access services while simultaneously facing staffing, skill, building, infrastructure, and financial challenges (Bertot, 2009). In short, there is increased demand on public libraries to provide enhanced public access services and adopt Internet-enabled roles in the face of substantial challenges.

CHANGING CONTEXT

The years 2008 and 2009 have been particularly rife with significant national events that have occurred or have been exacerbated and may cast a new perspective on the current context in which U.S. public libraries find themselves. These include:

- *Complicated and changing national and state politics and library policies.* While issues of information policy were prominently discussed in the 2008 elections, the impacts of these issues on libraries received little attention (Jaeger, Paquette, & Simmons, 2010). Limited cooperation among the various key political players and parties contributes to a range of policies—federal and state aid to libraries, national telecommunications and broadband policy, Internet security and privacy, and use of public libraries for e-government services—that fail to account for the affects on and needs of libraries. The degree to which national politicians are aware of these issues seems limited, and the degree to which it is possible to resolve the policy concerns that affect libraries is problematic. Within this context the Obama administration is planning to invest $7.3 billion through the *American Recovery and Reinvestment Act of 2009* in broadband deployment and access.

- *Reduced Travel.* Energy prices continue to fluctuate and in general increase, and airfares have also increased. Some immediate impacts from this include the inability of librarians to travel to meetings, to engage in additional community activities, and operate bookmobiles. For library users, it is likely that they are reducing overall car travel and may be more likely to engage in online and Web-based use of the library. In short, many Americans are quickly changing and/or reducing their travel activities.

- *Increased costs for consumer goods.* Many residents in the United States have found that food prices, due in part to increased costs associated with oil and petro-products and limited production of corn to make ethanol, have increased significantly. This rise of basic living costs, combined with the current worldwide recession, translates into less available money for luxuries such as travel, entertainment, and a range of household purchases (such as books, videos, DVDs, etc.). Thus, one impact from this situation is greater demand on libraries for the resources and services they provide since many people will not wish to use their disposable income for services and resources they might otherwise obtain from the local public library.

- *Increased costs for operations and declining budgets.* Another impact of increasing energy costs is that it simply costs more to keep the doors of the public library open. Heating, cooling, and electricity costs for library buildings continue to increase and consume larger portions of a library's operating budget. This is occurring at the same time that a recent study reported that over one-third of U.S. public libraries are operating with declining budgets and that many others operate significantly behind the current inflation rates for employee benefits, energy, and materials (De Rosa & Johnson, 2008).

- *Reduced local tax base.* Because of the mortgage/housing loan crisis, many areas of the country are experiencing falling values of homes. The number of home foreclosures has increased significantly, and some states such as Florida have passed laws that have reduced the amount local governments can tax property owners. Since many public libraries rely almost entirely on local property taxes to operate the library, the impact from the mortgage/housing crisis and reduced local tax base can result in reduced library budgets and in some cases (such as Florida) library systems that have been forced into wholesale reductions in staff and services. A reduced local tax base will also increase the pressure on public libraries to seek alternate sources of funding (e.g., grants, fund raising through library foundations) to support basic library services and operations.

- *National and international financial crisis.* Due in part to the U.S. housing market, the collapse of national stock market values, and the subprime mortgage financial crisis, there has been a huge loss of individuals' net worth and severe declines in retirement and other investment accounts. The degree to which this financial crisis will continue or be resolved is unclear; nor is it clear how long it will last. An implication for libraries, however, is that in severe economic hardships there has been significantly increased use of and demands placed on libraries by people applying for jobs, seeking social support, and looking or free entertainment options (Carlton, 2009; CNN, 2009; Van Sant, 2009). In addition, states and local governments have been even more disinclined to invest in public libraries given badly declining tax revenues and the financial uncertainties of the future.

- *Reduced consumption.* A full year into the global recession, there is evidence that consumer consumption habits are changing substantially. Doing less with less is becoming a trend, and this has impacted public libraries through increased visits, additional demand for public access workstations and Internet access, increased use of library programs such as story time, and more.

- *New computing and telecommunications products and services.* Google continues to offer improved resource discovery tools for network services and resources; Apple has just released its new iPhone 4 which includes a set of services and Internet-enabled resources; the Kindle electronic book/reader is being widely received; and a range of social networking products and services now exist that are redefining the manner in which people access, use, and create information resources and services. Increasingly, some people have much more sophisticated computing, telecommunications, and connectivity than their local public library. The ability of libraries to stay current with these new computing and telecommunications products and services is problematic at best—especially in light of the trends previously identified and the public library's ongoing inability to attract adequate staff training in technology use, administration, and deployment.

In addition to the environment around libraries, there are also changes in the users of libraries. For example, Google is gaining greater currency in the minds of many information seekers as being as good as the library at meeting their information needs (Waller, 2009).

The findings from the 2006–2007, 2007–2008, and 2008–2009 PLFTAS clearly show the decreasing capacity on the part of libraries to respond to user needs related to computing and telecommunications support. Indeed, PLFTAS findings and the above trends suggest the possibility of the "perfect storm" for public libraries—decreased library funding, increasingly out-of-date physical facilities, inadequate technology and staffing, and demand for computing and telecommunications capacity occurring at the same time as ineffective government information and broadband policies and increased user demands for library computing services, equipment, and resources. The potential for such a perfect storm can be seen in library support and infrastructure, access differences among libraries, usage of library resources, the rise of social networking, assessment challenges, partnerships and collaborations, and government polices.

EVOLVING MODELS OF SUPPORT AND INFRASTRUCTURE

The evolving public access technologies environment in which public libraries operate involves multiple types of technologies, configurations, requirements, and implementations. Moreover, the technology infrastructure continues to grow in complexity, and thus requirements for management and expertise also continue to increase. The current context not only involves a range of hardware, software, and networking architecture, but also incorporates a range of applications and content that libraries license (i.e, databases, ebooks) or provide access to (i.e., flickr, YouTube, Second Life). This context requires public libraries to consider how best to manage their technology infrastructure to meet the demands of the networked environment.

Given the range of hardware, software, and networking infrastructure, as well as planning and public access management requirements, public librarians need a range of skills to successfully implement and maintain their public access computing environments. Moreover, the skill needs depend on the librarian's position—for example, an actual IT staff person versus a reference librarian who does double duty by serving as the library's IT person. The skills identified include (Bertot, 2009, pp. 90–91):

- General computer troubleshooting;
- Basic maintenance such as mouse and keyboard cleaning;

- Basic computer repair (i.e., memory replacement, floppy drive replacement, disk defragmentation, other);
- Basic networking (i.e., troubleshooting an "Internet" issue versus a computer problem);
- Basic telecommunications so as to understand the design and maintenance of broadband networks;
- Searching and using Internet-based resources;
- Searching and using library licensed resources mouse replacement;
- Ability to train patrons on the use of the public access computers, general Internet resources, and library resources;
- Ability to design curriculum for various patron training courses;
- License/contract negotiation for licensed resources, various public access software and licenses, and maintenance agreements (service and repair agreements);
- Technology plan development and implementation (including budgeting);
- Integrated library systems;
- Web design;
- Grant writing and partnership development; and
- Building design.

The list is not exhaustive, but the above provides a broad cross-section of the skills that various public library staff may need to offer to maintain a robust public access computer environment.

Public libraries may or may not have a formal technology management structure or access to the technical skills listed above. Some libraries have their own technology support staff; others have an employee who is technology savvy and self-taught; others have the library director who does it all—from toilet repair to installing a wireless router; others are part of a centralized county or city technology support structure. Some libraries have a well-conceived technology plan that consistently adjusts to technological innovations and demands. Others are simply reactionary and engage in what could be at best described as ad hoc planning. Where ever libraries may fall on this spectrum—sophisticated planning with dedicated technology staff to ad hoc with no dedicated technology staff—it is increasingly clear that the public library community needs to rethink how it engages in the planning, implementation, and support of its public access technology services and resources.

If one parses apart the public access technology environment, there are four critical components: (1) hardware, which can include public access computers, laptops, servers, routers, etc; (2) software, which can include application software as well as operating software; (3) connectivity, which can include internal networking as well as broadband connectivity; and (4) content, which can include licensed and purchased resources; and services, which can include digital reference, instruction, video conferencing, etc. The key questions that public libraries need to ask are: what is the best way to work within an increasingly complex technology environment? Should the library carry the technology burden on its own?

There are several traditional organizational models for supporting public access technologies that libraries adopt (Bertot, 2009):

1. *No Technology Support:* Libraries in this group have neither technology support staff nor any type of organized technology support mechanism with existing library staff. Nor do they have access to external support providers such as county or city IT staff. Libraries in this group might rely on volunteers or engage in ad hoc maintenance, but by and large have no formal approach to supporting or maintaining their technology.

2. *Internal Library Support without Technology Staff:* In this model, the library provides its own technology support but does not necessarily have dedicated technology staff. Rather, the library has designated one or more staff members to serve as the IT person. Usually this person has an interest in technology, but he/she has other primary responsibilities within the library. There may be some structure to the support—such as updating software (e.g., Windows patches) once a week at a certain time—but it may be more ad hoc and as needed in approach. Also, the library may try to provide its designated IT person(s) with training so as to develop his/her skills further over time.

3. *Internal Library Support with Technology Staff:* In this model, the library has at least one dedicated IT staff person (part- or full-time) who is responsible for maintaining, planning, etc., the library's public access computing environment. The person may also have responsibilities for network maintenance and a range of technology-based services and resources.

    At the higher end of this approach are libraries with multiple IT staff with differing responsibilities such as networking, telecommunications, public access computers, ILS, etc. Libraries at this end of the spectrum tend to have a high degree of technology sophistication, but may face other challenges (i.e., staffing shortages in key areas).

4. *Library Consortia:* Over the years, public libraries have developed consortia for a range of services—shared ILS; resource sharing; resource licensing; etc. As public library needs evolve, so too do the roles of library consortia. Consortia increasingly provide training and technology support services, and may be funded through membership fees, state aid, or other sources.

5. *Technology Partners:* While some libraries may rely on consortia for their technology support, others are seeking libraries which have more technology expertise, infrastructure, and abilities with whom to partner. This can be a fee-for-service arrangement that may involve sharing an ILS, maintenance agreement for network and public access computer support, and a range of services. These arrangements allow the partner libraries to have some input into the technology planning and implementation processes without incurring the full expense of testing the technologies, having to implement them first, or hiring necessary staff (e.g., to manage the ILS). The disadvantage to this model is that the smaller partner libraries are dependent on the technology decisions

that the primary partner makes, including upgrade cycles, technology choices, migration time frames, etc.

6. *City/County/Other Agency IT Support*: As city or county government agencies, some libraries received technology support from the city or county IT department (or in some cases the education department). This support ranged from a full slate of services and support available to the library to support only for the staff network and computers. Even at the higher end of the support spectrum, librarians gave mixed reviews for the support received from IT agencies. This was primarily due to competing philosophies regarding the public access computing environment, with public librarians wanting a fairly open access policy to allow users access to a range of information service and resources, and IT agency staff wanting to essentially lock down the public access environment, and thus severely limit the functionality of the public access computers. Other limitations might include prescribed public access computing technologies, specified vendors, and bidding requirements.

7. *State Library Support*: The state library of West Virginia (West Virginia Library Commission) provides a high degree of service through its statewide approach to supporting public access computing in the state's public library. The state library has IT staff in five locations throughout the state to provide support on a regional level, but also has additional staff in the Charleston location. These staff offer training, in-house technical support, phone support, and can remote access the public access computers in public libraries. Moreover, the Commission also built a statewide network through a statewide application to the federal E-rate program, thus providing at least a T1 to all public libraries in the state. This model extends the availability of qualified technical support staff to all public libraries in West Virginia—by phone as well as in-person if need be. As a result, this enables public libraries to concentrate on service delivery to patrons.

8. *Online Technology Support*: Online communities continue to evolve to support and assist public libraries in managing their technology resources. Two notable communities include WebJunction (http://www.webjunction.org) and TechSoup for Libraries (http://www.techsoupforlibraries.org/). Both provide a range of tips, tools, tutorials, and documentation regarding public access technology management and other technology issues.

But in the current context, the library community would do well to look at these approaches not as distinct ways in which to manage their technology, but rather as building blocks that libraries can use to design their technology management and planning approaches. For example, a library could review material in WebJunction or TechSoup for Libraries to gain an understanding of a particular set of technologies and how libraries use them, receive training from the state library or regional cooperative, work with county or city IT to plan for wireless access, etc. In short, the public library needs to regard these technology options as part of an overall portfolio to best serve its community and meet its own technology needs—and thus move away from the all too prevalent, particularly in rural communities—"no technology support" model.

DIGITAL DIVIDES AMONG PUBLIC LIBRARIES

The PLFTAS data clearly show that many rural and small public libraries are severely strained to provide adequate and high quality public access computing and the necessary infrastructure to support such services. In effect, there currently exist three broad categories of public libraries in terms of their public access technology infrastructure:[1]

- *Inadequate and below average computing services and infrastructure.* These have connectivity speeds of under 3 mbps limited or no wireless connectivity; outdated public access workstations; limited to no technical support staff; physical facilities that cannot be expanded, renovated, or modernized for the networked environment; and are largely dependent on statewide electronic resources (typically from the state library). These public libraries cannot meet existing public demands for networked services, staff support, and resources.

- *Adequate or average computing services and infrastructure.* These have connectivity speeds in the range of 3–5 mbps limited or some wireless connectivity; soon-to-be outdated public access workstations; limited to some technical support staff; physical facilities that only with some effort and costs can be expanded, renovated, or modernized for the networked environment; and some local as well as the statewide electronic resources (typically from the state library). These libraries increasingly find themselves at capacity or strained to meet public demands for networked services, staff support, and resources.

- *Better than adequate and above average computing services and infrastructure.* These have connectivity speeds of 10 mbps or more; significant wireless connectivity; relatively new and current public access workstations; onsite technical support staff; physical facilities for which there are resources for expansion, renovation, modernization of the networked environment; and significant local electronic resources as well as statewide electronic resources (typically from the state library). These libraries are currently able to meet public demands for networked services, staff support, and resources.

Data from the *Public Libraries and the Internet* national surveys conducted by the authors suggests that these categories have existed since at least 2000.

One might speculate, based on the 2006–2007 and 2007–2008 PLFTAS data that increasingly, those public libraries in the above average category and those in the adequate category may find themselves slipping down into the next category below them. Such may occur because of the current context described throughout the chapter and because of the general inability of public libraries to meet future demands and continue to update and expand the existing public computing infrastructure. One implication of this situation, ultimately, is that different venues for public access computing—other than access through public libraries—may need to occur or perhaps there will simply be less public access computing available to residents of the United States.

In short, there currently exists a digital divide between the haves and have-nots of public libraries in terms of their current ability and future capacity to provide public access computing and the necessary infrastructure to support that computing. Recognition of this situation is welcome, but there is a lack of study or exploration of strategies to address the situation. Perhaps a first step is to recognize that the situation exists, and develop a tiered referral system in which public libraries refer public access computing services beyond their capacity to others in a local, regional, or virtual system. Other solutions may exist, but currently little to no attention has been given to resolving this issue and ensuring equal public access computing to users regardless of the public library they visit.

LOCATION OF SERVICES AND RESOURCES

The importance of traditional in-library services—such as children's story time, adult programming, and community meeting place—are certainly likely to continue as important services that libraries provide. There are a number of studies that document the importance of the library as "place" or a facility where people can meet face-to-face and community activities can occur (Bushman & Leckie, 2006). But data from the PLFTAS clearly indicate that the demand for library networked services continues to increase. These services include provision of traditional library services via the library Web page (e.g., request an interlibrary loan); access to unique library or statewide data bases; ask-a-reference librarian; and others.

There are three possible responses from the library to try to meet these increased demands:

- The library might reallocate existing resources from print and traditional services/staff to networked services/staff;
- The library might be able to obtain additional resources from its funding agencies or other organizations such that more networked services and infrastructure can be supported; or
- The library increasingly is not able to meet demand for such services, nor does it adequately update the infrastructure to support such services.

The degree to which libraries can make *additional* reallocations of resources from traditional and print based services to networked services is problematic, and so too is the degree to which libraries can obtain additional resources to support networked services.

It is important to remember that there is a wide range of public access computer and Internet user skills—from the novice who has rarely, if at all, used a computer or the Internet, to the expert user. The ability of library users to access electronic resources through the library's Web site or other electronic portals without the library having to provide significant staffing support is unclear. The demand for these services may continue, but only to the point that the services are acceptable and meet user needs. But there are signs appearing that for some libraries, users of electronic services are beginning to consider venues other than the library to access electronic information. For example, users of electronic information clearly prefer to begin their Web-based search with Google rather than via a library Web site with links to a broad range of databases. The cumbersome nature of logging into library Web sites, moving through firewalls, and confusion about how the databases can be accessed and searched are only some of the factors that encourage the user to Google rather than use the library Web site or the library building.

The extent to which demands for increased library networked services may continue is problematic given the strained capacity of many public libraries. Competition from other vendors and services to provide a range of public access computing services, increasingly, may be easier and more effective for the user than access through the public library. Movement away from public library public computer use may be exacerbated if public libraries are unable to supply users with the most current, effective, and desired computing services and resources and at very fast connectivity speeds.

THE ROLE OF SOCIAL NETWORKING

In a recent paper, Lankes, Silverstein, and Nicholson describe library service in terms of participatory networks in which the library is a "conversation." They go on to state:

> A core concept of Web 2.0 is that people are the content of sites; that is, a site is not populated with information for users to consume. Instead, services are provided to individual users for them to build networks of friends and other groups (professional, recreational, and so on). The content of a site, then, comprises user-provided information that attracts new members of an ever-expanding network. (Lankes, Silverstein, & Nicholson, 2007, p. 19)

Of special interest to the topic being discussed here are several important questions: to what degree will these participatory network conversations include the public library or be developed by the public library? To what degree will public librarians be able to develop exciting and dynamic services that are participatory and draw on social networking principles successfully? To what degree will public libraries be able to facilitate user involvement in participatory networks through their public access technology infrastructure?

At the heart of all of these various social networking applications is a peer to peer relationship of community members that is not well-understood in terms of how it will affect public library Internet-enabled service roles. Many of the social networking applications "push" services to users, offer links to other information—much of it directly from other peers—and ultimately allow internet users to define and create information services that are personalized or customized to meet their specific needs. Perhaps more importantly, they encourage the development, content, and services to evolve based on participants' needs and creativity—as opposed to the needs and perspective of the public library.

Lankes, Silverstein, and Nicholson (2007) conclude that "libraries have a chance not only to improve service to their local communities, but to advance the field of participatory networks" (p. 32). While this may be true, libraries also have a chance to *not* be effective players in the development of participatory networks, to *not* develop internet-enabled service roles that build on social networking, and to *not* develop valid and reliable measures to gauge the success of their involvement in such service roles. While participatory technologies open up new opportunities in library services, such technologies also create new demands on and expectations for libraries, as well as many accompanying assessment, staffing, economic, and service pressures. The future of Web 2.0 public library services is one laden with challenges and issues—and one that will be increasingly decided by individual internet users—not public librarians.

In the current context of public library services there simply are inadequate staff trained in and knowledgeable about Web 2.0 applications; there are inadequate finances to support the purchase and application of these new services; and to a large degree, public libraries have been bystanders in this development as other services, e.g., YouTube, Facebook, etc., continue to evolve. But there are significant opportunities for public librarians to work together in virtual systems and initiatives to offer and manage such services. A national initiative, directed perhaps by the Public Library Association, to explore these evolving services and determine: (1) national public library Web 2.0 services that all public libraries can use; and (2) the best roles for public libraries to play in this environment, certainly would be welcome.

ASSESSMENT CHALLENGES

There is also a need to consider how to evaluate "successful" public access technology services. Evaluating Internet-based services as opposed to traditional services would need to consider a number of factors:

- Traditional evaluation approaches typically base assessment on an imposed or organizationally accepted set of service goals/objectives. Services based on social networking activities build on dynamic, personally self-driven goals/objectives which are constantly evolving and changing.

- Outcome measures (for example) that assess changes in knowledge, behavior, skills, and/or attitudes may be of less importance in Internet-based services where learning, contacts, quality of life, and other individually-based measures are most important. Moreover, individually-based measures may have greater validity for measuring user success than system-based outcomes.

- Comparing the "success" of users across various types of Internet-based services, especially social networking service applications, presents numerous challenges given the situational nature of users of these applications.

- Defining and operationalizing "page views," "full text downloads," and other online statistics in the context of federated searching, firewalls, and complex network configurations continues to be problematic.

- The nature and definition of "community" as it relates to the library's service population changes significantly in a networked environment. Existing definitions from library standards (e.g., ISO 2789 and NISO z39.7)[2] for "population served" simply do not apply in a networked environment. Indeed, successful services that rely on "virtual" communities span the globe and are not "local" communities as defined by an artificial geographical or political boundary.

- Separating the evaluation and measurement of the technological infrastructure of the service from the actual use of that application may be impossible. In short, to what degree are evaluators measuring the quality of the technology and the technology infrastructure as opposed to the use of that technology?

- Success of an individual's use of an Internet based service is dependent on the skills and knowledge of the user—one person's success versus another's may have little to do with the application or service itself.

These are but a few of the challenges that the future holds for successful evaluation of public library services in the networked environment.

Yet, national, state and local agencies, (e.g., U.S. Institute of Museum and Library Services, state libraries, and individual public libraries) continue to rely on a range of measurement approaches (outcomes assessment) and statistics describing traditional services which comprise smaller components of overall public library services. The library and information science research community has not addressed these and related issues regarding evaluation in a networked environment. Meanwhile, the current context described above will desperately need data to describe, analyze, justify, and plan for a range of public library networked-based services.

RETHINKING PARTNERSHIPS AND COLLABORATIONS

The terms "partnerships," "resource sharing," and "collaboration" have a long and checkered history in libraries in general and public libraries in particular. But due to the manner in which public libraries are organized, successful resource sharing, partnerships, and collaborations are difficult to establish. Successful resource sharing, partnerships, and collaborations are those that:

- Produce tangible and intangible benefits for each member participant;
- Require less administrative overhead to operate than the benefits that result;
- Detail clear guidelines as to which members have what responsibilities—including the administrative unit of the effort;
- Allow individual members flexibility to select and choose those services and activities of most importance/impact to them;

- Do not include personality and power conflicts among the key individuals engaged in the effort; and
- Do not result in the "rich" members subsidizing the "poor" members nor the "rich" members getting "richer."

Many of the successful resource sharing efforts are those with statewide purchase of databases or are in similar situations where costs can be reduced by larger number of purchases.

Because most U.S. public libraries receive 85% or more of their financial support from their local community, there is also a strong resistance to external controls and administrative involvement in local public library activities. Nonetheless, the ongoing call for public libraries to establish better/more resource sharing, partners, and collaborators is likely to continue and become much louder in the future.

Will the new context of public library public access computing change the ease with which public libraries can engage in more and/or better resource sharing, partnerships, and collaborations? The answer, it seems, is maybe. But there are too many factors in play that mitigate better resource sharing. Indeed, the current context of reduced/stagnant funding for public libraries reduces the staff and time available to establish such efforts.

In the past, resource sharing, collaboration, and partnerships were developed within a clearly defined geographic area. For example, a number of the states have "regional library systems" or "multi-type library systems" that are state mandated and are established for a specific region of the state. Typically these efforts, e.g., Multi-type Library Cooperatives (MLCs in Florida) and Public Library Systems, as well as Reference and Research Library Resources Councils (in New York), form the basis for public library resource sharing, partners, and collaborations. In short, libraries typically with limited resources and budgets share their limited resources and budgets with other libraries that have limited resources and budgets.

The networked environment allows for the establishment of virtual public library systems, multi-type library cooperatives, and partners/collaborators not within a specific geographic area. Indeed, it is possible for a public library in Illinois, a public library in Texas, a database producer in New York City, and a special library in Boston to establish a partnership or collaborative effort and conduct their activities virtually. A model of virtual resource sharing, partnerships, and collaboration may have some potential to better assist public libraries leverage existing resources and services. This is largely unchartered territory, though one finds experimentation with distributed services and collaborative models for digital reference and digitization projects, as examples. It is unclear as to the extent to which it is possible to expand such collaborative service approaches across a wide range of libraries and services.

While not understating the importance of resource sharing, partners, and collaboration, the traditional models for such efforts need to be re-examined and analyzed in light of the networked environment and conditions described in the current context above. Research to identify best practices innovative resource sharing efforts, and how such models might be transferred to other settings and applications, may assist public libraries weather a perfect storm.

CHANGING GOVERNMENT ROLES AND RESPONSIBILITIES

Federal, state, and local governments do not currently provide broad-based support for public libraries—either financially or in terms of policy. Data from the PLFTAS generally show a stagnant or declining role for federal, state, and local governments in their financial support of libraries. The current national, state, and local economic condition does not suggest that significant increases in the support of public libraries from government will occur, unless there is a national and carefully orchestrated effort, which the broadband deployment and access stimulus money from the *American Recovery and Reinvestment Act of 2009* might affect. But such an effort would need to be tied to the role of public libraries in addressing specific national, state, and local priorities such as:

- Promoting national, state, and local economic development;
- Helping citizens and residents access and use government services more effectively and economically;
- Providing more formalized support for job seekers;
- Reducing overall national health care costs;
- Contributing to emergency/disaster preparedness and response;
- Improving the social conditions and/or quality of life for selected population groups; and
- Helping veterans—especially those from the Iraq and Afghanistan wars—return to a productive life.

While there certainly may be other areas for attention, the key here is asserting the things that public libraries can do for governments, as opposed to maintaining the argument that governments should support libraries so they can continue to do what they have done in the past.

If public libraries can clearly demonstrate value in their ability to address national, state, and local social and economic concerns—even if only on a small scale—then public libraries would have a much stronger argument to make in terms of how governments should provide them with additional or different types of resources than they currently receive from government. Unfortunately, little concerted research and thought has been given as to the ways in which public libraries, at a national level, can move from some of the more traditional roles they have taken on to new and different roles—roles that public libraries might be much better able to address in a networked environment, e.g., employment assistance, technology training, or e-government services.

Another aspect of the relationship between governments and public libraries is the information policy perspective. Federal information policy initiatives in recent years have not been favorable to public libraries:

- The *USA PATRIOT Act* has increased national secrecy and decreased access to government information;
- National Security Letters have been used to access library records and other records without formal recourse;

- The *E-Government Act of 2002* failed to strengthen the role of public libraries as a possible vehicle for access to government information;
- E-rate and universal service as outlined in the *Telecommunications Act of 1996* continue to be under attack;
- Increased restrictions on copyright and intellectual property rights affect libraries' ability to provide access to electronic information and to own the electronic resources they purchase;
- The lack of a national broadband policy and program has limited libraries' ability to obtain adequate Internet bandwidth; and
- The *Children's Internet Protection Act* (CIPA) requires public libraries to adopt filters if they wish to receive federal support (E-rate or *Library Services and Technology Act* funding).

This list is illustrative and not comprehensive. A key theme across these laws has been the lack of thought about the impact of the laws on libraries during the crafting of the laws (Bertot et al., 2006a, 2006b; Gorham-Oscilowski & Jaeger, 2008; Jaeger, Bertot, & McClure, 2004; Jaeger et al., 2004, 2007; Jaeger & Yan, 2009).

Without widespread knowledge and understanding of these issues and how they affect public libraries and their provision of information, it is unlikely that public libraries and organizations that support them will successfully resolve these, and other, information policy issues. Working with governments to support public libraries as opposed to the current environment of actively hurting public libraries, will require more than a letter writing campaign or signing an email petition. The effort will require sustained long-term political activism on the part of public librarians, their supporters, and political leaders, that has hitherto been unknown in the public library community.

RIDING OUT THE PERFECT STORM

Clearly, the current environment presents a difficult scenario for the ability of public libraries to sustain high levels of Internet access, training, and assistance. A range of papers have highlighted many of the data that support this scenario over the years (e.g., Bertot, 2004; Bertot & Davis, 2007; Bertot & McClure, 1997, 1999, 2007; Bertot, McClure, & Jaeger, 2008a, 2008b; Bertot, McClure, Owens, 1999; Jaeger et al., 2006; McClure, Jaeger, & Bertot, 2007). But only with the careful review of the most recent years' data and the current social, economic, technological, and government factors shaping the environment around public libraries does this image of the perfect storm for public libraries begin to take shape. Responding to the storm after its arrival is likely to be too little, too late.

In the current environment, without a national focus on these issues, many libraries will face unpleasant and unpopular choices such as:

- Reducing overall service levels and options on an ongoing basis;
- Limiting traditional services and print materials to better support electronic services and resources;

- Limiting electronic services and resources to better support traditional services and print materials; and
- Curtailing support and training for patrons.

None of these options would be welcome to librarians, patrons, or policymakers.

To ride out this perfect storm, libraries must look to the challenges as opportunities in disguise, providing the chance to redefine the role, organization, and funding of public libraries in the networked environment. A core part of this response will be emphasizing coordination and cooperation among the groups with a stake in maintaining the quality and scope of public library Internet access and services:

- The American Library Association and especially the Public Library Association and the ALA Washington Office;
- Federal, state, and local government officials;
- Researchers, especially those in the Library and Information Science (LIS) research community;
- Foundations (especially the Bill & Melinda Gates Foundation) and other funding organizations (such as the U.S. Institute of Museum and Library Services);
- State Library Associations;
- Friends and trustees of public libraries;
- Concerned citizens and residents;
- Public library database and other vendors;
- State Libraries; and
- Individual public library leaders and innovators.

Although this list is long and other groups could also be included, the success of public libraries in this country has always depended on many groups and on the involvement of many leaders. To weather these difficult economic times and meet increasing demands on access and training, libraries will particularly need to focus on two key areas.

First, libraries and the stakeholders in libraries must be creative in finding ways to build partnerships and cooperatives to share expenses and resources and to use economies of scale to negotiate cost savings. State libraries and library consortia would be well-positioned to take the lead in such ventures. However, libraries that are not currently part of consortia or cooperatives should carefully explore the potential benefits of banding together in the face of the current extenuating circumstances. While libraries are a widely trusted and respected public institution, that status does not make them immortal. In fall 2009, major systems were facing reductions in hours of operation and numbers of open branches. For example, until a budget compromise was reached, the libraries of Philadelphia were slated to close indefinitely due to insufficient funds. In short, libraries and interested stakeholders in libraries need to work together nationally, regionally, and locally to preserve their ability to meet patron, community, and government needs and expectations.

Second, libraries need to work to educate policymakers and taxpayers about the quandary they have been placed in. Public libraries cannot continue to meet ever-greater demands and expectations for public access computing at the same time that significant limitations on infrastructure, capacity, and staffing continue to occur. Libraries must articulate and demonstrate their value to individuals, to communities, and to governments through education and advocacy. Libraries do many things, and are generally taken for granted. If libraries are to benefit from a coordinated national response to the current situation and take part in the development of some form of national library policy, libraries must clearly demonstrate their value and educate stakeholders about this value.

MAINTAINING THE PUBLIC SERVICE TRADITIONS THROUGH THE STORM

Libraries have existed for millennia, having gone through many permutations, functions, and levels of availability (Jackson, 1974). Difficulties in the surrounding environment are, in fact, nothing new to library service. The Middle Ages in Europe stands as the low point for libraries—scientific knowledge became equated with paganism, making the educational mission of libraries very difficult to carry out without running the risk of meeting a fiery ending (Manchester, 1993).

Since its origins as isolated colonies, America has maintained an especially strong relationship with libraries. At the beginning of American Revolution, nearly a hundred libraries existed in the colonies; one hundred years later, there were more than 3,500 libraries in the United States (McMullen, 2000). While 1876 is considered the beginning of the modern library movement, thousands of libraries in the United States were founded before then—social, circulating, subscription, academic, church, hospital, asylum, government, military, commercial, law, town, scientific, literary, and philosophical society, mechanics, institute, antheneum, and lyceum libraries, among others (Green, 2007; Jackson, 1974; McMullen, 2000; Raven, 2007).

American towns began passing legislation to create tax-supported school libraries in the 1830s and public use libraries in the 1840s, while states made legislation for public funding of libraries commonplace shortly thereafter (Conant, 1965; Davies, 1974; DuMont, 1977; Gerard, 1978). Many early public libraries were established with support from philanthropists, none more prominent than Andrew Carnegie, who bestowed more than $41,000,000 to 1,420 towns to establish public libraries between 1886 and 1919 (Davies, 1974). Since becoming widespread due such philanthropic endeavors, public libraries, as demonstrated throughout this book, have become a widely trusted and virtually essential part of the fabric of American society.

Throughout history and through the modern era of librarianship, public libraries have proven themselves to be quite resilient. As social institutions, libraries "have evolved in response to certain problem situations and have been shaped by countless, relatively independent individual decisions" (Swanson, 1979, p. 3). The current difficulties and challenges, while significant, will not spell the end of public libraries.

For all of the extra responsibilities and costs that the Internet has created for public libraries, it has greatly expanded the resources and services that libraries can provide and has created vital new roles that libraries can play in the lives of patrons and communities. This book provides a catalogue of new ways that libraries help their communities and the specific populations who benefit from these services. While the Internet has forever changed the public library for both the good and the bad, the overwhelming majority of these impacts are positive. When addressing current challenges, these amazing and innovative ways to serve patrons, communities, governments, and society as a whole made possible by the Internet in public libraries must not be forgotten.

NOTES

1. Admittedly, "adequacy" is difficult to define and depends on a number of situational factors such as the number of public access computers using a connection and the types of applications in use at any given time, whether wireless connectivity shares the same connection as a library's public access computers, whether staff computers share the same connection as public access computers, etc.

2. See http://www.niso.org/home for additional information about library standards and definitions.

REFERENCES

American Library Association. (2007). *Libraries connect communities: Public Library Funding & Technology Access Study 2006–2007*. Chicago, IL: American Library Association. Available at http://www.ala.org/plinternetfunding.

American Library Association. (2008). *Libraries connect communities: Public Library Funding & Technology Access Study 2007–2008*. Chicago, IL: American Library Association. Available at http://www.ala.org/plinternetfunding.

American Library Association. (2009). *Libraries connect communities: Public Library Funding & Technology Access Study 2008–2009*. Chicago, IL: American Library Association. Available at http://www.ala.org/plinternetfunding.

Bertot, J. C. (2004). Libraries and the networked environment: Future issues and strategies. *Library Trends, 52*(2), 209–227.

Bertot, J. C. (2009). Public access technologies in public libraries: Impacts and implications. *Information Technology and Libraries, 28*(2), 84–95.

Bertot, J. C., & Davis, D. M. (2007). Public library public access computing and internet access: Factors which contribute to quality services and resources. *Public Library Quarterly, 25*(2), 27–42.

Bertot, J. C., Jaeger, P. T., Langa, L. A., & McClure, C. R. (2006a). Public access computing and Internet access in public libraries: The role of public libraries in e-government and emergency situations. *First Monday, 11*(9). Available at http://www.firstmonday.org/issues/issue11_9/bertot/index.html.

Bertot, J. C., Jaeger, P. T., Langa, L. A., & McClure, C. R. (2006b). Drafted: I want you to deliver e-government. *Library Journal, 131*(13), 34–39.

Bertot, J. C., & McClure, C. R. (1997). *Policy issues and strategies affecting public libraries in the national networked environment: Moving beyond connectivity*. Washington, D.C.: National Commission on Libraries and Information Science.

Bertot, J. C., & McClure, C. R. (1999). Public library Internet connectivity: Status and policy implications. *Library and Information Science Research, 21*, 281–298.

Bertot, J. C., & McClure, C. R. (2007). Assessing sufficiency and quality of bandwidth for public libraries. *Information Technology and Libraries, 26*(1), 14–22.

Bertot, J. C., McClure, C. R., & Jaeger, P. T. (2008a). Public libraries and the Internet 2007: Issues, implications, and expectations. *Library and Information Science Research, 30*, 175–184.

Bertot, J. C., McClure, C. R., & Jaeger, P. T. (2008b). The impacts of free public Internet access on public library patrons and communities. *Library Quarterly, 78*, 285–301.

Bertot, J. C., McClure, C. R., & Owens, K. A. (1999). Universal service in a global networked environment. *Government Information Quarterly, 16*, 309–327.

Bertot, J. C., McClure, C. R., Wright, C. B., Jensen, E., & Thomas, S. (2009). *Public libraries and the Internet 2008: Study results and findings.* Information Institute and Center for Library & Information Innovation: Tallahassee, FL. Available at http://www.plinternetsurvey.org.

Bushman, J. E., & Leckie, G. J. (2006). *The library as place: History, community, and culture.* Westport, CT: Libraries Unlimited.

Carlton, J. (2009, January 19). Folks are flocking to the library, a cozy place to look for a job: Books, computers and wi-fi are free, but staffs are stressed by crowds, cutbacks. *Washington Post,* A1.

CNN. (2009). Hard economic times: A boon for public libraries. *CNN.com.* Available at http://www.cnn.com/2009/US/02/28/recession.libraries/index.html.

Conant, R. W. (1965). *The public library and the city.* Cambridge, MA: MIT.

Davies, D. W. (1974). *Public libraries as culture and social centers: The origin of the concept.* Metuchen, NJ: Scarecrow.

De Rosa, C., & Johnson, J. (2008). *From awareness to funding: A study of library support in America.* Columbus, OH: OCLC.

DuMont, R. R. (1977). *Reform and reaction: The big city public library in American life.* Westport, CT: Greenwood.

Gerard, D. (1978). *Libraries in society: A reader.* London: Clive Bingley.

Gorham-Oscilowski, U., & Jaeger, P. T. (2008). National Security Letters, the USA PATRIOT Act, and the Constitution: The tensions between national security and civil rights. *Government Information Quarterly, 25*(4), 625–644.

Green, J. (2007). Subscription libraries and commercial circulating libraries in colonial Philadelphia and New York. In T. Augst & K. Carpenter (Eds.), *Institutions of reading: The social life of libraries in the United States* (pp. 24–52). Amherst, MA: University of Massachusetts Press.

Jackson, S. L. (1974). *Libraries and librarianship in the West: A brief history.* New York: McGraw-Hill.

Jaeger, P. T., Bertot, J. C., & McClure, C. R. (2004). The effects of the Children's Internet Protection Act (CIPA) in public libraries and its implications for research: A statistical, policy, and legal analysis. *Journal of the American Society for Information Science and Technology, 55*(13), 1131–1139.

Jaeger, P. T., Bertot, J. C., McClure, C. R., & Langa, L. A. (2006). The policy implications of internet connectivity in public libraries. *Government Information Quarterly, 23*, 123–141.

Jaeger, P. T., Langa, L. A., McClure, C. R., & Bertot, J. C. (2007). The 2004 and 2005 Gulf Coast hurricanes: Evolving roles and lessons learned for public libraries in disaster preparedness and community services. *Public Library Quarterly, 25*(3/4), 199–214.

Jaeger, P. T., McClure, C. R., Bertot, J. C., & Snead, J. T. (2004). The USA PATRIOT Act, the Foreign Intelligence Surveillance Act, and information policy research in libraries: Issues, impacts, and questions for libraries and researchers. *Library Quarterly, 74,* 99–121

Jaeger, P. T., Paquette, S., & Simmons, S. N. (2010). Information policy in national political campaigns: A comparison of the 2008 campaigns for President of the United States and Prime Minister of Canada. *Journal of Information Technology and Politics, 7,* 1–16.

Jaeger, P. T., & Yan, Z. (2009). One law with two outcomes: Comparing the implementation of the Children's Internet Protection Act in public libraries and public schools. *Information Technology and Libraries, 28*(1), 8–16.

Lankes, R. D., Silverstein, J., & Nicholson, S. (2007). Participatory networks: The library as conversation. *Information Technology and Libraries, 26*(4), 17–33.

Manchester, W. (1993). *A world lit only by fire: The medieval mind and the Renaissance; Portrait of an age.* New York: Little, Brown and Company.

McClure, C. R., & Jaeger, P. T. (2008). *Public libraries and Internet service roles: measuring and maximizing Internet services.* Chicago: American Library Association.

McClure, C. R., Jaeger, P. T., & Bertot, J. C. (2007). The looming infrastructure plateau?: Space, funding, connection speed, and the ability of public libraries to meet the demand for free Internet access. *First Monday, 12*(12). Available at http://www.uic.edu/htbin/cgiwrap/bin/ojs/index.php/fm/article/view/2017/1907.

McMullen, H. (2000). *American libraries before 1876.* Westport, CT: Greenwood.

Raven, J. (2007). Social libraries and library societies in eighteenth century North America. In T. Augst & K. Carpenter (Eds.), *Institutions of reading: The social life of libraries in the United States* (pp. 1–23). Amherst, MA: University of Massachusetts.

Swanson, D. R. (1979). Libraries and the growth of knowledge. *Library Quarterly, 49,* 3–25.

Van Sant, W. (2009, June 8). Librarians now add social work to their resumes. *St. Petersburg Times.* Available at http://www.tampabay.com/.

Waller, V. (2009). The relationship between public libraries and Google: Too much information. *First Monday, 14*(9). Available at http://www.uic.edu/htbin/cgiwrap/bin/ojs/index.php/fm/article/view/2477/2279.

Index

About the Editors
and Contributors

JOHN CARLO BERTOT, PhD, is Professor, the Director of the Center for Library & Information Innovation (clii.umd.edu), and the Associate Director of the Center for Information Policy and Electronic Government (www.cipeg.umd.edu) in the College of Information Studies at the University of Maryland. Prior to joining the faculty at the University of Maryland, Bertot served as Associate Director of the Information Institute and Professor at Florida State University. His research spans library and government agency technology planning and evaluation, information and telecommunications policy, and e-government. Bertot serves as chair of the International Standards Organization's (ISO) Library Performance Indicator working group and serves as a member of the National Information Standards Organization's (NISO) Business Information Topic committee. Bertot is past Chair of the American Library Association's (ALA) Library Research Round Table, and serves as president-elect of the Digital Government Society of North America. Also, Bertot is editor of *Library Quarterly* and *Government Information Quarterly*. More information on Bertot is available at http://terpconnect.umd.edu/~jbertot.

BRADLEY WADE BISHOP, PhD, was a Graduate Research Associate at the Information Use Management and Policy Institute at the Florida State University in Tallahassee, Florida when this chapter was written. He holds a Master's degree in Library and Information Science from the University of South Florida and a PhD in Information Studies from Florida State University. Bishop is currently an Assistant Professor at the University of Kentucky School of Library

291

and Information Science. Much of his research includes utilizing GIS as a tool in library and information science research.

ROBERT BOCHER is the Technology Consultant with the Wisconsin Division for Libraries, the state library agency. He has been instrumental in ensuring that all Wisconsin public libraries have broadband and over 97% are connected to BadgerNet, the state's telecommunications network. At the national level he is past chair of the ALA/OITP E-rate Task Force and the OITP Subcommittee on Telecommunications. In July 2009 Bob was appointed an OITP Fellow. He has an MLS from the University of Wisconsin-Madison.

JOHN BROBST is a PhD candidate at the Florida State University College of Communication & Information and a Graduate Research Associate with the Information Use Management & Policy Institute. His research interests lie primarily in the areas of information policy and the impact of technology on society. Mr. Brobst's dissertation research examines the usability of government Web sites, including an analysis of the current policy environment that attempts to promote Web accessibility.

LARRA M. CLARK is project manager for the ALA Office of Research and Statistics. She joined the office in January 2007 after working more than six years in the ALA Public Information Office as the manager of media relations. Ms. Clark completed her MLS at the University of Illinois at Urbana-Champaign in December 2006. Previously, she worked in nonprofit public affairs, media relations, and print journalism in Chicago and Arizona for more than 10 years.

DENISE M. DAVIS, director of the ALA Office of Research and Statistics, is overall project coordinator for the annual *Public Library Funding and Technology Access* study. Ms. Davis has managed multi-year research projects including the ALA annual librarian salary survey and an ongoing multi-part demographics study of ALA membership.

KENNETH R. FLEISCHMANN is an Assistant Professor in the College of Information Studies at the University of Maryland. He is also an Assistant Director of the Center for Information Policy and Electronic Government and a member of the Human-Computer Interaction Lab. He holds degrees in computer science, anthropology, and science and technology studies from Case Western Reserve University and Rensselaer Polytechnic Institute, where he received his PhD. His research examines the mutually constitutive relationship between information technology and human values. His current NSF-funded research projects include developing and evaluating an educational simulation for computing and information ethics; field research on the role of human values in the design and use of computational models; and developing systems to automatically detect and classify human values in information policy discussions.

ERIN V. HELMRICH holds an MLS from Wayne State University in Detroit, Michigan. She is currently a Teen Services Librarian at the Ann Arbor District Library in Ann Arbor, Michigan. Helmrich has worked with youth in public libraries for 15 years. She has published articles about pop culture and marketing as it relates to teen library services & videogaming in libraries. Helmrich has presented talks and workshops on these topics at conferences, cooperatives, and libraries all over the country. She's written the Teen Pop Culture Quiz for Voices of Youth Advocates (VOYA) since 1999.

CHARLES C. HINNANT, PhD, is an Assistant Professor in the College of Communication & Information and was Assistant Director at the Information Use Management and Policy Institute at the Florida State University. He is a former Fellow and Assistant Director in the IT Team at the U.S. Government Accountability Office. His research interests include social and organizational informatics, digital government, information management and policy, public management, social science research methods, and applied statistics. He is particularly interested in how public organizations employ Information and Communication Technology (ICT) to alter organizational processes and structures and how the use of ICT ultimately impacts institutional governance mechanisms. His research has appeared or is forthcoming in journals such as *Administration and Society, Government Information Quarterly, Journal of Public Administration Research and Theory*, and *IEEE Transactions on Engineering Management*. He earned his BS and MPA at North Carolina State University and his PhD in Public Administration from the Maxwell School at Syracuse University.

ERIN DOWNEY HOWERTON holds an MA in English from Kansas State University and an MLIS from Florida State University's College of Information. She is currently the School Liaison at Johnson County Library in Overland Park, Kansas. Howerton has worked with youth for nearly a decade in both library and higher educational settings. She has published various articles and book chapters about library collections, intellectual freedom, and technology topics concerning youth. Howerton blogs about education, libraries, and technology at http://www.schoolingdotus.blogspot.com and maintains an educational wiki at http://www.cyber64edu.wetpaint.com.

PAUL T. JAEGER, PhD, JD, is an Assistant Professor, the Director of the Center for Information Policy and Electronic Government, and the Associate Director of the Center for Library & Information Innovation in the College of Information Studies at the University of Maryland. His research focuses on the ways in which law and policy shape information behavior. Dr. Jaeger is the author of more than ninety journal articles and book chapters, along with six books. His most recently authored book is *Information Worlds: Social Context, Technology, & Information Behavior in the Age of the Internet* (with Gary Burnett) published in 2010 by Routledge. He is the Associate Editor of *Library Quarterly*. His research has been funded by the Institute of Museum & Library Services, the National Science Foundation, the American Library Association, and the Bill & Melinda Gates Foundation, among others.

DR. JONATHAN LAZAR is a Professor of Computer and Information Sciences at Towson University. He is the founder and Director of the Universal Usability Laboratory at Towson University, and currently serves as director of the undergraduate Information Systems program. His most recently authored book is *Web Usability: A User-Centered Design Approach*, published by Addison-

Wesley in 2006, and his most recently edited book is *Universal Usability: Designing Computer Interfaces for Diverse User Populations*, published by John Wiley and Sons in 2007. He is co-author of the new book *Research Methods in Human-Computer Interaction*, to be published in 2010 by John Wiley and Sons. He currently serves as national chair of the ACM SIGCHI U.S. Public Policy Committee, and also serves on the editorial boards of *Universal Access in the Information Society* and *Interacting with Computers*, as well as the executive board of the Friends of the Maryland Library for the Blind and Physically Handicapped.

LAUREN H. MANDEL is a doctoral candidate at the Florida State University College of Communication & Information and the Research Coordinator at the Information Use Management and Policy Institute. Her research interests include public library facility design, wayfinding, and geographic information studies. She earned a Bachelor's degree in History at Vassar College and received a Master's of Science in Library and Information Science from Simmons College.

CHARLES R. McCLURE, PhD, is the Francis Eppes Professor of Information Studies and the Director of the Information Use Management Policy Institute at the Florida State University (http://ii.fsu.edu/). McClure was principal investigator on the American Library Association-funded project that resulted in *Planning and Role Setting for Public Libraries* (1987) and *Output Measures for Public Libraries*, 2nd ed. (1987). Since 1994 he and John Carlo Bertot have conducted the national *Public Libraries and the Internet* surveys, which have been funded by the Bill & Melinda Gates Foundation and the American Library Association since 2004. McClure has written extensively on topics related to the planning and evaluation of information services, federal information policy, information resources management, and digital libraries. His most recent book is *Public Libraries and Internet Service Roles* (ALA, 2009) with Paul T. Jaeger.

DR. LORRI MON is an Assistant Professor at Florida State University's College of Communication and Information. She is a co-principal investigator on a 3-year Institute of Museum and Library Services grant, "A Virtual Learning Laboratory for Digital Reference: Transforming the Internet Public Library," which has included development of a virtual learning community for library and information science education. Dr. Mon studies and teaches about digital and remote reference services from traditional face-to-face settings to chat, e-mail, instant messaging, cell phone text messaging, social networking, and virtual world environments. Her research has explored evolving areas of library information services including the expanding use of new technologies in reference practice and LIS education, the online geography of chat reference, and information services by librarians in the virtual world of Second Life for which she received the 2007 ASIS&T SIG-USE Elfreda Chatman Research Award.

ELIZABETH NORTON is a librarian in the Specialized Information Services Division of the U.S. National Library of Medicine. She holds master's degrees in Public Health, Business Administration, and Library Science.

DAVID PIPER is an Intern at the Training and Development Department of the International Brotherhood of Teamsters in Washington, D.C. He has degrees in Anthropology (BA), and Library Science (MLS). His interests include lifelong learning, performing arts librarianship, and historical research.

JOE RYAN was a Senior Research Associate with the Information Use Management and Policy Institute at Florida State University when this chapter was written.

JOHN T. SNEAD, PhD, is an Assistant Professor in the School of Library and Information Studies at the University of Oklahoma. His areas of teaching and research interest include information policy, e-government, and the assessment of networked library resources and services. He has worked in an academic library, a medical school library, and as Manager of Research Development at the Information Use Management and Policy Institute at Florida State University.

CHADWICK B. STARK is a Public Librarian at the Prince George's County Memorial Library System (MD). He has degrees in Library Science (MA), English Literature (BA) and Linguistics (BA). His focuses include Instructional Role, Information Literacy, and Senior Outreach.

KIM M. THOMPSON, a Lecturer in the Charles Stuart University School of Information Studies, earned her MLS and PhD from the Florida State University. She has published articles on e-government, information management, information poverty, and physical, intellectual, and social aspects of information access.

AMY COOPER WHITE is a recent graduate of the MLS program at the University of Maryland and previously earned an MA in applied linguistics/TESOL from Ohio University. Over the past 12 years, she has enjoyed teaching adult students first as an ESL instructor and more recently as a librarian. Her research interests include adult education in public libraries, ESL reading/writing and librarian/faculty liaison programs.

BO XIE is an Assistant Professor in the College of Information Studies at the University of Maryland, College Park. She has degrees in Medicine (BS), Psychology (MS), and Science and Technology Studies (PhD). Her research focuses on the intersection of older age, health, and information technology.